GENRE THEORY AND HISTORICAL CHANGE

GENRE THEORY AND HISTORICAL CHANGE

THEORETICAL ESSAYS OF RALPH COHEN

EDITED BY

John L. Rowlett

UNIVERSITY OF VIRGINIA PRESS
Charlottesville and London

University of Virginia Press
© 2017 by the Rector and Visitors of the University of Virginia
All rights reserved
Printed in the United States of America on acid-free paper

First published 2017
First paperback edition published 2025

ISBN 978-0-8139-4011-3 (cloth)
ISBN 978-0-8139-5434-9 (paper)
ISBN 978-0-8139-4012-0 (e-book)

1 3 5 7 9 8 6 4 2

Library of Congress Cataloging-in-Publication Data
is available for this title.

Contents

Acknowledgments   vii
Editor's Note   ix
Introduction   xi

I. LITERARY THEORY AS GENRE THEORY

On the Interrelations of Eighteenth-Century Literary Forms	3
The Origins of a Genre: Descriptive Poetry	36
Literary Theory as a Genre	50
The Joys and Sorrows of Literary Theory	68
History and Genre	85
Do Postmodern Genres Exist?	105
Reviewing Criticism: Literary Theory	122
Materialities of Communication: Genre/Media	137
Genre Theory, Literary History, and Historical Change	145
What Are Genres?	170

II. LITERARY CHANGE AS GENERIC HISTORY

Innovation and Variation: Literary Change and Georgic Poetry	189
Historical Knowledge and Literary Understanding	221
Some Thoughts on the Problems of Literary Change 1750–1800	243
Literary History and Literary Theory	263

CONTENTS

A Propaedeutic for Literary Change	276
Generic History as New Literary History	291
The Generation of Conceptual Changes in Literary Study	307
Interpreting Interpretations	317
Renewing the Eighteenth Century	341
Generating Literary Histories	358

Bibliography of Ralph Cohen's Essays   375

Index   383

Acknowledgments

It is only fitting that I acknowledge my gratitude, first and foremost, to the late Ralph Cohen for his seminal contributions to literary history, his vision of education, his immensely stimulating presence for more than forty years at the University of Virginia, and—as teacher, mentor, colleague, and friend— for his exhilarating influence on my life as scholar and editor. This collection of his essays, part of a much larger editing project that involved preparing all of the 120 or so Cohen papers, was begun years before its completion and was being read at the Press during Ralph's final days, a fact that in no way suggests his sanctioning its appearance. At the source of his reluctance to review and collect his previously written papers was an indifference to anything but their expansive implications and releasing possibilities for other scholars; were his own papers of lasting value, their constructional procedures would be evident in the extensive writing of those he was reading. This indifference left his impatient life partner in a state of unresolved provocation. Yet had they lived to see this selection of his literary histories collected, I trust Ralph would have been pleasantly surprised, Libby surely elated.

I wish to thank Rita Felski for encouraging my early efforts, for some shrewd and judicious emendations, and for saving me from becoming too personal in my writing about Ralph. I thank Cliff Siskin, Larry Burton, and Michael Prince for their longtime support of collecting Ralph's papers and for their generous friendship. As Director of the School of Writing, Rhetoric, and Technical Communication at James Madison University, and later as Director of the Cohen Center for the Study of Technological Humanism, Larry kindly made available facilities for the transcription into editable form of Ralph's previously published papers. Herbert Tucker, Jerome McGann, Stephen Arata, Walter Jost, Alison Booth, James and Marcia Childress, and David Morris supported this effort in a variety of valuable ways, each with Ralph's best interest in mind. I'm sure they recognize that he must have hoped this assemblage of essays would defeat, while not disappointing, their expectations.

My insightful editor Eric Brandt has been unobtrusively helpful, and I thank him for the liberty he has given me to shape this manuscript. I also wish to credit my two outside readers with making useful suggestions. Project editor Morgan Myers directed a smooth editing process, and managing editor Ellen Satrom exercised uncommon prescience in selecting Ruth Melville to copyedit the manuscript. My debt to Ruth is more than considerable and her service to the reader cannot be overstated.

My most demanding and perspicacious reader has been my friend and Cohen student Jeffrey Plank, who cast a keen editorial eye over several versions of the introduction and delivered me from infelicities and indiscretion. My wife, Abbie, remains the touchstone of my taste and the foundation of my abiding continuity over the many years of grappling with Ralph's thinking and withstanding Libby's free spirit. Without her I could not have brought this to a close.

Editor's Note

Readers will find that most of Cohen's papers are not without imperfections, for few of them are editorially polished as they would be had he collected them for final publication. I have avoided the occasional temptation to correct an infelicity or smooth a construction for the sake of fidelity to the author. However, I have corrected grammatical errors, inaccurate quotations and citations, and mistakenly attributed quotations, supplied references that are made in the text but omitted from the citations, and introduced notes where I thought the reader would be assisted.

Eight of the essays have not been published, although they were all delivered to academic audiences, some of them to colleagues at Modern Language Association meetings, some to international conferences. These have been challenging to prepare because, as with every Cohen essay, multiple versions exist. I have attempted to find and select the latest revision prior to each paper's delivery, but I cannot be certain that a more updated draft does not exist. A few of the heretofore unpublished papers (including some not published here) have been difficult to date precisely, though the year of delivery is usually apparent. Regrettably, in the case of some presentations, I have found dates and occasions but have been unable to locate the papers. Some prestigious lectures—like the October 1984 Patten Lectures ("The Attack on Genre" and "The Regeneration of Genre") and the April 1987 Clifford Lecture (playfully entitled "Literary History at Mid-Century; or, Replacing Critical Furniture: Mirrors, Lamps, Pictures, etc.")—have not been published, yet are not included here owing to considerable overlap with published material. Some forty essays, all deserving of collection eventually, remain unpublished.

The bibliography of essays is as complete as I could make it, and any omissions are inadvertent. Not all brief prefaces or introductory notes to issues of *New Literary History* are included, as they are best read in close connection with the journal issues they open.

Introduction

Providing contemporary literary studies with the most adequate and compelling theory of genre available, Ralph Cohen has made accessible to scholars everywhere a systematic historical procedure for generating reliable explanatory narratives of literary, artistic, and cultural change. Such an extraordinary claim may seem extravagant and he would never have made it himself. Yet he would urge readers to weigh its legitimacy, a challenge now made possible with the collection of these transformative essays, eight of which are published here for the first time.

Ralph Cohen needs no introduction. However, introducing his theoretical papers is necessary because he never collected his essays for publication despite the clarity and coherence of that original work. Considering that he is so widely known for introducing the essays of others, both as the editor for forty years of *New Literary History* and as the editor of other interdisciplinary collections exemplifying continuity and change, it is at once lamentable and ironic that his own essays tracing the shift in our consciousness of theory and history have lain scattered like unaffiliated, unassembled stars across the literary firmament, no constellation to figure their concepts.

Why a collection of Cohen essays now? After all, as he pointed out indifferently, many of them are "out there"—languishing, his colleagues reminded him, in a diffuse array of publications, some obscure. In addition, all are from the century past, the bulk from the seventies and eighties. What bearing can they possibly have a half generation into the twenty-first century, well after "Theory" has been pronounced dead or dying on multiple occasions, well into the unfolding of an epoch or episteme many have called postmodern, or posthuman, or nonhuman? Yet don't contemporary literary historians remain in need of a more adequate theory of change to account for such a shift? We have that adequacy here in one comprehensive theory.

If we wish to understand the origins of our own epoch, if we want a conception and a procedure for understanding, explaining, and effecting change, if we wish to identify the individuality in the work of others while acknowledging the shared mode of intertextual discourse to which we contribute, if we desire a coherent vision for a robust educational system that serves democratic aims in a new technological age, we could not do better than to learn from—and extend—Cohen's remarkable essays. A careful reading of the work here collected is necessary to answer the question of its currency, adequacy, and range of applicability, but it is not sufficient as a rationale for collecting the work. A few points seek discovery.

I should emphasize that it was never Ralph Cohen's aim to collect his essays. He felt that without a second edition, life left no time for recycling papers. Besides, the continual future orientation of his prodigious work simply did not permit it. That aim has been mine, though he indulged, graciously if bemusedly, this paper-recycling project. I am responsible for gathering and editing the essays, yet I am by no means alone in the wish to see these essential papers assembled in one place or to acknowledge them as enduring contributions to our thinking—the shaping of our becoming as well as the understanding of our historical being and the origins of our assumptions. It is only in part with these scholars in mind—his students and the myriad colleagues who have learned from him—that these essays are collected.

Ralph Cohen worked alongside the most preeminent theorists of the late twentieth century in demonstrating that writing about historical change can be philosophically rigorous and philologically attentive. His exploratory essays—an interrelated assemblage spanning the theory movement—are not writings locked in the transitoriness of a moment or a movement. They exemplify innovative features and procedures by which theoretical essays become dominant, if developing, genres for the twenty-first century. The strategies of combination that Cohen describes and that are discernible in his papers, lectures, and editorial practices reveal the transformative mode of existence of contemporary discourse across the disciplines.

This collective procedure in no way limits scholarly creativity or individuality, since the generic act of combining varied conventions—say, autobiographical, anthropological, psychological, biological, neurological, technological, or ecological discourse—with the developed genres of literary theory and history is unavoidably specific, or particular, in nature. As Cohen states:

> No single genre—like a ballad or a tragedy—can be understood as changing by itself. It changes by establishing new combinatory discourses, and these develop changes in the meanings of the terms that are combined. Thomas Kuhn argues that changes in a paradigm involve changes in the definitions of terms previously used and incorporated into the new paradigm. Genres are

INTRODUCTION

indeed governed by developed discourses that become conventionalized. And as I have urged, generic terms like the epic undergo change as their construction is used to develop or articulate different modes of feeling.[1]

While Cohen's literary experiments have been salutary to his students and his other readers during a time of rapid and often incomprehensible change, they deserve a much wider audience, since Cohen himself is the scholar whose theoretical work on genre, I suggest, exceeds competing procedures, such as those more narrowly focused on lyric theory, novel theory, narrative theory, or cultural theory. That is because, for dealing with the implications of such historical change, his is the most precise, systematic, effective, and inclusive. It is also the most comprehensive, since in proposing a genre theory suited to describing and analyzing generic change, Cohen makes possible an exploration of the functions of change in the making of society. And to whom is this alien?

For Cohen all writing takes place in forms or genres, which have a behavioral basis and a social function. That is, forms of writing—literary genres—are groups of texts that define and promote behavior. "Genres are not versions of criticism or versions of theory; they are descriptions of the ways criticism, theory, all oral and literary phenomena operate."[2] Genre theory, Cohen elaborates, "is a system of explanation which attends to the historical continuities and discontinuities within texts or events, indicating the interrelations of these with other systems within and outside the genre. . . . In this sense texts themselves become implicit explanatory mechanisms. They are not merely texts to be explained but are extensive explanations themselves. This is what Harold Bloom means when he states that texts resist other earlier texts."[3]

Cohen's combinatory concept of genre—coupled with the recognition that every material instance of a genre changes the genre, if no more than slightly—is an exemplar for contemporary historical scholarship and continues to serve literary studies, now governed by varied hybrid forms of theory and history that reveal an interdisciplinary, intertextual mode of proceeding. In his heretofore most widely read theoretical essay, Cohen clarifies the inevitability of generic change, while stressing the recurrent human need for distinction and interrelation in the establishment of genres:

> Genre has been defined in terms of meter, inner form, intrinsic form, radical of presentation, single traits, family traits, institutions, conventions, contracts, and these have been considered either as universals or as empirical historical groupings.

xiii

INTRODUCTION

In recognition of this multiplicity of definitions, I wish to argue that genre concepts in theory and practice arise, change, and decline for historical reasons. And since each genre is composed of texts that accrue, the grouping is a process, not a determinate category. Genres are open categories. Each member alters the genre by adding, contradicting, or changing constituents, especially those of members most closely related to it. The process by which genres are established always involves the human need for distinction and interrelation. Since the purposes of critics who establish genres vary, it is self-evident that the same texts can belong to different groupings or genres and serve different generic purposes.[4]

Cohen's theorizing of genre and his attention to the nature of literary history may seem to have come from Bakhtin or Wellek or Frye or Crane, but some continuities with those antecedent thinkers cannot, I believe, account for at least four novel conceptual features: (1) a genre theory conceptualized not as a hermeneutical theory, a rhetorical theory, or a logical theory, but as a *historical theory* according to which groupings of texts constitute indeterminate categories instantiating processes of change as member texts accrue; (2) a visionary prioritization throughout his work of the *phenomenon of change*, resulting in his adoption of the *language of change* (generation, innovation, variation, alteration, modulation, transition, transformation, shift, etc.)—what Cohen calls "the generative metaphor"; (3) his conception that a text is *historical in nature,* that is, any text is an *individualized expression* of a *historically sedimented group or class,* namely, a unique instance of a genre; more completely put, a text is a singular combination of a received genre's conventionalized elements *and* contemporaneous constructional components—mixed, behavioral features from language (speech, rhetoric, developing discourses, and so forth); and (4) his hypothesis that genres are *descriptions of the ways oral and literary phenomena operate,* resulting in texts as *implicit explanatory mechanisms.*

Genres exemplify processes of textual change insofar as "any *instance* of a genre stems from a history of possibilities and from a language that is acculturated."[5] Any time we examine a text or artistic entity we are confronted with inherited components as well as components that have contemporary filiations with conventionalized discourse. Groups of texts form clusters that permit us to recognize the kind of knowledge organization we are dealing with. As Cohen puts it: "A genre is a group (or groups) of texts historically characterized by components in interaction toward some general purpose containing features that are intertextual, the whole forming an identity that

INTRODUCTION

can become a subgenre or can be the source of new genres. Genres occur in every language and many cross national borders. They are procedures for organizing knowledge, and for communicating it. They express our thoughts, feelings, and actions with regard to that knowledge."[6]

If varied iterations are called for in order to characterize, describe, and define such a capacious conception of genre, it is also necessary to stipulate more fully the nature of the historical existence of a written work in order to generate an adequate literary history. Here we can add another of Cohen's novel conceptual features: (5) the hypothesis of a *synchronic hierarchy of genres and member texts* (including those from other periods) that implies a knowledge hierarchy and a hierarchy of values—an ordering based on literary and cultural responses to social exigencies and political pressures. He explains that the historical existence of a written work is defined by the convergence of four systematic procedures, only one of which is generic:

> If a literary work is historical because it belongs to a genre, it is also historical because it is a member of at least two other temporally defined systems, neither of which is generic: it is part of a writer's total work, his oeuvre, part of his literary identity in whatever genre he composes, and it is, at the same time, part of the order of all other literary and verbal works synchronous with it. Thus "Lycidas" is a member of a subgenre called pastoral elegy, a part of Milton's oeuvre, and one of the total number of works composed in the years preceding the Civil War.
>
> The nature of the historical existence of a literary work is thus defined by the convergence of at least three systematic procedures: the genre, the oeuvre, and the synchronic hierarchy. I call such a work "historical" because by definition (1) it is a cultural alteration of an inherited form; (2) it is the expression of a historical being; and (3) it is a member of a chronologically identifiable literary norm.
>
> Besides the three, there is a fourth systematic procedure of which every literary work is a part: the transaction between it and the reader. A reader belongs to a historical ambience, and his literary hypotheses derive from interactions with a norm of which he himself cannot be fully conscious. Not fully conscious because, however self-aware he may be, he is living in the midst of a norm that can only be adequately perceived after it has been supplanted. The interpreter can overlook but he cannot deny that the work has a generic past identified by rhetorically inherited devices; whatever analysis he undertakes will presuppose—with his awareness or not—that there exists a relationship historically developed among particular conventions of construction and language.[7]

For Cohen, such a systematic reformulation was necessary in order "to establish reliable principles and procedures for dealing with literary and artistic change."[8] Indeed, new directions were provided by Cohen's published writings from the seventies into the nineties—consider the following half dozen seminal papers: "Innovation and Variation: Literary Change and Georgic Poetry" (1974), "Literary Theory as a Genre" (1975), "Historical Knowledge and Literary Understanding" (1978), "A Propaedeutic for Literary Change" (1983), "History and Genre" (1986), and "Genre Theory, Literary History, and Historical Change" (1991). If this work unveils the vision of but one man, the concomitant generic renewal engaged in variously by multiple genre critics from the seventies through the end of the century may be designated the "generic turn,"[9] perhaps more properly termed the "generic return," since generic turning, or the cyclical realignment of kinds, is characteristic of genres as conceptual shifts occur periodically throughout time. Of the various "turns" that have been stipulated since the "linguistic turn" in philosophy, only the generic turn in literary and cultural studies, the regeneration of genre, can account for the rest, since a concept of genres as cultural formations includes the others in communication and exchange and is capable of making the clarifying distinctions necessary for interrelating them all. This conceptual shift, this turn to genres as cultural formations, as historical procedures for organizing, valuing, and communicating knowledge, as implicit explanatory procedures for understanding historical change, may be thought of as Ralph Cohen's project in transformation.

Missing from the present volume are many of the insightful interpretations of eighteenth-century works that offer rereadings of the major writers, putting Cohen's genre theory to practice on texts from another episteme or norm—interpretations that exemplify his original model of literary and cultural history as generic in nature. Included in the bibliography, these uncollected essays displaying his variant of "conceptualist interpretations" are linked dialectically to the theoretical assemblage.[10] And though scarcely any of his writing for and about *New Literary History* is included here, brief mention can be made of the overlapping temporalities governing the journal and his own essays.

From 1969 the periodic unfolding of the journal has served as an exciting, necessary guide urging and enabling a collaborative involvement in issues concerning history, theory, and interpretation. Its founding editor played a director's role as the deliberative actions of theory and interpretation were performed throughout the close of the twentieth century. And while profiting immensely from the many rewarding contributions made in response to issues the journal raised, Cohen's own educational work was based on an understanding of the challenges that would present themselves pursuant to a conceptual shift, a shift that his essays disclose in the sixties. His scholarly papers collected here, all philosophical in nature yet steadfastly unpretentious, live and breathe in our twenty-first-century temporality. A literary/cultural movement, analogous to the Romantic movement and begun in the sixties, has been completed, more or less as of the beginning of this century, by the leading writers in all textual disciplines (the essays of numerous theory journals disclose this shift), an innovative epistemological norm now governs history writing, and disciplines are urging an abundance of theories and histories, albeit uneven in their adequacy. For this reason scholars should find it timely to have these papers now available, their concepts figuring a clarifying constellation.

Now let me say something about the nature and arrangement of the essays. That the influential editor of *New Literary History* had not used the journal to promulgate his own preferences and procedures for dealing with change has perhaps resulted in a readership assuming that he had no comprehensive view to contribute himself other than the challenging direction—widely acknowledged—that the shaped journal was shaping. And this assumption was exacerbated by Cohen's violating one professional norm: electing not to collect his essays as soon as he had a volume's worth; and scrupulously following another: recognizing that, as editor-teacher, he exercised authority—built on securing the trust of his readers—that could have been compromised had he used the journal's pages to broadcast his own explicit arguments.

Herein lies a paradox: indisputably central as editor-teacher, Cohen has remained peripheral as essayist-theorist, the extensive implications of his theoretical papers for the possibilities of a new history of aesthetics and cultural analysis largely unrecognized—at least to judge from the fact that his essays on genre are seldom cited, if not unnoted. Throughout the latter part of the twentieth century, literary scholars acknowledged Cohen as a brilliant eighteenth-century critic and a sagacious editor, shrewdly selecting subjects, conventions, issues, and controversies in need of rethinking; his invitation to international colloquies and conferences, often as plenary speaker or as commentator, demonstrated the esteem in which his demanding rigor and critical agility were held. However, his articles on genre theory and literary history, though jargon-free and plainly expressed, were difficult to comprehend because his subject—often, the nature of generic history—remained complicated, not to mention conceptually innovative; indeed, grasping his genius relied upon the individual critic's reconceptualization of certain terms— *genre, text, theory, history, innovation, norm, mode, interpretation*—rather than the coining of a new vocabulary.

Students and colleagues alike were treated to glimpses into a work in progress that would eventually be unveiled in further books. Yet, surprisingly, these further books turned out to be five collections of essays *by others*— collections he arranged and introduced with historical explanations and incisive interpretations, sequences that reconceived the book along the lines of the journal he was editing, introductions that served as clarifications of his genre technology at work.[11] Perhaps it was not recognized by his students, colleagues, and the readers of *New Literary History* that the journal essay, the professional paper, the scholarly article, itself had become the bounded form in which new literary narratives were being written on the dialogical model of the conferences he convened. What this paradox suggests to me is that Ralph Cohen's impact on humanistic scholarship, when accounts settle, will have come in two waves: his innovative guidance as editor-teacher, followed by adoption of his systematic procedures as essayist-theorist.

In 2003, after more than three decades of the journal's existence, during which time no issue had been devoted to genre, the self-effacing editor, after theorizing genres for thirty years, finally introduced, in collaboration with Hayden White, companion issues of *New Literary History* entitled "Theorizing Genres," issues that demonstrate the multivoiced, multigeneric nature of the inquiry. He opened the first number by calling attention to the vast range that systematic genre study enables:

> Many years have passed since Mikhail Bakhtin and later Tzvetan Todorov changed the direction of genre study from classification to its functions in human speech and behavior. And although much has been accomplished in the study of the novel and nonliterary writing, there have been few attempts to envision genre study as a theory of behavior or as one that can provide an insight into the arts and sciences.
>
> This issue and the following one "Theorizing Genres II" are an effort to expand the range of genre study as well as to examine its current practices. What is remarkable about such study is that examples of genre appear in language, in music, art, history, government, and human behavior. It is obvious that genres appear in popular culture—in films, television, journal-

ism, and comic strips. Similar genres cross national boundaries and thus create problems about the particular social nature of genres. Genres appear in precolonial, colonial, and postcolonial societies and some genres such as folktales and proverbs endure virtually unchanged despite immense social changes.

Genre study is more than another approach to literature or to social institutions or scientific practices; it analyzes our procedures for acquiring and accumulating knowledge including the changes that such knowledge undergoes.[12]

In addition, as he notes in his "Postmodern Genres" essay, "treating the essay as genre is a recognition that discourses cannot be an adequate substitute for the works that encompass them."[13] That is to say, the theoretical essay exemplifies "the necessity for genre" in delineating otherwise unbounded theoretical discourse or "writing"; after all, literary theory is enacted in lectures, papers, articles, essays that have different entries and exits, as well as distinct discourse networks. Whereas genre theorizing—because a genre itself—remains open, any particular instance of the genre, any theoretical essay, becomes a bounded, historical entity in which the constituents of change can be specified, described, and explained, while the nonessentialist theorizing remains "capable of being revised, corrected, or even refuted"[14] in response to the changes introduced by the genre member. This position further differentiates Cohen's conception of genre theory from those it displaces.

Indeed, for Ralph Cohen the form of self-shaping begins with an understanding, in writing, of the other. And he provides a model for such analyses in the five volumes of essays he introduces, as well as in the conferences and symposia he organized wherever he taught. His experimental, journalistic method of genre study resulted in seminars, essays, and presentations full of explosive insights, whether clarifying and relating the views of others or carefully and systematically shaping those of his own. Yet, setting aside the cognitive difficulty, the lack of widespread appropriation of his revisionary theory can best be accounted for, I suggest, by the lack of a comprehensive source to serve as an explanatory model for his concepts. Taken together now, these connected essays spanning the theory movement are regenerative and surprisingly forceful.

Whether the aim of a Ralph Cohen essay is predominantly descriptive, explanatory, interpretative, oppositional, or foundational, they all share quiet pleasures, a characteristic sensitivity, a theoretical imagination—and yet an unmistakable rigor. The procedure and rhetorical strategy of the essays written in the sixties and seventies tend to be that of rejection/affirmation, while those written in the eighties and nineties tend to be that of limitation/suggestion. This tempering in tone is indicative of the adequacy Cohen felt he had achieved with his genre theory/theory of change. Even so, the patient, modest tone is never combative, insulting, or demeaning in the earlier essays. The respectful and thoughtful voice, as exemplified in "Reviewing Criticism: Literary Theory," lends a moral authority seldom found in the essays of any but the most generous scholars. Since the lecture, or the performance of a paper's reading, was Cohen's preference for public delivery—at conferences, symposia, named lecture series, colloquia, seminars, the classroom—the rhythm of his characteristic voice, frequently beginning almost inaudibly and slowly modulating into a confident crescendo, is nigh silenced in these pages, his occasion-specific digressions and nonverbal gestures at rest. Yet in exchange, we are left with vibrant, material genre members and a distinctive style that is capable of rewarding manifold readings.

In a 2009 tribute to Ralph Cohen, after his stepping down as editor of the journal, Hélène Cixous comments on the nourishing, unobtrusive editor: "I realized that everything I am saying about Ralph belongs to ethical reflection. This is not by chance: Ralph Cohen's work is comparable—and I believe his example is unique—to that of an analyst who is wise enough to enable and encourage those seeking truths in the thickets where the unconscious speaks. He *does not discourage*. He keeps watch."[15] Although Cohen's essays constitute the interventions of a theorist, the ethical character Cixous lovingly discerns in the watchful analyst belongs to essayist and editor alike.

I have divided this selection of essays—and this collection is less than 20 percent of his papers—into two parts, publishing limits alone curtailing a more extensive collection. Part I, "Literary Theory as Genre Theory," deals predominantly with the nature of literary theory and reconceiving and theorizing genre. When theory emerged as a leading form of writing in the late twentieth century, genre theory was but one of many literary theories, most aimed at authorizing an ideological approach to, or a method of interpretation of, "literature." With Cohen defining literary theory as a kind of writing, the features of theorizing, along with the release of theory's subservience to literature, became apparent, permitting theoretical texts to be analyzed alongside contemporaneous nontheoretical texts. Hence these texts become *historical texts*, genres and subgenres possessing shared and oppositional aims and discourse elements in what had appeared seemingly unrelated and often conflicting literary and cultural writings.

INTRODUCTION

Part II, "Literary Change as Generic History," foregrounds Cohen's views of historical change, of a historical system, or systematic period concept, and the role of genres and forms, in their multiple dimensionality, for exploring, mapping, and explaining historical transformations. As I have noted, it is important to recognize that Ralph Cohen's historical theory of genre arises out of an effort to understand the literary interrelations of a historical Other. He presents, explains, and applies his innovative model in a 1974 essay "On the Interrelations of Eighteenth-Century Literary Forms," and subsequent papers continue to develop this diachronic-synchronic precondition for "literary understanding."[16] Though formulated in the seventies—the governing concept developed and refined over the next two decades—Cohen's combinatory theory of genre remains a vital twenty-first-century procedure essential to any study of historical change.

A succinct way to consider this division is to see the essays in Part I as theorizing genre, those in Part II as handling the problem of historical change. Yet since both parts are intimately intertwined, it will become evident that many of them are interchangeable: no theory without history, no history without theory. Although the essays have been arranged chronologically (by year) within each part, the sequence of Cohen's writing is not so important for the purposes of this collection because the essays are all governed by the same concepts; the essays reveal the systematic procedure Cohen followed in his thinking about theoretical matters and disclose the manner in which theoretical and historical essays proceed by incorporating additional combinations that supplement, complement, or correct the two genres.

As illustrated in both parts, there is a dialectical movement between the use of genre theory to contribute to a new history of the long eighteenth century and its use to extend the applicability of genre analysis to other cultural periods of the past and to our own time, thereby demonstrating its usefulness beyond literary behavior and literary histories to aesthetic/semiotic procedures of communication and histories of all kinds. Obviously, a reader can begin with any essay and skip from one part to the other without distortion, since the conceptually intertwined essays share Cohenesque constructional features. A Ralph Cohen essay, albeit directional, does not end in a conclusive destination but opens up, in the language of Deleuze and Guattari, a mapping of rhizomatic connections—and disconnections.

Cohen's papers reflect his determination to limit his insights and his findings to one systematic time frame—its origins, modulations, and passing— and to the transition from the subsequent (now also obsolete) time frame into the open temporality or contemporary mode that is our own. This represents a characteristic pattern of his thinking: by limiting himself to the long eighteenth century, he elaborates upon his procedures for dealing with the complexity of a closed norm and its variations; simultaneously, he notes contemporary linkages to eighteenth-century genres—for example, the critical essay and the periodical paper—while he notes that the nonlinear development and the constituent devices critics enumerate as characteristic of "postmodern" genres can be located in Augustan genres, like *Tristram Shandy*. By elevating and specifying the particularly apt value a historical study of the eighteenth century has for our time, he challenges critics to achieve insights by extending his innovation in novel directions. He joins those who wish to make current inquiry into the past once again replete with "the disturbing joys and pleasurable sorrows of literary theory."[17]

His essays are historical examples of genre theory, his earliest papers from the fifties revealing his preoccupation with literary theory. They follow the pattern of selecting and analyzing an issue pertinent to theory and history, characteristically engaging in genuine dialogue with other literary critics, describing and explaining their procedures, offering advances illustrating the value of his hypothesis in terms of its aims, generating original insights, and explaining his own procedures, before synthesizing exfoliated insights near the turn of the century. Thus we find his answers to "What Are Genres?" (1998), his retrospective on "Renewing the Eighteenth Century" (1993), his visionary "Generating Literary Histories" (1993), and his hortatory introductions to "Theorizing Genres" (2003) proffered near the culmination of his career as an essayist. The governing generic concepts of his theorizing remained stable from the midsixties, and the process of their development over more than forty years expanded from eighteenth-century historical poetics to range over all verbal, artistic, and cultural behavior.

This pattern of generic behavior also characterizes the disposition of his essays as if they were but waste in the wilderness of working papers. Seeking explanations relying on analyses of particular generic mixtures and continuous and discontinuous features rather than "grand narratives," Cohen elected to distribute his essayistic dialogues as transactive lectures and in journals and anthologies edited by colleagues in preference to publishing autobiographical essay collections that might be misinterpreted as self-promoting or as possessing unification and closure. Elevating his work was left, by design, to the reader who may use it. I am aware that unveiling unpublished lectures as essays disguises their unfinished condition and that extracting published materials from the collective sites in which they appeared cannot but distort their synchronicity and original, interventionist function. That is the risk this assemblage of Cohen's literary life assumes for the purpose of collecting and connecting the releasing concepts these living essays embody. Yet some contextual aspects of previously published papers can be restored with reference to notes specifying the date and place of each essay's original appearance.

The pattern of self-effacement, a form of withdrawal, is in keeping with Cohen's off-stage, directorial role as editor of *New Literary History* and his five collections of essays in the hands of others. Theorizing the practice of editing as a genre was another aspect of his teaching. He took it for granted that "authorship" was simply a form of editing, a means of arranging and creatively making use of the generic and discursive possibilities at one's disposal for treating one or more topics. Each issue of the journal served to investigate a single subject, a format that encouraged collaborative dialogues among contributors. His introduction of commentaries to each journal issue and his own role as commentator to the journalistic anthologies he edited display his concept of theorizing as open dialogue, as each issue, each book, was meant to process possibilities for further study in a common educative and moral enterprise.

In "A Tribute to Ralph Cohen," introducing one of the four twenty-fifth anniversary issues of *New Literary History*, the German theorist Wolfgang Iser puts it this way: "The journal represents a new form of writing insofar as it is Ralph Cohen's book, in which he self-effacingly hardly ever participates, though he orchestrates it by superbly conducting the chorus, the instruments, and the soloists of his own masterpiece."[18] His roles as teacher, editor, and essayist were educative in the dialogic manner he enacted, often redirecting contributors and students in the composition of their theoretical essays. Minimization of his imprint belonged to his view of education, the success of a teacher measured by his or her guiding with such restraint that self-elimination is achieved.

While far from encompassing the entirety of his oeuvre, these theoretical essays do constitute a conceptual whole, the full realization of which will require the completion of the reader. They are every bit as current, expansive, and necessary today as when they were penned during the theory generation. They invite amplification. Cohen's literary theory is needed in order to better understand and account for the regeneration of theory and its unceasing yet transformative impact on discourse studies, the novel, and other literary forms, on our rethinking technology and personhood, on computational analysis and the digital scholar, on the way we narrate history—indeed, on rethinking how it is that we think. His essays establish the basis of a new philology for the arts and sciences, or what he has termed "technological humanism." Indeed, they demonstrate that in order to construct more precise, systematic statements about the interrelations among language, texts, writers, and society, to produce coherent historical knowledge that can be passed on, and to better secure and shape, through education, the foundations and reformulations of a just society, the genre technology of Ralph Cohen will be essential. His new literary history is the history not only from which but toward which we proceed.

NOTES

1. Ralph Cohen, "Renewing the Eighteenth Century," p. 350 in this volume.
2. Cohen, "The Vagaries of Genre," unpublished seminar lecture (on audiocassette), delivered October 25, 1995, Centre of English Studies, University of London.
3. Cohen, "Materialities of Communication: Genre/Media," p. 138 in this volume.
4. Cohen, "History and Genre," p. 86 in this volume.
5. Cohen, "Literary History and Literary Theory," p. 265 in this volume.
6. Cohen, "What Are Genres?" p. 184 in this volume.
7. Cohen, "Historical Knowledge and Literary Understanding," p. 222-23 in this volume.
8. Cohen, Introduction to "Literary and Artistic Change in the Eighteenth Century," ed. Cohen, special issue, *Eighteenth-Century Studies* 2, no. 1 (1968): 6.
9. In "Genre Theory, Literary History, and Historical Change," Cohen credits in a note numerous writers whose vigorous and valuable productivity during this period demonstrates that "generic theory has reemerged as a critical force." However, he writes, "these few references cannot begin to convey the extent and subtlety of generic theory and practice at the present time."

It might be helpful to stress here that Cohen recognizes both "rhetorical genre theory" and "literary genre theory" as social constructions. For him "generic theory" employs both, and he sees no persuasive reason for separating these two language traditions, since any text, any utterance, is amenable to rhetorical and poetic explanations because any genre may have both communicative and aesthetic purposes. Rhetorical genre theorists may wish to see especially "What Are Genres?," included in this volume.

10. For Cohen's variant of what he calls "postformalist or conceptualist" interpretation, namely, "interpretation in terms of the functions of literary conventions," see his "On a Shift in the Concept of Interpretation," in *The New Criticism and After*, ed. Thomas Daniel Young (Charlottesville: Univ. Press of Virginia, 1975), 74-79.
11. These edited collections consist of *New Directions in Literary History* (Baltimore:

INTRODUCTION

Johns Hopkins Univ. Press, 1974); *Studies in Eighteenth-Century British Art and Aesthetics* (Berkeley: Univ. of California Press, 1985); *The Future of Literary Theory* (New York: Routledge, 1989); *Studies in Historical Change* (Charlottesville: Univ. Press of Virginia, 1992); and, with Michael S. Roth, *History and . . . : Histories within the Human Sciences* (Charlottesville: Univ. Press of Virginia, 1995).

12. Cohen, "Introduction," *New Literary History* 34, no. 2 (2003): v.

13. Cohen, "Do Postmodern Genres Exist?" p. 118 of this volume.

14. Cohen, "The Origins of a Genre: Descriptive Poetry," p. 37 of this volume.

15. Hélène Cixous, "Tribute to Ralph Cohen," *New Literary History* 40, no. 4 (2009): 753.

16. This comprehensive essay expanded upon an earlier innovative essay, "The Augustan Mode in English Poetry" (1967)—not included here—that was conceptually in keeping with "On the Interrelations" but limited to poetic forms.

17. Cohen, "The Joys and Sorrows of Literary Theory," p. 83 of this volume.

18. Wolfgang Iser, "Twenty-five Years *New Literary History:* A Tribute to Ralph Cohen," *New Literary History* 25, no. 4 (1994): 738.

GENRE THEORY AND
HISTORICAL CHANGE

PART I
LITERARY THEORY AS GENRE THEORY

On the Interrelations of Eighteenth-Century Literary Forms

I. THE HISTORICAL BACKGROUND

Modern critics, in discussing neoclassical genres, have insisted on the rigidity of forms, while acknowledging that eighteenth-century critics disagreed about and poets seemed to diverge from this "rigidity." Austin Warren wrote: "That genres are distinct—and also should be kept distinct—is a general article of Neo-Classical faith. But if we look to Neo-Classical criticism for definition of genre or method of distinguishing genre from genre, we find little consistency or even awareness of the need for a rationale."[1] James Sutherland, in *A Preface to Eighteenth Century Poetry,* declared: "You knew where you were with Pastoral, Elegy, Epic, and the rest; you were not called upon to adjust yourself to the untried or the unexpected. Even in the eighteenth century, however, men were not willing to bask forever in the traditional perfections.... The characteristic compromise was to seek variety within the established form: not to abandon the known Kinds, but to introduce a slight change of subject or treatment."[2]

Oliver F. Sigworth wrote that at the center of neoclassic criticism is "the conception of genre, of literary works existing as species in an absolute sense." "Each genre had its own rules, its own (to use the proper term) decorum, which extended not only to matters of form and structure—matters which we still vaguely understand—but also to verse and diction."[3] Emerson R. Marks declared that for neoclassical critics, "Each poem shines with its own peculiar beauty; and it more or less followed from this that the kinds

---

This essay was originally published in *New Approaches to Eighteenth-Century Literature, Selected Papers from the English Institute,* ed. Phillip Harth (New York: Columbia Univ. Press, 1974), 33-78, and is reprinted with permission of the publisher.

should never be mixed."[4] René Wellek, in *A History of Modern Criticism,* wrote: "The rules were rarely defined in general terms but rather specified according to genres. The distinction between genres was basic to the neoclassical creed, so basic that its assumptions were never, to my knowledge, properly examined during this time. . . . It was rarely clear whether the table of genres was closed or whether new genres could be admitted. In practice hybrids of existing genres or ruleless new genres outside of the table of categories arose and were at least tolerated."[5]

These critics posit the distinctiveness of the kinds, although some treat them as metaphysical absolutes, whereas others find them governed by rules and decorum. They recognize that although eighteenth-century critics do not always agree on the rules or the decorum of specific kinds, they do agree that distinct kinds exist, common responses to which are the result of shared beliefs in a general human nature. Each kind has its own specific effect—the single pointedness of epigram, the sweet communication of loss in elegy, the artful delivery of precepts in didactic poetry, the moral end of drama. The means by which the effects were achieved included subject (theme, fable, thought, sentiments, speaker), language (diction, imagery, rhetorical figures), style (sublime, low, etc.), and meter. Irène Simon puts it this way: "When approaching any poem the critic would first ask himself to what genre the work belonged, what instruction it intended to convey, whether the plot and characters did convey it, whether the design of the poem and the characters were such that nature was imitated all through, whether the style was suitable to the characters and to the sentiments they expressed, etc. Any critical examination would therefore consider in turn: the fable, the manners (i.e. the characters), the sentiments, the diction and the metre."[6]

My argument is that these critics are mistaken. They are mistaken in assuming that the distinctiveness of kinds was agreed upon; they are mistaken in assuming that the rules specified the kinds; they are mistaken in assuming that each kind was bound to a clearly defined specific effect. Rather, the poetic kinds were identified in terms of a hierarchy that may not have been all-inclusive (since not all possible forms were specified) but were all interrelated. And this hierarchy can be seen in terms of the inclusion of lower forms into higher—the epigram into satire, georgic, epic; the ode into epic; the sonnet into drama; the proverb into all preceptive forms. Edward Phillips refers to this hierarchy as "the *Epic,* the *Dramatic,* the *Lyric,* the *Elegiac,* the *Epoenetic,* the *Bucolic,* or the Epigram"—in them "the whole circuit of Poetic design is one way or other included." For Phillips the epigram is the "fag end of Poetry" as epic is "of the largest extent, and includes all that is narrative either of things or persons."[7] Dryden considered epic the top and epigram "the bottom of all poetry."[8] John Sheffield undertakes to rehearse the "differing kinds" of poetry, beginning with song, and moving through elegy, ode, satire and drama to epic, for "Heroick Poems have a just pretence / To be the chief effort of humane sence."[9]

The critics argued that, although each form had its own effect, it was, either in terms of its parts or as a whole, interrelated with other forms. Some types of poems were mixtures to begin with: Dryden pointed out that Varronian satire was a mixture of several sorts of verse and was also mixed with prose; moreover, these poems had various subjects. In praising the proper satire—that of Boileau—he describes it as "the majesty of the heroic, finely mixed with the venom of the other." And he refers to satire as a species of heroic poetry.[10] The georgic poem was a mixture of instruction and story: some lyric forms were closely related to the heroic poem; others to the pastoral or epigram. Norman Maclean remarks that the divine and heroic odes or lyrics are placed "near the top of the poetical hierarchy (along with epic and tragedy) and the minor lyric near the bottom (generally somewhere between pastoral and epigram)."[11]

The theory of interrelation of forms had been inherited from Renaissance critics such as Minturno, Patrizzi, and others. Sir Philip Sidney had noted in his *Apology*: "Now in his parts, kindes, or *Species* (as you list to terme them), it is to be noted that some Poesies have coupled together two or three kindes, as Tragicall and Comicall, wher-upon is risen the Tragi-comicall. Some in the like manner have mingled Prose and Verse, as *Sanazzar* and *Boetius*. Some have mingled matters Heroicall and Pastorall. But that commeth all to one in this question, for, if severed they be good, the conjunction cannot be hurtfull."[12]

The mingling of different "matters" within the heroic poem was only one of the very many ways in which Renaissance critics saw the forms as interrelated. Rosalie Colie has remarked that in the Renaissance a rigid system of genres "never existed in practice and barely even in theory. . . . We have been looking at far too many examples of works that involve mixed kind rather than a specific single kind to accept any such rule."[13] Late seventeenth-century critics continued to see the forms as interrelated, though their interrelations often differed from those named by Renaissance critics. Hobbes, for example, even when he objected to the "received" hierarchies, did so by suggesting an extended theory of mixtures. He listed only three "Sorts," "*Heroique, Scommatique* and *Pastorall*," and declared that the forms named by critics—"Sonets,

Epigrams, Eclogues, and the like Peeces"—were "but other Essayes and parts of an entire Poem."[14]

Joseph Trapp, professor of poetry at Oxford, wrote that the "Epic Poem... comprehends within its Sphere all the other Kinds of Poetry whatever; and is in this Art what the Organ is in Music, which with various Pipes, inflated with the same Breath, charms us not only with its own Harmony, but represents that of every other Instrument."[15] If the epic could include every other kind—satire, pastoral, ode, elegy, panegyric, epigram, etc.—then the epic can be seen, in Trapp's view, as a harmony of forms, and each form can be understood in terms of its interrelation with others, capable of containing, within itself, appropriate parts of others. This decorum, then, is the propriety by which forms can be included in other forms and the propriety by which elements of one form—diction, rhetoric, sentiment, thought—can become part of another. Even when critics objected to specific interrelations such as the inclusion of epigrams or minor lyrics in the epic,[16] thus limiting the form only to inclusion of features from the noblest poetry (panegyric, divine ode, etc.), they nevertheless accepted interrelations of forms or features of forms.

The source for this view was Aristotle, who, in comparing epic to tragedy, pointed out that its plot should "be constructed on dramatic principles." "The parts also, with the exception of song and scenery, are the same." Although Aristotle notes the different ends of tragedy and epic, these are defined by the formal possibilities resulting from interrelated parts. Epic is one kind of verse in narrative form; it has no fixed time. Tragedy and epic, Aristotle writes, differ in the sense that "all the elements of an Epic poem are found in Tragedy, but the elements of a Tragedy are not all found in the Epic poem." The principle of comprehensiveness by which tragedy was to be preferred to epic was based on the epic elements being included in tragedy: "superior it is, because it has all the epic elements—it may even use the epic metre—with the music and scenic effects as important accessories."[17] Thus the principle of interrelation was one of the principles governing tragedy's superiority to epic.

By the mid-seventeenth century, the inherited Renaissance hierarchy of forms had been altered by elevating georgic and satire and lowering the pastoral. For Puttenham the pastoral was an allegorical lyric that sought "under the vaile of homely persons in rude speeches to insinuate and glaunce at greater matters, and such as perchance had not bene safe to have beene disclosed in any other sort." He referred to the georgic poem only incidentally in a paragraph about "the forme wherein honest and profitable artes and sciences were treated."[18] For Sidney, following Scaliger and Minturno, eclogues or pastorals belonged to genuine poetry. As for the authors of georgic and didactic works, "whether they properly be Poets or no let Grammarians dispute."[19] By the turn of the century the altered hierarchy of forms was frequently endorsed. Addison praised the *Georgics* as "the most complete, elaborate and finished piece of all antiquity."[20] Tickell referred to didactic poetry as "this more noble part of Poetry, which is second to Epic alone."[21] Pastoral poetry, on the other hand, had its Virgilian scope reduced and became subject to parody and irony although still defended by some critics. Pope sought to purify the form by disengaging it from the life of man and offering it as an idealization of the past. But his major work dealing with the experience of his time was in the satiric and didactic forms. Trapp sought to explain the changed status of pastoral in the period. He granted the historical scope of pastorals, declaring that its subjects were as various as human passions and that it "may, in some measure, partake of every Kind of Poetry," provided that the scene was in the country and the thoughts not inconsistent with the scene. But he found that in modern times, pastoral was not quite suitable. It was "a Poem less suitable to modern Times, on account of the Difference in the Circumstances of human life, from what it was anciently. As the Condition of Shepherds is now mean and contemptible; it seems too forced a Prosopopoeia to affix to them any Character of Politeness, or to introduce them as Men of Wealth and Education: These Things are contradictory to truth, and therefore leave no Room for Fiction." And with regard to the subject of the didactic poem, he declared, "I would . . . observe that any Thing in the World may be the Subject of this Kind of Poem."[22]

A shift in the importance of georgic forms was part of the didactic shift,[23] altering the status of satire, epistle, and the fable, as well as that of smaller forms such as the epigram, aphorism, and the maxim, whether in prose or verse. I do not wish to imply that forms have a life of their own, some kind of metaphysical essence. Literary forms are written or spoken by people and they are addressed to people. When poets turn to one form rather than another, when critics defend one kind of hierarchy rather than another, they do so for reasons that are related to personal, public, and professional commitments.

The need for didactic mixtures can be related to the scientific, religious, and political developments of the seventeenth century. The microscope and telescope had enabled man to extend his eye and mind.[24] This extension resulted in a reexamination of external nature in terms of the variety of the seen and the unseen hand of God. Perceptual reconsideration was invoked to explain both the seen and the unseen, the historical present and the historical past. Moreover, the aftermath of the Civil War brought with it a body of controversial literature—in both poetry and prose—as well as appeals to subdue controversy. One solution was for literature to appeal to as many groups as possible, seeking to satisfy each. The premise of social, political, and natural variety had as its basis God's plenitude and the implicit harmony underlying the universe.

The perceptual reconsiderations implicit in such works as *Coopers Hill* and *Upon Appleton House* tied the idea of vision to that of history. Distance, prospect, spectator views—these joined the vocabulary of vision to that of history and society. In fact, the development of a comparative, historical consciousness underlies the didactic shift, the discovered relation between observations of nature and historical retrospection. It is not that Renaissance writers ignored historical change; Bernard Weinberg has shown that sixteenth-century Italian critics were aware of it.[25] But they did not consider change in terms of the scientific, naturalistic as well as political needs of a new audience.

The criterion of propriety or decorum identified literary expression with social action, and social action that distinguished between present and past propriety. Neoclassical critics substituted historical justification for formal ends; the interrelations of forms and the mixtures within forms are defended by comparative procedures, arrived at by distinguishing the propriety of Greek or Latin or Elizabethan usage from neoclassical. Propriety and decorum need to be understood as comparative social and literary terms: the argument, as Pope formulated it, was that what was appropriate for Greek or Roman society or for Shakespeare's audience was not appropriate for his own audience.

The shift to didactic forms can also be understood in terms of the mixtures such forms involve. Varronian satire, for example, was by derivation and by practice a medley, consisting "not only of all kinds of Verse, but of Verse and Prose mix'd together."[26] Its subject matter could include praise and blame, its form panegyric and epigram and maxim, its style could be low and sublime. It is less important that the critics did not agree upon the place of satire in the hierarchy than that its place was related to the kind of mixtures it could contain—heroic, burlesque, pastoral. The point to be made here is that these mixtures became, in the works of Augustan writers, related to political and religious factionalism, to a procedure by which different groups could be addressed, with some being supported and others attacked. Such satire in

Restoration comedy made use of diverse classes, ideas, and diction and was defended by Farquhar on the grounds that the dramatists must appeal to as many different responders as possible.[27] Types of mixture have also to do with the manner in which past and present meanings are interrelated, the manner in which surface and subsurface can be combined. But more about this later.

The argument from variety also applies to the practice of the periodical essay. And the model of this was, of course, Addison's aim as stated in *Spectator* 10 (March 12, 1711): "I shall be ambitious to have it said of me, that I have brought Philosophy out of closets and libraries, schools and colleges, to dwell in clubs and assemblies, at tea-tables, and in coffee-houses."[28] Johnson declared, in *Rambler* Number 23 (June 5, 1750), that "he who endeavours to gain many readers, must try various arts of invitation, essay every avenue of pleasure, and make frequent changes in his methods of approach."[29] The recognition of a new audience—"many readers"—that had to be won as well as taught accounted for the varied approach of the mixtures in the periodicals. The principle of variation also suggests the need of the reader to adapt to different works and different situations. Shaftesbury's reference to a "mixed character," one adaptable to all things, is to the kind of consciousness that such works can develop.[30]

J. Paul Hunter has argued that "almost all eighteenth century literature meant to influence specific attitudes and actions relative to particular events, persons, and ideas, as well as more general loyalties." The popular tradition, for example, included among its kinds, "guide books, anthologies of examples of God's judgments and mercies, spiritual autobiographies and biographies, sermons, devotional tracts, meditations upon physical objects, tracts for the times, and treatises arguing almost every conceivable philosophical, theological or ethical issue."[31]

As an example of the mixture of the smaller poetic didactic forms with the larger, I point first to the epigram. The fact that the epigram became part of nondidactic forms was generally accepted. What was not unanimously shared was the approval of such combinations. John Sheffield, the Duke of Buckingham, objected to epigram in elegy:

> Trifles like these perhaps of late have past,
> And may be lik'd awhile, but never last;
> 'Tis Epigram, 'tis Point, 'tis what you will,
> But not an Elegie, nor writ with skill.[32] (110-13)

Addison rejected the propriety of epigram in the ballad. He recognized that the subjects of these poems could be those of the epic or the elegy and he admitted into them features from descriptive poetry, but he drew the line at epigram, remarking that had the "old song been filled with epigrammatical turns and points of wit, it might perhaps have pleased the wrong taste of some readers."[33] But Addison was clearly cognizant that the epigram, the didactic wit-turn, was infecting nonsatiric forms, for it had already appeared in the lyric, as well as in the epic. Dryden's "Alexander's Feast" and Pope's "Ode for Music on St. Cecilia's Day" did contain epigrammatical turns; later in the century Joseph Warton objected to the fact that these poems conclude with "an epigram of four lines; a species of wit as flagrantly unsuitable to the dignity, and as foreign to the nature, of the lyric, as it is of the epic muse."[34] But some critics, contemporaries of Addison, did consider the epigram as appropriate to the epic; epigrams, wrote Trapp, can "breathe a Spirit of Sublimity, every way becoming them."[35] Didactic features could not only be included in lyrics, but some extended lyrics could be considered as didactic expressions. When Blair listed his four types of ode, one was clearly didactic: "moral and philosophical odes."[36] The didactic element could even be applied to tragedy, not merely in terms of poetic justice, but in the management of the form. Comedy mixed with tragedy, some critics argued, was a clearer approximation to actual life than either of the purer forms. And this is the basis of Johnson's well-known defense of the "mingled drama." "That the mingled drama may convey all the instruction of tragedy or comedy cannot be denied, because it includes both in its alternations of exhibition, and approaches nearer than either to the appearance of life, by shewing how great machinations and slender designs may promote or obviate one another, and the high and the low cooperate in the general system by unavoidable concatenation."[37]

The neoclassical interrelation of poems and parts within poems resulted in the redefining of older forms. Traditional pastorals came to be seen as combinations of forms. With regard to Theocritus's *Idylls* and Virgil's *Eclogues,* for example, the procedure was to subdivide these works into discrete poems, thus permitting a new definition of pastoral that would not clash with tradition. Eighteenth-century critics pointed out that the "idyllium," the kind of poem Theocritus wrote, meant not "pastoral" but little scenes or pictures, applicable to many kinds of subjects in nature. And the name that Virgil used for his early poems, *eclogae,* was by derivation a term for "select poems," and if they were to be restricted to poems about shepherds, they need not be confined to a specific subject matter like the "Golden Age." The arguments for and against pastorals—the publication of ironic "pastorals" such as *The Beggar's Opera,* or attempts to modernize the form—illustrate the introduction of a didactic (here satiric) version of what had been a lyric poem. Even when Pope sought to present himself as a conservator of pastoral conventions, he found it necessary to "use some illusion to render a Pastoral delightful; and this consists in exposing the best side only of a shepherd's life, and in concealing its miseries."[38] The rationale of the ideal was didactic, applied to his audience and to his time.

By midcentury, the combination or mixtures of forms and parts of forms had come to be taken for granted. When Bishop Lowth came to discuss the sacred poetry of the Bible, it was apparent that this was a model of mixed religious forms. Even within the psalms themselves, Bishop Lowth discovered many kinds. The Book of Psalms, he wrote, "is a collection, under the general title of hymns to the praise of God, containing poems of different kinds, and elegies among the rest."[39]

Bringing the old forms into a new hierarchy and providing explanations for the new forms that resulted, the critics and authors argued for the "newness," the "new sort of writing" of the poetry and prose. Thus Thomas Sprat wrote of Cowley's Pindaric odes that they "may perhaps be thought rather a new sort of Writing,"[40] the newness being the swiftness of transition, the sudden shifts of level. In his "Apology" to *A Tale of a Tub,* Swift wrote (and the irony supports my contention of repeated claims to newness) that he "resolved to proceed in a manner, that should be altogether new, the World having been already too long nauseated with endless Repetitions upon every Subject."[41] This newness included the mixing of prose fiction with nonfictional narrative, the parody of varied forms, the mixing of allegory with scatology. Fielding, in the preface to *Joseph Andrews,* declared, "It may not be improper to premise a few words concerning this kind of writing, which I do not remember to have seen hitherto attempted in our language."[42] And Johnson in the life of Denham declared that Denham was the author of a new species of composition "of which the fundamental subject is some particular landscape to be poetically described, with the addition of such embellishments as may be supplied by historical retrospection or incidental meditation."[43] I need not point out that "historical retrospection" could include panegyric, elegy, and didactic exposition, and that "incidental meditation" could be expressed in hymns and psalms.

A new combination can be understood as a demonstration of authorial individuality. The particular combination that Johnson described had political implications because it treated landed estates as prospects from which to view past and present. The estate could be a perceptual viewpoint as well as a mediating position between past and future. Thus the particular variety it encompassed tended to support the role of the gentry.

II. THE INDIVIDUALITY OF FORMS

I have been arguing that within the hierarchy of kinds, the major forms often included the minor. I now wish to argue that major and minor forms were interrelated in terms of their parts or features: all or some could embrace, in addition to common subject matter and characters noted above, portions of a shared diction, a shared rhetoric, a shared procedure for allusions, and a shared style. In fact, the distinction between "form" and "mode" can make this clear. "Form" refers to a combination of means to lead to a specific effect; "mode" refers to kinds of means. Thus there is a pastoral form—Pope's or Phillips's "Pastorals"—but pastoral as a mode can apply to different poetic kinds—to "Lycidas," a pastoral elegy, to drama, *As You Like It*, to prose fiction, *Arcadia*, to selected features of the pastoral form such as descriptions of shepherds or nature. And the pastoral form itself could include panegyric and elegiac elements and satiric subject matter; it did not exclude even the epigram. Rosalie Colie remarked of Renaissance poetry that there was an art to be mastered for the eclogue form and the pastoral mode, for tragedy as a form and the tragic mode. "Those arts mastered," she wrote, "there is no reason other than conviction why they should not be used together—but they cannot be used with utter indiscriminateness. We have to know *why* they are intermixed."[44] The distinction of form and mode that applied to pastoral applied equally to satire and the georgic poem. The form-mode distinction can be understood as an interpretative procedure. The mode of pastoral or satire presupposed a knowledge of the whole form, and in that way a satiric passage depended upon a depth knowledge of the form in order to explain the mode. For example, it gave the mode of satire an interrelation with all synchronic forms that could include it as well as with satire as a form. The form-mode distinction, therefore, functioned synchronically in contrast, for example, with a feature like allusion to a past work, which functioned diachronically. The interrelation of forms, therefore, provides a basis for interpretation that distinguishes the language of surface structure from that which draws attention to itself as part of a past work or other contemporary genre. Thus translations, reworkings of Latin passages, become part both of the continuity of literature in this period and the basis for recognizing different levels in the linguistic code. Moreover, the form-mode distinction, especially in satire, georgic, and mixed prose forms, introduces referential truth into literature to combine with nonreferential.

The point is that interrelations among forms were reinforced by the form-mode distinction, since modes of satire, for example, could appear in most other forms. The specification of parts of any form was minimally defined, and it was precisely because this specification of parts was left open that the critics relied upon "propriety" and "decorum" as comparative (historical) guides. These concepts need to be understood as hypothetical constructs dependent upon the critic's specific application. The effectiveness of any assemblage of parts was determined by the critic's adherence to a view of unity that specified interrelations. Whether one welcomed or opposed greater freedom of transition in some forms rather than others, resisted or welcomed the diction of one form in another, the grounds of the criticism led back to the justification of God's and man's variety.

Since genres or forms were interrelated, it is self-evident that each genre had a specific identity. How was this identity determined? Bernard Weinberg concludes his discussion of sixteenth-century Italian practical criticism by drawing attention to the community of problems treated:

> Among such problems, the most important was that of the genres; it took several forms. For each of the Italian works, the disputants had to decide to what genre it belonged. If it was an old, recognized genre, then one must ask whether the work satisfactorily fulfilled the traditional requirements of the genre. If it was a new genre, then it was appropriate to inquire whether it should be admitted to the canon of legitimate and proper genres, how it should be practiced, on the basis of what analogies to the old genres its conditions should be circumscribed. Sometimes it was extremely difficult to assign the work to any genre, and lengthy descriptions of the work and definitions of the genre had to precede a solution. At all times the solution involved those same topics that were foremost in theoretical discussion: the nature of poetry and its ends, criteria, and precepts for practice. Frequently, several quarrels came to turn about the same genre, thus creating an immediate community of problems.[45]

The problem of genre involved at least two distinctions: one was to identify the class of works that belonged to poetry and the other was to identify specific kinds within this class. The first, therefore, inevitably made interrelations possible among all poems; the second drew attention to the number of specific interrelations between different genres. Every new genre involved a synchronic relation to the other genres, and each traditional genre had a diachronic history as well as a synchronic one.

Eighteenth-century critics, like Trapp, saw the forms as hierarchical, comprehensively embodied or capable of being harmoniously embodied in the drama or epic. One theory of forms, therefore, identified the kinds by their appropriate means and ends in the harmony. Another theory of harmony that critics carried into the eighteenth century was that of a concord resulting from apparent discord (*concordia discors*). It, too, necessarily embodied a mixture of divergent features, and it was used didactically to support the combination of oppositions. Critics like Blair, who argued for the specificity of forms, recognized that even within the ode, somewhat different effects could be achieved by altering means, for example, the subject matter. In order for an identity to be specified, it had to be seen as related to other forms and as distinct from them. The eighteenth-century intermixtures extended far beyond those specified in the Renaissance; and not only were they more didactic, they also included new types of such mixtures. Among these were new forms such as the periodical essay, the novel, prose fictions, and the altered older forms such as the georgic and the epistle.

This concept of kinds or genre granted that the kinds had specific effects, but these tended to become loosened in terms of the interrelations possible for each kind. Inevitably the extension of the parts that could fit a form led to the alteration of the effect of that form. There are four types of interrelation that I wish to illustrate: diction, rhetoric, allusion, and style. One of the commonest aspects of interrelations among eighteenth-century poetry was the use of different dictions within a "kind." In this respect, Pope's remark to Spence about the purity of diction in his pastorals merits quotation: "Though Virgil, in his pastorals, has sometimes six or eight lines together that are epic: I have been so scrupulous as scarce ever to admit above two together, even in the Messiah." Upon this Geoffrey Tillotson has remarked: "Mixing the kinds, he [Pope] knew what he was doing and marked off the component parts by the use of different kinds of diction (diction brings with it other linguistic modes such as personification, apostrophe, exclamation)."[46] This view of limited interchangeability of diction was not only taken for granted by the critics of the eighteenth century, it was practiced by the writers.

As an example of the manner in which diction from pastoral and elegy was applied to diverse forms, I quote a recurrent image in seventeenth- and eighteenth-century poetry, first noted in 1785 by John Scott of Amwell,[47] and recently by James Sutherland, who uses the image as an example of the "way in which an eighteenth-century poet willingly availed himself of 'happy combinations of words' and 'phrases poetically elegant in the English language.'"[48] The image is of flowers that bloom, unseen, in the desert.

If the hypothesis that each kind had its own diction were true, it would be unlikely that a figure such as the desert flower would be found in a love song by Waller, a mock-heroic epic by Pope, a fable by Ambrose Philips, a satire by Young, a georgic by Thomson, an elegy by Gray, and a didactic poem by Dyer.

Waller's song "Go, lovely Rose" (1645) is an address to the rose that is an ironic song of love:

> Tell her that's young,
> And shuns to have her Graces spy'd,
> That hadst thou sprung
> In Desarts where no men abide,
> Thou must have uncommended dy'd. (6–10)

Pope's "rose" occurs in a passage spoken by Belinda under the influence of "beauteous grief" at the loss of her lock:

> Oh had I rather un-admir'd remain'd
> In some lone Isle, or distant *Northern* Land;
> Where the gilt *Chariot* never marks the Way,
> Where none learn *Ombre*, none e'er taste *Bohea!*
> There kept my Charms conceal'd from mortal Eye,
> Like Roses that in Desarts bloom and die. (4.153-58)

Ambrose Philips in "The Fable of Thule" wrote:

> Half human thus by lineage, half divine,
> In forests did the lovely beauty shine,
> Like woodland flowers which paint the desert glades
> And waste their sweets in unfrequented shades. (37-40)

Ten years later (1728), in a satire on women in the *Universal Passion,* Young wrote:

> How gay *they* smile! Such blessings *nature* pours,
> O'erstock'd mankind enjoy but half her stores:
> In distant wilds, by human eyes unseen,
> She rears her flow'rs, and spreads her velvet green:
> Pure gurgling rills the lonely desert trace,
> And *waste* their music on the savage race. (5.163-68)

In the Autumn pastoral narrative about Lavinia, Thomson wrote in the revised 1744 version:

> As in the hollow Breast of Appenine
> Beneath the Shelter of encircling Hills,
> A Myrtle rises, far from human Eye,
> And breathes its balmy Fragrance o'er the Wild;
> So flourished blooming, and unseen by all,
> The sweet Lavinia. (210-15)

Gray's "Elegy" (1750) contains the most famous of the unseen flower lines:

> Full many a gem of purest ray serene
> The dark unfathomed caves of ocean bear:
> Full many a flower is born to blush unseen
> And waste its sweetness on the desert air. (53-56)

And John Dyer in *The Fleece* (1757), a didactic poem, in a passage dealing with the journey through Russia, wrote:

>   and on each hand
> Roads hung with carcases, or under foot
> Thick strown; while, in their rough bewildered vales,
> The blooming rose its fragrance breathes in vain,
> And silver fountains fall, and nightingales
> Attune their notes, where none are left to hear. (4.418-23)

  The flower born to blush unseen is a topos that is not, so far as its diction is concerned, species bound. The image stands for the possibilities of nature that can either be used or misused. It forms a part of the large body of eighteenth-century retirement imagery that sees innocence as a consequence of one's natural situation rather than as deliberate rejection of unpleasant situations or the sacrifice of one possibility in order to retain others. The image is an example of God's fruitfulness at the same time that it suggests the unavailability of this variety to men; such an example, therefore, suggests that God's "Nature is but Art, unknown to thee."[49] The diction that derives from a language about nature in the pastoral can fit the song, elegy, satire, georgic, fable, pastoral, and mock-heroic; its maneuverability rests on the potentiality of forms to accommodate perceptual responses to nature as a norm. Each form had some kinds of diction considered appropriate to it, but the interrelation of the diction explains how the forms could be understood as resembling, comprehending, enhancing, or even contrasting with one another.

When Wordsworth continued the flower image in "Lucy Gray," it was concealed in a metaphor:

> No Mate, no comrade Lucy knew;
> She dwelt on a wild Moor,
> The sweetest thing that ever grew
> Beside a human door! (5-8)

The metaphor places Lucy within nature, a procedure that differed from the didactic separation of man from nature, a separation identified by the interaction of one kind of nature (flowers) with another ("distant wilds" or "desert air"). The response of the speaker to Lucy is to hold out the ambiguous possibility of her continued presence, like a natural force. This ambiguity, this mysterious possibility, is not, of course, the same limitation to be found in the unavailable beauty of eighteenth-century imagery.

The shift in implication can, perhaps, be used to indicate how even a pastoral image in the eighteenth century is used "didactically"—that is, to underline the apparent "waste" of nature, to draw attention to the need for belief and acceptance. For Wordsworth, the image becomes an instance of the extraordinary possibilities of the ordinary. The "footmarks" are the signs not of nature's limits, but of the manner in which nature's death-marks (her limitations) may become life-marks. Geoffrey H. Hartman refers to the Lucy poems by saying that "Lucy's fulfillment by nature and her passing into it (her death) coincide."[50] And he draws attention to the role of the speaker whose consciousness is altered by Lucy's death. The eighteenth-century speaker must again and again acknowledge and accept the limitation of "waste" and "death." What is apparent, then, is the manner in which the topos functions when it is part of the eighteenth-century hierarchy dominated by didactic forms and when it becomes part of the hierarchy dominated by lyrical forms.

The examples I have been giving of mixtures within forms apply to prose as well as poetry. The features of subject or language could fit more than one end. Thus the language of burlesque and parody, according to Fielding, could be admitted into his comic epic in prose on the grounds of the diverse audiences (here the classical reader is invoked). In his preface to *Joseph Andrews* he wrote: "In the diction, I think, burlesque itself may be sometimes admitted" in order to titillate "the classical reader, for whose entertainment those parodies or burlesque imitations are chiefly calculated." But he declared that "we have carefully excluded it from our sentiments and characters; for there it is never properly introduced, unless in writings of the burlesque kind."[51] The point that Fielding makes is that the mixed diction is directed at the classical audience, but that burlesque mixtures are not able to be tolerated in the characters or sentiments of a comic epic. Other mixtures, such as the use of inset stories and the introductory essays, were, however, acceptable practices, too common to be noted in the preface.

I wish to draw attention here to the principle of interrelation as it can appear in fiction. The levels of diction that Fielding permits are only one aspect of the variety of interrelation his novels reveal. For interrelation of characters—the relation between Parson Adams and Parson Trulliber in *Joseph Andrews,* or the relation among the varied innkeepers in *Tom Jones*—is based on the principle of degrees of difference within similarity. Interrelation that is necessary to distinction can be considered a principle of knowledge, a method of distinguishing by degrees of comparison. Characters, like diction, can reveal subtle differences by the interrelation of levels.

Discussions of diction should be distinguished from rhetorical features that could be applied to any form, though both are types of interrelation. Bishop Lowth, for example, pointed out that antithetic parallelism—"when a thing is illustrated by its contrary being opposed to it"—is "not confined to any particular form; for sentiments are opposed to sentiments, words to words, singulars to singulars, plurals to plurals."[52] This feature of style can occur in proverbs as it can in the superior kinds of Hebrew poetry. And although it is not frequent in sublime poetry, Bishop Lowth quotes several examples from Isaiah:

> In a little anger have I forsaken thee;
> But with great mercies will I receive thee again.
> In a short wrath I hid my face for a moment from thee
> But with everlasting kindness will I have mercy on thee.[53]

Rhetorical features that can appear in all forms provide yet another basis for harmony. If "antithetical parallelism" could apply to all forms, though to some more readily than to others, so, too, could repetition, allusion, and other figures. Bishop Lowth refers to rhetorical figures, but even specific images like that of the desert flower could appear in most kinds. The extension of a rhetorical feature or a specific diction was governed by propriety of function. The relation of part to whole, the manner in which a part could be fitted into the poem in terms of transition, combination, and effect, formed the basis for its approval or disapproval.

This is the point at which to introduce the concept of the sublime style as a feature locatable in the various kinds. Of the five sources or springheads of the sublime listed by Longinus three are the result of art. The last of these related to connection of selected parts to produce sublimity in the whole composition: "Now, as there are no Subjects, which are not attended by some adherent Circumstances, an accurate and judicious Choice of the most suitable of these Circumstances, and an ingenious and skilful Connexion of them into one Body, must necessarily produce the Sublime. For what by the judicious Choice, and what by the skilful Connexion, they cannot but very much affect the Imagination."[54]

The translator, William Smith, makes clear that he interprets "judicious choice" as applicable to a poem as a whole as well as narrative divisions. Thus he refers to Adam and Eve in *Paradise Lost* as the "finest Picture of conjugal Love." "In its Serenity and Sunshine, it is noble, amiable, endearing, and innocent."[55] Such a passage could be found in drama as well as epic, in heroic epistle as well as in odes or pastorals. The other two sources of art were figures and noble expression (choice of words and diction).

These formed sublime passages in their effect upon the reader or hearer, and one such example can be found in the allusion to a moment of immobility—a marble moment—in *Eloisa to Abelard*. Eloisa's cry: "I have not yet forgot my self to stone" (24) is an allusion to *Il Penseroso:* "Forget thyself to marble" (42), a line in which the goddess of melancholy is described in her accustomed state:

> Thy rapt soul sitting in thine eyes:
> There held in holy passion still,
> Forget thyself to marble. (40-42)

The propriety of the allusion rests on the kind of poem Pope is writing: the Ovidian epistle, a type of poem that because of its emotive contrasts could incorporate sublime expressions. "It is indeed no other," declares Joseph Warton, "than a passionate soliloquy; in which, the mind gives vent to the distresses and emotions under which it labours: . . . Judgment is chiefly shewn, by opening the interesting complaint just at such a period of time, as will give occasion for the most tender sentiments, and the most sudden and violent turns of passion, to be displayed."[56] The line from the pastoral suits the situation of passion while at the same time providing Pope with ironic overtones, since Eloisa is a nun without the purity or the calmness of serene Melancholy, and the "stone" is not "marble."

The propriety of allusions depends on the comprehensive range of diction in the epistle. The allusion moves beyond the single line to the two poetic kinds—the pastoral and the heroic epistle—as spoken addresses (dramatic monologues). One is addressed to contemplation and the consistent values of meditative melancholy. The other is addressed to the speaker's self with her inconsistent turns of meditation and melodrama. The common feature is the expression of meditation, and it is the different ends of pastoral and epistle that make Pope's irony possible. This point can be supported by reference to the mock epic and its requirement of a knowledge of the epic in order that the parody or irony be understood.

Augustan writers use allusion not merely to draw attention to species relations (parody and mock heroic) but to indicate competitive adaptation of a classical phrase or passage to the present situation. In this respect allusion resembles the concept of accretion of knowledge by degree because it is the degree of alteration or distortion that gives the allusion its significance. In addition, allusion is a form of "historical retrospection" because it calls attention to a past that is usable in the poet's present situation. And thus the concept of interrelation and intermixture is applied to historical as well as formal understanding.

Allusion, as it presents itself for interpretation, belongs to a different coding procedure from common rhetorical devices and themes. It belongs to the past used in the present to distinguish it from the present—as in translated passages from Virgil or Horace or Juvenal. It thus is part of the subsurface structure of historical meaning the form possesses, providing a guide to the comparative basis of the two poems (and societies), since two types of propriety or decorum are being intermingled.

If we accept the principle that a line from a pastoral poem can be appropriate to an epistle, and if the line retains some of its original context, then the notion of unity implied cannot be "indivisible." It is a unity that permits associations that are appropriate, and thus each work is a combination of features governed by the criteria of fitness to the passage and the form. This can only be judged in terms of how transitions are made, and this is, indeed, one of the considerations of this criticism. In Warton's discussion of *An Essay on Criticism,* he declared that each of the precepts "naturally introduce the succeeding ones, so as to form an entire whole." And he invoked Richard Hurd on Horace's *Epistle to the Pisos* in which "the connexions are delicately fine and almost imperceptible, like the secret hinges of a well-wrought box, yet they artfully and closely unite each part together, and give coherence, uniformity, and beauty to the work."[57] And Johnson in his Dictionary characterized the "greater ode" by "sublimity, rapture and quickness of transition."[58]

The principles of unity, therefore, whether of the didactic poem or ode, were governed by types of connection or association. These could be contrast, or resemblance, or cause and effect, or place and consequence, or time and its relations; indeed, as the century proceeded, the types of possible connection or transition grew so extensive that at the end of the century Dugald Stewart recognized that any relations could be associated provided the proper transitions were made. The hierarchy of forms thus became ambiguous, and many of the individual distinctions among elegy, ode, panegyric, song, idyll, georgic, satire were eroded so that when Wordsworth set up his six groups in 1815, one, narrative, was a new class; the dramatic included opera and the lyric excluded pastoral; and the last three—the Idyllic, the Didactic, and Philosophic Satire—could be recognized as the basis for a new "composite order" of poems "of which Young's *Night Thoughts,* and Cowper's *Task,* are excellent examples."[59]

The shift from a hierarchy adapted to didactic forms to one adjusted to lyric forms can be best noted in the ascendancy of the lyric and the decline of epic and dramatic forms. The lyric becomes, in the early nineteenth century, dominated by the principle of pure or spontaneous poetry. The didactic forms are, then, self-evident composites of purity and impurity. The associative or combinatory unity of the didactic poem is seen as a collection of fragments in contrast to the organic unfolding of the lyric.

As a result of the variety within works due to the subjects and to the mixtures, the transitions and combinations led to procedures for emphatic closures. Some works could be associatively expanded; the author sought for an assertive conclusion, one that clearly announced and satisfied the need for a conclusion, if, indeed, anything was to be concluded. The announcement of the "conclusion" to *A Tale of a Tub* or the insistent conclusion of *The Dunciad* demonstrates this procedure.

Barbara H. Smith, in dealing with the closural force of unqualified assertions, writes that "when universals and absolutes (words such as 'all,' 'none,' 'only,' and 'always') occur in assertions, they are themselves the expressions of the speaker's inability or refusal to qualify. . . . All such nonqualifying words and phrases tend to have closural effects when they occur as terminal features in an utterance or a poem, for they not only reinforce our sense of the speaker's conviction but are themselves expressions of comprehensiveness, climax, or finality."⁶⁰ She quotes the conclusion of the 1742 *Dunciad* as an example of such closure. I believe this argument is sound, but it needs amplification in dealing with Augustan poems. Closure needs to be asserted because, within the poem, additions can be and are fully and frequently made. *The Rape of the Lock, The Seasons, The Pleasures of the Imagination* were like *The Dunciad* expanded poems with strong closures, but the closure did not prevent expansion of the varied means. Interrelations and intermixtures could be increased and one of the consequences was that the conclusion had to be asserted in an unqualified way. Within the body of *The Dunciad* revisions could be and were made. *The Dunciad Variorum* of 1729 concluded:

> "In vain! they gaze, turn giddy, rave, and die.
> Thy hand great Dulness! lets the curtain fall,
> And universal Darkness covers all."
> "Enough! enough!" the raptur'd Monarch cries;
> And thro' the Ivory Gate the Vision flies.

Although Pope added a fourth book to *The Dunciad* in 1742, the ending remained equally assertive:

> Thy hand, great Anarch! lets the curtain fall;
> And Universal Darkness buries All.

The kind of unity that "Species" criticism propounded can be understood from Pope's didactic *Essay on Criticism*. The passage on the "Whole" reads as follows:

> A perfect Judge will *read* each work of Wit
> With the same spirit that its Author writ,
> Survey the Whole, nor seek slight Faults to find,
> Where *Nature moves,* and *Rapture warms,* the Mind. (233-36)

The ends of the poem are to explain what proper criticism is and who the model practitioners were and are. These two couplets form part of an explanation of the faults, for "Whoever thinks a faultless Piece to see, / Thinks what ne'er was, nor is, nor e'er shall be" (253-54). The different species imitate different kinds of human action, and the underlying metaphor of this imitation, for Pope, is a poem as a body with an informing soul or spirit that is "*it self unseen,* but in the Effects, remains" (79). The moving quality of poetry, its vigor, resides in the manner in which parts combine, join, or unite. Parts should neither be regularly dull nor monstrously irregular, but between regularity and monstrosity there looms the theory of species. Nature to all things "fix'd the Limits fit" (52), but the "fixity"—the rules—were governed by interrelations, and the discovery of the limits depended upon the knowledge of acceptable interrelations. Of course, each species was distinct in the sense that it had its own end (however ambiguous this was). But many of the features were interrelated with other forms so that "distinctness" was a matter of degree rather than of kind. And all forms were part of a family of forms, rather than distinct or isolated species. Critics who ignore this interrelationship whether by thinking of species as pure or denying that the concept of species is useful for us are both wrong. Species were part of an interrelated hierarchy and the parts of each species were related to others. Species were not "pure" even though critics sought to make them "pure" by reducing mixtures. But a theory of kinds is necessary if we are to understand how, and in what ways, eighteenth-century works can be interpreted.

Pope warned against making the whole "depend upon a Part," but he was aware of the need to make the parts unite; and this meant that the parts themselves—the figures, the meter, the light and dark shading—had to be carefully worked. The features that helped give life to forms—the careful sublime, the proper turn of wit, the description of detail and of the prospect, and, indeed, all the figures of poetry—became a source for inquiry because their various usages demanded distinctions between minute eccentricity and acceptable individuality within the range of the species. As time went on, these discriminations became more refined. And the increased refinement made the distinction of effect difficult to sustain.

III. THE MODEL APPLIED

In the late seventeenth and eighteenth centuries, "kind" was identified by its effect upon the reader, but since the higher forms could include the lower, "kinds" clearly could have multiple effects. The lower forms were interrelated in terms of their parts—character, subject matter, diction, and style—and thus the forms could be seen as sharing qualities, styles, and intermediate as against final effects. This concept of form meant that any particular kind was a combination of features, only the minimum of which was identified with the "kind" itself, and even this minimum was not agreed upon by all critics. Each form could, therefore, be understood as a combination or association joined together for a given effect. But whether that effect was achieved depended on the kinds of transitions, the idea of propriety or decorum that the critic held.

No critic denied mixtures or interrelations, but some claimed that the "purity" of form was to be obtained by limiting the mixtures from other forms.

In this section I shall discuss how eighteenth-century critics saw the historical development of interrelations of forms, and how two new forms support the premise I have been arguing.

The ascendancy of mixed didactic forms in the Augustan period can, perhaps, be understood in terms of the more general theory of the progress of literature. According to Hugh Blair, for example, odes, hymns, elegies, panegyrics, epics, and tragedies were originally all one: "None of these kinds of poetry, however, were in the first ages of society properly distinguished or separated, as they are now, from each other. Indeed, not only were the different kinds of poetry then mixed together, but all that we now call letters, or composition of any kind, was then blended in one mass.... When the progress of society brought on a separation of the different arts and professions of civil life, it led also by degrees to a separation of the different literary provinces from each other."[61]

Blair was not the only critic who identified all the forms as originally one, gradually assuming individual identities as society became organized into arts and professions. Poetic forms, argued these critics, had their genesis in social forms so that subsequently successful interrelations became instances of civilized harmony whereas their unfortunate mixtures—for example, Addison's remarks on the epigram included in "Chevy Chase"—were forms of disharmony. The progress was, then, from homogeneity to heterogeneity; when the principle is reversed one gets a work like *A Tale of a Tub*, which begins with clearly distinguished narrative and digressive sections that become indistinguishable. It moves from heterogeneity to homogeneity.

The interrelation of forms has not often been noted, and Ronald Paulson, one of the few who do note this, connects the seventeenth-century anatomy, sermon, polemical pamphlet, and heroic drama. But he does so to argue that in "all of these forms detail takes on a greater autonomy than is always consistent with the over-all aim of the work."[62] Paulson is correct in identifying features of mixed forms, but inaccurate in assuming that mixtures are forms of disorder.

Among the mixed forms not often noticed are the annotated editions of Greek, Latin, and English authors. Although these were inherited from the Renaissance, in the seventeenth and eighteenth centuries they were frequently addressed to audiences for purposes of edification. Indeed, at the end of the century (1795), Vicesimus Knox argued for the validity of "miscellanies" through the sanction of past works such as Seneca's *Epistles* and Horace's *Sermones*. "Nor let the grave and austere despise them as trifling amusements only," he wrote, "for the mind is nourished by variety of food . . . like the body by a commixture of fish, flesh, fowl, and vegetables."[63]

Both the annotations and miscellanies were parodied in works such as *A Tale of a Tub, Tom Thumb,* and *The Dunciad*. And the parody of *A Tale of a Tub*, for example, was to undermine false mixtures (of learning and religion) and, by implication, to suggest proper ones.

The first edition of *A Tale* was published in 1704; the fifth, with "An Apology" and additional notes, was issued in 1710. The latter work is the result of multiple authorship, or so we are led to believe: the Grub Street author, the bookseller, the group of commentators, and, in the 1710 Apology, the author behind the Grub Street author. The forms include, in addition to the Apology, a dedication by the "Bookseller," an address of the "Bookseller to the Reader," a dedicatory epistle to Prince Posterity by the author, a "Preface," and a narrative in the form of a folktale that turns into an allegory, a series of digressive essays, and a body of annotations. Of course, the prefaces are parodies of Dryden's procedures, but they function as do the digressions, to create disjunctions in the reading of the narrative which begins as a folktale: "Once upon a Time, there was a Man who had Three Sons by one Wife, and all at a Birth. . . ." But it is a tale never finished: "I can only assure thee, Courteous Reader, for both our Comforts, that my Concern is altogether equal to thine, for my Unhappiness in losing, or mislaying among my Papers the remaining Part of these Memoirs. . . ."[64]

Not only is the narrative of the brothers unfinished, but the irresponsibility revealed in the failure to keep the memoir together is unreproved. The narrative is based on papers—a memoir—by an unreliable keeper, who lacks respect for the past, yet who sees as his task the justification and restoration of the "Grub Street Brotherhood."

The *Tale* with its many forms is, on one level, an attempt to provide a justification of Grub Street writing by a cooperative authorship, with Wotton and others explaining the difficult passages of the tale and digressions. But on another level, the serial reading of the *Tale* is interrupted for the reader, the different forms are monstrous and they interfere with an understanding of the allegory, and, finally, in Section XI, they become mingled and destroy the harmony of form.

The disharmony of forms has its source in the failure of the Grub Street writer to discriminate true from false values of the past, just as the brothers are involved in the over-refined interpretation of the father's will and their consequent disregard of it. Both their disregard and, on the part of two brothers, their restoration of the will come from the pressures of their situations, not from a respect for or admiration of the father.

The interrelation of narrative and digression arises from an attempt to justify a "Brotherhood" that has become divided in itself, and the diversity of forms is an attempt to restore the eminence of one faction. But the consequence of this indiscriminate diversity is to alienate the reader and to create in him an opposition to this type of false learning. Swift indicates the manner in which diversity becomes madness, in which dismembered fragments form a grotesque harmony, whether it is the confluence of garbage in "A Description of a City Shower" or the confluence of narrative and digression in *A Tale*.

In *A Tale* the narrative itself becomes a form of digression, the object being to indicate the historical discontinuity, the corruption of judgment, and, finally, the corruption of human responsibility. I believe John Clark is right when he says that in "Section XI all coherence is gone. In a climax of sorts, tale and digression merge, become confounded."[65] The idea of a "digression" or a "wandering" belongs with the mingling of forms to suggest a harmony or a disharmony. The associated terms were "incident," "episode," and "diversion," the first referring to events in which the characters advance the main action of an epic, the second referring to actions collateral to the main one; "diversion," another of the metaphors of wandering, indicates that the author has turned from the narrative to relieve the tension of the reader or to provide him with a new object of interest. The diversion can be another narrative or an essay or, as is claimed in the "Preface" to *A Tale*, it can refer to the whole work: "at a Grand Committee, some Days ago, this important Discovery was made by a certain curious and refined Observer; That Seamen have a Custom when they meet a *Whale,* to fling him out an empty *Tub,* by way of Amusement, to divert him from laying violent Hands upon the Ship."[66]

The digression essay as a form belongs not only to the mingling of species in this period, but to Swift's special way of thinking about such mixtures. He seems obsessed with the transformations of norms to abnorms, of diversions to deviations. If we consider the use of forms in *Gulliver's Travels,* we can recognize that the four voyages are all forms that digress; they detail Gulliver's wanderings from the destinations for which he sets sail, but, contrariwise, he always returns to England from which he sets out. The repetitive digressions, each a narrative of interest in its own right, ultimately lead to alienation at home. I do not mean to imply that the voyages result in increasing alienation or that *Gulliver's Travels* is organized by any plan of progression. Rather, the voyaging or wandering accidentally leads Gulliver to a country that he admires. Being prepared there to desist from wandering, he is compelled once again to set forth. It is this sense of frustrated desire that makes his return a digressive voyage. What was previously a return to recognition becomes now a return to alienation.

The multiple authorship of *A Tale of a Tub* leads Denis Donoghue to suggest that the author is really anonymous. But this is to misunderstand the place of multiple authorship, whether fictitious as here, or actual as in the Scriblerus papers or the numerous poetical miscellanies. This authorship is used by Swift to insist on quite different identities that become entangled and unfortunately fused. Authors can be seen in prefaces, for example, that introduce poets, as quite properly maintaining their identity, decorum, and honesty. But not in *A Tale,* where the authors of the notes, the bookseller, the digressor are part of a family of falsely learned men and corrupted critics who perpetrate such works on readers.

The brotherhood is indeed the corrupted family of which the three brothers represent the model—one birth leading to three sons and many scholars leading to one misshapen birth. In its concern with sects and factions, *A Tale* is not only about the kinds of learned folly in a commonwealth, it is a fable of civil war, with brother plotting against brother.

Swift's use of forms is representative of the factionalism of society, and the dangers of this division. Addison, while agreeing on the existence of factions, sought to mediate among them in his writings. Indeed, this is precisely the use of forms developed in the periodical essay of which the *Spectator* can be taken as a standard. It included a fictional narrative of Sir Roger de Coverley and the members of his club, together with critical essays, prose fictions, sermons, epistles. Roy M. Wiles writes of the narratives of the *Spectator:* "In the 635 numbers there is an abundance of fables, moral tales, dreams, visions, allegories, and autobiographical letters."[67] To these should be added diaries, criticisms, arguments, and letters from correspondents. If one considers the *Spectator* with its varied fare and compares it with the periodical publication of Dickens's novels, one finds that Addison and Steele sought to contribute to an understanding of the world by addressing the different groups within it: "well-regulated families," "the fraternity of spectators," "the Blanks of Society," and the "female world" (*Spectator* 10). The aim of the periodical was "to make instruction agreeable" and "diversion useful" to the readers (*Spectator* 10). Dickens's view of his audience was more homogeneous, his fictions more tightly unified, his aim more consistent with the novel.

In the first number Addison identified the impartial character of the spectator with the concept of withdrawal as insight: by not participating in life one "can discern the errors in the economy, business and diversion of others, better than those who are engaged in them." The reason for this is that zeal is misleading. He related the diversity of his plan to political neutrality, the need to avoid party conflict. The diversity of forms was a way of providing a variety of interests that minimized the possibility of intense party commitment and violence. In *Spectator* 125 he wrote: "There cannot a greater judgment befal a country, than such a dreadful spirit of division as rends a government into two distinct people."[68]

If the periodical paper is seen as a combinatory form the purpose of which is to provide knowledge to a varied audience, to interest diverse groups, to reduce political pressures or factions, one of the methods is to welcome participation of the audience by providing the possibility of cooperative authorship through letters to the *Spectator*. Another is to create multiple expectations by writing diverse essays that interrupt a series, such as the papers on *Paradise Lost* (267, 273, 285, 291, etc.) or *The Pleasures of the Imagination*.

The interrelation of forms served to foster a consciousness of interrelation of interests in readers. It suggested a mode of harmony that had as its implicit analogy God's variety. At the same time the interplay of forms helped reduce the rigidity of a literary hierarchy, for as subjects and languages were shared, the aims of the forms themselves grew more heterogeneous.

The primacy of didactic mixed forms has been identified with the awareness of religious and political factionalism. The hospitality to diversity, the desire to insist on proper discrimination or taste or decorum, the addresses to readers with instructions are all literary features that, by imitating human action, illustrated how diversity could or should be properly pursued. The principle of variety of features can thus be seen as corresponding to defenses of general principles of human nature by indicating the kinds of variations within any form.

The political underpinning of mixed forms necessarily gave to didactic works direct or indirect political implications. For Augustan writers and readers, these forms had to combine truth with fiction if their teaching was to be realized. The truth statements that combined with fictional narratives did not suddenly themselves become fictions. Because works were not indivisible wholes, truth and fiction could be related without being fused. Consider an example from the "Apology" to *A Tale of a Tub*. Swift writes: "The greatest Part of that Book was finished above thirteen Years since, 1696, which is eight Years before it was published." This is a true statement and all our additional evidence supports it. When he writes, "In the Author's Original Copy there were not so many Chasms as appear in the Book; and why some of them were left he knows not,"[69] this statement so far as we know is false. I have chosen two simple instances, but truth-value was also to be found in an *Essay on Man* with its moral and metaphysical precepts. And it was to be found in Fielding's addresses to the reader. Truth statements were a necessary part of didactic poems and could be found in panegyric, elegy, most prose forms. Readers, therefore, were addressed, challenged, guided, and goaded to discover the proper distinctions, not because earlier theories had not made them, but because mixtures had become so prevalent. The mixtures created a new kind of reader whose reading procedures undermined the overt statement about general human nature the works contained.

This discussion of the Augustan concept of species has dwelt on the critics' awareness of and the authors' practice of and the readers' responses to genre mixtures and interrelations. And the critics were not unaware of the individual responses they were cultivating. In explaining that under the general title of hymns were included many forms such as panegyrics, lyrics, and elegies, as well as hymns, Bishop Lowth remarked that the classification of forms in the book of Psalms "is a matter dependant in a great measure upon opinion, and not to be clearly demonstrated upon determinate principles; since the nature of the subject, the complexion of the style, or the general form and disposition of each poem, must decide the question; and . . . different persons will judge differently upon these points."[70] Their procedure was to assume that various combinations of features could be subsumed under the usual ends. But their statements about species and their practice of composition can only be made clear by an approach to genre that accounts for change synchronically as well as diachronically, by the nature of received forms and the alteration these undergo as a result of the commitment to mixtures, in this period, characteristic of didactic forms.

As the number of possible combinations of features increased in the course of the eighteenth century, the ends of the species began to change as well. Species criticism then ceased to provide the generalizations governing variety, generalizations necessary to explain how art provided models for mediation or meditation.

IV. SOME CONCLUSIONS

What are the implications of my thesis that neoclassical forms were mixed and interrelated, dominated by didactic models? With regard to the theory of genres, this view undermines the hypothesis that forms were pure or rigid. Some forms, like the epic and drama, were never considered "pure," and in the late seventeenth century the ideas of "purity" of form implied the removal of interrelations considered inappropriate, but appropriate interrelations were sanctioned.

The hierarchy that writers and critics of this period inherited from the Renaissance was altered in terms of the elevation of the longer didactic forms: the georgic, the epistle, and satire. But my argument is that the practice of all forms was infected by the didactic shift so that the elegy, lyric, ode, even drama and epic came to incorporate features of didactic forms or sometimes the forms themselves. Critics did not always agree on the propriety of such interrelations, but no critic denied that they existed.

The consequence of this for a theory of genre is that generic studies cannot be understood merely in terms of family traits or variation of a form studied diachronically. A genre is a part, at any period in literary history, of a family of forms. To study a form or genre one must grasp it in relation to other forms within the poetic hierarchy, just as one must understand prose forms—when no hierarchy exists—in terms of the principle of interrelation. This means that a genre course needs to be taught not merely in terms of a single kind, but of a hierarchy of kinds—for tragedy cannot be properly understood in its own traits or terms.

Critics referred and still refer to the principle of propriety or decorum and to the "rules" as a basis for judging the adequacy of any interrelation. These criteria were rooted in claims about the propriety of human relations and about the specific effects that works were to have upon readers or hearers at a particular time in history. The principle of interrelation, governed as it was by didactic procedures, altered the received effects by altering the means by which effects were achieved. Thus what needs to be emphasized is the freedom encouraged by the comparative critics and the procedures of interrelation. As the eighteenth century moved on, the justification of interrelations became a matter of the critic's acceptance or rejection of transitions, combinations, relation of part to whole. And these were inevitably tied to the critic's historical consciousness, his view of propriety as a comparative response to a modern reader's expectations.

ON THE INTERRELATIONS OF EIGHTEENTH-CENTURY LITERARY FORMS

The stipulation of "rules" was primarily cautionary and relative, urging writers not to take certain freedoms. But the interrelation of forms made such guides questionable, especially since the forms were part of a hierarchy not fully understood.

The implication of this thesis for interpretation is extensive. No literary work in the period can be understood without recognizing that it is a combination of parts or forms. This provides a basis for understanding "unity" as a *combination or interrelation of parts*. This unity will make it possible to relate a particular work to other works of the period. As I have demonstrated in regard to *A Tale of a Tub* and the *Spectator,* works that are considered disorganized or a series of discrete items can be seen as wholes in terms of the harmony of forms. Interpretation of eighteenth-century forms involves the recognition of features like allusion or mode as subsurface elements. Allusion draws attention to historical reexamination of a past work or passage or idea; mode involves the relation of a form like satire to its reduced function as part of another form. Such elements need to be compared to rhetorical procedures like repetition or antithetical parallelism that are available in other synchronic forms; these rhetorical procedures are parts of a common code in contrast to allusion or mode, which are parts of a different coding procedure. Combinations within a work permit different codes governed by the same procedures, but also different codes with different procedures.

The theoretical position of interrelation of forms and mixture of parts also leads to a view of language that combines two kinds of truth—referential and nonreferential—in the same work. Thus the idea of associative, composite, or combinatory forms requires the modern reader to adjust to depth as well as surface variations of language and to locate his selection of values within these rather than within the work as a self-reflexive whole.

Thus there becomes available a procedure for relating annotated forms like Latin poetry or English models to their parodies, such as *Tom Thumb* and *The Dunciad.* And forms not considered wholes—*Miscellanies,* periodical papers—can be understood as related by a common principle to the organization of literary forms contemporary with them.

Not only does this procedure widen the scope of what "literature" was considered to be, but it provides a basis for explaining why a particular principle of interrelation was enacted or recognized. In terms of literary history, this common procedure provides a basis for period analysis, distinguishing the interrelations of the late seventeenth and eighteenth centuries from those that preceded and those that followed.

Such a hypothesis provides a systematic basis for dealing with literary forms in all periods, and in doing so it takes account of the continuity of forms and their interrelations, the changes that occur in these forms, the introduction of new and the abandonment of old forms. And it is a hypothesis that explains more works and more features within works than the premise of rigid, distinct, and continuous genres that it supplants.

NOTES

1. René Wellek and Austin Warren, *Theory of Literature*, 3rd ed. (1942; New York: Harcourt Brace, Jovanovich, 1962), 229.

2. James Sutherland, *A Preface to Eighteenth Century Poetry* (1948; Oxford: Clarendon, 1962), 124.

3. Oliver F. Sigworth, *Criticism and Aesthetics, 1660-1800* (San Francisco: Rinehart Press, 1971), xv, xvi.

4. Emerson R. Marks, *The Poetics of Reason* (New York: Random House, 1968), 92. See also Francis Gallaway, *Reason, Rule and Revolt in English Classicism* (1940; Lexington: Univ. of Kentucky Press, 1965), 228: "the distaste for any mixture of 'kinds' indicate[s] the preoccupation of neo-classicists with the Rules of specific literary forms."

5. René Wellek, *A History of Modern Criticism: 1750-1950* (New Haven, CT: Yale Univ. Press, 1955), 1:19, 20.

6. Irène Simon, ed., *Neo-Classical Criticism 1660-1800* (London: Edward Arnold; Columbia: Univ. of South Carolina Press, 1971), 14.

7. "Preface to Theatrum Poetarum (1675)," in *Critical Essays of the Seventeenth Century*, ed. J. E. Spingarn (Oxford: Clarendon, 1908), 2:266, 267.

8. John Dryden, "A Discourse Concerning the Original and Progress of Satire," in *Of Dramatic Poesy and Other Critical Essays*, ed. George Watson (London: J. M. Dent & Sons, 1962), 2:82.

9. John Sheffield, "An Essay Upon Poetry," in Spingarn, *Critical Essays*, 2:295.

10. Dryden, *Of Dramatic Poesy*, 2:113-15, 149.

11. Norman Maclean, "From Action to Image: Theories of the Lyric in the Eighteenth Century," in *Critics and Criticism*, ed. R. S. Crane (Chicago: Univ. of Chicago Press, 1952), 410.

12. Sir Philip Sidney, "An Apologie for Poetrie," in *Elizabethan Critical Essays*, ed. G. Gregory Smith (1904; London: Oxford Univ. Press, 1950), 1:175. The terms "kindes," "species," "forms," and "genres" are used interchangeably throughout the paper.

13. Rosalie L. Colie, *The Resources of Kind: Genre-Theory in the Renaissance* (Berkeley: Univ. of California Press, 1973), 114-15.

14. Thomas Hobbes, "Answer to Davenant's Preface to *Gondibert*," in Spingarn, *Critical Essays*, 2:55, 56.

15. Joseph Trapp, *Lectures on Poetry* (London: C. Hitch and C. Davis, 1742), 10; also 328.

16. Dryden, *Of Dramatic Poesy*, 2:82.

17. Aristotle, *Poetics*, trans. S. H. Butcher, in *Criticism: The Major Texts*, ed. W. J. Bate (1952; New York: Harcourt Brace Jovanovich, 1970), 5.22, 13.34, 24.35, 26.38.

18. George Puttenham, *The Arte of English Poesie* (1589), in Smith, *Elizabethan Critical Essays*, 2:40, 46.

19. Philip Sidney, "Apologie," in Smith, *Elizabethan Critical Essays*, Smith, 1:159.

20. Joseph Addison, "An Essay on Virgil's *Georgics*" (1697), in *The Works of Joseph Addison*, ed. T. Tickell (London: printed by T. Maiden, 1804), 5:454.

21. Thomas Tickell, "De Poesi Didactica," in *Thomas Tickell and the Eighteenth Century Poets (1685-1740)*, by Richard Eustace Tickell (London: Constable, 1931), 199.

22. Trapp, *Lectures*, 180, 186, 200.

23. R. S. Crane, "Critical and Historical Principles of Literary History," in *The Idea of the Humanities* (Chicago: Univ. of Chicago Press, 1967), 2:85. Johnson's *Dictionary* (1765) under "Didascalick," a synonym for "didactic," contains a quotation from Prior indicating the ambiguous interrelation of "didascalick" and "heroic."

24. See M. H. Nicolson, *Newton Demands the Muse* (1946; Princeton, NJ: Princeton Univ. Press, 1966), *Science and Imagination* (Ithaca, NY: Cornell Univ. Press, 1956), and *The Breaking of the Circle* (Evanston, IL: Northwestern Univ. Press, 1950).

25. Bernard Weinberg, *A History of Literary Criticism in the Italian Renaissance* (Chicago: Univ. of Chicago Press, 1961), 2:1110-11.

26. Trapp, *Lectures*, 223. See also Dryden, *Of Dramatic Poesy*, 2:113.

27. "A Discourse Upon Comedy, in Reference to the English Stage" (1702), in *Eighteenth-Century Critical Essays*, ed. Scott Elledge (Ithaca, NY: Cornell Univ. Press, 1961), 1:92-93.

28. Addison, *Works*, 1:32. This passage and the following are quoted in the essay by Roy M. Wiles, "The Periodical Essay: Lures to Readership," in *English Symposium Papers II*, ed. Douglas Shepard (Fredonia: SUNY, 1972), 3-40.

29. Samuel Johnson, *The Rambler*, ed. W. J. Bate and Albrecht B. Strauss, in *The Works of Samuel Johnson* (New Haven, CT: Yale Univ. Press, 1969), 3:129.

30. Anthony Ashley Cooper, *The Life, Unpublished Letters and Philosophical Regimen of Anthony, Earl of Shaftesbury*, ed. B. Rand (London: Swan Sonnenchein, 1900), 26.

31. J. Paul Hunter, "'Peace' and the Augustans: Some Implications of Didactic Method and Literary Form," in *Studies in Change and Revolution: Aspects of English Intellectual History, 1640-1800*, ed. Paul J. Korshin (London: Scolar Press, 1972).

32. John Sheffield, "An Essay Upon Poetry," in Spingarn, *Critical Essays*, 2:289.

33. Addison, *Spectator* 74, in *Works*, 1:195.

34. Joseph Warton, *An Essay on the Writings and Genius of Pope* (London: printed for M. Cooper, 1756), 1:62.

35. Trapp, *Lectures*, 157.

36. Hugh Blair, *Lectures on Rhetoric and Belles Lettres,* vol. 3 (London: printed for W. Strahan, 1783), Lecture 39.

37. Johnson, "Preface" (1765), in Shakespeare, *Works,* 7:67.

38. Alexander Pope, "A Discourse on Pastoral Poetry" (1709), *The Poems of Alexander Pope,* ed. John Butt (New Haven, CT: Yale Univ. Press, 1963), 120.

39. Robert Lowth, *Lectures on the Sacred Poetry of the Hebrews* (1753), trans. G. Gregory, 2nd ed. (1787; London: printed for Ogles, Duncan, and Cochran, 1816), 2:144.

40. Thomas Sprat, "Account of the Life and Writings of Abraham Cowley" (1668), in Spingarn, *Critical Essays,* 2:132.

41. Jonathan Swift, *A Tale of a Tub,* ed. A. C. Guthkelch and D. Nichol Smith (Oxford: Clarendon Press, 1920), 4.

42. Henry Fielding, *Joseph Andrews and Shamela,* ed. Martin C. Battestin (Boston: Houghton Mifflin, 1961), 7.

43. Samuel Johnson, *Lives of the Poets,* ed. G. Birkbeck Hill (Oxford: Clarendon Press, 1905), 1:77.

44. Samuel Johnson, *Lives of the Poets,* ed. G. Birkbeck Hill (Oxford: Clarendon Press, 1905), 1:77.

45. Weinberg, *A History of Literary Criticism,* 2:1108.

46. Geoffrey Tillotson, *Augustan Poetic Diction* (London: Athlone Press, 1964), 25.

47. John Scott, *Critical Essays on Some of the Poems of Several English Poets* (London: 1785), 206.

48. Sutherland, *A Preface to Eighteenth Century Poetry,* 132-33.

49. Pope, *Essay on Man,* Epistle I, 289.

50. Geoffrey H. Hartman, *Wordsworth's Poetry, 1787-1814* (New Haven, CT: Yale Univ. Press, 1964), 158.

51. Fielding, *Joseph Andrews,* 8.

52. Lowth, *Lectures,* 2:45.

53. Lowth, *Lectures,* 2:48.

54. Longinus, *Dionysius Longinus on the Sublime,* trans. William Smith (London: B. Dod, 1743), 27.

55. Longinus, *On the Sublime,* 136.

56. Warton, *An Essay,* 1:286-87.

57. Warton, *An Essay,* 1:100-101.

58. Quoted by Maclean, "From Action to Image," 419.

59. Wordsworth, "Preface to Poems (1815)," in *Wordsworth's Literary Criticism,* ed. Nowell C. Smith (London: Henry Frowde, 1905), 153.

60. Barbara Herrnstein Smith, *Poetic Closure: A Study of How Poems End* (Chicago: Univ. of Chicago Press, 1968), 183.

61. Blair, *Lectures,* Lecture 38, 91-92.

62. Ronald Paulson, *Theme and Structure in Swift's Tale of a Tub* (New Haven, CT: Yale Univ. Press, 1960), 25.

63. Vicesimus Knox, "On some Peculiarities in periodical Essays," *Winter Evenings* (1788), 3rd ed. (London: 1795), 1:27.

64. Swift, *A Tale,* 204.

65. John R. Clark, *Form and Frenzy in Swift's Tale of a Tub* (Ithaca, NY: Cornell Univ. Press, 1970), 140.

66. Swift, *A Tale,* 40.

67. Wiles, "The Periodical Essay," 22-23.

68. Addison, *Spectator* 125, in *Works,* 1:308, 310.

69. Swift, *A Tale,* 4, 17.

70. Lowth, *Lectures,* 2:144.

The Origins of a Genre
Descriptive Poetry

I. THE NATURE OF THE PROBLEM

The problem I have set for myself—the origins of a genre: descriptive poetry—belongs to the area of historical poetics (within the larger domain of historical semiotics). Such an inquiry I take to be central to the question: How do literary works relate to one another diachronically or synchronically? The genesis of a genre presupposes that "genre" is a proper and valuable theoretical concept; I shall argue that it is, but it seems reasonable to draw attention to two types of antigenre argument. The first is that every work has its own form and is important only to the extent that it possesses its own identity. But this identity or form cannot be fixed. Blanchot writes: "The book alone is important, as it is, far from genres, outside rubrics—prose, poetry, the novel, the first-person account—under which it refuses to be arranged and to which it denies the power to fix its place and to determine its form."[1] The second argument, which can be seen as complementary to the first, is that identifying a work with a particular genre inevitably delimits its range of possible meanings. Geoffrey Hartman, for example, writes that the so-called descriptive poem "Yew-Trees" contains features of numerous genres—the ghostly ballad, the meditative poem, and funerary inscription. He points to the "danger of such hypostatized genres as 'descriptive poetry'" and claims "no method can determine what findings are to be emphasized."[2]

These views are directed at certain naive interpretations of "genre" in which forms are fixed and methods prescribed. But "genre" need not deny that a literary text can have features from different genres, nor that a text—say, an ode—can be considered part of the group called lyrics. That different critics identify the same poem in different genres is cause for inquiry into

This essay is published here for the first time.

critical constructs, not a denial that texts have form. Indeed, both critics—Blanchot and Hartman—would grant that literary works exist as entities that engage the critic in a transaction. Since the nature of the entity is implicit in the transaction, any interpretative effort presupposes a hypothesis about forms and their interrelations. And although the term "form" is ambiguous, it is necessary to note that I see genre theory operating at the level of literary continuities and discontinuities; these critics see genre as a hermeneutical theory rather than as a historical theory that is a precondition for interpretation.

I assume that what I have said thus far is an accurate description of the state of affairs regarding genre. I add only that the identification of features and their interrelation in any given work depends upon the critics' knowledge of *other* works. When a critic declares that "no method can determine what findings are to be emphasized," he evidently identifies his own method as exploratory and other methods as prescriptive. But his own hypothesis-discovery is surely not random. The question in dispute, therefore, is the adequacy of a genre hypothesis, not its existence.

What both these critics bring to our attention is the problem of the individual identity of a literary work. Put this way it is immediately apparent that a text's individuality or uniqueness is inevitably bound up with similarity of this work to others. Thus tradition and originality can be redefined in terms of genesis and difference. The fact that each work is similar to and yet different from every other makes classifying a necessity, for without it tradition becomes pointless and interrelations arbitrary. The problem, therefore, is not whether genre hypotheses are useful, but what uses they serve.

II. THE SPECIFICATIONS OF A GENRE HYPOTHESIS

To begin with, a genre hypothesis would be heuristic, capable of being revised, corrected, or even refuted. Such a hypothesis would have to assume that works have diverse features but common aims. A genre theory would have to distinguish between a diachronic genre system and a synchronic genre system. The diachronic deals with the possibilities of a form through time, the synchronic with particular actualizations. Propp's plot functions are an example of a diachronic system, providing a definition of the plot of a folk tale by separating it from the totality of each tale and from the specific relation of this genre to all other genres. A synchronic genre system would indicate how each tale is interrelated, at any one time, with all other literary genres. As a class, a diachronic genre would be capable of expansion but would have boundaries that mark it off from other classes. It would have to have a chronological beginning and a possible end. And any diachronic genre system would have to be included in a synchronic genre system in which all works identified as literature would be genre members, and all genres would form an interrelated whole.

If "genre" is to be a concept, it ought to provide the possibility of a hypothetical class. It ought to include all possible literary works, not merely those that have been written. Thus genre as a concept is based on a definition of the literary text and a definition of the class to which the literary text belongs. It will also, as a theory of genre, indicate the relation of genre classes to each other. Thus a literary text is a combination of rhetorical, stylistic discourse features combined for ends identified by critics as literary. A diachronic genre system would be a possible class of such works distinguished by its possible combinations from all other such classes. And a synchronic genre system would be the actual interrelation of all possible genres into a hierarchy (recognized by comprehensiveness or dominance). Thus any particular literary work represents the actualization of a genre; it broadens, complements, supplements, resists, criticizes, or opposes works within the class, and by doing so makes possible the grouping of a work within a received class or as a work that will become part of a new class.

I write "become part of a new class" because, by definition, every work is to some extent unique. Thus "new" may refer to a slight variant of the synchronic genre system, or it might be seen as the initiation of a group of works that offer an alternative mode of combination, which is a way of knowing and perceiving. Newness, thus, can only be claimed as a genre after the synchronic system in which it was initiated has been altered. In this respect, a genre concept is essential for charting the distinctions within literary change.

And if I may be permitted a digression, I would point out that the verbal procedures involved in theorizing are themselves a genre, being at different times interrelated with other expository prose forms. "Description," however we define it philosophically, is thus a part of the genre, as are quotation, evidence, and logical claims. What a generic theory undertakes to explain is why theorizing should take the particular form that it does in our time, since theories, my own included, arise from the interrelation of personal, social, and disciplinary needs.

Offering a genre theory at this time cannot be justified merely by the classifying of literary works; even if it explains why certain classes of works are possible but neglected, why others that were once considered unimportant are now primary. It must justify itself as a study not only within the discipline, but through the discipline for the human beings it serves. I see genre theory in this light, as answering certain historical problems of literary change—of tradition and innovation, of individual difference and similarity—central to the actualities of change in our time. Analogously, genre theory is a precondition for the analysis of a poem's individuality.

The definition of genre that I have proposed is meant to take account of the problems implicit in genre theorizing by contemporary critics. Northrop Frye, for example, suggests that genre is defined by the radical of presentation; that there are modes of narration in which the author's self is primary (lyric), the author's self is absent (dramatic), or where the author's self is mixed with that of the impersonal narrator (narrative). Such a theory of genres minimizes the different types of presentation in the same work and the varied subsystems a genre contains. It is not that modes of presentation do not exist, but rather that the lyric can include impersonal narration, can—in a work like *Prometheus Unbound*—include dialogue, just as the dramatic mode can include within the statements of the speakers lyrical declamations and narrative presentations. Since *Prometheus Unbound* contains combinatory features of the lyric and the drama, the decision of generic identity in this case could be either or both.

It is not that modes of presentation—that lyric, dramatic, narrative as genres—are wrong, but rather that they are inadequate to take account of varied features of which works are composed. Another genre theory is one that refers to ode, song, encomium, elegy, satire, etc. In this "theory," forms are grouped restrictively by features and ends, so that these become prescriptively narrow. Hypothetically, it would be possible to reduce each such group to a single member. The difficulty with such a grouping is its neglect of the interrelations of groups with one another. It is to this particular difficulty that the Russian formalists addressed themselves, arguing that every literary work is a combination of interrelated features and that these are related to features in other works. In Lotman's theory, the concept of genre undergoes a major transformation from the position it has in Tynyanov's view of evolution of genres—it becomes subordinated to a text-code relationship. A text is a particular instance of a literary code, and "every literary code contains a typology of literary texts: what . . . the various kinds of literature [are], what identifies each of them, what differentiates each of them from all others."³ Thus genre becomes a synchronic dimension of the existing code; typologies in different period codes have different interpretations.

In this theory, genre is treated pragmatically, the different genres being dependent on the codes and their specifications. What is important to Lotman is the code and the assumption of the literary text as a discrete entity. These permit him to argue for a totality of culture: "In the study of culture," he writes, "the initial premise is that all human activity concerned with the processing, exchange, and storage of information possesses a certain unity. Individual sign systems, though they presuppose immanently organized structures, function only in unity, supported by one another."[4]

However one may argue, as I do, with his syncretic definition of a literary text, namely that "all significant units of literary analysis are . . . discourse units, which need not coincide with those of the language system,"[5] it is necessary to point to the difference between a literary work as a discourse unit and as a particular form or genre. For Lotman, the analysis of the literary text becomes based on units of discourse; in my theory of genre the units of discourse are subordinated to the role of constructional rather than discourse features—a dialogue, an invocation, an imprecation, a quatrain, a folktale within a longer narrative, an interpolated play, a quotation, etc. It is the *combination* of these rhetorical, literary, and stylistic features that defines the literary work as a form. And each form is interconnected with others to compose genre groups or families, and all are part of a hierarchy governed by comprehensiveness or dominance. Thus Homer's epics are seen in early Greek commentaries to be the highest of genres because as epics they contain all possible genres; just as the drama for Aristotle represented the apogee of all literary forms.

The major objection to Lotman's demotion of genre is that it overlooks the concept of generic hierarchy; for the dominance of certain genres in the hierarchy indicates ideological and combinatory modes of knowing and perceiving. The movement from subordinate roles of satire and georgic in the Renaissance to their primacy in the mid-seventeenth century, and their reduction in the hierarchy at the end of the eighteenth century, indicate this shift. I shall reserve my discussion of the social nature of literary forms for my comments on the origins of descriptive poetry. But the issue of *form* change and *form* stability cannot adequately be dealt with in a theory which places codes as primary. For what is to be studied and theorized about is the range of forms possible within a genre or the kinds of associated genres or family of genres that interconnect and amplify related ends. Here the difficulty of genre as discourse is apparent: genre is essential for the continuity and discontinuity of forms. It is thus not a method of text interpretation, but a condition for it. To confuse the two is to lead to a misconception of the link of constructional features. Here I wish to stress the need for the level of system construction. The system required is not a syntactical one or a semantic one. What is needed is a system that deals with constructional units that are interrelated. For this, rhetorical and literary features can be identified for study as they combine and interrelate.

III. COMBINATIONAL FEATURES AND GENRE CHANGE

Some of the difficulties in treating works in terms of codes rather than genres (which can, of course, include codes) are apparent in some recent studies of anthropologists. The Russian anthropologist Meletinsky, in distinguishing between "myth" and "tale," drew attention to features from myth that make clear the syncretic unity of the literary work. For example, the folktale retains features of ritual, features of the culture hero, features of local classifications and places; but these features, he points out, do not function in the same way as they do in myth. But in seeking the criteria for differentiating a mythic from a literary work, he admits to considerable difficulty: "One and the same text," he writes, "can before one and the same audience, function as both myth and folktale, for example, if it simultaneously describes some link in cosmogenesis, sanctions a given ritual, demonstrates the bad consequences of violation of taboo, and at the same time inspires and amuses listeners with the bold or cunning escapades of the mythical hero."[6] It would seem reasonable to assume that both these narratives form a group in which each supplements and complements the other.

The argument that in the tale we have a new genre would in Lotman's view (if I am correct) be based on the fact that two different codes were operative in myth and tale, one that was applied to the narrative as myth and the other to the narrative as tale. Such a hypothesis would appear difficult to sustain, since the same text is responded to in contrary ways. A much simpler assumption would be that the elements of the tale permit it to be accepted in some features as myth and in others as tale because the features and ends of both types of narratives are similar, and that "tale" does not involve a special literary code.

Meletinsky suggests that the major change between myth and literature or the tale is clearly marked in time by changes in the function of formal features. These, he argues, are "deritualization" (if the myth was attached to ritual), desacralization, demythologizing of the hero and time of action, reduction from cosmic to human scale (in the lives of individuals), detachment from actual beliefs, weakening of reliability, and conscious admission of poetic invention. But these features do not change at once; in fact, as they change in time they continue to be taken either as myth or as folktale. The point at which the genre clearly disengages itself from myth and becomes a folktale requires some distinction such as I have suggested between variants of a synchronic system and alternatives to it. The argument against function with regard to the origin of genres has been made by Francis Cairns in his study of the origin of Greek genres. According to Cairns, the combination of varied rhetorical features constituted the earliest genres, but the rhetorical function and the literary function remained undifferentiated. The genre was merely an accumulation of associated rhetorical functions, whether of encomia or of farewell to a place. The literary form was a class of associated rhetorical features. "Literariness" was then no necessary feature of literary genres; rather, literary genres were identical with combinations of rhetorical features.

It can now, perhaps, be understood why a theory of forms based *either* on codes or on genres confronts the theorist with serious difficulties. Whether one proceeds historically or theoretically, one is committed to a theory of form change. Such a theory will need to explain the kinds of changes that forms may have without being characterized by different codes. Any theorist of codes who argues for a typology of forms has to explain how a language code can generate form typologies. On the other hand, any theorist of genres will be committed to show the ways in which a concept of forms can permit the eclogues of Virgil, for example, to include songs about pastoral and social unrest, whereas the eclogues of Pope are confined to songs about love totally divorced from conflicts in his own time. I might mention here one of the pseudo problems connected with genre study. "Satire" can refer to a person, a drama, or a narrative. Is the term "satire" a genre, or is "narrative" a genre? The answer, of course, depends on the range of genre systems one needs to answer a particular inquiry. Since the criteria are features and their combination, "satire" as a diachronic genre will include all possible combinations. If one's genre system requires a narrower range—say, satiric poetry—the diachronic system should include all possible combinations of these. Any single type of satire is actualized in a particular synchronic genre system and is interrelated with other genres.

Although a diachronic genre system is a hypothetical concept of possible combinations that can exist, these are nevertheless not indefinite, since other genres provide the limitation of combinations and ends. Every *actualization* of a genre exists in chronological time and has a societal basis. Thus at any moment in literary history there exists a particular system of genres with social ties, while at the same time prior generic systems are known and occasionally invoked by writers.

Every genre hierarchy which actually exists is characterized by a norm of combination. The types of combinations that appear in books of proverbs, or in sonnets, or in odes, or in dramas, or in epics are governed by underlying principles of the combination of features. It is these modes of combination that indicate how knowledge is connected and acquired. Such a synchronic or period norm coincides, I believe, with Lotman's view of period code; it insists, however, on the interconnection of features rather than the relations of words. (I shall not in this paper argue the case for norms, though I recognize the need to do so.) The kinds of possibilities a norm provides are determined by the nature of the synchronic hierarchy. When the georgic and satiric poem become the dominant forms, the structures of all genres come to include antithetical connections, series, and cycles that are associatively joined. New forms thus become amplifications, divergences, extensions, analogues of the norm. Tzvetan Todorov is quite right when he says that new genres are derived from existing genres by "the transformation of one or several old genres; by inversion, by displacement, by combination."[7] But such a statement, although true, is far from adequate. For new genres may appear within a norm and new genres may result from the supplanting of a norm. One of the difficulties of theorizing about genre origins has been—as I have indicated—the failure to distinguish changes within a norm and changes of a norm.

The development and disintegration of the norm is a study in itself, but I can only point out that each writer in seeking to distinguish his particular work from others of the same kind engages in processes that make his combinations less and less reliable as versions of knowledge, so that he is compelled to imitate combinations that do not support customary ways of knowing or make his work, whether he is aware of it or not, a parody of the norm.

IV. THE ORIGINS OF DESCRIPTIVE POETRY

The theory that I have been developing will, I trust, serve as the encompassing frame in which to deal with the origins of the genre *descriptive poetry*. I am dealing therefore with the actualization of a genre within a synchronic genre system. Although description as a rhetorical feature was present in the *Odyssey* and in poems since the *Odyssey*, it was only in the middle of the seventeenth century that it began to appear as a form, derived from the georgic, the encomiastic poem, the epic, the eclogue. We can now see that it was part of a synchronic genre system that developed combinations identifying place with actions and that saw knowledge as cumulative based on the necessary existence of diverse objects and events. More than a hundred years later after the publication of many poems modeled on what critics came to call the first loco-descriptive poem—*Coopers Hill* by John Denham—the definition of a descriptive poem was given by Samuel Johnson and John Scott: a poem that describes a particular place and related the "most remarkable events to which it [the place] has been witness, and from either the prospect or the narrative to introduce such moral sentiment as will easily arise."[8] As I pointed out earlier, the stipulation of this poem as a genre by critics followed long after a body of similar poems had become acknowledged.

The poem as a form placed in the foreground a particular place, and with this feature were connected others—narratives, historical retrospection, invocations, contemporary allusions, moral injunctions. I have said that literary forms have a social basis, and the descriptive poem reflects an effort to make the harmony of nature in its effects the basis for social harmony. As a descriptive poem, for example, *Coopers Hill* begins by relating place to perception, Cooper's Hill to the poet's perception of Parnassus:

> Sure there are Poets which did never dream
> Upon *Parnassus,* nor did tast the stream
> Of *Helicon;* we therefore may suppose
> Those made not Poets, but the Poets those,
> And as Courts make not Kings, but Kings the Court,
> So where the Muses & their train resort,
> *Parnassus* stands; if I can be to thee
> A Poet, thou *Parnassus* art to me. (1–8)

In connecting Cooper's Hill to perception, to the historical retrospection of Windsor Castle and the kings who inhabited it, Denham sought to provide a naturalistic basis for kingly authority and social harmony. But, further, the mode of combination of features is that of succession—in space and time. Historical retrospection becomes an example of chronological development connected with the deeds of the past. The spatial overview connects the different places from the perspective of the poet playing at Parnassian power. The importance of harmonizing king and country places the descriptive poet in the position of councillor to the state, a position which argues against revolution and for harmonious relationships between king and subjects.

Since it is the feature of place that is important rather than description of objects, an argument has to be made for the selection of place rather than objects in this form. Here it is necessary to draw attention to the language of natural science and of physical theology: natural scientists like Roy, Derham, and others argued that nature and natural objects were but the external effects of God's inner presence and harmony. This language of description, therefore, was calculated to reflect the inner force present in external objects and to relate it to political will as religious authority.

The procedure then was to introduce a verse form—the heroic couplet—that served often as a series of maxims, the model for which came from *Coopers Hill*. These came to be known as the Thames couplets. They are:

> O could I flow like thee, and make thy stream
> My great example, as it is my theme!
> Though deep, yet clear, though gentle, yet not dull.
> Strong without rage, without ore-flowing full. (1655; 189-92)

In relating these lines as a feature of descriptive poetry, I wish to explain the use of this couplet as a maxim: the image is the relation of subject (theme) to model (example).

The subject is the Thames River, and as a natural, nationalistic reference, the scene of England's commerce, it suggests that description is related to incipient nationalism. Moreover, this is an invocation in which the poet asks to be naturalized (become like a river) and addresses the river in terms of personification. The invocation is characterized by separation of speaker and river; the appeal is for features similar to those possessed by the river. The invocation follows a historical narrative, relating the prosperity of the nation to the movement of the river. But although the invocation is to the river, the power that governs the river and man is God, so that the wish expressed by the poet contains an undertone of hopelessness that such features can be granted.

This invocation which describes nature's (the river's) norm by concession ("though . . . yet") and by affirmation through negation of excess ("without rage") is an aesthetic and social model for man. Insofar as the feature is also statement about poetry, it is an example of how verse flows; as poetic example, it is pragmatic. As a social theory, it is hortatory: it serves as a hope or ideal.

I offer these comments not as a reading of a descriptive poem, but as an example of combinatory processes. I turn now to a so-called descriptive poem, Wordsworth's "Yew-Trees," 150 years later, to indicate how combinatory changes can be observed and how they serve as preconditions for analysis. I reserve the analysis for a later occasion.

Perhaps the clearest way to illustrate my procedure of genre theory as a precondition for such analysis is to compare it with a type of linguistic analysis. Michael Riffaterre, in discussing "Yew-Trees" and descriptive poetry in general, writes that in a descriptive poem the interpreter starts with the "very way the descriptive sentence is generated, that is, the way a kernel statement is *expanded* into its semantic components, or homonyms or antonyms (a word being transformed, in the generative sense, into a phrase, a phrase into a sentence), this precisely enables the critic to interpret what the text is aiming at, to watch the description changing into the sign of something else."[9]

Now my first objection is to the generative hypothesis; the arguments that I rehearsed earlier about a literary work as a combination of features—literary and discursive—would seem seriously to damage this claim. It would insist on the feature-combination as the basis from which to proceed to the smaller units. Riffaterre's generative-linguistic assumption, for example, commits the critic to an a priori view of poetic language, a denial of the accuracy or validity of place-names such as Crecy or Poitiers, arguing that any referential quality in such names is a mistake because poetic language is nonreferential.

Such an argument inevitably results in a rejection of the possibility that different codes are implicit in a poem, subduing all differences to the same code. But an even more troubling problem is at issue: namely, *the level at which a poem is a historical object* and the manner in which this is to be distinguished from its uniqueness as a text or as a model of a Wordsworthian text. For if one seeks to discover Wordsworth's individuality, it becomes apparent only through his actualization of the combined features of description. That this is how he proceeds can be seen from a reading of "Yew-Trees":

> There is a Yew-tree, pride of Lorton Vale,
> Which to this day stands single, in the midst
> Of its own darkness, as it stood of yore:
> Not loth to furnish weapons for the bands
> Of Umfraville or Percy ere they marched
> To Scotland's heaths; or those that crossed the sea

> And drew their sounding bows at Azincour,
> Perhaps at earlier Crecy, or Poictiers.
> Of vast circumference and gloom profound
> This solitary Tree! a living thing
> Produced too slowly ever to decay;
> Of form and aspect too magnificent
> To be destroyed. But worthier still of note
> Are those fraternal Four of Borrowdale,
> Joined in one solemn and capacious grove;
> Huge trunks! and each particular trunk a growth
> Of intertwisted fibres serpentine
> Up-coiling, and inveterately convolved;
> Nor uninformed with Phantasy, and looks
> That threaten the profane;—a pillared shade,
> Upon whose grassless floor of red-brown hue,
> By sheddings from the pining umbrage tinged
> Perennially—beneath whose sable roof
> Of boughs, as if for festal purpose, decked
> With unrejoicing berries—ghostly Shapes
> May meet at noontide; Fear and trembling Hope,
> Silence and Foresight; Death the Skeleton
> And Time the Shadow;—there to celebrate,
> As in a natural temple scattered o'er
> With alters undisturbed of mossy stone,
> United worship; or in mute repose
> To lie, and listen to the mountain flood
> Murmuring from Glaramara's inmost caves. (1815; 1-33)

I merely note the generic features in order to indicate how these alter those inherited from Denham and others. The poem's speaker begins with a statement of an object (yew-trees) and a place, relating the place to activities of the past. He then, in an apostrophe (to the reader?), identifies the tree as a magnificent and eternal form. He next establishes a hierarchy between this tree and place with the "fraternal Four" trees at Borrowdale. Their more worthiness—in comparison to the single tree—results from their intertwined union. There follows a description of the poet's fantasy or vision in which personified feelings and abstractions—related to present and future—are seen in worship under the trees as a temple or in repose listening to the waters murmuring in "inmost caves."

The first part of the poem that relates the place to history—and is, therefore, in the tradition of the early genre—is replaced by a vision which urges the reader to conceive of a similar constellation in a different (symbolic) code. The first yew-tree is a single separate entity related to man by providing branches for weapons (moving outside itself as earlier descriptive poems); it creates the harmony characteristic of the descriptive poems, as well as the separation of man from nature. Yet there is already implied in the tree's solitary, dark magnificence an eternal quality, an unbounded view of knowledge as sustained in objects. But the poem is clearly divided into two parts—the second being "worthier" as well as more comprehensive. The worthier example of fraternal trees not only offers a fantasy landscape with allegorical figures in symbolic language, it offers a union of ghostly abstractions, a union of the natural with the supernatural.

Thus in this "descriptive" poem the historical retrospection is syncopated because the relation between place and political power is supplanted by the inner resources of place as self-sustaining. Spatial continuity and successive events to imply knowledge as additive are replaced by the idea of place as an interlocked moment of eternity. The apostrophe in the earlier couplets clearly separated the poet and nature; it indicated the need for relation by example. In Wordsworth's poem, the apostrophe follows upon England's military use of the tree (for bows), uses long past and forms of war outmoded (decayed), and reveals the eternity of nature in contrast to the temporality of nationalism. As for the poet, he is who sees the fantasy or vision: nature is not his example. Rather his vision sees in the temple of nature a symbolic enclosure of his own mind. Instead of the combinations that specified careful boundaries, concessions, affirmations through negation of excess, the fraternal trees present an enclosure in which the natural and supernatural meet in concord, through which the distant sounds of innermost caves are drawn into the perception of eternal repose.

If the mode of combination in Denham was associative, was distributive, each object seen individually in space and time though related, if body and soul were separable entities, then Wordsworthian combinations operate quite differently. They move hierarchically from the individual to the group, from historical time to timelessness, from natural intertwining to the union of ghostly opposites. The process of intertwining identifies how the external becomes the source of the internal and all part of eternal concord. The poem, therefore, begins by taking account of genuine features and implications and rejects them for an alternative. It is thus a poem in which the history of its kind is implicit.

The features of the descriptive poem as a hypothetical form are present, and the poem deliberately indicates its past as form and the need to supersede it. The combination of features implies a synchronic system not conformable to that of *Coopers Hill*. How the other genres relate to it, what the organizing features of this norm are, is another paper. In this one my purpose has been to argue that the genre of a "descriptive poem" and the actualization of particular instances of the genre require a genre theory to establish the continuity and discontinuity among forms. These are, as I have said, a precondition for the analysis of the poem as revealing its unique identity.

NOTES

1. Maurice Blanchot, *Le livre à venir* (Paris: Gallimard, 1959), 293; this translation is given in Tzvetan Todorov, "The Origin of Genres," trans. Richard M. Berrong, *New Literary History* 8, no. 1 (1976): 159.

2. Geoffrey H. Hartman, "The Use and Abuse of Structural Analysis: Riffaterre's Interpretation of Wordsworth's 'Yew-Trees,'" *New Literary History* 7, no. 1 (1975): 168.

3. Uri Margolin, "Juri Lotman on the Creation of Meaning in Literature," *Canadian Review of Comparative Literature* 2, no. 3 (1975): 273.

4. Yuri M. Lotman, B. A. Uspensky, et al., *Theses on the Semiotic Study of Culture (as Applied to Slavic Texts)* (Lisse: Peter de Ridder Press, 1975), 3.

5. Margolin, "Juri Lotman," 262.

6. E. M. Meletinsky, "Structural-Typological Study of the Folktale," trans. Robin Dietrich, *Genre* 4 (1971): 249-79.

7. Todorov, "The Origin of Genres," 161.

8. John Scott, "On Denham's Cooper's-Hill," in *Critical Essays on Some of the Poems, of Several English Poets, with an Account of the Life and Writings of the Author*, by John Hoole (London, 1785), 2.

9. Michael Riffaterre, "Interpretation and Descriptive Poetry: A Reading of Wordsworth's 'Yew-Trees,'" *New Literary History* 4, no. 2 (1973): 237.

Literary Theory as a Genre

My argument in this paper shall be as follows: literary theory is a literary genre. In consequence of this, literary theory has generic continuity, while undergoing changes in its parts and functions. It is interrelated with other genres in terms of parts and methods, and it is analyzable with them as a member of a group, movement, or period. By considering literary theory as a genre, I mean to eliminate the following as redundant or meaningless questions: Is literary theory nonhistorical? Is literary theory cumulative? Is literary theory modeled upon scientific theory? Is a literary theory verifiable? Is literary theory possible?

To write a theory in words, in contrast to writing it in mathematical formulas, is to identify theory as a form of discourse. Literary theory is a kind of writing, a genre, a literary form that seeks to provide us with a procedure for understanding problematic areas, not particular works, in literary study. As such, it resembles as well as differs from philosophic discourse, historical writing, narrative writing, scientific explanation, poetry of various kinds, though it can contain proverbs, epigrams, lyrical passages, mathematical formulas, and varied levels of diction and rhetorical procedures. The phenomenon of interrelation of parts is characteristic of all literary forms that extend beyond the sentence. The specific aim of a literary theory is to theorize about literary forms, including itself, in all their varied relations to each other, to the author, audience, and society.

A literary theory need not provide solutions to problems in a logical sense; rather, it provides ways of understanding problems. Logic is used to avoid errors in coherence or consistency, but it need not be the central technique for persuading readers to grasp conventions, perceive relations, or consider

---

This essay was originally published in *Centrum: Working Papers* 3, no. 1 (1975): 45-64, and is reprinted here with permission of the publisher. © Minnesota Center for Advanced Studies in Language, Style, and Literary Theory 1976.

the problem as worthy of their attention. This is done by teaching the reader, by encouraging him to make connections among works and within works, to recognize structures, and to understand how literary works function. It is because a literary theory uses these techniques of analysis and persuasion that it contains historical references, descriptions of the reader and examples of his responses, irrespective of the particular problem under investigation.

I have deliberately used the words "need not be" because I do not wish to deny that a literary theory may make logical procedures central. But such a theory is merely one of a number of possible ways to use the genre. It is neither especially privileged nor always appropriate.

As a form, literary theory is history-bound. It is tied to its time by its aim or function in relation to the problems it proposes to explain or understand. Now this is not a view that is widely held, theory being considered by some critics as a logical rather than a literary procedure which may use logic. Consider the following statement of John Ellis in his 1974 book, *The Theory of Literary Criticism: A Logical Analysis:*

> Literary theory is, in part, first and foremost theory; the literary theorist is, or should be, first and foremost a theorist among other kinds of theorists. In large measure, their aims and methods are his. He must understand what critics are doing to be able to function properly; but he must perform the job of a theorist, not that of a critic. The performance has much more in common with that of other theorists in other fields of theoretical inquiry than with that of critics. I do not wish to be misunderstood on this point.... What I am asserting is that theory itself (not criticism) is a matter of logical analysis. As such, logical analysis cannot be contrasted with any other kind of input into literary theory (e.g., modern linguistics); it must be uniquely at the center of literary theory.[1]

This statement equates literary theory with logical analysis. But this is a reduction of what all literary theorists do, including the theorists who are supposedly confined to logical analysis. Take, for example, the claim that literary theory is a matter of logical analysis. On what logical ground is such a claim made? Surely there is no logical ground for assuming that literary theory ought to be based on logic, since the claim itself is a matter of belief, or, as John Ellis might say, a matter of reasonable inference from the premise of logical analysis. But theory, or what critics call theory, as it is practiced by Aristotle, Longinus, Hume, and Wordsworth is not a matter merely of logic, nor is logic at the "center" of these theories any more than it is at the "center" of any argument that uses rhetoric, logic, and other arts of persuasion.

Two explanations are called for at this time. One is that I use the term "theory" to refer to what critics call "theory," exploring their reasons for such naming. This means that critics can and do disagree about what is to be so called. I treat such disagreements by explaining or illustrating the particular limits involved, my aim being to understand what critics do when they advocate a particular version of "theory."

The second explanation has to do with what I mean by "discourse" or "form of writing." Literary theories are written; they present an organized body of thought about writing. Such theories refer to works, present a way of conceiving them, and elicit from the reader a response both to the theories as art and to the theories as content. A literary theory, therefore, is always more than the logic it employs.

If "theory" is a form of writing, it is inevitable that the process of generic form-change must also apply to form-change in theory-writing. Aristotle, Longinus, Hume, and Wordsworth wrote literary theory, and although parts of their theories were often the same, the functions and connections differed. By neglecting the fact that theorists write in literary forms, John Ellis endows theory with an implicit yet unchanging single, logical function. Also, although theorists in literature share some of the methods and aims of theory-writers in the humanities and even some in the social sciences, they share relatively little with theory-writers in the mathematical and physical sciences.

The identification of literary "theory" with modern views of scientific theory is not only anachronistic; it rests on a misconception of the kind of proof a scientific theory offers and the confirmation that a literary theory offers. Ernest Nagel distinguishes three components in a scientific theory—and he is referring to the physical sciences: (1) an abstract calculus that is the logical skeleton of the explanatory system; (2) a set of rules that in effect assign an empirical content to the abstract calculus; (3) an interpretation or model of the abstract calculus.[2] The empirical data to which the abstract calculus applies does not depend on any historical situation as it does in literary theory. The validity of the scientific theory based on repetitive duplication cannot be applied to literary theory. And the model which is an interpretation of the abstract calculus does not correspond to the model in literary theory, because the latter has no equivalent for the abstract calculus but is, rather, a purely historical and heuristic procedure.

Meyer H. Abrams in his essay on theorizing in the arts criticizes the limitations of the idea of literary theory as developed by the analytic philosophers and offers his own views of theory:

> Some observations are in order about what Aristotle does, as against what a number of analysts assume that, as a critical theorist, he must be doing:
> (1) The whole of the *Poetics*, according to the criteria of the analysts, counts as theory and not as applied criticism, for its basic statements are all generalizations about the arts, or about a class of art such as poetry, or about a species of poetry such as tragedy and its typical elements, organization, and effects; Aristotle refers to particular works only to exemplify or clarify such general statements. Of this theory, however, definitions certainly do not constitute a major part, but are used only briefly and passingly, as a way of introducing one or another area of investigation. And the body of the theory does not consist of an attempt—whether vain or successful—to support and "prove" the definition. It consists instead of putting to work the terms, distinctions, and categories proposed in the initial definition (which are supplemented, in a way consistent with this definition, as the need arises) in the analysis of the distinctive elements, organization, and characteristic powers of various kinds of poetic art.[3]

Meyer Abrams is quite right in arguing that "definitions certainly do not constitute a major part" of the *Poetics* and are merely used to introduce one or another area of investigation. But the muddle of the logical analyst goes further, for he neglects to differentiate the making of statements from their function in a particular discourse. And even Abrams, who describes what Aristotle does accurately, does not discuss the aim of Aristotle's theorizing. Aristotle's theorizing is directed at recognizing that all types of learning are a form of imitation, and he wishes to distinguish artistic imitation from other human acts of imitation and within artistic imitation to distinguish among the various kinds. The process of theorizing, in this example, is to provide a way of conceiving of works of art as distinctive objects of imitation. It is not an attempt to establish the basis for a theory of the passions or of the spectator's response or of the nature of artistic knowledge. And yet the *Poetics*, despite its specific function, includes parts that refer to the passions, to the spectator and reader, and to artistic knowledge.

Literary theory as a form invokes general principles of behavior to explain readers' responses to literature. It can seek to persuade the reader to pursue the argument by calling attention to the privileged knowledge of art. It can initiate inquiries of a particular kind, because the critic wishes to trace the artistic context of general human principles; whatever choice of problems the critic makes, it is not a logical, but a historical one. Thus remarks, definitions, or arguments may be subordinated in one theory, but may become the dominant inquiry of another. Why this is so is a matter of critical and historical change; and the shift in critical problems cannot be explained as a matter of logic, nor are the logical processes involved "central" to the formulation or the development of the formulation.

As an example, I wish to trace the relation between Aristotle's incidental hypothesis of the pleasure in imitation and its dominance in the theories developed by Hume and Wordsworth. My purpose is to demonstrate the nature of continuity of parts and the difference in their function. This will serve as an example of generic continuity.

In his discussion of imitation, Aristotle points out that there is universal "pleasure felt in things imitated":

> 3. We have evidence of this in the facts of experience. Objects which in themselves we view with pain, we delight to contemplate when reproduced with minute fidelity: such as the forms of the most ignoble animals and of dead bodies. 4. The cause of this again is, that to learn gives the liveliest pleasure, not only to philosophers but to men in general; whose capacity, however, of learning is more limited. 5. Thus the reason why men enjoy seeing a likeness is, that in contemplating it they find themselves learning or inferring, and saying perhaps, "ah, that is he." For if you happen not to have seen the original, the pleasure will be due not to the imitation as such, but to the execution, the coloring, or some such other cause.[4]

This explanation of pleasure in imitation is connected with a discussion of the origin of poetry, and it is ancillary to Aristotle's analysis of poetry and the kinds of imitation. But in Hume's discussion of tragedy, the problem of the pleasure in tragedy (which is an imitation) becomes the inquiry itself. For although Hume grants that man takes pleasure in imitation, his explanation of how dead bodies provide pleasure in painting is based on a psychological principle which he considers primary: the conversion of passion. And it is this principle which, without denying that pleasure in imitation is a factor, becomes predominant and alters the relationship of parts and functions in Hume's theory: "It seems an unaccountable pleasure, which the spectators of a well-written tragedy receive from sorrow, terror, anxiety and other passions, that are in themselves disagreeable and uneasy. The more they are touched and affected, the more are they delighted with the spectacle; and as soon as the uneasy passions cease to operate, the piece is at an end."[5]

Hume builds on the remarks of l'Abbé Dubos and Fontenelle on this subject, thus relating his theory-writing to contemporary discussions of the problem. But he finds their conclusions insufficient to clear up the dilemma. He offers, therefore, the hypotheses that "all the passions, excited by eloquence are agreeable in the highest degree, as well as those which are moved by painting and the theatre."[6] Hume's explanation of the conversion of pathetic circumstances into pleasurable ones rests on a theory of the transformative power of artistic expression in tragedy. Hume confirms his "theory" by giving instances from everyday life, for the principle he discovers in art is neither extraordinary nor paradoxical; it is, he assumes, a principle of human nature. And he provides examples to argue the converse of the principle—i.e., if the subordinate passion is not converted into the dominant, then the dominant grows in intensity. Hume takes his examples from Cicero's oratory, Lord Clarendon's *History*, and incidents in life so that the explanation of tragedy is but one instance of a principle operative in artistic and nonartistic, dramatic and nondramatic actions that involve sublime or intense passions.[7]

Hume's argument of artistic predominance in tragedy does not apply to lyric poetry or to other imitative literary works that can be called "beautiful." These lack the intensity to create the linguistic dominance achievable (though not always achieved) in tragedy. The failure of Hume to establish a theory of artistic conversion is not a matter of logical inference, but the commitment to a theory of the passions that contemporary knowledge sanctioned. It should be pointed out, moreover, that the applicable range of subject matter of a theory is dependent on the claims the theory makes. Thus, for Hume, "tragedy" refers to those works that are artistically successful; the tragedies that do not move the reader and do not give pleasure are unworthy of consideration within the framework of his theory.

Hume's purpose is to demonstrate that art, like life, is governed by common principles of the passions, and tragedy is distinguished merely by having a context—the procedures of imitation, eloquence, organization, etc.—which serves to make the psychological principle operate with greater force. Hume is not interested in arguing how, in any particular drama, the language of tragedy serves to support his claim. His theory functions to explain why people surround themselves with art that deals with painful subjects, why they find "pleasure" in tragedy; it is the role of art in human life that is important to Hume because in a theory in which disinterested benevolence or utility serve as a moral guide, art is valuable only if it can be of use or can reinforce men's ability to convert suffering or pain into pleasure.

In that section of the 1800 "Preface" in which Wordsworth turns to the "general grounds" (or theoretical grounds) of his argument about the nature of poetry and the poet, he declares that the "Poet writes under one restriction only, namely, the necessity of giving immediate pleasure to a human Being possessed of that information which may be expected from him ... as a Man."[8] This principle of pleasure is defined as that complex of emotions which men have in contemplating objects, acts, and men and which excite in them sympathies that are accompanied by an overbalance of enjoyment.

> We have no sympathy but what is propagated by pleasure: I would not be misunderstood; but wherever we sympathize with pain, it will be found that the sympathy is produced and carried on by subtle combinations with pleasure. We have no knowledge, that is, no general principles drawn from the contemplation of particular facts, but what has been built up by pleasure, and exists in us by pleasure alone. The Man of science, the Chemist and Mathematician, whatever difficulties and disgusts they may have had to struggle with, know and feel this. However painful may be the objects with which the Anatomist's knowledge is connected, he feels that his knowledge is pleasure; and where he has no pleasure he has no knowledge. What then does the Poet? He considers man and the objects that surround him as acting and reacting upon each other, so as to produce an infinite complexity of pain and pleasure.[9]

Wordsworth defends the use of meter by referring to the testimony of ages (the norm of readers) who find that meter improves the pleasure that coexists with it. Wordsworth refers to the "theory" he is developing and remarks that he would, if he were providing a systematic defense, argue that metrical pleasure is based on a general principle of mind, "namely, the pleasure which the mind derives from the perception of similitude in dissimilitude. This principle is the great spring of the activity of our minds, and their chief feeder."[10]

Wordsworth's theory of the origin of poetry can be seen as related to this principle, for the spontaneous overflow of powerful feelings is different from feelings recollected in tranquillity. The tranquillity gradually disappears and the emotion that overflows "is qualified by various pleasures." In this particular passage Wordsworth provides a quite different function for the Humean problem:

> I have said that poetry is the spontaneous overflow of powerful feelings: it takes its origin from emotion recollected in tranquillity: the emotion is contemplated till, by a species of reaction, the tranquillity gradually disappears,

and an emotion, kindred to that which was before the subject of contemplation, is gradually produced, and does itself actually exist in the mind. In this mood successful composition generally begins, and in a mood similar to this it is carried on; but the emotion, of whatever kind, and in whatever degree, from various causes, is qualified by various pleasures, so that in describing any passions whatsoever, which are voluntarily described, the mind will, upon the whole, be in a state of enjoyment.[11]

Wordsworth shares with Hume the belief that art and life are governed by common principles; both insist on the importance of pleasure. Hume's theory rests on a distributive view of the passions—each passion operates singly and contrary passions may be related but they are not fused. Hume's view of predominance is not a fusion but an overpowering, the subordination of one passion to another. But Wordsworth accepts the complexity of passion, and his theory makes possible a fusion that Hume cannot manage. He relates the mixed pleasures to the language and action of common men. What he has done, therefore, has been to declass Hume's theory and to provide an alternative based on a more complex hypothesis.

The function of his theory as Wordsworth saw it was to enlarge the sensibility of his readers by demonstrating that exciting poetry could be written about ordinary people and actions. Thus the important contribution of Wordsworth's theory was its reconsideration of the role of depth perception, conscious and unconscious—of the submergence of feeling, of the widening and declassifying of the audience and subjects of poetry, and of the complex interrelation, the deepened fusion of pain and pleasure.

With regard to the feature that I have been tracing, it seems appropriate to inquire whether these theories are valid. To what extent is Hume's view of tragedy or Wordsworth's view of the origin and writing of poetry still acceptable? Hume's view of tragedy takes too elementary a view of passion so that its ambiguous nature, including the ambiguity of "pleasure," is overlooked. Hume tends to posit an elite audience that is unchanging, though he acknowledges that its capacity for responsiveness can change. Indeed, it is apparent that the response to literary works changes, as witness Hume's dismissal of Bunyan. But Hume was dependent on an inadequate theory of the passions, and on a view of cultural change that was undeveloped as a theory. His statements about changes of taste were lodged in a body of generalizations about unchanging responses and the exceptions to such responses. His theory was an impressive contribution to a theory of tragedy in his time, but his psychology and his belief in a static norm of responders has not been sustained by later study. Wordsworth's depth procedure in describing the origin of poetry and in explaining the complexity of emotion has endured successfully. It has been transposed into contemporary psychological theories without serious distortion. His theory of poetic language, however, was refuted by Coleridge in Wordsworth's lifetime, and his principle of similitude in dissimilitude was too naive to win support as a principle of the human mind.

I hope that these examples have made clear the cumulation as well as the change in an aspect of literary theory, and that it has removed any question about the historicity of literary theory. Some features of literary theory can survive much longer than others, as Aristotle's method of distinctions has been disengaged from the limited views of art to which Aristotle restricted it.

But if one wishes to inquire not about cumulation, but about the aim of a good critical theory, the answer can only be historical: to provide a reliable understanding of the problems the theorist raises. This can be an understanding of why relations function as they do within a work, or between works, or between works and audience, society, or creator. Such an understanding is subject to the same testability as other forms of discourse which are written at the same time. And a theory is reliable for so long as its explanation of the available data meets the criteria for adequacy of argument. To claim that all literary theory has a single aim is to make the same mistake as those who attribute to literary theory a single method. Meyer Abrams writes: "This is the primary service of a good critical theory, for in bringing us, with new insights and powers of discrimination, to individual works of art in their immediacy, it enhances our appreciation of the only places where artistic values are in fact realized."[12] But a theory leads to insights into a system; not into specific qualities of particular works. These may occur, but they are incidental to the process of theorizing.

The idea of influence or tradition, when applied to a theory of genre, implies continuity within the reworking of earlier forms of the genre. The attempt of the Cambridge Platonists to write a Platonic philosophy or of the neo-Aristotelians to write theory in accordance with the *Poetics* is an activity that is tied to history. These later applications are inevitably directed at readers with different experiences of methods, aims, language, and theory from those of the original audiences. In seeking, for example, to apply the method of past writing to the present, there is an inevitable distortion. Past uses of a form can be valuable to present critics only if they understand that, to make them viable, they must consider the changes the forms have undergone. It is thus self-evident that the process of theorizing, the manner in which the aims of theory are selected, and the kind of evidence needed to support these do change despite the continuity of particular features. Theorizing always involves subordinating individual instances to a general principle, analyzing how classes of works or groups of features can be understood.

A literary theory proceeds by theorizing, by exploring the bases of particular problems—not how a literary passage means, but the nature of literary meaning; not how a particular passion is raised, but the principle governing the raising of the passions in literary work. Theorizing is the procedure that characterizes literary theory as a genre and it provides a basis for distinguishing between this genre and others. Certainly this process can include parts from other forms just as Aristotle notes that "all the elements of an epic poem are found in tragedy; but the elements of a tragedy are not all found in the epic poem."[13] Analogously, one might say all the parts of literary criticism are included in literary theory, but those of theory are not all included in criticism. That parts of theory appear in other literary forms is to be assumed. In fact, it seems reasonable to argue that every literary work, not merely literary history or literary criticism, will assume some generalizations that are theoretical, make some use of inference, analogy, and examples.

But the making of assumptions which underlies any kind of writing cannot in criticism be identified as an implicit theory. Theory is a way of writing itself, quite distinct from that of criticism. But even if this argument is rejected, a critic's assumptions must not be confused with the quality and significance of the statements he makes. He may assume a particular kind of audience or a particular theory of imitation, but the actual writing defines what he says. Unless one is prepared to claim that all writing is inherently theoretical, the words are in no necessary relation to theoretical assumptions. Indeed, a critic's assumptions can be religious or psychological or philosophical without being systematic. Such assumptions or points of reference are not theorizing nor are they literary theory; they are incidental parts of historical or critical writing. Still, a number of critics have argued that to have parts of theory is to have a literary theory.

René Wellek declares that "no criticism or history is possible without some set of questions, some system of concepts, some points of reference, some generalizations."[14] Tzvetan Todorov writes that "no literary scholar can avoid adhering to some theory of literature. The very use of descriptive terms, whatever they may be, implies one, in spite of protestations to the contrary."[15] The statements speak confusedly of a "system of concepts," "some theory of literature." The argument for this position was put most effectively by R. S. Crane:

> The reference of any critic's statements, general or particular, to the things he professes to be talking about is mediated, in the first place, by the special framework of concepts and distinctions which, out of all others that might be, or have been, thought relevant to the things in question, he has chosen for one reason or another to employ . . . it follows that, before we can judge fairly of either the meaning or the validity of any critical statement, we must first reconstruct the underlying and often only partly explicit conceptual scheme in which the statement appears.[16]

To reconstruct a conceptual scheme that is often only partly explicit is to assume that "partly explicit" implies "fully explicit." To avoid fictionalizing, such reconstruction must clearly distinguish statements that are to be taken as hints for a theory from those that are merely strategic or trivial. Moreover, these theorists accept the premise that all practical critics have conceptual schemes, even if they do not know that they have such schemes. I do not wish to discuss the idea of unconscious theorizing, but even if such theorizing were examinable, it would still be necessary to differentiate between a *construction* of a scheme by someone other than the critic and the presentation of a literary theory by the critic himself. How is one to discover whether the construction is indeed the "scheme" that was implicit, since more that one scheme can be derived from fragmentary evidence? The perplexities of this procedure can be seen in "The Theoretical Foundations of Johnson's Criticism" by W. R. Keast, an essay often used as an example of this criticism at its best.[17]

Mr. Keast undertook "a recovery and restatement of Johnson's theory of literature and criticism and of his critical method."[18] But, as he acknowledges, Johnson did not have either a theory of literature or of criticism; to "recover" it is to "invent," not to "discover," it. Johnson posited certain critical principles in discussing particular works—that these constitute a "framework" rather than some ad hoc working principles is what Mr. Keast sought to demonstrate. Mr. Keast proceeds by selecting phrases and sentences and converts these into generalizations about the nature of literature. Johnson, in the "Preface to Shakespeare," declared that "Shakespeare's plays are not in the rigorous and critical sense either tragedies or comedies, but compositions of a distinct kind; exhibiting the real state of sublunary nature which partakes of good and evil, joy and sorrow, mingled with endless variety of proportion and innumerable modes of combination."[19]

The "real state of sublunary nature," as the poet's object, does not, in itself, constitute a general principle for Johnson. The imitation of reality does not apply, even in the drama, to the punishment of the innocent or to irreligious actions such as that of Hamlet refusing to slay the king at prayer lest he go to heaven. The attempt to construct a generalization about reality from Johnson's work must be hedged by reservations which do not indicate the level of generality that can be sustained nor how Johnson would see reality in the drama in contrast to reality in any other literary form.

The theorist who seeks a framework for the practical critic must make certain distinctions not only about critical language, but about levels of generality, about the range of forms discussed. He must be able to distinguish commonplaces from general statements that imply a theory, recognizing the particular problems to which such statements refer. Johnson's acceptance of general human nature was a critical commonplace, and Johnson did not seek to provide evidence for its existence, just as he did not provide evidence for his idea of the common reader. It is one thing to interpret Northrop Frye's essays on Shakespeare in terms of his general theory, another to do as much for Samuel Johnson, who has no such theory. Practical critics make theoretical statements in the act of analyzing particular works, but a discussion of a poem is neither an explicit act of theorizing nor an implicit act of theorizing.

In our time an effort has been made to convert all critics to theorists, even to convert all poets to theorists. If every poem is about the writing of poetry, then the premises of poetry are implicit in every poem. For the first time in the study of literature, critics have insisted that there is a "need" for theory. In 1949 René Wellek had written: "Literary theory, an *organon* of methods, is the great need of literary scholarship today."[20] And in 1957 Northrop Frye wrote: "Criticism seems to be badly in need of a coordinating principle, a central hypothesis which, like the theory of evolution in biology, will see the phenomena it deals with as parts of a whole."[21] And in a recent essay Tzvetan Todorov has pointed to the shift from studies of individual works to an emphasis on theory or "a coherent body of concepts and methods aiming at the knowledge of underlying laws."[22]

Why do these critics find the need for literary theory especially great at this time? The institutionalization of literary study has made it necessary to pass on a body of knowledge, and without an agreed upon systematization of such knowledge, the transmitting can only be haphazard. It is significant that the call for literary theory occurs at a particular historical moment, implying the need for a scientific or systematic theory. Thus previous theories are considered, in this sense, as pretheoretical. This historical moment has resulted in a very wide variety of speculative "literary theories," each of which seeks to move beyond particular works to some general principles governing the processes of writing. The need for theory at this time is the need for theory to inquire into writing itself—into its social and personal powers. Theory looms more important than other kinds of writing because it self-consciously analyzes itself and other literary works; parts of theory can now be found in fiction, poetry, and other literary forms. Its attempt at system construction is, in this procedure, an attempt to become the supreme fiction.

But the call for the "need" for literary theory does not call such theory into existence. What it does is to draw attention to such study, for Northrop Frye has admitted that "the main principles of [this theory] are as yet unknown to us."[23] In order for it to begin to be known, the theorist must inquire into certain initial principles, one of which is whether theory is a form of discourse and, if so, what type of discourse it is. This I have tried to answer; then the term "theory" itself as applied to literary study seems to be used in at least two different ways: theory of literature and literary theory.

A theory of literature, which is what Northrop Frye and Tzvetan Todorov refer to, is a theory of all possible writing. It is a theory, the body of facts for which is not yet known. To theorize about genres, for example, is to theorize about genres in Western literature, not all literature. To theorize about all "literature" is to presuppose some definition of literature that is ahistorical or universal. Such theorizing can be understood as speculation about knowledge rather than the attempt to understand knowledge already possessed. To illustrate that a comprehensive theory of literature is committed to huge generalizations that are based on belief rather than knowledge, I offer as an example Ralph W. Rader's effort: "The specific aim of a comprehensive theory of literature, then, would be to conceive and render explicit the objective basis of our tacit experience, accepting the task of accounting for all the general discriminations just indicated as well as of specific problematical facts that have come to be associated with particular works."[24]

Now a theory which undertakes "to conceive and render explicit the objective basis of our tacit experience" is aiming to remove empirical relativity of judgment by claiming that there exists, tacitly, one fixed and fundamental judgment. It is clear that such a criticism seeks to provide coherence among diverse responses, especially among literary disagreements, by assuming that "our perception of literature is not fluid and subjectively indefinite but in some fundamental sense fixed and objective."[25] Thus this comprehensive theory begins with a personal commitment to a view of human nature and judgment, and accounts for diverse discriminations by reference to this view. Such theories must exist as speculations. But literary theory, which relates to a limited set of facts about examinable literary data, is the kind of theory that has existed and does exist, and I have described some of its features. And among these one can point to areas of agreement without invoking absolutes.

One of the consequences of treating literary theory as a genre is that it provides a method for considering the areas of agreement in widely different theories without neglecting the grounds of disagreement. In dealing with Aristotle, Hume, and Wordsworth I sought to explain how literary theory functioned diachronically. I wish now to analyze two contemporary literary theories in order to illustrate how they function synchronically. The theories I have selected are the reader's response theory of Hans Robert Jauss and the semiotic theory as developed by Jonathan Culler in *Structuralist Poetics*.

Jauss begins "Literary History as a Challenge to Literary Theory" by reference to formalist and Marxist theories that he finds limited because of their neglect of the reader. For him, the reader is an active agent in shaping the communication of the literary work: "If the history of literature is viewed . . . as a dialogue between work and public, the contrast between its aesthetic and its historical aspects is continually mediated."[26] Jauss sees as the function of his study the revival of the history of literature by the aesthetics of reception, a revival of which will illuminate "our present literary experience" and provide a more adequate basis for understanding past literature.

The concept of reading is central to his theory, and reading is redefined as a dialogue between work and reader. By "reader" Jauss means a "receptive reader, the reflective critic," though Jauss grants that other kinds of readers have different sets of expectations which do not involve dialogue. A receptive reader has a set of expectations, from his previous understanding of the specific genre, from the form and themes of already familiar works, from the contrast between poetic and practical language. Such expectations are formed in part by the conventions of genre and style. The author, too, possesses these expectations and he predisposes the reader by certain strategies, signals, allusions. Thus works provide a continuous horizon setting and horizon changing that in turn affect new works, and the reader finds that a work satisfies, disappoints, or surpasses his expectations. Jauss offers a series of discriminations which define and clarify these distinctions. He is aware that not all works of a genre survive changes in the horizon of expectations, and he offers some hypotheses about such works. The changing horizon also makes it possible for Jauss to attack the sociological view that art is a mere reflection of its time because such a premise neglects the active role of readers.

The aesthetics of reception becomes essential to understanding past works because it presents a reconstruction of the original horizon of expectations; how the original readers understood the work. It thus makes clear the different bases for understanding past and present works, since a past work, without such reconstruction, does not reveal itself to the modern reader.

Jauss concludes with the society-forming function of literature. The aesthetics of reception can lead the reader to a new perception of his environment and to an openness to experience. It can help him surmount the boredom of everyday experience. It can even alter his moral consciousness.

Jonathan Culler, like Jauss, begins his study with a review of linguistic critics who seek to apply linguistic procedures to literature. Culler takes from them the necessity of conceiving the study of literature as a system of rules and conventions which make meaning possible: "Studying signs which, whatever their apparent 'naturalness,' have a conventional basis, [the critic] tries to reconstruct the conventions which enable physical objects or events to have meaning; and this reconstruction will require him to formulate the pertinent distinctions and relations among elements as well as the rules governing their possibility of combination. The basic task is to render as explicit as possible the conventions responsible for the production of attested effects."[27] Culler shares with Jauss the procedure of indicating the limitations of a group of critics beyond whose conclusions he wishes to move. And he shares, too, the hypothesis about the systematic nature of theory. Culler, however, derives his idea of system from the model of the analysis of language, whereas Jauss takes his from phenomenology. However, the range of the two systems varies. Jauss is providing a system for the study of literary history whereas Culler is providing a theory of the lyric and the novel, and, more speculatively, a theory of fictional forms.

Both critics agree that the concept of reading is central to their enterprise. Jauss analyzes reading in terms of the expectations of the reader; these expectations are built into the literary work by the author, who provides clues to expectations but also can defeat them. These "expectations," encountered in dialogue by the reader, include conventions, but they also include the reader's preparedness to find unexpected ways of dealing with the work. Jonathan Culler writes of "conventions" although he also uses "expectations," but he includes in "conventions" the expectation of significance in a work, metaphoric coherence, and, indeed, all possible aspects of the literary work. Genres are for him sets of expectations. "The conventions of poetry, the logic of symbols, the operations for the production of poetic effects, are not simply the property of readers but the basis of literary forms."[28]

Although Jauss and Culler agree upon the function of the reader and his use of conventions, Culler seeks to make the reader's competence testable. This test, it turns out, is precisely what defined the reader to begin with, a knowledge of poetic conventions. Other readers, adds Culler, would find a substantial part of their own interpretation in that of any competent reader. Jauss's reader is identified as perceptive, but the function of his reader is limited by his horizon. There is no competent reader who can read a past work without a reconstruction of its horizon, and every reader governed by a different horizon inevitably reads differently.

This historical consciousness of Jauss gives a different function to the features of agreement and distinguishes his theory from that of Culler's. So, too, the relation of a text to society provides another basis for distinction. For Culler sees the work, at least on one level, as a reflection of society, and Jauss resists this view of art, arguing that a valuable literary work has a society-forming function.[29]

Each of these theorists moves in his own direction—Jauss in discussing literary evolution and the special nature of literary as compared with general history; Culler in his discussion of the structures of the lyric and the novel. Both deal with individual works only as examples for theoretical procedures: a study of literary history in terms of aesthetics of response, or a study of particular genres such as the lyric or novel in terms of linguistic structures governed by conventions.

Hans Robert Jauss's theory answers the question, why do literary responses function as they do? Jonathan Culler's theory answers the question, what forms the basis for the literary structures of the lyric or novel? Both theories agree upon the primacy of the reader and the role of conventions; but they imply a study of the reader that moves beyond the mere discipline of reading, just as a study of conventions entails a knowledge of how conventions begin and where they come from. These theories still reveal the limits within which their conceptions develop. A reader needs not merely the experience of books, but the experiences which make books accessible and valuable. To attribute to literature the power to change the reader's consciousness is to ignore the relation of reading to action, to the other pressures which shape the mind at any one time. And as for a theory of conventions, the combination of conventions that form a genre merely isolates the different genres. What is needed is to interrelate them as well. Moreover, conventions change, and if this is granted, then what is needed is a theory that will explain why conventions change in the order in which they do.

Thus two different contemporary literary theories can be seen to share premises about the manner of making distinctions, offering examples, proposing models, generalizations, and definitions. But in doing so they also share certain limits of theorizing—due to the beliefs on which theories rest, the hypotheses of selection, the nature of the problems, and the reasons for theorizing.

To conceive of literary theory as a genre is to recognize that its functions are conditioned by previous theoretical writings and present knowledge. Thus, although the varied versions of modern theory—as logical analysis or aesthetics of response or structural conventions—have different links to past writing, synchronically they share a method of proceeding, a process of theorizing in terms of functions and of problems. Not to conceive of literary theory as a genre is to render such writing a matter of unrelated or ad hoc discourse about related subjects, that is, unrelated, unconnected theories about related subject matter. The first step to establish literary theory as a systematic study is to consider it as a form of discourse related to other forms of discourse but with a history of its own. It is itself a form of writing and a particular analysis of forms of writing. To acknowledge this is to accept its historicity, and, by doing so, make possible a study of literary theory as a coherent, continuing, yet changing, activity.

NOTES

1. John Ellis, *The Theory of Literary Criticism: A Logical Analysis* (Berkeley: Univ. of California Press, 1974), 10-11.

2. Ernest Nagel, *The Structure of Science* (New York: Harcourt, Brace, 1961), 90.

3. Meyer H. Abrams, "What's the Use of Theorizing about the Arts?," in *In Search of Literary Theory*, ed. Morton W. Bloomfield (Ithaca, NY: Cornell Univ. Press, 1972), 20-21.

4. Aristotle, *Poetics*, trans. S. H. Butcher, in *Critical Theory since Plato*, ed. Hazard Adams (New York: Thomson Learning, 1971), 50; hereafter cited in text.

5. David Hume, "Of Tragedy," *Of the Standard of Taste and Other Essays*, ed. John W. Lenz (Indianapolis, IN: Bobbs-Merrill, 1965), 29; hereafter cited in text.

6. Hume, "Of Tragedy," 31.

7. Hume, "Of Tragedy," 31-36.

8. William Wordsworth, "Preface to Lyrical Ballads (1800)," in *Wordsworth's Literary Criticism,* ed. Nowell C. Smith (London: Henry Frowde, 1905), 25; hereafter cited in text.

9. Wordsworth, "Preface," 26.

10. Wordsworth, "Preface," 34.

11. Wordsworth, "Preface," 34-35.

12. Abrams, "What's the Use," 22.

13. Aristotle, *Poetics,* 51.

14. René Wellek and Austin Warren, *Theory of Literature* (New York: Harcourt, Brace, 1949), 31.

15. Tzvetan Todorov, "Structuralism and Literature," in *Approaches to Poetics,* ed. Seymour Chatman (New York: Columbia Univ. Press, 1973), 156.

16. R. S. Crane, Introduction to *Critics and Criticism,* ed. Crane (Chicago: Univ. of Chicago Press, 1952), 7.

17. W. R. Keast, "The Theoretical Foundations of Johnson's Criticism," in *Critics and Criticism,* 389-407.

18. Keast, "Theoretical Foundations," 392.

19. Samuel Johnson, "Preface to Shakespeare, 1765," in *Johnson on Shakespeare,* ed. Arthur Sherbo, Yale Edition of the Works of Samuel Johnson (New Haven, CT: Yale Univ. Press, 1968), 7:66.

20. Wellek, *Theory of Literature,* 8.

21. Northrop Frye, *Anatomy of Criticism* (Princeton, NJ: Princeton Univ. Press, 1957), 16.

22. Todorov, "Structuralism and Literature," 154.

23. Frye, *Anatomy of Criticism,* 11.

24. Ralph W. Rader, "Fact, Theory, and Literary Explanation," *Critical Inquiry* 1, no. 2 (1974): 249.

25. Rader, "Fact, Theory, and Literary Explanation," 248.

26. Hans Robert Jauss, "Literary History as a Challenge to Literary Theory," in *New Directions in Literary History,* ed. Ralph Cohen (Baltimore: Johns Hopkins Univ. Press, 1974), 12.

27. Jonathan Culler, *Structuralist Poetics: Structuralism, Linguistics and the Study of Literature* (Ithaca, NY: Cornell Univ. Press, 1975), 31.

28. Culler, *Structuralist Poetics,* 117.

29. Jauss, "Literary History," 36ff.

The Joys and Sorrows of Literary Theory

I call this essay "The Joys and Sorrows of Literary Theory" because literary theory is a deliberate form of human action, of writing, and all such actions have consequences that range from joy to sorrow for the actors and the audience. My allusion to *The Joy of Sex* and *The Sorrows of Young Werther* is neither accidental nor arbitrary. The pleasures of the text and the anxiety of deconstruction are but two aspects of modern theory, but they do serve to indicate the passion with which theorists write theory. Roland Barthes has described the different pleasures of a text, including those of reading and writing theoretical texts.[1] Such pleasures arouse and express desires with regard to the nature, methods, and aims of writing; no one theory, whether erotic, Marxist, or phenomenological, has come to dominate our thinking about writing. But it is apparent that the multifariousness of theoretical writing has made our time especially cognizant of theoretical formulations.

There are formalist theories, Freudian theories, phenomenological, hermeneutical, historical, semiotic, and genre theories; there are structuralist and deconstructuralist theories, aesthetics of reception, reader response, and speech act theories; there are sociological, anthropological, and Marxist theories; there are affective, institutional, contextual, procedural, archetypal, and Jungian theories; there is a Marxist-Freudian-reader response theory, and there is a hermeneutical-phenomenological-historical aesthetics of reception theory.

I do not take delight in this disorder, but I do wish to suggest that each theory, being an attempt to order some aspects of literature, becomes part of a larger theoretical framework that is far from complete. In this essay I

This essay was originally published in *Innovation/Renovation: New Perspectives on the Humanities,* ed. Ihab Hassan and Sally Hassan (Madison: Univ. of Wisconsin Press, 1983), 111–30, and is reprinted with permission of the Estate of Ralph Cohen.

sketch a historical map of contemporary theory, indicating why it has become prominent, what kind of literary studies it has undertaken, what kind of unity or disunity it reveals, what are its triumphs and failures, and what types of exploration we still need to undertake.

Inevitably my map shall be incomplete—not because I do not have time to make it complete, and not because I introduce my biases in drawing the boundaries or formulating problems—but because living among the theories I describe I can only speculate about where they lead, what their dominant features will prove to be, which will be absorbed, which dissolved, which preserved. Human actions, as we know, often have consequences far different from those intended by the actors. But I shall try to minimize my difficulties in this historical account by considering theory not merely as a form of human action but of such controversial actions as are involved in dialogues, arguments, agreements, and disagreements.

I shall try to answer such queries as, why theories which clearly have as their aim the propagation of values about the ends of writing, of interpretation, of literary systems and their relation to other kinds of systems, why such theories which are addressed to all literate members of a society become so technical that they estrange members of the very group they aim to serve. And why it is that literary theories no less than poems are subject to transactions with readers who help construct their meanings. Contemporary theorists have moved from broad questions, such as the nature of interpretation, to narrower questions, such as the nature of the reader or of reading, to help remove the impasses of the original inquiry. I shall conclude, therefore, with directions for what I take to be still narrower but necessary inquiries.

For our time, theorizing may be understood as an effort to systematize interpretation by disentangling the problems that were implicit in formal analysis. For example, theorists raised basic questions about poetic analysis by inquiring not into the specific analyses of particular poems but into the subject matter of literature, which meant inquiring into the shared structure of poems and the nature of literature. Were poems different in kind from biographies or journalistic accounts? Was Gibbon's *Decline and Fall* literature? Ought literature to be confined to self-referential, to imaginative works that were considered "autonomous"? Theorists raised these questions from within the discipline because groups within the profession insisted that the literary canon was the result of an undemocratic aim in teaching "literature," or a consequence of the fact that the human mind operated in certain binary oppositions.

The *desire to theorize* developed from a dissatisfaction with particular empirical analyses, and it moved in two directions. On the one hand, it led to speculations beyond the empirical, speculations that related it to all art. On the other, it led to a more precise use of the empirical, what some theorists identified as a more "scientific" methodology, by grounding it in scientific, linguistic, or psychological assumptions. The desire for theory can be understood as part of a more general search for the origins of our assumptions. Theory has become for us a dramatic spectacle, and Kenneth Burke's dramatistic terms are philologically appropriate because the term "theory" is related to "theater," to "speculation," to "spectacle."[2] Finally, the desire to theorize was a desire to move beyond the limits of a single discipline, to reach for a literary study that could be made part of a general humanistic inquiry.

Indeed, in other humanistic disciplines, scholars concerned themselves with many of the same problems that led literary critics to turn to theoretical explanations. When Clifford Geertz, the anthropologist, described and analyzed a Balinese cockfight, he was interpreting another culture in his own language; his task engaged a number of the problems that confronted the literary critic, and he recognized this. To what extent did he, as an American anthropologist, distort what he saw because of his Western prejudices, and by the fact that he had to describe behavior in a language that had connotations from a different culture? When Thomas Kuhn analyzed the structure of scientific revolutions, he sought the grounds of periodization in science, and these replicated inquiries by literary and art critics into concepts of literary norms or periods.

My point is that theorists who aim at systematizing literary study are part of a broad group of humanistic scholars who seek to theorize about human actions. Moreover, they agree in rejecting the view that interpreting or theorizing is value-free. They reject the view of a disinterested study of human action, or to put it in literary terms, they reject the belief that the literary work is "autonomous," or self-reflexive, or unconnected with the external world. The procedure, therefore, is to identify the kind of values implied or stated in a text. Such a task results in reconsideration of the writer, the text, and the reader. For the writer is both a member of society and a maker of it; the text embodies his intentions and those of a tradition or genre; and the reader who helps construct the work is shaped by his past readings and his social or group values.

These reconsiderations account for varieties of theoretical hypotheses. The *issue* for theorists is *not a question* of the presence or absence of value, but what literary values are and how they can be located. I take as my first example of a shift in values the case of Paul de Man. In 1963 Paul de Man subscribed to the procedures of the New Criticism, and he contributed to a collection of essays edited by Reuben Brower and Richard Poirier called *In Defense of Reading*.[3] De Man's essay interpreted Wordsworth's sonnet "Composed by the Side of Grasmere Lake."[4] The sonnet reads as follows:

> Clouds, lingering yet, extend in solid bars
> Through the grey West; and lo! these waters, steeled
> By breezeless air to smoothest polish, yield
> A vivid repetition of the stars;
> Jove, Venus, and the ruddy crest of Mars
> Amid his fellows beauteously revealed
> At happy distance from earth's groaning field,
> Where ruthless mortals wage incessant wars.
> Is it a mirror?—or the nether Sphere
> Opening to view the abyss in which she feeds
> Her own calm fires?—But list! a voice is near;
> Great Pan himself low-whispering through the reeds.
> "Be thankful, thou; for, if unholy deeds
> Ravage the world, tranquillity is here!"

De Man argued that the poem was unified by tension and, he declared, "the juxtaposition of two very different attitudes toward a landscape, [which are] held together by a dramatic progression which constitutes the key to the interpretation."[5] These two attitudes—of ruthless wars and a peaceful haven held in tension—underlay the entire sonnet. This emphasis on a single "key" to interpretation, on the controlling concept of "tension," was the response of an independent critic whose transaction with the poem resulted in what he considered a "proper" interpretation.

The social aim of this criticism was spelled out by Reuben Brower: the essays in the book had as their aim, he wrote, "to get the student in a position where he could learn for himself. If we succeed, we have reason to believe that he may acquire a lifetime habit of learning independently."[6]

The purpose of the interpretation was to teach the student a "method," one that the student would come to apply by himself. One can admire the intention behind such an aim—to make the student independent—but can only regret the neglect of the student or reader as an individual. The kind of learning, training, and values that the student brought to the class could not make him independent, only an independent dependent. The student did not help construct the text, he discovered what was there. The very concept of independence, as Brower defines it, is a fiction, for such independence is dependent on another's guidance and method.

But even more perturbing is how the reader is to respond to tranquillity as a virtue, to accept a retreat alongside Grasmere Lake as a form of value which permits him to ignore the sights and sounds of "earth's groaning field." The practice in which Paul de Man had engaged took as its aim independence in reading and learning. It attempted neither to understand the nature of the institutions that fostered this learning nor to ask whether the canon, including the particular poem of Wordsworth's, urged the kind of values that deserved support. The critic-teacher seemed unaware of the social and political values that this fiction of independence nourished. Eight years later, 1971, Paul de Man published *Blindness and Insight*. In the introduction the following statements appeared:

> The picture of reading that emerges from the examination of a few contemporary critics is not a simple one. In all of them a paradoxical discrepancy appears between the general statements they make about the nature of literature (statements on which they base their critical methods) and the actual results of their interpretations. Their findings about the structure of texts contradict the general conception that they use as their model.... I suggest that this pattern of discrepancy, far from being the consequence of individual or collective aberrations, is a constitutive characteristic of literary language in general.... we no longer take for granted that a literary text can be reduced to a finite meaning or set of meanings, but see the act of reading as an endless process in which truth and falsehood are inextricably intertwined.[7]

What took place in the writing of Paul de Man was a shift from construction to deconstruction, from "tension" to "contradiction." He discarded his belief in "the key to interpretation": not only did he find no key, he rejected the possibility that a set of keys could unlock meaning. The act of reading was now an "endless process in which truth and falsehood are inextricably intertwined." De Man's absolute view of language replaced his absolute view of method, and we note the untying of assumptions implicit in his earlier statements.

There was no longer a belief in the possibility of learning from key readings; instead, there was a skeptical view of language, a view that language was an untrustworthy means of communication requiring skeptical readers.

Such readers need to familiarize themselves with the varied strategies of mixing truth with falsehood. But does this not imply that the words of Paul de Man are subject to the same deconstruction? Is not this strategy as unreliably transient as all others? Indeed, it is, and he would not deny it.

What he arrived at was a theory suited to a time of public hypocrisy and betrayal. The theory that Paul de Man and other deconstructionists offered was directed at the distrust of language and the reeducation of readers. This distrust, what Hillis Miller calls language as host and parasite, language that undermines itself, is only one of several competing hypotheses about aspects of a text. But this theory and its competitors, despite their many differences, *do share two assumptions: first,* that every text has a subtext, another text concealed in it or implied in it or capable of being derived from it. Whether the subtext undermines the text or supplements it, this hypothesis implies a *second:* every text involves a reader or critic who transacts with it and helps construct it. These two assumptions do away with the earlier limited view of reader independence; rather, they suggest a view that writing and reading involve a *communal* partnership or enterprise, including a way of questioning or testing this partnership. Writing is not a matter of one person issuing a message and another receiving it. The message is constructed by the issuer and receiver. One might say that the linguistic distinction between signifier and signified is undermined by the receiver who mediates or constructs relations between signifier and signified. The situation I am describing implicates sender and receiver in every message; thus betrayal is not the act of another but of oneself, just as partnership is a mutual, not an individual, act.

I quote Wolfgang Iser's phenomenological explanation of the reader-text transaction to convey some of the distinctions involved in his interpretation of this transaction. "The literary work cannot be completely identical with the text, or with the realization of the text, but in fact must lie halfway between the two. The work is more than the text, for the text only takes on life when it is realized, and furthermore the realization is by no means independent of the individual disposition of the reader—though this in turn is acted upon by the different patterns of the text. The convergence of text and reader brings the literary work into existence."[8] The distinctions between "text" and "literary work," distinctions among "text," "realization of the text," and a convergence of the two, confirm the point I made earlier—that theory proceeds by refining or untying concepts taken for granted. Thus for the formalists, the subtext is a series of expectations that the text defeats or alienates. For Freudians, the subtext consists of the nonconscious conflicts submerged in the text. For the phenomenologists the subtext is the realm of Being, the open space implicit in the text or the gaps and indeterminacies which the reader must fill. For the Marxists—or at least for some of them—the subtext is the description of social oppression which the text conceals.

I wish to focus on the Marxist position—or Fredric Jameson's version of it—in order to discuss not only the concept of reader as a collective figure but the concept of reading as a historical dialectic. Jameson writes:

> We must try to rid ourselves of the habit of thinking about our (aesthetic) relationship to culturally or temporally distant artifacts as being a relationship between individual subjects (as in my *personal* reading of an *individual* text written by a biographical individual named Spenser or Juvenal, or even my personal attempt to invent an individual relationship to an oral story once told by an individual storyteller in a tribal society). It is not a question of dismissing the role of individual subjects in the reading process, but rather of grasping this obvious and concrete individual relationship as being itself a mediation for a nonindividual and more collective process: the confrontation of two distinct social forms or modes of production. We must try to accustom ourselves to a perspective in which every act of reading, every local interpretive practice, is grasped as the privileged vehicle through which two distinct modes of production confront and interrogate one another. Our individual reading thus becomes an allegorical figure for this essentially collective confrontation of two social forms.[9]

The forcefulness of this argument is impressive—not only because Jameson is conducting a dialogue with other contemporary critics but because he is absorbing and redefining their arguments. He does not dismiss "the role of individual subjects in the reading process," but restates the relationship as a "mediation for a nonindividual and more collective process: the confrontation of two distinct social forms or modes of production." He finds the individual to be both an individual and a part of a larger cultural process, and he conceives of a text as a social form or a mode of production.

This is a subtle procedure for reintroducing the concept of collective behavior into theory; still, if each individual reading is an allegorical figure for collective confrontation, are we not left, once again, with multiple distinctions in reading, only this time *within* a single trope—allegory? And has not Frye argued that all interpretation is allegorical because it constructs its own meaning from another text, and does not Jameson's claim lead to the same dilemma as Frye's?[10] When critics move from individual readings to analyses of the nature of reading, are we necessarily involved in the same type of collectivism or cultural process? In fact, does not the introduction of mediation create a special dilemma because mediation as criticism or theory is itself a form of writing, which creates values as well as describes them? What becomes problematical is the act of confrontation between two modes of production. What sort of historical relation is involved? How can the critic control the perspective through which he sees the modes of production? What does the term "mode of production" conceal? Is not "mode of production" as collective a term as "individual critic"?

The hermeneutical critic (I refer to Heidegger here), who also assumes (with some Marxists) that texts interrogate each other, adds a belief in their "immanence" and "truth"; these further assumptions are necessary for his text to speak for itself. For example, David Hoy writes: "On the hermeneutic account . . . immanence and truth must be seen not only as properties of the text, but also as assumptions granted to the text by the reader in the process of letting the text speak for itself. The text does not exist except in a dialogue between text and interpreter."[11] But we must be wary of the dialogue metaphor because the dialogue is conducted through a monologue. The critic who speaks for the text is the same critic who speaks to it. The dialogue is filtered through one mind; what we have is a partnership; but the thoughts and words of the silent partner are filtered through the mind of the vocal one. "Truth" and "immanence," therefore, can be filtered out as well as permitted to drip in.

If the hermeneutic theorist and the Marxist critic both wish to avoid total relativism, they at least realize that this act cannot be performed by returning to Kant and to value-free objectivism. The alternatives to relativism may prove complicated, even insurmountable, involving questionable questions and answers. But these critics are aware that the questions they ask are conditioned by their own culture, not released from it. I would, however, be an inadequate guide to contemporary theory if I did not inform you that there *still* are critics who argue that value-free judgments exist in literary study. Gerald Graff has declared that "we all become value-free objectivists to some extent when we attempt to make sure our value judgments rest on an unbiased understanding of the object. In other words, value-free objectivity is a necessary first stage of making value judgments—the descriptive, disinterested determination of what it is that is to be judged."[12]

But it is precisely the assumption of selectivity—"what it is that is to be judged"—that governs canon making. The establishing of the subject matter is governed by what theorists take to be the aims or ends of a discipline, the values they want to convey. I do not claim that there exists only one set of values—there are, after all, personal as well as public values. But the selection of a subject matter is tied to the values that those in control believe are best for the discipline. Even the language of literary study—such terms as "literature," or "belles lettres," or "genre," "novel," "poem," "narrative," are value laden. Does it help to claim, as Graff does, that "value itself is objective in that it rests on prior understanding," since "prior understanding" is no more than a term for values established at some prior time by an institution, class, or group?[13]

Gerald Graff's *Literature against Itself* is a historical study of contemporary criticism and theory, but its version of "history" is one that the theorists I have been discussing would reject. Graff maintains that there are indeed certain objective truths that need to be accepted despite the fact that the very process of arriving at them marks them as relativistic and transient. But why do theorists continue to hold fast to theories that are being undermined, that are being dissolved or untied? There is the desire to maintain stability, to cling to views that are familiar. There is the belief that the overthrow of authority, literary or otherwise, includes the overthrow of logic and reason even though the newer theories are based on accommodations to logic and reason and, indeed, call for "rational inquiry."

I have introduced Gerald Graff not because he opposes what Michel Foucault or Jacques Derrida do, but because the reasons he gives exemplify the disjunctions they describe. His objectivism belongs to an earlier time frame, and the point of some contemporary theoretical writing is that a *period* contains within itself contrary theories from different time frames, and that this awareness is one of the characteristics of modern writing, including the writing of theory considered as "modern."

Graff's literary history, based on his version of logic and objectivism, does not describe the kind of "reality" to which Foucault, Derrida, and others point. It is not surprising that modernist writing, of which recent theory is an example, develops a series of rhetorical traits that, according to David Lodge, reflect the breakup of earlier forms. Lodge writes: "Now the characteristics . . . of modernist writing in particular have been often enough described: formal experiment, dislocation of conventional syntax, radical breaches of decorum, disturbance of chronology and spatial order, ambiguity, polysemy, obscurity, mythopoeic allusion, primitivism, irrationalism, structuring by symbol and motif rather than by narrative or argumentative logic, and so on. And it is easy to see how these strategies and themes reflect the sense that the modern period has a special historic destiny, perhaps to abolish history itself."[14]

David Lodge's irony in writing a modern historical account suggesting that "the modern period has a special historic destiny, perhaps to abolish history itself," reveals that the "history" which is being abolished is not the "history" written by Foucault or Derrida. Their "history," like contemporary "literary theory," invents or redefines the vocabulary of discourse. Foucault declares: "We must also question those divisions or groupings with which we have become so familiar. Can one accept, as such, the distinction . . . between such forms or genres as science, literature, philosophy, religion, history, fiction, etc., and which tend to create certain great historical individualities? We are not even sure of ourselves when we use these distinctions in our own world of discourse, let alone when we are analysing groups of statements which, when first formulated, were distributed, divided, and characterized in a quite different way."[15]

So, too, Derrida's substitution of "text" for "work" is a deliberate effort to remove the metaphysical implications of linearity and succession inherent in the earlier term. But "text" and "history" are words with their own pasts, and the effort to erase this fact and rebaptize the terms creates deliberate disjunctions of meaning and equally deliberate hostility to such disjunctions.[16]

One can appreciate the desire to start anew; to begin with a vocabulary constructed by the critic and to provide a series of relations among works that are the result of uncontaminated concepts. But if a theorist conceives of his theory in terms of new beginnings, we find that all theorists who stress their novelty *share* a search for differentness. If we consider our time as disjunctive with explanations of previous events in history, we can understand this disjunction only by knowing previous explanations.

Can there be a complete rejection of the language that deals with history, with past actions—a complete rejection of the expressions of past events? If a text is a form of human action and human actions undergo change, some continuity is essential to define any action. If a text is identified with a genre, then any particular text can only be understood in terms of past traditions or examples of its genre. If a text is understood as a series of conventions, history is necessary to explain these conventions. But what if one believes a text is constituted by a self-referential language? Is not such a text to be understood only in its own terms and without any past conventions, traditions, or actions? What use would historical procedures be in understanding such a work? But even as one asks this question, the answer is self-evident: how does one know a language if one has never used it? How does one know a poem if one has never seen or heard a poem? How does one know what "understanding" is if one has no prior understanding of "understanding"?

The issue is not, "Are historical procedures necessary for the understanding of theory?" but "What kind of historical procedures are necessary for such understanding?" Contemporary theory that accepts disjunctions and discontinuities is inevitably confronted with how past meanings can be recaptured. The hermeneutic circle suggests that the critic interprets past texts in terms of present premises. It is only critics who, like Gerald Graff, urge ideal objectivity by denying empirical objectivity who can overlook the hermeneutic paradox in interpretation. Others, like Hans Robert Jauss, Stanley Fish, Wolfgang Iser, have undertaken to circumvent this dilemma by providing restraints on subjectivity. Jauss's aesthetics of reception is one of the most comprehensive attempts to reduce individual subjectivity by tracing the subjectivity of past critics.[17] Jauss sees any response to a work as part of a historical series which begins with the generic nature of the text. Each response is then related to responses to other works of the same time. Responses to the work are thus controlled by synchronic as well as diachronic texts. The consequence is that the modern response is not unrestrained but defined and delimited in terms of prior historical awareness. Of course, the subjective element is never eliminated. But at least it is brought to consciousness and is confined by the frame that has been historically traced.

Such a historical theory offers contemporary critics an opportunity to redefine key terms; for example, what a "genre" is and how "genre" is part of a series and a literary system. It also leads us to consider the relation between popular writing and sophisticated or elite writing, for, surely, there is writing which consciously supports the prejudices of bourgeois readers, as there is writing which attacks or subverts these prejudices. A novel by Judith Krantz may fit uneasily with a novel by Thomas Pynchon, but a theorist would have to explain the interrelations of such different works within the same genre.

But theorists are not always ready to engage the problems that empirical acts impose or to make such inquiries accessible to the common reader. Theory in our time has had to face the charge that it has become all too often a technical study. On the one hand, theorists seek to relate their study to human values and concerns; on the other, they must render their study highly technical in order to accomplish this.

The argument against the scientific or technical vocabulary of contemporary theory is, I believe, misdirected. There is no reason to assume that theory need or need not be simple: different theoretical inquiries have different ends. What needs to be simple and clear is the explanation of the value that theoretical study has for any layman, because such discourse is addressed to laymen. The practice of theory requires a special competence, and theorists recognize this. One of the practitioners of institutional theory, Charles Altieri, puts it this way: "The essential properties of literary response are created by education and exposure rather than by necessary and sufficient conditions in the object. . . .When we read a text, we have implicitly operating a history of other texts and of questions we put often without being self-conscious about them. The competent reader is like a trained athlete, whose skills far outweigh his explanatory powers and whose actions combine required moves with a continual possibility for free improvisation."[18]

The practice of theory requires a special competence, but every human being is engaged in one way or another with interpreting language and other social forms. The need to possess this competence is what should be made clear to all thinking human beings: to learn which verbal actions to trust, which to distrust; to recognize the value-laden qualities of such actions, to distinguish between the continuities and discontinuities of value (between a living and a dead tradition).

But it is all too easy to admire so seductive an institutional theory, especially for scholars who are themselves members of an institution. If readers learn by imitating teachers and critics, the importance of these acts may elevate our pride but not always their knowledge. For such theories are subject to the same objections that were leveled against the statements of Reuben Brower. Students do not come naked into the classroom; they bring values and attitudes. And they select aspects of a teacher to imitate that do not necessarily duplicate his values: Paul de Man can stand as such an example. Moreover, an institutional theory that does not explain why or how an institution changes cannot offer an adequate explanation of its value structure. In a sense, an institutional theory addresses itself to the collective nature of the individual, but it cannot adequately define the institution without placing it within a context of other societal institutions: those of religion, politics, the family, the law, and science.

I wrote above about Clifford Geertz and Thomas Kuhn, writers who deal with institutions other than that of literary study. And I suggested that the approach they had to human problems resembled that of literary theorists. For purposes of institutional study, I want to note now that a number of critics from other disciplines use literary criticism and theory as models. Indeed, in the sociology of Robert Brown, in the anthropology of Dell Hymes and Victor Turner, in the history of science of Gerald Holton, literary theory has become a model. Its analysis of interpretation, of writers who are readers and readers who are writers, of the relation between text and critic, have all served to establish not only a concept of communal responsiveness in verbal actions but a closer relationship among the different disciplines and institutions.

I want to conclude my study of contemporary theory by examining two examples—one of which aims at scientific precision and the other which deliberately avoids it. Both are open theories: they await and invite evidence and confirmation. And they display the joys of invented vocabularies that are meant to encourage humanistic discourse. The German theorist and concrete poet Siegfried J. Schmidt, in "Empirische Literaturwissenschaft als Perspektiv," argues that *rational inquiry* can and should be applied to literary study. Ihab Hassan, in "Desire, Imagination, Change: Outline of a Theoretical Project," among other essays, seeks to illustrate that literary and scientific discourses are indeed interrelated.[19]

Schmidt seeks to do away with speculative, imaginative theorizing and offers as an alternative an empirical, "scientific" literary theory based on a series of propositions for which evidence still needs to be assembled, but which, he is convinced, can be assembled. Schmidt explains that he uses "empirical" in a special sense: "the empiricity of a statement cannot be decided in relation to reality as such, but only in relation to a model of reality consensually adopted by a community of investigators. The value of methods used to prove the empirical contents of statements or arguments can consequently only be judged by the interpretation of this model of reality."[20]

As for "theoreticity," he declares: "The fundamental theory predicate must be identifiable; the logical structure of problem solving strategies must be explicit or at least explicable; the theory must be empirically interpretable (or: the empirical content of the theory must be expressible)."[21] The three preconditions that Schmidt finds essential for a proper *Literaturwissenschaft* pertain to the kind of intellectual activity that is to be performed in the framework of theory; the classification of the concept of literature; the aims and functions of theoretical investigations and the social relevance of such activities. His text includes references to historians of science, to theorists of science and literature; it includes formulas—$T = (K, I)$, where T = Theory; K = Kernel; I = Intended Application—it includes diagrams, different type fonts. It is also composed of sentences and sentence fragments. In his critical writing, he seeks to bridge the gap between the verbal and the visual, between the word and the nonverbal formula, and his literary theory includes elements of scientific and of linguistic (diagrammatic) notations.

There is an element of pseudoscience in Schmidt's formulas; they can, after all, be written without the equational mystique. And the precision that he calls for requires evidence not yet assembled. But his plea for "rational inquiry" is another version of the contemporary communal enterprise shared by those who participate in a method of arguing or a manner of writing or a procedure for thinking. His argument for the empiricity of a statement makes the communal element clear: "The empiricity of a statement" can be judged "only in relation to a model of reality consensually adopted by a community of investigators." Different investigators do adopt different reality-models, and Schmidt leaves unresolved the conflicts between such models.

Schmidt's model for literary theory is coherent and consistent, but can the evidence for it be assembled? Can the classification of the concept of literature be defended on rational grounds when it is selected for historical rather than rational reasons? Does the term "rational" activity take account of the learning that is done by imitation or—to be paradoxical—by model following? Is not Schmidt's theorizing speculative and imaginative rather than scientific and experimental? Is not his theory constructed as an imaginative whole prior to the data that are to fit it?

The kind of theorizing that he rejects is the speculative intertextual writing that Ihab Hassan practices. Hassan's text offers quotations from A. N. Whitehead, J. D. Bernal, William Blake, Nietzsche, Freud, Heisenberg, Haldane, etc., and organizes them into an inquiry about interrelating the systems of science and art. He asks, "Can the gnosis of science and the prophetic dream of art converge on some idea(s) of change that criticism has yet to acknowledge, let alone explore?" Hassan does not argue for a thesis; rather, he is intent on provoking the reader to consider or reconsider certain theoretical issues. Because of this, he and some other contemporary theorists have been accused of competing with literary texts. But ought we to be guided by Matthew Arnold's hypothesis that criticism must prepare the way for creative writing or be the handmaid of such writing? If writing is a form of human action, then at some times types of verbal action such as Plato's *Symposium* or Nietzsche's *The Birth of Tragedy* or Shelley's *A Defence of Poetry* can be, and indeed have been, considered by critics as works of art. What constitutes "literature," "works of art," or "creative" writing depends upon the values and functions one attributes to these. In our time theory is causing us to rethink the nature of past texts; as such, it is initiating a rewriting of past poetry and prose; it leads us to new responses to old poetry.

It used to be considered a devastating attack upon criticism—and even theory—to declare that there would be no criticism or theory if there were no literature. The idea was that theory was parasitical upon literary texts. Whether or not it was the theorists' revenge, the Russian formalists began—and some contemporary theorists continue—to argue that every literary text is a form of theory. Each text exemplifies certain principles of composition and is, by example, an instance of theory. Thus the argument can be reversed—there can be no poetry without theory.

This interpretative reversal leads me back to the nature of a text, for if a text includes a subtext, both include principles of composition. The term "text" needs further division and analysis; the concept of intertextuality—the inclusion of quotations from and references to other texts—in a theoretical work indicates one possibility of dealing with the multiform character of a text. This is, therefore, one of the three directions we can take in theory: an investigation of the collective, combinatory nature of a text; a study of the nature of literary value—its kinds and functions, especially in relation to other kinds of values; and, finally, a study of the nature of and reasons for literary change—of styles, subjects, genres, periods, and so forth.

Hassan posits quotations from a variety of thinkers, and he designs the printed page with numerous typological innovations. Many of these prove trivial and unsuccessful, but the aim of his text is to challenge the imagination of the reader to cooperate in the construction of theoretical ideas. When a text includes quotations that come from different times, it urges the reader to interrelate them, to make unexpected and unanticipated temporal connections, to reconstitute tradition. The fragments of time embodied in such quotations urge readers to compare a fragmented quotation with the whole of which it is a part and with the new whole of which it has become a part.

I began by indicating some of my own literary presuppositions, hearing in my ear the voice of Geoffrey Hartman: "Interpreter: define thyself."[22] I then explained why theory had become prominent in our time both from the demands of the discipline and from the external recognition of inquiry into human actions. This was followed by the study of a specific example of a critic, Paul de Man, who turned from criticism to theory. It was a theory that answered, I said, to certain public needs, and I then illustrated that a body of contemporary theorists agreed upon certain formulations expressing shared values. I focused in detail on two specific statements dealing with theoretical issues involved in reading and introduced a standard opposition to the formulations. I sought to show that this opposition was based on a misconception and explained how this misconception could arise from the ambiguity of theoretical language. I then illustrated several theories that sought, not always successfully, to restrain relativism without succumbing to untenable claims. No theory has yet proved entirely satisfactory, but the impact of theorizing and criticizing has affected disciplines other than literary study and has called into question the conventional assumptions about theory.

Theory has, for us, been freed from its subservience to literature, and it now appears as a genre on its own. In this respect, its history has not yet begun to be written, and we have before us a challenging and provocative task. Confronting it, we can envision once again the disturbing joys and pleasurable sorrows of literary theory.

NOTES

1. Roland Barthes, *The Pleasure of the Text,* trans. Richard Howard (New York: Hill & Wang, 1975), 16-17.

2. Kenneth Burke, *A Grammar of Motives* (New York: Prentice-Hall, 1945).

3. Reuben A. Brower and Richard Poirier, eds., *In Defense of Reading: A Reader's Approach to Literary Criticism* (New York: E. P. Dutton, 1963).

4. Paul de Man, "Symbolic Landscape in Wordsworth and Yeats," in Brower and Poirier, *In Defense of Reading,* 22-37.

5. De Man, "Symbolic Landscape," 22-23.

6. Reuben A. Brower, "Reading in Slow Motion," in Brower and Poirier, *In Defense of Reading,* 8.

7. Paul de Man, *Blindness and Insight: Essays in the Rhetoric of Contemporary Criticism* (New York: Oxford Univ. Press, 1971), ix.

8. Wolfgang Iser, "The Reading Process: A Phenomenological Approach," in *New Directions in Literary History,* ed. Ralph Cohen (Baltimore: Johns Hopkins Univ. Press, 1974), 125.

9. Fredric Jameson, "Marxism and Historicism," *New Literary History* 11, no. 1 (1979): 69-70.

10. Northrop Frye, *Anatomy of Criticism* (Princeton, NJ: Princeton Univ. Press, 1957), 89-92.

11. David Couzens Hoy, *The Critical Circle: Literature, History, and Philosophical Hermeneutics* (Berkeley and Los Angeles: Univ. of California Press, 1978), 145.

12. Gerald Graff, *Literature against Itself: Literary Ideas in Modern Society* (Chicago: Univ. of Chicago Press, 1979), 86.

13. Graff, *Literature against Itself,* 87.

14. David Lodge, "Historicism and Literary History: Mapping the Modern Period," *New Literary History* 10, no. 3 (1979): 550.

15. Michel Foucault, *The Archaeology of Knowledge,* trans. A. M. Sheridan Smith (London: Tavistock, 1972), 22.

16. Jacques Derrida, *Of Grammatology,* trans. Gayatri C. Spivak (Baltimore: Johns Hopkins Univ. Press, 1976), 18.

17. Hans Robert Jauss, "Literary History as a Challenge to Literary Theory," in Cohen, *New Directions in Literary History,* 11-41.

18. Charles Altieri, "A Procedural Definition of Literature," in *What Is Literature?,* ed. Paul Hernadi (Bloomington: Indiana Univ. Press, 1978), 70.

19. Siegfried J. Schmidt, "Empirische Literaturwissenschaft als Perspektive," *Poetics* 8 (1979): 557-68; Ihab Hassan, "Desire, Imagination, Change: Outline of a Theoretical Project," *Studies in the Literary Imagination* 12 (1979): 129-43.

20. Schmidt, "Empirische Literaturwissenschaft," 560.

21. Schmidt, "Empirische Literaturwissenschaft," 560-61.

22. Geoffrey H. Hartman, "The Interpreter: A Self-Analysis," *New Literary History* 4, no. 2 (1973): 219.

History and Genre

I

I call this paper "History and Genre" though history is a genre and genre has a history. It is this interweaving between history and genre that I seek to describe. In *The Political Unconscious* Fredric Jameson wrote that genre criticism has been "thoroughly discredited by modern literary theory and practice."[1] There are at least three reasons for this. First, the very notion that texts compose classes has been questioned. Secondly, the assumption that members of a genre share a common trait or traits has been questioned, and thirdly, the function of a genre as an interpretative guide has been questioned.

But what is this genre that has been discredited? The term "genre" is relatively recent in critical discourse. Previous to the nineteenth century the terms used for it were "kinds" or "species." Genre has its source in the Latin *genus,* which refers in some cases to "kind" or "sort" or "class" or "species." But in others, "species" is considered a subclass of "genus." Its root terms are *genre, gignere*—to beget and (in the passive) to be born. In this latter sense it refers to both a class and an individual. And it is, of course, derived from the same root terms as *gender.* The connection of "genre" to "gender" suggests that an early use of the term was based on division or classification. Two genders are necessary in order to define one, and sexual genders implied not merely classification but a hierarchy or dominance of one gender over the other. Genres included, in the Attic age, poems written in a distinctive meter

This essay was originally published in "Interpretation and Culture," special issue, *New Literary History* 17, no. 2 (1986): 203-18, and is reprinted here with the permission of the publisher; a slightly different version of the essay was published in *Neohelicon* 13, no. 2 (1986): 87-105. At the beginning of the essay in *New Literary History*, Cohen noted that it was "part of a work in progress dealing with genre, history, and narrative." The intellectual historian Dominick LaCapra and the sociologist Richard Harvey Brown were asked to comment on Cohen's paper in the same issue; only Cohen's reply to their remarks is included here.

like elegiac or satiric poetry. With regard to the number of genres, critics have suggested that every work is its own genre, that there are two genres (literature and nonliterature), that there are three genres (lyric, epic, and drama), that there are four genres (lyric, epic, drama, and prose fiction), and, finally, that genres are any group of texts selected by readers to establish continuities that distinguish this group from others. As one critic puts it, genre is "any group of works selected on the basis of some shared features."[2] Genre has been defined in terms of meter, inner form, intrinsic form, radical of presentation, single traits, family traits, institutions, conventions, contracts, and these have been considered either as universals or as empirical historical groupings.

In recognition of this multiplicity of definitions, I wish to argue that genre concepts in theory and practice arise, change, and decline for historical reasons. And since each genre is composed of texts that accrue, the grouping is a process, not a determinate category. Genres are open categories. Each member alters the genre by adding, contradicting, or changing constituents, especially those of members most closely related to it. The process by which genres are established always involves the human need for distinction and interrelation. Since the purposes of critics who establish genres vary, it is self-evident that the same texts can belong to different groupings or genres and serve different generic purposes.

Have all the theories of genre from Menander to Morson been discredited? Contemporary critics continue to invest in genre, and I shall urge that there are critical tasks that can best be undertaken by genre. But it is necessary to understand what aspects, what assumptions of genre theory are being attacked. The first is that the classes or groupings that are called genres are no longer acceptable because we cannot be sure how to understand the texts as a class.

Michel Foucault states the general objection that dividing genre into groups like literature or philosophy is not useful since users of such distinctions no longer agree on how to take them. "We are not even sure of ourselves when we use these distinctions in our own world of discourse, let alone when we are analysing groups of statements which, when first formulated, were distributed, divided, and characterized in a quite different way."[3]

Jacques Derrida argues, characteristically, for the need and futility of genre designation. He points out that any generic classification system is untenable because individual texts although participating in it cannot belong to it. Individual texts resist classification because they are interpretatively indeterminate. He asks: "Can one identify a work of art, of whatever sort, but especially a work of discursive art, if it does not bear the mark of a genre, if it does not signal or mention it or make it remarkable in any way?"[4]

In putting the question in this manner Derrida wishes to confront all possible definitions of genre. For example, "literature" can be considered a genre which includes novel, elegy, tragedy, and so forth. It is a genre that includes other genres that define it: again, a genre can intermix genres—as a novel can contain poems, proverbs, sermons, letters, and so forth. The mark of belonging to a class need not be conscious (to author or reader) though it obviously is conscious to the critic who notes it. Indeed, a work can refer to itself even in its title, as *The History of Tom Jones, a Foundling* does, although subsequent critics and readers distinguish "history" from "novel." Or a text can refer to itself as a travel description when it is, like *Travel into Several Remote Nations of the World, by Lemuel Gulliver,* an imagined prose fiction. For Derrida, no generic trait completely or absolutely confines a text to a genre or class because such belonging falsifies the constituents of a text. He writes: "If . . . such a [generic] trait is remarkable, that is, noticeable, in every aesthetic, poetic, or literary corpus, then consider this paradox, consider the irony . . . this supplementary and distinctive trait, a mark of belonging or inclusion, does not properly pertain to any genre or class. The re-mark of belonging does not belong. It belongs without belonging" (64-65).

Belonging without belonging. With it but not of it. Why should an author, reader, or critic wish to classify a work or to identify it as belonging with other works of a similar kind: What acts and assumptions are concealed in the infinitive "to identify"? After all, classifications are undertaken for specific purposes. Derrida assumes that such classes are determinate and thus fix a text within them even though a text may be "fixed" in several different genres. But if one considers genres as processes, this criticism does not hold. Considerations of purposes are historical; different authors, readers, critics have different reasons for identifying texts as they do. The reasons for identifying texts differently do not interest Derrida; the identifications themselves do. He wishes to demonstrate that generic traits cannot *belong* to genres: "this supplementary and distinctive trait, a mark of belonging or inclusion, does not properly pertain to any genre or class." And not because a text is "an abundant overflowing or a free, anarchic, and unclassifiable productivity, but because of the *trait* of participation itself, because of the effect of the code and of the generic mark" (65). No text which is denominated "novel," for example, has traits that will identity all texts within the class.

Derrida both affirms and denies genre, and the basis for this inclusion and exclusion is the manner in which the individual text *participates* in the class and denies the class. Derrida does not pursue the historical inquiry of the types of "participation" involved in specific works; he assumes that all such participations are to be distinguished from "belonging." Indeed, for him, the individual text has so many contrary markings that participations undo belonging.

Derrida wishes to lead us away from the analysis of a class to an analysis of a text; textual interpretation will then support the paradox of belonging and not belonging. How persuasive is his undoing of a class? He does not deny the necessity for grouping texts, for showing that a text participates in a group. But he points out that "at the very moment that a genre or a literature is broached, at that very moment, degenerescence has begun, the end begins" (66). No sooner is a genre stipulated than it proceeds to be ungenerated. But it must be noted that this is a historical procedure—both the broaching of a genre and the beginning of its end. For in order for the end to have a beginning we must be in time; temporal history, however, insofar as it pertains to the process of undoing, is not what Derrida examines. By failing to do so, he takes a road that leads not to a history of generic purposes in a study of individual texts, but to a study of individual texts as distinct from genre. He creates a Herculean dilemma where none exists. Thus, to understand the aims and purposes of genre, to understand beginnings and endings it is necessary to take the road Derrida has not taken.

II

Francis Cairns points out that genres are as old as organized societies and that early genres were classifications in terms of content. The functions of these were to aid the listener in making logical connections and distinctions; generic distinctions aided him in following oral communications from the poet. Genre markers served to distinguish one type of communication from another, since such communications shared many secondary elements. Oral communication demanded primary markers. Members of the same oral genre shared at least one primary trait for purposes of recognition by hearers.[5] From these early beginnings of communication between poet and audience, we can note that genres possessed social purposes in a community, and that genres arose to contrast, complement, define each other's aims.

When an oral society is replaced by a literate one, the reasons for generic classification undergo change. The functions of markers or traits become the bases for value distinctions as well as for artistic distinctions and interrelations. When Aristotle deals with tragedy, for example, he lists plot as the primary marker within tragedy; he suggests the proper model for tragedy and he compares tragedy with epic in terms of generic value. He continues to note the interrelation of genres by showing the similarities and differences in qualitative elements and quantitative parts of tragedy and epic. "Again, tragedy has everything that epic has (it can even use its metre), and moreover has a considerable addition in the music and the spectacle, which produce pleasure in a most vividly perceptible way. . . . So much for tragedy and epic, their nature, the number and differences of their qualitative parts, the reasons for success and failure in them, and criticisms of them and how to answer them."[6]

Even for Aristotle generic markers are not absolutes; they indicate stages through which a genre passes. Moreover, the traits that are shared do not necessarily share the same function. Trait sharing may be, but need not be, the way to characterize a genre. A genre does not exist independently; it arises to compete or to contrast with other genres, to complement, augment, interrelate with other genres. Genres do not exist by themselves; they are named and placed within hierarchies or systems of genres, and each is defined by reference to the system and its members. A genre, therefore, is to be understood in relation to other genres, so that its aims and purposes at a particular time are defined by its interrelation with and differentiation from others. Thus critics can classify a Shakespearean "tragedy" not merely as a tragedy, but as a poem, a performance, a narrative, and so forth, depending on the points a critic wishes to make. What is at stake is not some single trait that would place it in each of these classes, but the purpose for so classifying it within a generic system. Only if one dehistoricizes genre does the notion of classification with one or more traits shared by each member become a problem; such a claim would make it impossible for a class to undergo change, since its traits would be essential rather than existential.

Contemporary critics do not find classification to be the purpose of genres, nor do they find that classifications serve evaluative purposes. When Northrop Frye sets up four genres based on the radical of presentation, he returns to the view that genres are rhetorical "in the sense that the genre is determined by the conditions established between the poet and his public."[7]

The trait called "radical of presentation" is the marker of a genre: "Words may be acted in front of a spectator; they may be spoken in front of a listener; they may be sung or chanted; or they may be written for a reader" (247). It is apparent that, given this single trait, Frye has to provide numerous qualifications and interrelations in the texts he consults. If Frye were a historical critic concerned with actual texts, he would proceed to illustrate the kind of interrelations that empirical critics develop, interrelations that show the choral chanting, riddling, and other oral devices in works acted in front of a spectator. He would undertake to explain how his genres interrelate historically with earlier genres as well as with each other. His efforts, however, are directed at traditions and affinities rather than the actualities of changing traditions and changing affinities. He knows that genre is determined by conditions that vary between poet and public, and that the terms "conditions" and "public" are both problematic. Generic distinctions, he points out, "are among the ways in which literary works are *ideally* presented, whatever the actualities are" (247). "Milton, for example, seems to have no ideal of reciter and audience in mind for *Paradise Lost;* he seems content to leave it, in practice, a poem to be read in a book" (247). "The purpose of criticism by genres," writes Frye, "is not so much to classify as to clarify . . . traditions and affinities, thereby bringing out a large number of literary relationships that would not be noticed as long as there were no context established for them" (247-48).

Frye's approach accepts the ideal of markers even though he has reservations about their use in practice. But he desists, in the *Anatomy,* from attributing the weakness of markers to different historical situations. The attempt to "recuperate" Frye's approach by historicizing it was undertaken by Fredric Jameson. He set out to convert aspects of Frye's approach to a Marxist theory of genres which coordinates "immanent formal analysis of the individual text with the twin diachronic perspective of the history of forms and the evolution of social life" (105). Jameson sees genre as a literary institution, as a social contract between a writer and a particular public "whose function is to specify the proper use of a particular cultural artifact" (106). Like Frye, he argues that genres exist in performance situations, but he notes that genres do undergo changes: "as texts free themselves more and more from an immediate performance situation, it becomes ever more difficult to enforce a given generic rule on their readers" (106). The generic contract can indeed be broken: "The generic contract and institution itself . . . , along with so many other institutions and traditional practices, falls casualty to the gradual penetration of a market system and a money economy. . . . The older generic categories do not, for all that, die out, but persist in the half-life of the subliterary genres of mass culture, transformed into the drugstore and airport paperback lines of gothics, mysteries, romances, bestsellers, and popular biographies, where they await the resurrection of their immemorial, archetypal resonance at the hands of a Frye or a Bloch" (107).

The contract theory of genre avoids the concept of specific markers; it rests on an agreement between a writer and a particular public that specifies the proper use of a cultural artifact. But is there only one public that specifies "proper" use? And how can such a contract negotiate for the present, let alone for the future? Each new text that critics join to the genre results in interrelations with other genres. How does a contract come to be established and how is it abrogated? How many contracts exist for the same text at any given time? Jameson claims that each genre is "immanently and intrinsically an ideology in its own right," but insofar as a genre retains past elements in a text, and insofar as different texts become members of a genre, how is this ideology determined?

Jameson's contract theory of genre presupposes a devolution of genres that follow the economic pattern, "the gradual penetration of a market system and a money economy." But the homology between genre and Marxist economic history disregards the contrasting aims of contemporary readers, as witness the diverse views about genre. Moreover, the reconceptualization of one genre often coincides with the initiation or restancing of others because of the process of interrelation. Thus a genre like tragedy continues despite the fact that it is reconceptualized by "domestic" tragedy; it is not abandoned despite serious changes in the economy. It seems a logical misstep to compare a kind of writing with an economic system rather than with the writings about an economic system. When such writings intersect with those of different genres they do not trivialize or dispose of such genres; they establish combinations that can make their contributions subservient rather than dominant in the genres that include them. As for genres possessing immanent ideologies, it would appear that such an assumption disregards the differences among the members of a genre. This is not to deny that texts—as generic members—can be interpreted as possessing ideologies, but rather that these cannot be deduced from generalizations about the genre.

For example, the characters, narrative, language—indeed all aesthetic strategies of *Lord Jim*—form, for Jameson, one specific instance of the symbolic act of the end of capitalist expansion. In the history of forms, *Lord Jim* "may be described as a structural breakdown of the older realisms, from which emerges not modernism alone, but rather two literary and cultural structures, dialectically interrelated and necessarily presupposing each other for any adequate analysis: these now find themselves positioned in the distinct and generally incompatible spaces of the institutions of high literature and what the Frankfurt School conveniently termed the 'culture industry,' that is, the apparatuses for the production of 'popular' or mass culture" (207). Jameson argues that *Lord Jim* represents in its structure the breakdown of the novel as a genre in terms of what he calls "older realisms." From this breakdown emerge two literary or cultural structures that are interrelated—"necessarily presupposing each other for any adequate analysis"—institutions of high literature and the apparatuses for the production of "popular" or mass culture. Since my concern is with genre theory and how a member of the genre "novel"—*Lord Jim*, for example—alters the genre while remaining a member of the class, the question arises, How are we to understand the persistence of a classification without charting the processes of classification change? It is, after all, through interrelation and competition with other genres, alterations or omissions of generic traits, and so forth that a modernist text begins to replace an "older realism."

My argument about text classes or genres can be summarized as follows: Classifications are empirical, not logical. They are historical assumptions constructed by authors, audiences, and critics in order to serve communicative and aesthetic purposes. Such groupings are always in terms of distinctions and interrelations, and they form a system or community of genres. The purposes they serve are social and aesthetic. Groupings arise at particular historical moments, and as they include more and more members, they are subject to repeated redefinitions or abandonment.

Genres are open systems: they are groupings of texts by critics to fulfill certain ends. And each genre is related to and defined by others to which it is related. Such relations change based on internal contraction, expansion, interweaving. Members of a genre need not have a single trait in common, since to do so would presuppose that the trait has the same function for each of the member texts. Rather the members of a generic classification have multiple relational possibilities with each other, relationships that are discovered only in the process of adding members to a class. Thus the claim that genre study should be abandoned because members of a genre do not share a single trait or traits can be seen not as undermining genre but as offering an argument for its study. Aimed as an attack against an essentialist theory, this claim fails to address those theories that begin by denying essential generic traits altogether.

III

Finally there is the attack on genre as an interpretative guide. The attack rests on two premises: that of genre and that of the text. With regard to genre, the argument is that a class generalization cannot help to interpret a specific member of the class; with regard to text, the argument is that a specific text is indeterminate: thus no determinate statements are useful in its interpretation. Genre defenders have at least two important answers: genres provide expectations for interpretations, and, a variant of this, genres provide conventions for interpretation. Elizabeth Bruss, for example, writes: "The genre does not tell us the style or construction of a text as much as how we should expect to 'take' that style or mode of construction—what force it should have for us. And this force is derived from the kind of action that text is taken to be."[8] A knowledge of genre, says another critic, provides "invaluable clues about how to interpret" a poem,[9] and the strongest argument for generic expectations is made by Hans Robert Jauss. In his essay on theory of genres and medieval vernacular literature, he writes: "The new text evokes for the reader (listener) the horizon of expectations and 'rules of the game' familiar to him from earlier texts, which as such can then be varied, extended, corrected, but also transformed, crossed out, or simply reproduced. Variation, extension, and correction determine the latitude of a generic structure; a break with the convention on the one hand and mere reproduction on the other determines its boundaries."[10] Jauss offers as an explanation of genre the view that "the relationship between the individual text and the series of texts formative of a genre presents itself as a process of the continual founding and altering of horizons" (88). Jauss deals with the individual text as well as with a group of texts; yet it is difficult to see how a single text can fuse its horizons with a body of texts each of which has its own individual fusions.

The assumption of generic expectations makes or implies the claim that generalizations about a class can help interpret any particular instance of that class. What kind of expectations does *Oedipus Rex* or *Hamlet* or the genre tragedy offer us in understanding *Death of a Salesman* that we couldn't achieve without them? Such a conclusion does Jauss an injustice, since the aim of his genre theory is to trace the succession of responses to a text and to explain its relation to society, author, and reader. He thus pursues history, in Jameson's terms, as a history of forms and as a history to be compared with histories of other genres and disciplines. Jauss seems minimally interested in how a text as a member of a genre is constituted. But such a procedure is necessary for an interpretative theory.

Jauss realizes that readers extend beyond the original responders to a text, and it is to the continuity or succession of responders that he turns in order to explain the responses a text elicits. One might, therefore, point out that whereas Frye directs his generic inquiry toward traditions and affinities that a writer has, Jauss directs his to the historical responses of readers who are governed by "rules of the game." But both, it should be noticed, are concerned with the changing responses toward a text and with textual affinities.

"Rules of the game" are but another name for "conventions," and some genre theorists argue for the interpretative importance of genre conventions. Here is Gary Morson: "Texts are . . . classified according to what I shall call their 'semiotic nature,' which is to say, the conventions acknowledged to be appropriate for interpreting them. . . . Readers can and do disagree about conventions for interpreting a work; when they do, I shall say they disagree about its genre. Strictly speaking, therefore, I shall not be stating that given works belong to certain genres. I shall, rather, describe the hermeneutic consequences entailed by classifying a work as one of a particular semiotic type."[11]

This genre theory substitutes "reading conventions" for "genre," thus avoiding the problem of generic consistency or constituents by placing them upon "conventions." The notion of convention as a basis for interpreting works within a class refers to "conventions acknowledged to be appropriate for interpreting them." But conventions of interpretation are themselves writings (or genre members) that control readings, and thus they are subject to the same kind of changes that genres undergo. For example, conventions about treating a work as literature are not conventions applicable to one genre but to all genres included under the genre "literature." Moreover, the notion of "convention" is clearly not shared by informed readers of the same time, since interpretative disagreements do indeed arise. My point is not that interpretative conventions do not exist, but that they exist within literary criticism and literary theory and that the attempt to define such conventions merely leads—as the examples of Wolfgang Iser, Stanley Fish, and Jacques Derrida illustrate—to different views of reading conventions. If reading conventions fall within the genres of criticism and theory, are we not involved in a circular argument? Genres are identified by reading conventions. But reading conventions are themselves parts of genres or genres. Thus reading conventions are themselves involved in the problem of generic specification.

The difficulty with this semiotic approach to interpretation is that the critics assume "interpretation" exists nongenerically. If they considered interpretation as text- and genre-bound, as I have suggested, they would be dealing with the changes in and transformation of texts. They would thus be led to reconsider the function of textual constituents and to analyze "conventions" in the same manner that they analyze other generic texts.

Consider Eric Havelock's discussion of the interpenetration of oral procedures in written tragedy. Discussing orality as a genre that includes many oral genres, he illustrates that a number of the practices characteristic of oral genres enter into Attic tragedy, and the example he chooses for illustration is *Oedipus Rex:* "The *Oedipus* therefore is, under one aspect, a personally produced product embodying a degree of personal creativity. Nevertheless its composition, like that of all Greek drama, involves a partnership between the oral and the written, the acoustic and the visual, a dichotomy which can also be rendered in terms of tradition versus design, generic versus specific, communal versus personal. It is a combination which lies at the heart of all high classic Greek 'literature' from Homer to Euripides."[12]

The point to be made here is that an individual instance of a genre—*Oedipus Rex*—can reveal its individuality not only by comparison with other tragedies within the genre and within the oeuvre of Sophocles, but also by comparison with older oral genres. The conceptual change brought about by literacy permits us to identify a historical process of change. This process includes the absorption of elements from nontragic forms to tragedy, and, in particular, to Sophoclean tragedy. If, in other words, we wish to study literature as an interrelated system of texts and society, generic distinctions offer us a procedure to accomplish this.

Havelock outlines the interpenetration of one type of orality in the plays of Sophocles. I quote: "The riddling of the *Oedipus,* then, while giving to this particular play a peculiar degree of dramatic tension, can be seen as a revival of a traditional device, mnemonic in character and having its roots in the habits of primary orality" (190). Here a constituent of oral performance enters into a later form, and so we come to understand how a text is multitemporal. *Oedipus Rex* has sedimented in it elements from older genres or elements from earlier examples of the same genre. In this respect generic composition expresses diverse communal (or ideological) values.

Some defenders of genre theory find no inconsistency between the claim that texts are indeterminate and their own assumption that a text can have diverse interpretations. The expectations of readers change and the conventions of readings change and both these hypotheses are advanced by genre critics. I have indicated that these hypotheses can be made more adequate, but I do not find that they have been discredited. Critics who assume that every text is self-contradictory still have to grant that types of contradiction exist and that such types, including their own writings, presuppose generic groupings. The view of genre that I have been advocating has considerable potential for interpretation and literary history, and I shall indicate some of this in my final section.

IV

It is unfortunate that one of the difficulties with genre is that we have the same term to describe a genre like novel or a particular novel like *Finnegans Wake*. One designation for a whole and for parts of the whole creates the impression of an organic linkage. But knowledge of the relation between the genre "novel" and members such as Austen's *Emma* and Faulkner's *The Sound and the Fury* is useful for literary study only if we can explain how they are continuous, how discontinuous. What inquiries can a genre study undertake to explain changes in individual texts or genres and literary and historical reasons for them? One is to examine the different genres an author undertakes; Joyce, for example, writes short stories, poems, a play, novels, letters. What is involved in these generic variations? Another is to relate generic changes to changes in the writing of history, granting that there are special and general histories, Marxist and other approaches to history. Another is to analyze the reasons for generic omissions or neglect of genres that can be but are not written, as the neglect of the sonnet after Milton until the end of the eighteenth century. Another is to analyze generic transformations, as, for example, the "ballad" and the "lyric" are joined by Wordsworth to form "lyrical ballads." Still another generic inquiry is to examine a single narrative as it undergoes generic variations, becoming, in turn, a ballad, a prose fiction, a tragedy, a memoir, as well as a member of other genres. This is the inquiry I shall offer in order to consider the potentialities of generic criticism. My assumption is that an author in making a generic choice involves himself in an ideological choice, and that the critic in reconsidering the generic choices he attributes to a text involves himself in certain ideological, social, and literary commitments.

There is an early seventeenth-century ballad (ca. 1600-1624) called—in short—"The Excellent Ballad of George Barnwel." Like most ballads, it was sung in the streets, and the sheets on which it was printed—broadsides—

usually wound up on the bottom of baking dishes or in the fireplace. The ballad is a confession addressed to the youths of London, and it serves as a moral warning at the same time that it notes the erotic pleasures of immorality. Its subject matter undergoes numerous generic transformations, indicating the persistent audience appeal of sexual seduction, criminal licentiousness, and parricide while paradoxically invoking the need for morality. The action of the ballad is as follows:

1. George Barnwel, a youth apprenticed to a merchant, is accosted by a woman.
2. She is an experienced harlot and seduces him.
3. As a result of his infatuation and incapacity to resist sexual pleasures, she persuades him to embezzle his master's money. He does so and flees to her when his exposure is imminent.
4. She instigates him to murder and rob his rich uncle, and he does so.
5. When the money is spent, she betrays him to the authorities.
6. He escapes and betrays her to the authorities in turn and she is hanged.
7. He flees to Poland and is hanged for an unrelated murder.

This ballad was republished several times during the seventeenth century and at the end of the century there appeared a prose fiction chapbook based on the poem to which was appended a version of the ballad. The poetic song with its first-person narrative was converted into a third-person prose narrative. The prose version has a different generic history from the ballad. It is modeled upon criminal biographies with quotations from Proverbs, a life history in outline, with episodes from fabliaux. Why should a popular form be rewritten in another popular form? (1) The rewriting is addressed to a more literate audience than the original, since it goes into detail about the effects of the reading of classical romances; (2) it seeks to mitigate the criminality of Barnwel by making him an innocent who can't distinguish between an angel and a whore; (3) it makes the narrative more erotic while becoming more didactically religious; and (4) it is an attack upon the dangers of reading pagan texts. The change of form nevertheless continues a narrative that is recognizably that of the original ballad. What we have, therefore, is a generic change that expands upon the narrative of the ballad, but selects certain features—like the character of the harlot—to concentrate upon. There is an antifeminism that surfaces in the prose version, and a structure that resembles other criminal biographies.

In 1731 the ballad was rewritten as a tragedy, called *The London Merchant*.

Here we have an elevation of a low genre into a high one: a tragedy about common people addressed to common people, altering the genre of tragedy that characteristically was about kings and aristocrats and dealt with affairs of state. The subject matter and characters altered the constituents of the tragedy. In his introduction, the author, George Lillo, argued for the need to extend the characters and subject matter of tragedy to include common people and the events in which they were involved. What this implied was a conceptual change in tragedy. The genre was now a model for what critics called "domestic" tragedy. The question for the genre critic is why and how such a subgenre is initiated. The most obvious explanation is ideological: the plot of a known popular form becomes the subject of a traditionally elite one. The intermingling of the two suggests an elevation of the merchant's role that is one of the tragedy's themes. It also indicates a reshifting of the hierarchy of generic kinds. It will not do to talk here about a reader's contract or reading conventions, since key sections of the "contract" are abrogated and conventions disregarded. This classification shift of ballad from subliterature to high literature involves generic procedures of transformation and incorporation too complicated to discuss here. But I can point out that the claim for the elevation of the ballad was made by Joseph Addison in a new genre, the periodical essay, a "newspaper" genre; it justified, by analogy, the periodical essay itself as a literary form. Moreover, ballad elevation was made analogous to the class elevation of the merchant. Generic consciousness is not, in the early eighteenth century, separated from social consciousness. It does not matter that critics parodied Addison's interest in ballads; what does matter is that his argument for genre elevation offered a procedure for treating class elevation. In this respect, generic considerations do indeed suggest that they can shape how critics look at social life rather than merely reflect it.

Some of the problems that such a genre theory invites include the interrelation of forms; for example, in the ballad opera individual ballads become interrelated with music, dialogue, spectacle, and comedy. Then again, there is the phenomenon in which a single sonnet is joined to others to form a sequence. Or a single prose narrative or short story joined to form a series of stories.

In Bishop Percy's *Reliques of Ancient English Poetry* (1765), which became the central transmission agency by which the ballad genre entered English literature, there was published a version of the Barnwel ballad. Percy rationalized ballads as literature by claiming they were individual compositions; he consciously sought to identify them with a national tradition and he sought to illustrate them as "literature" by including in his collection a number of esteemed contemporary poems. But an important aspect of this effort at gaining establishment acceptance of the popular genre was his editing of them. He imposed on Barnwel the standards of decorum and correctness practiced by established eighteenth-century poets, standards that he found consistent with the needs of his audience. He deliberately revised the ballad of George Barnwel, therefore, to meet their assumed social and literary criteria.

What conclusions can one draw about history and genre from this limited example? Most obviously, genres have popular and polite functions and statuses. Generic transformation can be a social act. Generic transformation reveals the social changes in audiences and the interpenetration of popular and polite literature. Within a common audience different genres complement or contrast with one another. Some processes of generic alteration — for example, of the single text leading to a collective text (sonnet to sonnet sequences) — tend to repeat themselves regardless of cultural change. The success of one genre — for example, *The London Merchant* — can lead to ideological changes in an earlier genre — the ballad — now prepared for an audience familiar with the tragedy. Generic differentiation serves different ends, but each new rewriting of the ballad involves a selection from the original narrative. The ballad dealt with the mercenary, the economic behavior of the prostitute, but the tragedy dealt with the noble behavior of the merchant who had no role in the poem. The elements selected thus provide a clue to the social and cultural implications of genre. The process of sedimentation involves, in the different genres, elements from other genres that preceded them. Some of the ballad repetitions interpenetrate the prose fiction, and others are explored in greater detail. Since genres are understood in terms of their interrelation, they can be seen as renewing a distance which earlier genres sought to erase, to renew a justification for separating once again popular and polite literature, once ballads are established as polite literature. Narrative can function to establish an element of continuity among different genres and thus provide a guide for historical continuity while making possible the recognition of historical changes in attitude — to merchant, merchant's apprentice, and harlot.

In this paper I have sought to answer three types of discreditation of genre theory and to offer an alternative theory. The claim that generic classes are indecipherable or indeterminate I have answered by showing how to decipher them and how a process theory can explain their transformability. The claim that members of a genre share a common element or elements in consequence of which genre is an essentialist study, I have answered by showing the historical naïveté of this argument and by illustrating that genre theory is not dependent on such essentialist assumptions. The claim that genre cannot be a guide to interpretation I have answered by showing how a process theory of genre explains the constituents of texts that it seeks historically to explain. The whole direction of my paper may thus be seen as a contribution to the regeneration of genre theory.

REPLY TO DOMINICK LACAPRA AND RICHARD HARVEY BROWN

I appreciate the comments of Dominick LaCapra and I welcome his invitation to expand upon some of the statements made in "History and Genre." Mr. LaCapra is quite right in noting that I conceive of genre as a classification system and as a discursive institution. I would add, however, that I conceive of both as expressed in writing. Writing about genre—about classification systems, about institutions and transformations—presupposes writing in a genre or genres. Genre discussions such as mine and his fall within the genres of literary theory, of criticism, of dialogues. Such genres undergo changes no less than epic, tragedy, or the ode.

Genre writing—of whatever kind—is historical in the sense that at a particular time certain works are identified as belonging together by an author or critic. And this grouping is made in order to relate such writing to literary, social, and other ends. When such ends become unimportant, the writing of a particular genre diminishes or is discontinued while other genres assume importance. Thus in the Renaissance serious objections arise to including *De rerum natura* in the genre "poetry," but during the Restoration and eighteenth century Lucretius's georgic poem becomes once again an important literary genre, and thus is included in the comprehensive genre "poetry."

Mr. LaCapra recognizes that my use of genre stresses "the interchange between past and present as well as the interaction between recurrence and change." In this respect, my own essay is directed at certain shortcomings of critical writings on genre. I take as my example Jacques Derrida's questioning of the usefulness of naming and interrelating kinds of writing in "The Law of Genre." It is a questioning that seems not to realize that an individual text such as Derrida's own "The Law of Genre" is generically related to literary theory, literary criticism, and fictive narrative. A study of genre need not disregard analyses of individual texts; on the contrary, my view of genre makes the interpretation of texts more precise and their historical interrelations more apparent. The mixture of genres, the incorporation, merging, and transformation of genres, may appear a monstrosity to some critics and theorists and an impasse to others, but only because they misconceive the actualities of genre. The mixed character of genres provides a basis for establishing identifiable chronological or "period" norms. The historical dimension of the theory leads the critic to offer reasons for positing such norms and for the alterations, conflicts, and replacement of norms.

The questions that Mr. LaCapra raises about stereotypical texts in a genre and about texts that challenge their own genres are pertinent and important. He notes the paradox "that texts hailed as perfections of a genre also appear to test and contest generic limits." The notion of "perfection" of a genre is implicitly (and sometimes explicitly) evolutionary; one such view, for example, was developed by Aristotle in terms of increasing comprehensiveness and maturity. But an evolutionary theory is not for us a satisfactory historical hypothesis for genre; thus a historical, interactive, processural theory which makes room for discontinuities as well as continuities seems an appropriate replacement.

I agree that texts identified as "classics" come in time to repress or downplay those processes or constituents in them that would resist the canonical interpretations. But critics can also use "classics" to support noncanonical views, as witness Addison's reference to Virgil's *Aeneid* in order to raise a noncanonical ballad, "Chevy Chase," to epic or canonical status. How and why this occurs is a discussion for a different occasion.

This leads to the question of ideology and genre because if the same text can be used antithetically, the attribution to it of a single ideology is untenable. Indeed, since the same text endures through time, it seems inevitable that readers will attribute to it different ideological assumptions or give different values to the same assumptions. I have suggested that there are social and political as well as literary and personal reasons for choosing to write or not to write in a particular genre, for initiating new species of writings called "novels" or "tragedies of private lives." Mr. LaCapra rightly notes that such choices and the relation of genres to each other involve distinctions within a level of culture as well as between levels. Within the same level, a genre can undergo slight variations as well as conceptual changes (tragedy is a typical example here). Between cultural levels, genres move from addressing one audience to another that is higher or lower (an example is Swift's *Gulliver's Travels,* which begins by addressing an adult audience and is abridged to address children). A shift in cultural levels takes place when the Bible moves from a sacred text to a literary one. The theory I propose has as one of its aims an explanation of just such historical and critical interchanges. I thank Mr. LaCapra for his valuable and challenging comments, and for encouraging me to expand upon some of the remarks in my paper.

Richard Brown is a sociologist interested in having his discipline undertake extensive cultural analysis; his book *A Poetic for Sociology* (1977) sought to break down the division between a positivist and a romantic sociology. This strategy involved urging the exploration of continuities between discourses in science and those in literature and the arts, and his commentary exemplifies this procedure. It is a strategy I support. Mr. Brown recognizes that my theory of genre applies to writings of all kinds, but he obviously feels more at ease with a historian of science than a historian of literature. Thus his remarks provide a sociological application to literature of Thomas Kuhn's ideas in *The Structure of Scientific Revolutions* rather than an analysis of "History and Genre."

A Kuhnian aesthetic is an interesting possibility, though it must be pointed out that Kuhn eschews it and that Kuhn's theory has met with considerable opposition from philosophers and historians of science because of his ambiguous use of "paradigm." The paradigm theory has been applied by some literary historians to literature, but the results have not been particularly illuminating. For an essay dealing with a few such applications, I can recommend Joseph F. Musser's "The Perils of Relying on Thomas Kuhn."[13]

Mr. Brown presents only a sketch of a Kuhnian aesthetic, and one must await a fuller picture before discussing it in detail. But I find the sketch in its historical explanations insufficiently rigorous, especially in addressing the continuing conflicts between holders of generic theories. My essay is devoted to a view of historical contestation within and among genres that, at the very least, seriously questions the use of metaphors like "victory" of new and "survival" of old paradigms, metaphors that do not take adequate account of the complex generic interactions. Moreover, Mr. Brown's hypothesis that "'genres,' 'families of positions,' and 'paradigms' can be understood as expressions of political economic organization" may be defensible in some historical instances, but it overlooks the conflicting ideological premises that texts reveal. And it does seem that the hypothesis oversimplifies the relation between genre and "political economic organization."

I can certainly understand Mr. Brown's desire to have a sociology of art and literature in which the "proper unit for analysis" is "not so much specific works as it is genres, schools, 'art worlds,' or paradigms." But I am puzzled by the claim that genres are "reflected by but not contained within, any work itself." Can genres be originated by having texts reflect them? Particular works interact with and thus lead to revisions of generic generalizations. Since genres are generalizations about groups of texts that critics and theorists posit for particular purposes, these groups and purposes change in consequence of works that come to be included in a genre.

I agree that rhetoric is a proper method for analyzing texts, whether these texts deal with discourse theories or with poems. But here, again, the statements any rhetorical analysis makes are made in a generic text; and we must not forget that different genres invoke different rhetorical conventions and limits.

I support Mr. Brown in his aim to develop a sociological discourse that applies to cultural inquiry. I appreciate his initiative in offering a sketch of what such an inquiry might be, and I hope that my remarks indicate the importance of the task he has undertaken.

NOTES

1. Fredric Jameson, *The Political Unconscious: Narrative as a Socially Symbolic Act* (Ithaca, NY: Cornell Univ. Press, 1981), 105; hereafter cited in text.

2. John Reichert, "More than Kin and Less than Kind: The Limits of Genre Theory," in *Theories of Literary Genre,* ed. Joseph P. Strelka (University Park: Pennsylvania State Univ. Press, 1978), 57.

3. Michel Foucault, *The Archaeology of Knowledge,* trans. A. M. Sheridan Smith (1969; New York: Pantheon, 1972), 22.

4. Jacques Derrida, "The Law of Genre," *Critical Inquiry* 7, no. 1 (1980): 64; hereafter cited in text. A translation of this essay by Avital Ronell also appeared in *Glyph* 7 (Baltimore: Johns Hopkins Univ. Press, 1980), 176-232.

5. Francis Cairns, *Generic Composition in Greek and Roman Poetry* (Edinburgh: Edinburgh Univ. Press, 1972), 6-7, 34.

6. Aristotle *Poetics* 26.1462a-b.

7. Northrop Frye, *Anatomy of Criticism* (Princeton, NJ: Princeton Univ. Press, 1957), 247; hereafter cited in text.

8. Elizabeth Bruss, *Autobiographical Acts* (Baltimore: Johns Hopkins Univ. Press, 1976), 4.

9. Heather Dubrow, *Genre* (London: Methuen, 1982), 135.

10. Hans Robert Jauss, *Toward an Aesthetics of Reception,* trans. Timothy Bahti (Minneapolis: Univ. of Minnesota Press, 1982), 88; hereafter cited in text.

11. Gary Saul Morson, *The Boundaries of Genre: Dostoevsky's "Diary of a Writer" and the Traditions of Literary Utopia* (Austin: Univ. of Texas Press, 1981), viii-ix.

12. Eric Havelock, "Oral Composition in the *Oedipus Tyrannus* of Sophocles," *New Literary History* 16, no. 1 (1984): 186; hereafter cited in text.

13. *Eighteenth-Century Studies* 18, no. 2 [1985]: 215-26.

Do Postmodern Genres Exist?

Critics and theorists who write about postmodern texts often refer to "genres" as a term inappropriate for characterizing postmodernist writing. The process of suppression results from the claim that postmodern writing blurs genres, transgresses them, or unfixes boundaries that conceal domination or authority, and that "genre" is an anachronistic term and concept. When critics offer examples of postmodern novels, for example, they cite omniscient authors who are parodied or undermined. They point to self-conscious addresses to the reader in *If on a Winter's Night* and note the self-conscious foregrounding of literary artifice that undermines the generic assumption that a novel is referential or that it is a construction that bears a real relation to society.

These critics assume that a genre theory of the novel is committed to backgrounding literary artifice, to demanding coherence, unity, and linear continuity. But though such an assumption may apply to some generic theories, there are others that are perfectly compatible with multiple discourses, with narratives of discontinuity, with transgressed boundaries. To mention the multiple discourses that Bakhtin defines as characteristic of the novel is to note only one of the modernist theorists who accept multiple discourses and discontinuous structures. Not only are there genre theories based on these premises but there are texts like *Tristram Shandy* and *Joseph Andrews* that exhibit what are now referred to as postmodern features. Ihab Hassan, one of the leaders of postmodernist theorizing, remarks that we now perceive "postmodern features in *Tristram Shandy* precisely because our eyes have learned to recognize postmodern features."[1]

Ihab Hassan is correct in noting that what we call "postmodern" writing

---

This essay was originally published in "Postmodern Genres," ed. Marjorie Perloff, special issue, *Genre* 12, nos. 3-4 (1987): 241-57, subsequently published as *Postmodern Genres*, ed. Marjorie Perloff, Oklahoma Project for Discourse and Theory, vol. 5 (Norman: Univ. of Oklahoma Press, 1989), and is reprinted with permission of the publisher.

is espied in an earlier time, but eighteenth-century genres exhibited some of the same features. We rename these features in terms of our critical language, but *Tristram Shandy*'s marbled pages were transgressions then as now, as were the foregrounding of literary artifice, the nonlinear narration, the insertion into the narrative of sermons, letters, and stories. The basis for a genre theory of mixed forms or shared generic features is as old as Aristotle's comparison of tragedy and epic. Rosalie Colie has pointed out that numerous Renaissance writers self-consciously worked with mixtures of generic features, "self-conscious, carefully worked mixtures, which counterpoint against one another the separate genres Petrarca was trying to reestablish."[2] And such mixtures were not isolated cases but rather a way of thinking, of assuming that genres, mixed or unmixed, were the appropriate carriers of ancient knowledge. In fact the mixtures found in Homer's works were considered by some critics as the source of all poetic kinds. Colie points out that "there were many more kinds [genres] than were recognized in official literary philosophy; and it is by these competing notions of kind that the richness and variety of Renaissance letters were assured."[3]

Postmodern critics and theorists are often unaware of the various generic theories that have been created, and when they attack genre assumptions, they select these most often from modernist critics. Jonathan Culler, for example, in his 1975 essay, "Towards a Theory of Non-Genre Literature," took as his modernist model the assumption that genre was a set of expectations between reader and text. This was a modernist assumption that could have been derived from Northrop Frye's *Anatomy of Criticism* (1957). By the mid-1970s there were several modernist formulations of a "set of expectations." But this phrase is always part of a comprehensive statement or theory. For example, for Hans Robert Jauss the "set of expectations" forms one part of his system of the aesthetics of reception and influence: "The analysis of the literary experience of the reader avoids the threatening pitfalls of psychology if it describes the reception and the influence of a work within the objectifiable *system of expectations* that arises for each work in the historical moment of its appearance, from a pre-understanding of the genre, from the form and themes of already familiar works, and from the opposition between poetic and practical language."[4] And the relation of expectations to a particular public as addressee was formulated by Maria Corti: "every genre seems to be directed toward a certain type of public, sometimes even to a specific class, *whose expectations* are directed toward that genre as long as social conditions warrant."[5]

Culler formulates the concept of expectations as follows: "genre, one might say, is a set of expectations, a set of instructions about the type of coherence one is to look for and the ways in which sequences are to be read."[6] This is a reader-based definition, one that can accommodate to many variations within a genre. But it does not take account of how this generic claim actually fits into a genre theory. These theories attend to the historical moment of a work's appearance or to the social conditions that provide a warrant to a particular public for a specific genre.

When a theory of expectations is divorced from its theoretical frame it can be treated as an unstated "contractual" relation of author to reader, although the formulation of such a contract is a legal image, not an actual situation. Culler argues that postmodern novels void the contract because they alter conventions and become "unreadable." But this argument presupposes some hypothesis about how conventions begin, how they become commonplace, and how they are altered or abandoned. Postmodern genres, as many critics point out, have features that are inherited from modernist genres. Since genres are interrelated, there seems always a basis for some readability. And at the end of the essay Culler seems to concede that even abstruse postmodern novels come to be read because of a basic human capacity for ordering disorder. There is, he writes, an "astonishing human capacity to recuperate the deviant, to invest new conventions and functions so as to overcome that which resists our efforts."[7] In fact Joyce's *Finnegans Wake,* a text often used as an example of postmodern writing, is treated by Frye as an encyclopedic form and ironic epic. The text requires no abandonment of a genre system: on the contrary, it can fit quite readily within it.

Postmodern critics have sought to do without a genre theory. Terms like "text" and "écriture" deliberately avoid generic classifications. And the reasons for this are efforts to abolish the hierarchies that genres introduce, to avoid the assumed fixity of genres and the social as well as literary authority such limits exert, to reject the social and subjective elements in classification. But these reasons apply to a genre theory that Austin Warren calls "classical" and that argues for the "purity" of genres. As he points out, modern genre theory is descriptive: "It doesn't limit the number of possible kinds and doesn't prescribe rules to authors. It supposes that traditional kinds may be 'mixed' and produce a new kind (like tragi-comedy)."[8] Modernist genre theories minimize classification and maximize clarification and interpretation. Such genre theories are part of semiotic theories of communication that relate genres to culture. Indeed, modernist critics who resort to genre theory—Todorov,

Jameson, Fowler, Bakhtin, Gilbert and Gubar—undertake to explain and analyze the relation between trivial or ignored genres and canonized genres.[9] And this is a procedure that seems most applicable to a postmodern inquiry.

The initiation or use of one genre is determined by its relation to others. If writing were always identical, there would be no kinds and no need for generic distinctions about whole works. And if each piece of writing were different from all others there would be no basis for theorizing or even for communication. But since one piece of writing tends to be based on other pieces—some theorists refer to genres as families of texts with close or distant relatives—a genre theory offers the most extensive procedure for dealing with this phenomenon. It not only inquires into the reasons for intertextuality; it inquires into the significance of the combinatory procedures that result from it. The generic concept of combinatory writing makes possible the study of continuities and changes within a genre as well as the recurrence of generic features and their historical implications. But this particular genre theory is one among many. Theorists who propose genre theories no less than those who oppose them need, therefore, to explore the aims that govern any genre theory. Whether the purpose of a genre system (however constructed) be evaluative, as it was for Aristotle or Dryden or Irving Babbitt, or educative as it was for Renaissance theorists, or evolutionary as it was for Brunetière, or a system of communication as it is for Maria Corti, or an ideological structure as it is for Fredric Jameson, or a basis for understanding literary transitions and history as it was for the Russian formalists, genre theorizing is itself a genre. It can be an essay, literary criticism, literary theory, literary history, etc. And writing in genres is demonstrated by a text itself.

When Derrida asks of what genre is genre, he draws attention to the fact that his own essay belongs with essayistic genres like literary theory or philosophical discourse. This is not the place to discuss the issues involved in the naming of genres, but to point out that every text is a member of one or more genres. What needs to be studied are the constituents of a text and what kinds of effects these have or can have upon readers. It is these constituents in a mixed or combinatory form that make some theorists refer to genres as "blurred." In this respect, many critics who find postmodern writing nongeneric because it is combinatory or reader oriented or discontinuous seem to be unfamiliar with the available generic theories upon which they can draw.

Clifford Geertz's essay "Blurred Genres" is a noteworthy example of assuming that the blurring or mixing of genres is indicative of a new way of thinking. Although his essay is directed at studies of social thought, it also refers to literary examples. He describes the phenomenon of blurring as follows:

> ... scientific discussions looking like belles lettres *morceaux* (Lewis Thomas, Loren Eiseley), baroque fantasies presented as deadpan empirical observations (Borges, Barthelme), histories that consist of equations and tables or law court testimony (Fogel and Engerman, Le Roi Ladurie), documentaries that read like true confessions (Mailer), parables posing as ethnographies (Castaneda), theoretical treatises set out as travelogues (Levi-Strauss), ... Nabokov's *Pale Fire,* that impossible object made of poetry and fiction, footnotes and images from the clinic, seems very much of the time; one waits only for quantum theory in verse or biography in algebra.[10]

Geertz finds interactions and intertextuality in and out of "literary" texts. I add to his examples by noting that genres such as ballads, lyrics, proverbs, short stories, etc., become part of other texts—of novels, of tragedies, of comedies. He notes that parts of a genre, such as autobiography, can be mixed with a scientific disquisition (James Watson's *The Double Helix*). One can add that a theoretical essay (Annette Kolodny's "Dancing through the Minefield: Some Observations on the Theory, Practice, and Politics of a Feminist Literary Criticism") can also contain autobiographical discourses. For Geertz, this procedure represents a refiguration of social theory; he sees it as indicative of a change in social inquiry from one concerned with *what knowledge is* to "what it is we want to know."[11] He assumes that "modernist" inquiry studied the dynamics of collective life in order to alter it "in desired directions." Postmodern inquiry studies the anatomization of thought, not the manipulation of behavior. In *The Double Helix,* however, the purpose of mixing laboratory politics with scientific inquiry serves to undermine the "objectivity" of scientific procedures and the assumption of a unified scientific community. And Kolodny's essay, in its combinatory procedures, describes her actual indoctrination by male critics in order to support her argument urging the need for an adequate feminist criticism. It is an attack on the "objectivity" of literary criticism, on the need for an overt acknowledgment of the authority implied in such criticism, on the need for recognition of gender as an overlooked or repressed aspect of academic instruction.

In these works, the combination of autobiography, laboratory or classroom practice, and politics is related to social and political attitudes. Combinations not only present the procedures of scientific or literary inquiry, but serve to illustrate the procedures by which they conceal antagonisms, prejudices, and disunity. This generic analysis redirects textual analyses: from studying behavior to studying the grounds of behavior; from the overt desire to manipulate behavior to studying the nature of this desire, the actual processes of manipulation.

The texts that I have been describing still fall within accustomed genres: the history of a scientific discovery or the theoretical essay about literary study. Nevertheless they do transgress the modernist generic bounds by introducing subjective elements and insisting on the ideological bases governing inquiries. Still, the very concept of transgression presupposes an acknowledgment of boundaries or limits. Such transgressions, as some theorists of postmodernism recognize, presuppose genres, presuppose that postmodern practices have not homogenized writing; rather they continue to introduce distinctions even though these differ from modernist practices. Certain models of modernist literature—Dos Passos's *U.S.A.*, Pound's *Cantos*, Faulkner's *Absalom, Absalom!*—are cited repeatedly as combinations of multiple discourses found in modernist genres. Thus the issue is not a matter of multiple subjects or discontinuous narration, but of the shift in the kinds of "transgressions" and in the implications of the revised combinations. And Bakhtin, Jameson, and other modernist genre theorists do provide insights into the social basis of generic structures.

What alternatives exist if one rejects the study of genres in analyzing postmodern texts? One can discuss themes, one can discuss periods, one can discuss rhetorical strategies. None of these, however, are incompatible with generic study. If we conceive of postmodernism as a style, it must be defined or described by being shown to be different from the modernist style. And yet any such change will inevitably call upon similarities or continuing features. If we conceive of postmodernism as a period, such description will have to include genres like tragedy or new mass culture genres like TV sitcoms and the detective or spy story and film. A period study will have to include genres like Shakespeare's plays and Milton's *Paradise Lost,* genres from earlier periods that are kept alive by the curricula of academic institutions and stage or TV productions. A period study, therefore, unless it degenerizes all previous texts within a given chronological segment, will inevitably have to retain the language of genres as a part of the period.

It is one of the ironies of postmodern criticism that critics who are rightly cognizant of the constraints imposed by boundaries, who seek to reveal what boundaries conceal about "the nexus between knowledge and power," often do so within boundaries they seem not to recognize. In the introduction to an anthology of theoretical essays entitled *Criticism without Boundaries*,[12] the editor sees boundaries in terms of disciplinary demarcations. But the anthology of essays is itself a genre, a genre that has been practiced by modernist no less than by postmodernist critics. The essays themselves are collected into a fictitious unity, and they are written, each of them, in the linear tradition of the modernist essay with intersections of sociological, educative, and Marxist discourses. What this generic combination implies, since the essays were given or intended as lectures, is the disregard of the difference between oral delivery and the written text in an anthology, between the relation of an audience to a speaker in contrast to a reader reading an essay. We have generic continuity of a modernist genre that aims, as Robert Stallman's anthology did, to undermine earlier critical positions. An awareness of this enterprise as generic would have introduced an aspect of cultural continuity requiring explanation. After all, this postmodern enterprise displays a readiness of critics to operate within the academy, using modernist generic conventions to undermine modernism and its values. This generic procedure operates within familiar categories and constituents including the insistence on the need to defamiliarize them and to politicize them.

One can point out that the journal and the anthology as genres present options of beginning with any selection, of providing multiple thematic approaches or variations of one approach. The texts within an anthology call attention to shared features of essays or poems or stories no less than to differences and they thus permit distinctions to be made regarding individual examples. But these combinatory texts, when they deny their generic identity, serve to repress the difference between what they say and what they are. What lurks in the denial of generic combinations while employing them is the fear that boundaries are conservative, that to admit that bounds or limits are inevitable is to submit to them. But as I have pointed out, there need be no such confinement. "Postmodernist" writing without boundaries is as much a fiction as postmodernist writing fixed by them.

The combinatory nature of genres moves in our time to mixtures of media and to mixtures resulting from the electronic world in which we live. Films,[13] TV genres, university educational programs, our very explanations of identity and discourses all indicate combinations of one kind or another. The precise nature of these combinations differ, but what genre critics and theorists can now study are the interactions within combinations and how these differ from earlier combinations, whether in epic, tragedy, novel, lyric, etc.

This generic procedure, this combinatory genre theory no less than that of the postmodern "novel" or surfiction, has significant antecedents in the writings of the early eighteenth century. Marjorie Perloff has suggested that this might be the case with postmodern poetics: "Postmodern poetics, it may yet turn out, has more in common with the performative, playful mode of eighteenth-century ironists than with Shelleyan apocalypse."[14] Here the recognition of the anthology as a genre reveals a substantial clue for grasping what might be called generic history, the discontinuous recurrence or the continuity of certain genres or features of genres.

To pursue one example of this that is pertinent to postmodern genres, I wish to consider some of the innovative genres that occur at the beginning of the eighteenth century. One of the characteristic features of that species of writing that came to be called the novel reveals a narrator who quite consciously addresses the reader and suggests how the text should be read. The obvious example, *Tristram Shandy*, resists narrative closure, linear narration, includes genres such as the sermon, letter, and story, produces interventions of musical and other nonverbal genres. Certainly with regard to the postmodern palimpsest assumption that each new text is written over an older one,[15] one need only consult a satire like Swift's *A Tale of a Tub*. And Henry Fielding's *Joseph Andrews* announces itself as "Written in Imitation of Cervantes, Author of Don Quixote." I am not suggesting that Fielding is Borges or that *Joseph Andrews* is equatable with "Pierre Menard, Author of the *Quixote*" or that "imitation" as used in the eighteenth century is anything but resisted and discarded by postmodern critics. What I am arguing is that Fielding's self-conscious addresses to the reader, that his use of inset stories and thus of multiple narrators who result in making the primary characters become secondary while some of the trivial characters become, for the inset story, the primary narrators, that these practices are analogous to some in postmodern genres. When the inset story of Leonard and Paul is interrupted and left uncompleted in *Joseph Andrews* we have a further instance of the discontinuity characteristic of postmodern writing. A generic history will not merely point to these recurrences, but suggest that these are tied to social and cultural no less than literary phenomena. Thus these procedures are not merely engaged in rejecting inherited hierarchical genres, but, by parodying them, they offer a consciousness of certain limited eighteenth-century alternatives.

Since I am proposing a historical linkage between eighteenth-century and postmodern genres, I wish to relate the innovative periodical essay to the postmodern presence of the critical and theoretical essay. My purpose in drawing attention to the prevalence of innovative early eighteenth-century genres and those in our time is to indicate shared features. These reveal relations between generic constituents and societal changes. The eighteenth-century genres that appeared in periodical papers—letters, stories, critical and political essays, etc.—were addressed primarily to a female audience deprived of a university education. They sought to educate a new audience and in so doing helped create in readers a consciousness that some transgressions were an acceptable and even desirable practice. If, as Douwe Fokkema claims, postmodernism is "the most 'democratic' of literary codes,"[16] the generic developments of the earlier time sought to provide generic changes that would make it possible to legitimate a bourgeois society. However different a postindustrial society is from one moving into a bourgeois economy, genre theory may indicate that we are dealing with beginnings and endings. If an analysis of eighteenth-century generic instances and intersections reveals that these served to elevate folk genres (or popular genres ignored by critics) then it seems reasonable to inquire what shifts are involved in modern and postmodern critical acts that elevate formerly ignored genres like slave narratives or popular romances so that they merit academic research and critical analyses. In both situations we find the retention of some older genres, whether the sermon or comedy. In both periods there develop popular genres that serve readers not yet a coherent part of a bourgeois class or of a postmodern non-elite audience. The limits imposed by postmodern writing surely narrow its audience, an audience that responds more fully to rock music of the sixties, to TV sitcoms, and to other genres current in the modernist period.

Critics and theorists disagree about how to explain the phenomenon of postmodernism; some even believe that such explanations are unnecessary. But it is especially important to observe that by rejecting generic procedures, such critics deprive themselves of explanatory tools. In order to demonstrate the characteristics of postmodern writing, critics need to distinguish these from those found in modernism. Postmodern critics resist the usefulness that generic critics find in discussing entities. But writings of different kinds do begin and stop. Constituent parts require that they be considered both within the text and in connections with other texts that begin and stop differently. Some generic procedures are essential to any such effort. Derrida, in discussing the genre of a text by Maurice Blanchot, declares that it reveals the madness of genre: "in literature, satirically practicing all genres, imbibing them but never allowing herself to be saturated with a catalog of genres, she, madness, has started spinning Peterson's genre-disc like a demented sun. And she does not only do so *in* literature, for in concealing the boundaries that sunder mode and genre, she has also inundated and divided the borders between literature and its others."[17]

But this very attack upon genre falls within the genres of satire, parody, and literary theory. To note that genres are necessary in order to be rejected is to remain within the discourse of genres. That a short work can have reference to or be the basis of all other genres is to parody the claim that Homer's epics included them all (however ironic one treats or parodies this claim).

Derrida's parodic essay does, of course, have an ending regardless of its "openness." And it is this writing against genre while being in it that Linda Hutcheon identifies with parody: "The collective weight of parodic *practice* suggests a redefinition of parody as repetition with critical distance that allows ironic signaling of difference at the heart of similarity."[18] This definition applies to parody as a constituent of a text as well as a genre of its own. And it is as a genre that parody displays itself in the playful/serious text that Derrida has written.

I have emphasized the constituents of a generic text, the combinatorial parts that together produce effects upon readers. But it is necessary, also, to stress the notion of an entity, of the consequences of particular kinds of combinations, mixtures, multiple discourses, intertextuality. The language that critics—modern and postmodern—use in discussing texts implies images of the human body as a system, as a biological organism (gender), as a machine. They refer to voice, to sight, to hearing, to smelling, moving, etc. Overtly or implicitly the image of the body of the reader (sometimes of the narrator) is present in the transaction with a text. In drama, of course, the actor's body is a constituent of the drama whereas in postmodern fiction the body can be a theme as it is in Sukenick's "The Death of the Novel."[19] But there is another sense in which the image of the text as a member of a genre is appropriate. Just as a human body has physically descriptive limits, so, too, does any text. The body is dependent on oxygen, on drawing into itself and excreting from itself substances that make it possible to endure as a physical entity, so texts depend upon the language of generic forms in order to be considered as verbal entities. These make it possible to distinguish texts that at any one time are considered unknown or even unknowable genres from those that are known. How does the unknown genre become knowable? That the concept of a genre changes because its members change is self-evident. What is not self-evident is how the constituents of a text begin to undermine the usefulness of a genre so that critics offer replacements.

Two examples should be mentioned here. One is M. H. Abrams's positing of "the Greater Romantic Lyric" as a genre. His procedure is to argue that no known genre describes the texts to which he refers. The new genre is a combination of parts from the loco-descriptive poem, the Romantic meditative lyric, the conversation poem. For Abrams, the new genre "displaced what neoclassical critics had called 'the greater ode' . . . as the favored form for the long lyric poem."[20] Abrams sought to fill a gap in our understanding of Romantic literary invention. He thus proceeded generically in locating the origins of the new genre for which numerous examples existed but remained unnamed or misdescribed.

The second example of generic initiation occurs in Rosalind Krauss's essay "Sculpture in the Expanded Field." Her argument is that critics have expanded the genre "sculpture" to include earthworks, "narrow corridors with TV monitors at the ends; large photographs documenting country hikes," and other structures so that the category has become "almost infinitely malleable."[21] The reasons for such inclusion she attributes to the desire to make the new familiar by assuming that the new forms evolved from past forms. In this respect genre serves to avoid discontinuity by expanding the members of the category. Krauss argues that the genre is a "historically bounded category" with its "own internal logic, its own set of rules, which, though they can be applied to a variety of situations, are not themselves open to very much change."[22] But if the reliance on the internal logic of sculpture is a problematic use of "logic," her subsequent explanation is much more persuasive. It is that the genre "sculpture" must be understood in relation to the genres of landscape and architecture (and not-landscape and not-architecture): "within the situation of postmodernism, practice is not defined in relation to a given medium—sculpture—but rather in relation to the logical operations on a set of cultural terms, for which any medium—photography, books, lines on walls, mirrors or sculpture itself—might be used."[23] For Krauss, the remapping of genres is the result of forces reshaping history contemporaneous with the new genres. And the durability of these genres, established by ruptures in concepts of history, would seem to be contemporaneous with the history that initiated it.

For Fredric Jameson, the history that initiates postmodern views of sculpture is not a matter of the rational logic of a genre, but what he calls "cultural logic." Postmodernism is a historical period concept characteristic of the late stage of capitalism. In his projection of a "new systematic cultural norm,"

Jameson names as the constituents of postmodernism he plans to discuss "a new depthlessness," "a consequent weakening of historicity," "a whole new type of emotional ground tone," "the deep constitutive relationships of all this to a whole new technology, which is itself a figure for a whole new economic world system."[24] I cannot rehearse here Jameson's remarkable study of sophisticated and complex features that change as a result of economic changes, his distaste for the dominant cultural norm he finds in postmodernism, his desire to replace Hutcheon's key term "parody" with "pastiche," a term that makes "parody" blank, "a statue with blind eyeballs."

The very same concept of a cultural "dominant" is developed by Brian McHale except that the latter finds critics discovering various "dominants" demonstrating the reciprocal linkages between modernism and postmodernism: "Clearly, then, there are *many* dominants, and different dominants may be distinguished depending upon the level, scope, and focus of the analysis. Furthermore, one and the same text will, we can infer, yield different dominants depending upon what aspect of it we are analyzing.... In short, different dominants emerge depending upon which questions we ask of the text, and the position from which we interrogate it."[25]

The writings of Jameson and McHale fall into established genres of critical theory and literary criticism. Alterations of views about dominant features do not result in changes of genre. It thus appears that Jameson's Marxist interventions and McHale's formalist interventions still aim at reader persuasion. Thus we can note that the ideology in the linear essay can be seen as resisting postmodernist emptiness of form or aligning some aspects of modernist ideology while others involve an attack upon it. The two texts thus render paradoxical the arguments they make.

The writings of the critics and theorists who argue for "postmodern" as a turning away from modernism find themselves, with few exceptions, continuing to write in the essay genres that were characteristic of modernism. Whatever thematic discourses of generic interpretations they introduce into their essays, they combine them with the traits of modernist essays. Even an essay that seeks to free itself from the modernist genre does include some modernist devices. Thus an essay by Ihab Hassan entitled "POSTmodernISM: A Paracritical Bibliography" undertakes the creation of the essay as encyclopedic genre, as a verbal object typographically innovative, deliberately disjunctive, rejecting linear development, including parts that are normally excluded from the text itself (a bibliography), blank lines for the reader to fill in as he wishes and to become an author, participating in the writing of the essay: "I offer . . . some rubrics and spaces. Let the readers fill them in with their own spaces or grimaces. We value what we choose."[26]

Yet even as he experiments with the transformation of the essay, Hassan expresses reservations about postmodernism's transformative characteristics. Is it, he asks, "somewhat more inward with destiny? Though my sympathies are in the present, I cannot believe this to be entirely so."[27] This essay was published in 1971; in *The Postmodern Turn,* published in 1987, he writes of postmodernism with considerable uneasiness about its usefulness as a category: "Though postmodernism may persist, like modernism itself, a fiercely contested category, at once signifier and signified, altering itself in the very process of signification, the effort to speak it can not be wholly vain."[28]

Critics are divided about the constituents of postmodernism and about its relation to modernism. But most essays confine themselves to constituents of texts rather than to texts as examples of genres. Matei Calinescu writes that as long as we compare and contrast postmodernity with modernity, "modernity survives, at least as the name of a cultural family resemblance in which, for better or for worse, we continue to recognize ourselves."[29] Even Linda Hutcheon, in her comprehensive attempt to theorize about postmodernism, points out that postmodernism's relation to modernism is typically contradictory: "It makes neither a simple and radical break with it nor a straightforward continuity with it: it is both and neither."[30]

Now this description occurs in an essay developed in a linear manner, including, however, some of the discourses of postmodernism in fiction and the other arts as well as discourses from Marxist and other critics, and, in conclusion, arriving at pluralism, at pragmatism, at an understanding of signifying processes (at epistemology), and even (perhaps in a parodic demonstration of postmodernist contradictions) at a version of humanistic aims: "To move from the desire and expectation of sure and single meaning to a recognition of the value of differences and even contradictions might be a tentative first step towards accepting responsibility for both art and theory as *signifying processes*. In other words, maybe we could begin to study the implications of both our making and our making sense of our culture."[31]

The critical and theoretical essay—and my essay is another example of this—is a genre that has come to be practiced more frequently in the late modernist and postmodernist periods than at any time previously in English literary history. To recognize it as a kind of writing, as a genre, is to demonstrate some of the functions it has for us. The essay is not merely a part of anthologies; it is a genre of its own and critics have traced its changes from

Montaigne to the present. The academic essay serves postmodernism by exemplifying how a genre can embrace discourses that attack genres, how a genre can be the site of contrary ideologies.

Roland Barthes's view of the essay, as quoted by Réda Bensmaïa, is that it is a question "'with intellectual things . . . of combining . . . *at the same time* theory, critical combat, and pleasure.'" And Barthes's experimentation with the essay as a unique form offers "the possibility of a 'plural' text made up of multiple networks 'that interact without any one of them being able to dominate the others' . . . 'it has no beginning; it is reversible; we gain access to it by several entrances, none of which can be authoritatively declared to be the main one.'"[32]

This is a postmodern view of the essay and it does not refer to the essays I have quoted, but it does draw attention to the fact that the theoretical essay is a historical kind. If this is a postmodern definition, then the multiple networks argument is itself a dominant for postmodern essays. Treating the essay as genre is a recognition that discourses cannot be an adequate substitute for the works that encompass them. The rejection of genre falsifies the situation in which entrances are many and exits are many. For it conceals the fact that in different kinds of postmodernist writing, in novels, dramas, essays, entrances and exits are not the same.

Do postmodern genres exist? This question can now be seen in the context I have set for it. If one wishes to trace the relation between modernism and postmodernism, if one wishes to understand the diverse ways of distinguishing postmodern fiction from postmodern surfiction and from the romance and spy story as fictions equally contemporary but not postmodern, then genre study is the most adequate procedure to accomplish this aim.

Do postmodern genres exist? If we wish to understand the proliferation of academic anthologies, journals, collections of critical essays, then we need names for such omnibus volumes and genre theory provides them. If we wish to study the kinds of writing with reference to the social environment of which they are a part, then genre study helps us relate institutions and economics to the production of texts. If we seek to understand the historical recurrence of certain kinds of writing, the rejection or abandonment of other kinds, genre theory provides the most adequate procedure for this inquiry. If we wish to analyze an individual text, genre theory provides a knowledge of its constituents and how they combine. Not only do these actions recognize the value of a genre theory in analyzing modernist writing, but they demonstrate that postmodern theorists, critics, authors, and readers inevitably use the language of genre theory even as they seek to deny its usefulness.

NOTES

1. Ihab Hassan, *The Postmodern Turn* (Columbus: Ohio State Univ. Press, 1987), xvi.

2. Rosalie Colie, *The Resources of Kind: Genre-Theory in the Renaissance* (Berkeley: Univ. of California Press, 1973), 19.

3. Colie, *The Resources of Kind*, 8. Colie writes: "I would like to present genre-theory as a means of accounting for connections between topic and treatment within the literary system, but also to see the connection of the literary kinds with *kinds* of knowledge and experience; to present the kinds as a major part of that *genus universum* which is part of all literary students' heritage" (29).

4. Hans Robert Jauss, "Literary History as a Challenge to Literary Theory," in *Toward an Aesthetic of Reception*, trans. Timothy Bahti (Minneapolis: Univ. of Minnesota Press, 1982), 22; my italics. An earlier version of some sections of this essay was published in 1970 in *New Literary History*.

5. Maria Corti, *An Introduction to Literary Semiotics*, trans. M. Bogat and A. Mandelbaum (Bloomington: Indiana Univ. Press, 1978), 118; my italics.

6. Jonathan Culler, "Towards a Theory of Non-Genre Literature," in *Surfiction*, ed. Raymond Federman (Chicago: Swallow Press, 1975), 255.

7. Culler, "Towards a Theory," 259. A point similar to Culler's on the unreadableness of some postmodern genres is made by Charles Caramello. Referring to essays by Edmond Jabès, Ihab Hassan, Campbell Tatham, and Raymond Federman, he writes: "What they *are* is impossible to ascertain. 'Impossible to classify these books,' Rosmarie Waldrop writes of Jabès's *Le livre des questions*. 'They have the texture of poetry, but are mostly prose'" (Caramello, "On Styles of Postmodern Writing," in *Performance in Postmodern Culture*, ed. Michel Benamou and Caramello [Milwaukee: Center for Twentieth Century Studies, Univ. of Wisconsin-Milwaukee, 1977], 227).

8. Austin Warren, "Literary Genres," in *Theory of Literature*, by René Wellek and Austin Warren (New York: Harcourt Brace, 1949), 245.

9. Discussions of this aspect of genre theory can be found in the essays of Yury Tynyanov and Roman Jakobson in *Readings in Russian Poetics: Formalist and Structuralist Views* (Ann Arbor: Michigan Slavic Publications, 1978); Mikhail Bakhtin, *Problems of Dostoevsky's Poetics*, ed. and trans. Caryl Emerson (Minneapolis: Univ. of Minnesota Press, 1984), *The Dialogic Imagination: Four Essays*, ed. Michael Holquist, trans. Caryl Emerson and Michael Holquist (Austin: Univ. of Texas Press, 1981), and *Speech Genres and Other Late Essays*, ed. Caryl Emerson and Michael Holquist, trans. Vern W. McGee (Austin: Univ. of Texas Press, 1986); Tzvetan Todorov, *The Fantastic: A Structural Approach to a Literary Genre* (Cleveland, OH: Press of Case Western Reserve Univ., 1973); Alastair Fowler, *Kinds of Literature: An Introduction to the Theory of Genres and Modes*

(Cambridge, MA: Harvard Univ. Press, 1982); Fredric Jameson, *The Political Unconscious: Narrative as a Socially Symbolic Act* (Ithaca, NY: Cornell Univ. Press, 1981); Sandra M. Gilbert and Susan Gubar, *The Madwoman in the Attic: The Woman Writer and the Nineteenth-Century Literary Imagination* (New Haven, CT: Yale Univ. Press, 1979).

10. Clifford Geertz, "Blurred Genres: The Refiguration of Social Thought," *American Scholar* 49, no. 2 (1980): 165-66.

11. Geertz, "Blurred Genres," 178.

12. Joseph A. Buttigieg, ed., *Criticism without Boundaries: Directions and Crosscurrents in Postmodern Critical Theory* (Notre Dame, IN: Univ. of Notre Dame Press, 1987).

13. See Rick Altman, *The American Film Musical* (Bloomington: Indiana Univ. Press, 1987); Christian Metz, *The Imaginary Signifier* (Bloomington: Indiana Univ. Press, 1982); and S. J. Solomon, *The Film Idea* (New York: Harcourt Brace Jovanovich, 1972), among others.

14. Marjorie Perloff, "Postmodernism and the Impasse of Lyric," in *The Dance of the Intellect* (Cambridge: Cambridge Univ. Press, 1985), 176.

15. Caramello, in "On Styles of Postmodern Writing," quotes Julia Kristeva: "Every text takes shape as a mosaic of citations, every text is the absorption and transformation of other texts. The notion of intertextuality comes to take the place of the notion of intersubjectivity" (224).

16. Douwe Fokkema, *Literary History, Modernism, and Postmodernism* (Amsterdam and Philadelphia: John Benjamins, 1984), 48.

17. Jacques Derrida, "The Law of Genre," trans. Avital Ronell, *Glyph* 7 (Baltimore: Johns Hopkins Univ. Press, 1980), 228.

18. Linda Hutcheon, "The Politics of Postmodernism: Parody and History," *Cultural Critique* 5 (1986-87): 185. The entire issue is devoted to the subject "Modernity and Modernism, Postmodernity and Postmodernism."

19. Ronald Sukenick, *The Death of the Novel and Other Stories* (New York: Dial Press, 1969).

20. M. H. Abrams, "Structure and Style in the Greater Romantic Lyric," in *From Sensibility to Romanticism,* ed. F. W. Hillis and Harold Bloom (New York: Oxford Univ. Press, 1965), 528.

21. Rosalind E. Krauss, "Sculpture in the Expanded Field," in *The Originality of the Avant-Garde and Other Modernist Myths* (Cambridge, MA: MIT Press, 1985), 277.

22. Krauss, "Sculpture," 279.

23. Krauss, "Sculpture," 288.

24. Fredric Jameson, "Postmodernism, or The Cultural Logic of Late Capitalism," *New Left Review,* no. 146 (1984): 59-92. See also an earlier version, "Postmodernism and Consumer Society," in *The Anti-Aesthetic: Essays on Postmodern Culture,* ed. Hal Foster (Port Townsend, WA: Bay Press, 1983).

25. Brian McHale, *Postmodernist Fiction* (New York and London: Methuen, 1987), 6. The concept of the "dominant" is applied by Todorov to a theory of genres in *The Fantastic.*

26. Hassan, "POSTmodernISM: A Paracritical Bibliography," *The Postmodern Turn,* 35.

27. Hassan, "POSTmodernISM," 45.

28. Hassan, *The Postmodern Turn,* xii.

29. Matei Calinescu, *Five Faces of Modernity* (Durham, NC: Duke Univ. Press, 1987), 312.

30. Linda Hutcheon, "Beginning to Theorize Postmodernism," *Textual Practice* 1, no. 1 (1987): 23.

31. Hutcheon, "Beginning to Theorize," 26.

32. Réda Bensmaïa, *The Barthes Effect: The Essay as Reflective Text,* trans. Pat Fedkiew (Minneapolis: Univ. of Minnesota Press, 1987), 99.

Reviewing Criticism
Literary Theory

I. WHAT IS "LITERARY THEORY"?

Literary theory has joined a host of other subjects that in our time have been pronounced dead: the author, the novel, God, concrete poetry, archetypal and genre criticism. As Terry Eagleton inters literary theory, he finds that from its grave arise the blossoms of a theory of culture. Literary theory, which once seemed the counterpart of scientific theory, has ceased to search for the "method" by which literature could be studied.[1]

Like scientific method, literary method has turned out to be a fiction. The need to give coherence to literary study has met with grave doubts about the coherence or unity of writing. And it is not surprising to find the late Paul de Man explaining that he cannot find in his own collection of essays a coherence that would give it consistency and unity.

> The fragmentary aspect of the whole is made more obvious still by the hypotactic manner that prevails in each of the essays taken in isolation, by the continued attempt, however ironized, to present a closed and linear argument. This apparent coherence *within* each essay is not matched by a corresponding coherence *between* them. Laid out diachronically in a roughly chronological sequence, they do not evolve in a manner that easily allows for dialectical progression or, ultimately, for historical totalization. Rather, it seems that they always start again from scratch and that their conclusions fail to add up to anything.[2]

Whether or not de Man was a reliable critic of his own work, the point is that "literary theory" is no single-voiced phenomenon. To review "literary theory" in 1987 is not a simple, readily recognized choice; it is, for example,

This essay was originally published in *Literary Reviewing*, ed. James O. Hoge (Charlottesville: Univ. Press of Virginia, 1987), 1-18, and is reprinted with permission of the publisher.

difficult to know whether Eagleton's *Literary Theory* is a theoretical or historical study. It begins with a chapter entitled "What Is Literature?" but has no chapter called "What Is Literary Theory?" Eagleton claims that literary theory is an "illusion." He writes that "it is an illusion first in the sense that literary theory, as I hope to have shown, is really no more than a branch of social ideologies, utterly without any unity or identity which would adequately distinguish it from philosophy, linguistics, psychology, cultural and sociological thought; and secondly in the sense that the one hope it has of distinguishing itself—clinging to an object named literature—is misplaced."[3] Literary theory is, in his argument, a small part of the larger study of "culture." But in reviewing this claim it must be noted that Eagleton assumes that different generic writings have neither unity nor identity. If literary theory cannot "adequately" be distinguished from philosophy or linguistics, it cannot be an independent subject. But hiding behind "adequately" is the basis for distinct subjects. Who, if not critics, determines whether "literary theory" is an independent subject? And is it not reasonable for them to argue that the writings called literary theory can be discussed more adequately as an independent discipline than as part of a discipline called "social ideologies"? The reviewer of *literary theory* may indeed object to the selection of ideology as the chief basis governing such theory. He might, at the very least, indicate the unimportance of the idea of art or pleasure for Eagleton, since these are, for him, always subordinated to ideology.

Is "literary theory" a theory of works that fall into the genre "literature" or is it a theory of any work that can be generalized about and analyzed in the procedures applied to poems and novels? Barbara H. Smith and Murray Krieger reserve "literary" theory for theorizing about works that are considered by them to be part of "literature." Paul de Man and Harold Bloom, for example, refer to "literary theory" as a way of theorizing about any text, using the term "literary" to refer to writing rather than to a specialized category of writing. The reviewer will, therefore, point to the concept of "literary" that is being used and note the examples that an author offers of "literary" texts.

When René Wellek and Austin Warren published their *Theory of Literature* in 1949, the book contained a chapter called "Literary Theory, Criticism, and History," written by Wellek. And he made the point then that literary theory, criticism, and history "cannot be used in isolation . . . they implicate each other so thoroughly as to make inconceivable literary theory without criticism or history, or criticism without theory and history, or history without theory and criticism."[4]

It is unnecessary to point out that "scientific theory" in the view of Thomas Kuhn is a term for the way scientists practice their discipline; it characterizes solutions that result from problem solving. And problem solving does not result from one particular "method." So, too, literary theory is not some isolated study despite the fact that some practitioners seem to conceive of it as a purely abstract enterprise. Giving it the kiss of death is usually the result of this separation of theory from the actual study of literary texts. But no thoughtful practitioner of literary theory would want to make this separation. Even F. R. Leavis, who had little patience for literary theory, did not seek to eliminate it but to find the proper (secondary) place for it in literary study; the primary place he reserved for the attainment of "a peculiar completeness of response" to the concrete fullness of the poem: "I am sure," Leavis wrote, "the kind of work I have attempted comes first, and would, for such a theoretical statement to be worth anything, have to come first."[5]

The notion of primacy is, perhaps, a mistake, since the interaction between theory and practice is such that simple hierarchizing is misplaced. After all, to refer to Shelley's "Mont Blanc" as a *poem* is to assume knowledge of what a "poem" is, and that is a theoretical assumption, not the result of a completeness of response. And many contemporary theorists recognize this. Murray Krieger, for example, draws attention to this interaction when he declares that each "new work challenges our theory and our theory challenges each new work."[6] Any literary theory as he conceives it generalizes about texts, but since such generalizations are based on past texts they are challenged by present and future texts. Thus theory is challenged by new texts and needs to be rethought and rewritten to accommodate those writings for which it was not intended. Krieger quite rightly discusses the relation between theory and practice. Any theory demonstrates its adequacy by its applicability. Its value lies in its usefulness in helping scholars and students deal with problems that literary texts raise.

Thus far I have been dealing with the ambiguities latent in "literary theory," the last two words of my title. Since texts identified as "literary theory" are passed on to a reviewer, what are the assumptions that govern such a classification and designation? What is it that a reviewer of theory reviews? He reviews any text that is primarily concerned with the nature of literary language, the problems pertinent to interpretation, the nature and kinds of genre, the place of value in literary study, and the construction of systematic statements about relations among the author, the text, society, and other texts. Theoretical texts are intertwined with critical and historical studies so that a theoretical text may be considered a historical text or even a "fictional" text as well. The consequence of such intertwining is that the reviewer will need considerable malleability in describing a theoretical text, since its theoretical character cannot readily be identified without specifying a series of interrelations that make it more than one kind of text. One of the tasks of a reviewer, therefore, is to describe the text as a combination of elements involving historical, critical, and other discourses.

II. READERS AND REVIEWERS

When writing a "scholarly" review, the reviewer obviously seeks to familiarize himself with his audience. He seeks to discover, if he does not already know, for whom the review is written. Students, scholars, and critics constitute in large part the audience for theory and for theoretical reviews. Robert Scholes puts it this way: "A substantial portion of the audience for theory is composed of teachers. Teachers read theory in order to 'keep up'—as we say— with the field of literary study, partly in response to the pressure all fashions or modes of behavior exert in this most modish of all possible worlds; partly, perhaps, for the pleasures of concentration and controversy; but also, surely, for ideas that will enhance their performance as teachers in the field of literary studies."[7] One should not, however, overlook those readers of theoretical books and their reviews who disdain theory, and read it in order to parody it. For such readers, literary theory is less a corpse than a clown.

Fashion, controversy, instruction, use, amusement—these are some of the reasons for reading theory and reviews of theory. But review readers do not often read the books under review. Rather they read reviews to discover the issues theorists are raising, to learn about the theoretical books reviewers consider important, to familiarize themselves with different theoretical vocabularies. Moreover, scholars read reviews not only to learn about the books under review; they read them to learn what the reviewer thinks and to familiarize themselves with his theoretical ideas.

Since a reviewer, in describing a text, selectively rephrases it, the reader will look for a description that takes account of the varied writing of theoretical discourses. It is not merely that such discourses combine literary theory with literary criticism and literary history; they also combine it with autobiographical and other writings. The reader is no single entity but a body of more or less knowledgeable responders. Some of these will want an explanation of the consequences of any particular theoretical combination.

Some readers of reviews expect distinctions to be made between an author's use of rhetoric to develop new thoughts and his use of it to shield or support old ones. The review reader knows that the prejudices of a reviewer are written into a review, and he knows this because he is familiar with other writings of the reviewer or the author or with other reviews of the same book. Since a reviewer's prejudices and assumptions may be minimized but not avoided, the review reader will expect to have them exposed. A reviewer who makes his own views clear by juxtaposing them with the author's reduces the most obvious sources of distortion. But reviewers, like other people, often do not know or recognize their deep-seated prejudices, those that are intertwined in their very style of writing. A reviewer's exposure of his distortions can be revealed in his statements of an author's limits—his claim of what an author is resisting, supplementing, attacking, or avoiding. He exposes his own views in relating those that confine the author, in judging the confinement as reasonable or trivial.

I have been using the terms "reviewing," "review," and "reviewer" in the formal sense of a critical article on a recent book or books that is published in a periodical or other reviewing organ. But the terms "review" and "reviewing" apply to activities that are not published but written and circulated in academic departments, usually to members who have not read the original materials. Such "reviews" form part of academic decision making. There, as well as in published reviews, the process of reviewing carries within it the assumption of authority and the distancing of the audience from reviewed texts.

So, too, in publishing, "reviewing" provides the publisher with a so-called authoritative decision about accepting or rejecting a manuscript. It is not necessary to point out that "reviewing" grants authority to individuals or groups that is normally vested in those who bear responsibility for decisions. Reviewing as a procedure can easily become the basis for bureaucratic control and the continuance of prejudice. And this is especially the case when those who read manuscripts and those who publish reviews of them share the same views and even the same roles at different times.

Considering the number of books written in any field during a year, the reviewing procedure may seem a reasonable one, but the secondary processing of information that it produces cannot be denied. Reviews may be useful, even necessary, to help readers keep abreast of work in a field, but they often familiarize the reader with the ideas of the reviewer rather than with those of the author.

III. TYPES OF THEORETICAL REVIEWS

Any competent review inevitably restates the premises of the author, and even though a reviewer may quote the author himself, he reassembles the argument for the reader. But no review can substitute for the reading of a book. What it does, is indicate what values the reviewer finds or misses in the book. In this respect the reviewer finds himself, whether he wishes it or not, in a judgmental role. No matter how careful he is in seeking to present the book's argument, he has to render it by selection and by his own words. Every reviewer is a writer, and in this procedure he differs from the nonreviewing reader who is under no obligation to write.

The reviewer becomes an author and his own review competes with the book he is reviewing. In this he resembles the authors he reviews. It is not surprising that contemporary theorists are intent upon developing "original" theories. Whether it is Bloom's version of Emerson and Freud, or de Man's particular variation of rhetorical theory, or Jameson's Marxist literary theory—all such theorists seek to announce their originality. Reviewing theory very often results in the imitative contamination of originality because the reviewer seeks to match the ingenuity of the author. In such a situation similarities among theoreticians are made to dwindle and differences—no matter how trivial—come to be emphasized.

Since theoretical reviewing is a relatively narrow field, it is especially troubled by the internecine conflicts among the participants. For the reviews are very often written by the theorists who are themselves authors and who in their reviews reiterate the positions they espouse, stressing minor differences rather than major agreements. Thus Eagleton has his Marxism, which differs from Jameson's and Lotman's. Other differences rather than similarities are stressed between the writings of French and American psychoanalytical critics, between the various phenomenologists, between the reader-response theorists and those who deal with aesthetics of response, between the deconstructionists and the neonaturalists—any one of these theorists can predictably respond to a given text regardless of his individual generosity, meanness, or more or less felicitous writing style. No matter how unbiased reviewing theorists may seek to be, they discover in the text under review the flaws, gaps, ruptures, contradictions, that their own theory sets out to expose. Books that support one's view are obviously much easier to praise than those that question or attack it.

The theorists known as the neo-Aristotelians (also called the "Chicago

Critics") had a systematic way of reviewing theoretical books based on their premise that various literary criticisms and theories were distinct and more or less incommensurable "frameworks" or "languages." The approach to any theoretical language, therefore, was a matter "of assumed principle, definition and method." R. S. Crane declared that these "are not likely to show themselves, save indirectly, on the surface of a critic's discourse, and hence not likely, even in controversy, to force themselves on his attention. They pertain rather to what he thinks with than to what he thinks about—to the implicit structure and rationale of his argument as a whole than to the explicit doctrines he is attempting to state."[8]

Such a procedure makes reviewing systematic and comprehensible, but it also gives a false uniformity to the reviewing and writing process. It misconceives the way writing of theory takes place, and it neglects the interconnections among various types of "frameworks" or "languages." It creates systematic and coherent frameworks that belie what the authors are actually doing. In this procedure the reviewer conceals, though not consciously, the social and political interests which govern him and which a Marxist like Eagleton makes primary. But as feminist critics have argued, a disregard for recognizing or acknowledging one's own preferences makes prejudices seemingly nonexistent. By systematizing the unsystematic, this procedure reduces the complexity and often eliminates the insights a book possesses.

This kind of reviewing was an attempt to bring a "framework" system to the study of literature, an attempt to give it an analytical rigor. It provided a pluralistic approach while disregarding how theorists reviewing other theorists were entangled with their own and society's values. Reviewing was never a neutral enterprise, and from its beginning it was tied to journals as "institutions."

Reviewing as a professional activity dates from the establishment of reviewing journals in the eighteenth century. John Gross noted in *The Rise and Fall of the Man of Letters* that "with the rise of the professional author came the rise of the professional critic." The extension of the publishing industry brought with it reviewing journals that helped publicize and thus increase distribution of books: "The first successful reviews, the *Monthly* and the *Critical*, were both established in the reign of George II, and by the end of the eighteenth century other competitors had taken the field. At their worst these periodicals were little more than thinly-disguised publishers' catalogues, at their best they carried competent, respectable, even original work."[9] But the professional author and the increase in the number of publications were not the only bases for the development of reviewing journals. John Clive has pointed out that the numerous eighteenth-century clubs and societies in Edinburgh provided the "essential fertile soil for cooperative literary projects such as the [*Edinburgh*] *Review*" founded in 1802. He remarked that the earlier reviews—the *Monthly Review* (from 1749), the *Critical Review* (from 1756), the *Analytical Review* (from 1788)—were primarily abstracts of "the latest works on politics, literature, science and art. The emphasis on abstracts lasted, in varying degrees, throughout the century."[10] It was the *Edinburgh Review* that became at the beginning of the nineteenth century the most successful reviewing journal available. Its reviewers were, of course, professional literary men.

IV. REVIEWING AND VALUING

At present, reviewers and authors of theoretical books are almost always members of academic institutions. This means that they are involved in departmental as well as professional reviews. Thus their reviews are not merely scholarly exercises but instances of power. They have impact on the academic and economic advancement of the author, but also of the reviewer as author. For this reason scholarly reviews in our time have become an occasion for publicity and scholarly exposure. Scholarly reviewers are, if they give thought to their task, confronted with moral dilemmas as a result of the institutionalization of authors, since reviews are among the determinants of advancement. First books, especially, constitute a moral problem for the reviewer. This may result in an eminent scholar like W. J. Bate reviewing and praising the book of his student or it may result in a senior reviewer refusing to review the book of a young scholar if he finds that he disapproves of some of the arguments in it. It is one thing to quarrel with the arguments of Stanley Fish or M. H. Abrams or Jacques Derrida; quite another to quarrel with the book of an unknown assistant professor.

It may seem that matters of academic appointment or economic advancement are irrelevant in reviewing books and that the examples I have given of reviewing or not reviewing are relatively infrequent. It may even be claimed that in loosening the meanings of "review" and "reviewing," I have muddled what is a very specific activity. To these objections I would reply that "reviewing" is an activity that in our time has become intimately connected with authority and power in contrast to early forms of reviewing as abstracts and summaries. Moreover, reviewing for us has connected the members of the academy with the production of reviews and the writing of books—and these are academic and economic interrelations. But I would make a further point, namely, that theoretical texts are especially concerned with moral issues. No matter whether a literary theory involves the nature of reading or the deconstruction of language, the theorist offers it as a value that will enhance the lives of those who pursue it. If a theorist defends "slow reading," he does so because it enhances the reader's appreciation and understanding.[11] And such activities are valuable because they make individuals more adequate members of society. If a scholar proposes a genre theory, he may do so because he wishes to explore generic change and, through this, the functions of change in society.

In the writing of a review, the reviewer acts as adviser to readers (and sometimes to the author). But the basis of his description, analysis, and judgment is some larger view of the aim of the text. Whether the book deals with the rise or nature of the novel, the function of rhetoric, the nature of meaning or imagination, the reviewer assesses it in terms of its contribution to a field. But a literary field is worked by students, scholars, and teachers and they judge contributions by their "value." In this sense a reviewer envisages certain values for his field, and his review is governed by his explicit or implicit claims for literary study. And this applies as well to deconstructionists who find the languages of reviewers as well as those of texts self-contradictory. For even though it may appear pointless to write what is in itself unreliable, the very act of writing can be considered a moral gesture demonstrating the need to be skeptical of such gestures.

Given the varied views of reviewers, it may be asked how far a reader can trust a reviewer. What reliance can a reader place in a reviewer's comments, descriptions, evaluations? If reviews are governed by the premises of a reviewer, if his decisions are moral because they are related to his concern for the fate of society or for the author's fate or for his own, how can the reviewer offer his audience a reliable description and judgment of a text?

The trust that a reader gives to a reviewer should, under present reviewing conditions, be withheld. Until the reader has made an effort to read the book and assess the remarks of the reviewer, such remarks are untested and uncontested. It may, however, be useful to know whether a review can be tested or examined; whether mediated language can be weighed, or prejudices discounted, or hidden assumptions exposed. Since the mediated language introduces distortions, can the nature of the distortions be gauged by the reviewer's recognition of the difference between his language and the author's? Efforts toward this have been made by including extended quotations from the text, by sifting the vocabulary under review. Theorists employ terms like "text," "absence," "presence," "transaction," "other," "discourse," etc., in special ways. The reviewer who seeks to redefine these to convey the author's private use of a theoretical language is, at the very least, not resisting the special vocabulary an author introduces. He makes an effort to distinguish between an author's language and his own. This does not eliminate mediated language, but it makes the review reader conscious of it.

The reviewer brings to his task his own theoretical commitments and he reads the book under review against these. If he believes that theoretical books are written within language frameworks, he will seek to present the framework in detail, laying out the principles, definitions, methods. But if he believes that a work is composed of discursive formations, he will seek to explicate the epistemological assumptions of these formations. The reviewer, in describing these hypotheses, often notes that they can be completely circular and thus self-confirming. M. H. Abrams puts it this way: "The reason that all these modes of Newreading work is that each practitioner brings to the language of a text a ruling hypothesis about the kind of things it must necessarily mean or fail to mean, then deploys tactics that provide ample degrees of interpretive freedom to ensure that the hypothesis applies, by ruling out in advance any possible recourse that might serve to disconfirm it."[12]

But confirmation or disconfirmation is not the issue. Theoretical constructs are not inherent in language or literature; theorists formulate them for varied purposes. Such constructs are demonstrated in practice; they provide explanations for the pertinent subject matter. A reviewer, therefore, finds himself examining the specific examples offered or he offers his own in order to examine the construct. But no theory can or should be disengaged from explanations offered by other theorists; rather, any theory leads back to the question, what aims are served by its explanation or interpretation? The reviewer may thus find himself involved in questions about interpretive communities or the nature and aims of educational institutions, or the relation of art to morals.

It is easy to see how tempting for the theoretical reviewer is the pluralistic approach—the acceptance of different theories each of which seeks to be, even though it seldom is, consistent and coherent in its own terms. And tempting, too, is the assumption that although different approaches are acceptable, one's own is preferable to that of others. These are the lines reviewers take, along with the search for chinks in the system—for contradictions, inconsistencies, incoherence. But none of these seem to me to question the reasons for the initiation of a theory or the changes it makes in previous theories. A reviewer of a theoretical book ought to ask where, in the present realm of theoretical thinking, does the text belong? The problems it deals with are self-evidently a reviewer's task to consider, but why the selection of these problems and to what purpose? Why propose a generic theory, or a theory of "literature" in contrast to "nonliterature"? Why a theory of deconstruction or of capitalist production?

Why in studying Bunyan's *Grace Abounding* is it useful or perhaps necessary to raise the generic question of what constitutes an autobiography? Why is it necessary or even desirable to posit a theory of metaphor or allegory in order to discuss the specific uses of these in *The Waste Land?* What educational and social purposes are served by such theoretical works as Frye's *Anatomy of Criticism,* Wellek and Warren's *Theory of Literature,* Derrida's *Of Grammatology?* A reviewer of a theory book can easily avoid such questions by analyzing the theory itself, but the aims of a theory no less than the aims of poetry ought not to be ignored. A theoretical reviewer needs to see his task in terms of the discipline of letters and literature, in terms of the role it plays in the drama of society.

Psychoanalytic theories may deal with the transaction between the reviewer's self and that of the author in the text; they explore how the language of the self shapes and is shaped by the language of the text. But the larger social aim is the rehumanizing of the individual and thus the rehumanizing of society. Feminist critics who rely on psychoanalysis as the basis for gender criticism are equally concerned with identifying the feminist self in the reading transaction. My point is that any theory—whether it be deconstructive, structural, rhetorical, etc.—is concerned with the function of texts in the making of society.

It is apparent that a reviewer, in analyzing the societal aims of a theory, may find himself having to explain a theory that deals with an aspect of language such as metaphor rather than with poetic language in general, with the Gothic novel rather than with the novel. Theories are more or less comprehensive, and those of Northrop Frye or Kenneth Burke or R. S. Crane or Jacques Derrida, who seek to theorize about "literature" or all writing, are more comprehensive than Paul Ricoeur's in *The Rule of Metaphor.* It is the task of the reviewer to point out the range of theory, and in doing so, to indicate which theories the author is opposing and which he is supplementing by variations, or revising by omissions or alterations.

V. THEORETICAL REVIEWING AS HISTORICAL INQUIRY

This implies that any "literary" theory is a historical text; it is composed to deal with, to explain, to initiate, to oppose certain kinds of writing of a certain place and time—no matter whether the place is the Western world or the year 2000. A theory is to be understood in terms of the kinds of texts to which it refers, and to other texts—theoretical and nontheoretical—with which it is contemporaneous. A theory is itself a kind of writing and it belongs with them as part of a historical period or movement or school.

Confirmation or disconfirmation of a theory is not often possible, even though specific references may be disconfirmed. But even if it were possible, it would not explain why such a theory should be proposed at this particular time. The reviewer who sees himself as a historical being will wish to know what elements or features or aspects of past theories are being continued. He will see his review as a group of statements relating the book under review to others in the past, carrying on some of the views of literature, of unity, of intention, of value. This he does by attending to redefined terms, to the initiation of new ones, to the problems neglected or confronted, to the continuities and changes based on previous theories, to discourse elements and their interrelations with other kinds of writing.

The most obvious historical procedure is for the reviewer to note the changes that take place with the author's own theoretical premises. Thus Paul de Man's early essay "Symbolic Landscape in Wordsworth and Yeats" (1963) was an example of New Critical analysis with its search for tension, complexity, and an underlying unity and wholeness, a belief that there is a "key" to interpretation of the poem.[13] The close reading is not abandoned with its analysis of individual terms and images. But the concept of the whole is and with it the assumption of the special power of poetic imagery. The reviewer of *Blindness and Insight* or *Allegories of Reading* would have to explain how a shift in the conception of poetic language and unity undermined the previous views that sought the independence of the student reader as one of its goals.

The author who writes self-consciously of the changes in his own writing— as Paul de Man, Jerome McGann, and Elaine Showalter do—provides the reviewer with an autobiographical awareness of historical change. But such awareness places the reviewer in a position to describe an author's revision and to evaluate an author's sense of self. There is no reason to assume that an author's judgment reflects anything more than his own limitations—but these become apparent to reviewers through his particular form of self-consciousness.

Consider the recent recantation of Jerome McGann in *The Romantic Ideology* (1983): "I should like to conclude with an illustrative case from Byron, partly because I have been to some extent responsible for perpetuating certain misconceptions about his work, and partly because Byron's late achievements can sometimes appear to have transcended his own Romantic illusions. The 'poetic development' of Byron which I argued in *Fiery Dust* now seems to me a most misleading critical formulation." What the reviewer faces here is the claim that Byron's late poetry remains a romantic delusion and that it does not avoid the inadequate self-assessment of the Romantics. Byron's art can make readers miss "the ideas and the ideologies which lead him into a disclosure of his world's contradictions by tempting him to believe that they can be transcended in imaginative thought.... In the end Byron's poetry discovers... that there is no place of refuge, not in desire, not in the mind, not in imagination."[14]

The reviewer who finds McGann's earlier book on Byron, *Fiery Dust*, a more adequate interpretation than his later will present the reasons for such disagreement. Is the quality of a poem determined by its awareness of its contradictions? This would seem a peculiar argument to offer, since the very qualities that Byron is aware of would not be those that are located by the theorist. The very concept of concealed contradiction is imposed by the theorist, and there is no reason for assuming that the poet in making such contradictions evident becomes a better artist. McGann does not deny the value of the English stanzas of *Don Juan*, but it is not at all clear in what this value consists, since, for him, the stanzas illustrate the inadequacy of thought characteristic of all Romantic poetry.

The reviewer who sees himself as a historical inquirer realizes the tentative role he performs in our time. His role as middleman between author and reader has become ambiguous; his obligation as narrator is neither neutral nor objective. He often competes as author with the author of the book he is reviewing. His own views of theory are written into the review he writes—intentionally or unintentionally. His guidance is suspect, since it is often governed by motives that are concealed from the reader. In a time of competing and burgeoning theories, the historical reviewer can, at best, disclose his own preferences and prejudices. He becomes, therefore, not a reliable guide but an advocate of a theoretical position. Reviewing is becoming in our time an analogue to literary theory; it becomes an independent genre often discussing the reviewer's interests rather than those of the text under review.

Can reviewing become a reliable guide? It can but only if the reviewing procedure is reconceived. If reviews were published with answers by the author, the reader would be in a position to examine contrary arguments. Reviews of this kind would be dialogues between authors and reader-reviewers. Reviews *could* then be part of an ongoing inquiry into the theoretical problems raised; such dialogues would deal with specific issues that would engage both participants in noting agreements and disagreements. Such a procedure would present author and reviewer together and the reader would thus have before him a sample of the oppositional views and the styles in which they are composed. Scholarly journals often publish forums or letters in which replies to reviews are made months after the reviews have been published. Such procedures make performances out of such interchanges; they have little to do with clarifying issues.

Publishing an author's response together with a review would not alter the institutional pressures exerted on reviewers, but it would modify the search for originality and the emphasis on theoretical differences. It would help to clarify for the reader the arguments that are offered, and it would make possible a conception of reviewing as a cooperative inquiring. And it might, just might, create a sense of common enterprise in the study of theory that is clearly absent today.

The solution is not meant as a panacea or as an effort to provide some single unified theory with which all theorists will agree. Reviewers will remain as varied as before. But they will at least realize that they are addressing the author and are subject to his reply. This may make them less untrustworthy and more responsible as interpreters and judges. But what if, in this dialogue, reviewer and author agree? Here, surely, review readers have grounds for suspicion. Perhaps, then, we can turn to the book itself.

NOTES

1. Terry Eagleton, *Literary Theory: An Introduction* (Minneapolis: Univ. of Minnesota Press, 1983), 204.

2. Paul de Man, *The Rhetoric of Romanticism* (New York: Columbia Univ. Press, 1984), viii.

3. Eagleton, *Literary Theory,* 204.

4. René Wellek and Austin Warren, *Theory of Literature* (New York: Harcourt, Brace, 1949), 30-31.

5. Eric Bentley, ed., "A Reply to F. R. Leavis," in *The Importance of Scrutiny* (New York: Grove, 1948), 32.

6. Murray Krieger, *Theory of Criticism: A Tradition and Its System* (Baltimore: Johns Hopkins Univ. Press, 1976), 7.

7. Robert Scholes, *Textual Power: Literary Theory and the Teaching of English* (New Haven, CT: Yale Univ. Press, 1985), 19.

8. R. S. Crane, *The Languages of Criticism and the Structure of Poetry* (Toronto: Univ. of Toronto Press, 1953), 13.

9. John Gross, *The Rise and Fall of the Man of Letters* (New York: Collier Books, 1970), 1.

10. John Clive, *Scotch Reviewers:* The Edinburgh Review, *1802-1815* (London: Faber and Faber, 1957), 21, 31.

11. Reuben Brower, "Reading in Slow Motion," in *In Defense of Reading*, ed. Brower and Richard Poirier (New York: Dutton, 1963), 19-20.

12. M. H. Abrams, "Literary Criticism in America: Some New Directions," in *Theories of Criticism: Essays in Literature and Art,* ed. Abrams and Jesse Ackerman (Washington, DC: Library of Congress, 1984), 29.

13. Paul de Man, "Symbolic Landscape in Wordsworth and Yeats," in Brower and Poirier, *In Defense of Reading,* 22-37.

14. Jerome J. McGann, *The Romantic Ideology: A Critical Investigation* (Chicago: Univ. of Chicago Press, 1983), 138, 145.

Materialities of Communication
Genre/Media

I begin by positioning myself within this colloquium on "Materialities of Communication." I use the term "positioning" to note the physical presence of the speaker's table and the obvious fact that now I am observed as yesterday I was an observer. Let us say that I am a conscious instrumentality of transmitting and receiving communications. I am prepared to accept the notion that I and each of us is a complex system, but clearly systems that are complexly intertwined with other systems.

One such intersection is with the persons and their papers and commentaries at the colloquium. My consciousness of "materialities" is shaped and defined by my cultural hypotheses as they diverge from or intersect with theirs. I see this paper as a proposal of an alternate view of systems from that proposed by Professor Luhmann, but I see both our papers as belonging to a class or genre in which the presentation of hypotheses, the description of data to support a hypothesis, aim to persuade listeners to accept the argument. I accept the claim that genre is a system and I use it to indicate that a system of writing can intersect with a system of nonverbal as well as verbal signs. I mean for this to be an open system.

Supposing we think not of a body but of a masculine and feminine body, would we be able to assume that the feminine body can produce another body without some type of intervention? And can we say that a similar process of copying or duplication takes place on the Xerox machine? Do we not refer to two different kinds of genres, and to talk of human reproduction and machine reproduction as similar is to imply either—as in La Mettrie's term— "man is a machine" or—in artificial intelligence terms—that machines can act

---

This paper is published here for the first time. It was delivered April 1987 to the colloquium "Materialities of Communication," University of Dubrovnik, Croatia.

as humans? *And yet,* we would wish to know the purpose or consequences of such comparison.

I position myself within this colloquium on "Materialities of Communication" by assuming that our inquiry has certain ends among which are the role of media in communication, the function of nonverbal elements such as rhythm, meter, music, of visual and bodily movements. Our inquiry also raises the question whether communication, if any, takes place and how we are to know that it has taken place. Perhaps we ought to inquire into the question of the persistence or direction of communicated "meanings" or "mismeanings." Such ends are posited for us in our thematic notes. Such ends are historical. They reveal a history of the body in the production of meaning, a history of the intersection of visual and verbal signs in painting, a history of visuality in tactile or architectural structures whether these visual products are on floors, walls, or ceilings. For this historical procedure no model has been presented. Nevertheless, the prospectus and the papers do indeed indicate the need to supplant a discourse theory with a theory that accounts for communicative factors other than discourse.

One such theory is a "genre" theory. This is a system of explanation which attends to the historical continuities and discontinuities within texts or events, indicating the interrelations of these with other systems within and outside the genre. If we consider tragedy a genre, then we can begin with *Oedipus Rex* by relating the chorus, for example, to early oral narratives. We can proceed to show the usefulness of such explanation by pointing to the shared features of this text with those of other texts. And, of course, no genre can be identified unless it is distinguished, as Aristotle does distinguish it, by comparing tragedy with another structure—the epic—that has numerous similarities with it, sufficient to make a distinction worthwhile. But genre, like all systems, has an end or ends. These are historical and they change as the nonshared elements of a genre become dominant and thus need to be distinguished from genres of which they were merely parts. I do not wish to go into the theoretical aspects of generic conflict or generic transformations, but I wish to note that Aristotle's use of genre served him to establish the basis for a model tragedy and to indicate why that kind of spectacle was important to the state. Need I add that he was cognizant of this genre as natural spectacle?

The other aspect of genre that is appropriate for our inquiry is that genre refers to texts or events that relate to one another. In this sense texts themselves become implicit explanatory mechanisms. They are not merely texts to be explained but are extensive explanations themselves. This is what Harold Bloom means when he states that texts resist other earlier texts.

It is not at all surprising that genre theory should sometimes be treated as mere classification, and that some critics should find it inappropriate for explaining literature or events. They can surely select a historical occasion like the English Renaissance or late nineteenth-century France to indicate its particular reference to genres as absolute categories. Take, for example, Derrida's essay "The Law of Genre." In it he assumes that genre is a fixed category that functions as a boundary-fixed group of texts. Or Foucault, in "The Discourse on Language," in which he argues that genre is no longer appropriate for contemporary discourse theory. It really does not matter that they prefer to construct nongeneric systems. What does matter is that in constructing such theories they are prepared to shift or enlarge the meaning of such terms as "text," "supplement," "discourse," but refuse to redefine other terms, including "genre."

Why should this be so? In Derrida's case, he uses the essay genre to deny the genre "essay." This is because the system he constructs can call into question texts that are bounded. But the term and system that I am proposing comes from a theory that has, in the Italian Renaissance, assumed that genre, any genre, is combinatory, combined with elements from different genres. Derrida's essay is notable, therefore, for positing an opposition to any genre, while offering as an alternative a theory which is generic in its constituents. Derrida seeks to illustrate the inevitable contradiction within language, but if we remove the names of kinds of writing, we are left with the term writing itself—and that then becomes a genre. The distinctions made within this genre become far fewer than those within less extensive categories. For such categories are not fixed; we can call Alexander Pope's *Essay on Criticism,* for example, a didactic poem, a critical text, a history of criticism, a poem in couplets, depending on the kind of system we are constructing. Genre in this usage is a group of poems each of which in some way redefines the class, crosses boundaries of other genres, and provides a basis for assessing historical continuity and change or change through continuity.

"Genre" is a contested concept in contemporary critical theory. If Derrida and Foucault are prepared to abandon it, to forget it, Bakhtin, Todorov, Jean-Marie Schaeffer seek to redefine its use. In Bakhtin's discussion of the novel, for example, he finds it composed of mixed and varied discourses, the term for which—translated into English—is "heteroglossia." He is prepared to see the historical changes that have taken place in the novel, and, indeed, other Russian formalists saw a value in the historical evaluation of generic changes. Among some contemporary Marxists—I refer to Fred Jameson and Franco Moretti—a genre theory marked by various boundary crossings is important in explaining various and subtle changes in literary history.

I take the aim of the genre theory I am offering as the most adequate procedure for explaining literary, artistic, and cultural change. Why one should wish to do this at this time and in this place is probably self-evident.

I now point to some of the features of genre that relate to issues that have arisen this week. Since genre can be understood as a historical system undergoing change, there are continuities between members of the genre though they are not always the same. Tragedy may be considered a reading text at one time and a performance at another, and the historian of genre will seek to explain the change in the "materialities" of this genre. But any tragedy will share either or both of these by continuing some elements of past tragedies. Genre makes it possible to see elements of past materialities manifest in the present. This is obvious in medieval paintings and medieval architecture which create a multiple sense of time consciousness in the present. Within a single genre we often find opposing contents—as failure novels and success novels. New genres arise and older genres are forgotten—as is the case of the novel or some medieval poetic forms. At this colloquium we have had contributions of painting genres that include texts and we could easily have had poetic genres that include music. Genres have tended to be hierarchical—the georgic poem and satire were dominant forms in the early eighteenth century, the novel in the nineteenth. But I do not wish in this lecture to develop a full-scale theory, only to indicate its relevance for historical interpretation and to explore its usefulness in at least one medium.

To make clear what such a theory might produce, I want to treat this colloquium as an example. Our meetings are referred to by the directors as a "colloquium." As a genre it belongs to those events in which the participants are both speakers and listeners. The genre of this particular colloquium is best identified with reference to its earlier versions. But this genre is part of a family of genres, such as conferences, seminars, and classes. Indeed, the IUC [Inter-University Centre, Dubrovnik] lists it among its classes. Thus the name of this even can be any one of these depending upon the system which one aims to explain. It is a conference if one wishes to note the printed papers that will follow from it; a seminar if one wishes to develop the faculty and student presentations; it is a class if one wishes to treat it as resulting in grades for students; it is a colloquium if one wishes to systematize the exploratory or inquiring aspect.

All of these will have filiations with whatever generic name we give it. If we seek the constituents of the genre, we can begin with its materialities. The colloquium is held in a seminar classroom in a graduate institution. The confined space relates it to the closed institutional spaces to be found in other classrooms. The colloquium is time-bound; it has a set duration as a whole and a somewhat set duration for papers and discussion on the days it meets. This procedure relates it to seminars just as the excursion relates the colloquium to tourist entertainment. It thus implies that the space in which it is held might be treated as foreign space. Thus the participants can be interpreted as involved in a social as well as educational function.

The participants are all university trained, some are teachers, others graduate students. In this particular colloquium we come from a wide variety of countries and converse in three different languages. We are thus distinguished from other colloquia by our subject, our representations, and our performances. The colloquium provides each of us with an alternative to other learning genres. It moves us outside our own classrooms; by the frequency and duration of the papers, we find our consciousness engaged by diverse lines of thought and our patience tried. These are palliated by the wit and wisdom of our directors, who find that they have continually to readjust a program that refuses to be fixed.

I put aside the discussion of papers in this description of a genre. But I wish to mention other materialities that are involved in this genre. As we sit, we observe nonverbal indications in the movements of our bodies, the clothes we wear, the ways we get and drink our coffee. We thus bring to this genre filiations from other behavior patterns; this genre is inevitably connected with other genres or rituals or frames in which we live. This genre, therefore, is defined by its other-generic affiliations, its boundary crossings, while at the same time generating shared experience and responses. This generic view indicates how each of us is shaped by the class experiences through which we have all been and how we process the information we receive. There is no simple way to determine what has been communicated, although through the question period some information is shared. But what about the nonverbal communication? Are we able to read contexts from different countries and their different behavior patterns?

When this colloquium concludes, we may then see this genre as a sublimely harmonious event or a rupture or an interference in terms of the genres by which we live or in which we normally participate. Seeing it in contrast to these other genres helps to define the change this one has provided—if it has.

I hope you will forgive the length of this discussion of our genre, but I have tried your patience in order to discuss a subject that began yesterday, namely the relation of genre to the media. Since Monica and Thomas and Peter initiated a rewarding discussion of TV and, indeed, urged it, I have decided to confine my remarks to television.

What might a generic approach to TV be? We might wish to note the history of the technology. (Here we might note that the technology for the visual transmission and reception of messages existed for military purposes before the content was found for commercial exploitation.) We might wish to inquire into the innovative genres that television developed. We might select existing forms and study what happened to them when absorbed by television. To begin with, we would distinguish the different aims of television stations by noting, for example, that in the United States there is commercial television, cable television, and public television. And although they share the same technology, they are organized in different ways. Commercial television is free but contains advertising, cable TV requires purchase, and public television is supported by donations from listeners, business patrons, and the government. By its structure, we recognize that we are dealing with an industry, not merely formal events. Within each of these there are sub-genres: the news broadcasts, serials (soaps) that carry on from week to week, miniseries (they carry on for several days), sports events, situation comedies, movies, made for TV movies, information programs about nature, science, and human beings, educational lectures, and numerous other such genres.

In terms of genre, we might begin by noticing that television reframes non-TV genres. Movies that were made with another technology for larger screens are either shown (whole) on cable TV or censored and interfered with by advertising on commercial TV. We can take for granted the distortion involved in placing a cinemascope film on the small screen. The ingestion of one genre by the other results in a revamping of the production and distribution of the absorbed genre. It results in films aimed for a special audience on the one hand and films that are experimentally and artistically produced by individuals. The process has positive and negative effects. It has resulted in the closing down of movie theaters all over the U.S. But in another sense the absorption of one genre into the technology of another supports a consciousness in which mergers and what are called "takeovers" in business are seen as positive acts benefitting the consumer.

If we take the subgenre of the newscast, we must compare it to another medium—the newspaper. The print media is visual and verbal; the newscast, visual and oral. The newscast is time-bound, not the newspaper. But the first page of the newspaper is marked by unfinished stories; it is discontinuous. It takes for granted visual fragmentation. Indeed, it should be noted that the news text has a history in print going back to ballads. The newscast is marked by what Raymond Williams has called a "flow" of time. But this is not merely pertinent to news. What is important for a generic study of the newscast is that it is presented by an anchorman or anchorwoman. Here is an innovative procedure. These are like the chief actors in a play and they are always identified by name or identify themselves. The news provides a body of visual information edited for the time slot and photographed to show limited aspects of a situation. The oral commentary indicates the line to be taken toward the visual material. In contrast to this, the print medium has come to include more and more editorializing in columns written by journalists on current events. The genre critic will seek to explore the impact of one medium upon another and conceive of these as competitors for an audience.

The audience or the observer can perhaps be considered in terms of actual sporting events. In these we are shown not only the event but the observers present at the event. Watching them watch the game, we as viewers find the observers to be things, anonymous masses that become part of the game. Is it useful to raise the question of reality when one has a representation? Would it not be simpler to study the kind of distortions involved in a particular televised game?

To exemplify this inquiry I ask you to consider the televising of a session of our colloquium. The likelihood would be that we would be more firmly time-bound than for this session. Where the cameras would be placed would indicate who is to be highlighted. The segment would require that more order be shown so that the speaker would not be interrupted and questions would be asked without intruding jokes, incidental remarks, or occasional interruptions of the speaker's role. We would find ourselves as performers. And when our live telecast was presented, what would precede or follow it? We would exist not as a generic colloquium with a past, but an isolated remnant of a genre. What would take place if the readings of the papers were properly recorded? Would we find that in our shrinkage we had lost the filiation that helped define our genre? Would we find that being absorbed by the screen in a visual and auditory technology, we had been deprived of the nonverbal world and had become mere verbal bodies? When this colloquium dissolves and becomes a part of history, we shall recognize that our example of the genre has also dissolved. Perhaps we shall then be aware that television in its various subgenres is also in the process of historical change and that, already, the educational lecture has begun to be replaced by a computer that talks to the viewer who is no longer passive. Genre theory helps us to see, define, describe, and cope with such transformations.

Genre Theory, Literary History, and Historical Change

In the last half of the twentieth century generic theory has reemerged as a critical force, in part owing to discussions of genre by Northrop Frye, R. S. Crane, and Rosalie Colie. More recent genre theory has reexamined the novel (Michael McKeon's *The Origins of the English Novel 1660-1740*), the essay (Alexander J. Butrym's *Essays on the Essay: Redefining the Genre*), the short story (Susan Lohafer and Jo Ellyn Clarey's *Short Story Theory at a Crossroads*), satire, elegy, lyric, tragedy, and others. New theories of genre had been advanced by Mikhail Bakhtin in his work on Dostoevsky and in translations of his essays entitled *The Dialogic Imagination* and *Speech Genres and Other Late Essays*. Richard Rorty has practiced genre criticism in an essay dealing with historical explanation in philosophy, "The Historiography of Philosophy: Four Genres." Alastair Fowler's *Kinds of Literature,* Adena Rosmarin's *The Power of Genre,* Arnold Krupat's *The Voice in the Margin: Native American Literature and the Canon,* and numerous feminist discussions of autobiography, journals, novels, memoirs, and other genres have offered examples of generic analysis dealing with theory and practice. So, too, Henry Louis Gates Jr., Houston Baker, Deborah McDowell, and other African American critics occasionally use generic analyses when they discuss the works of black authors. Marxist critics like Louis Althusser, Fredric Jameson, Franco Moretti, John Frow, and others use genre as a frame for relating literature to social formations.[1]

In their reemergence, genre criticism and theory have moved from assumptions of genres as fixed to genre as process of textual change. Indeed, the generic emphasis on change is introduced by examination of the varied texts

This essay was originally published in *Theoretical Issues in Literary History,* ed. David Perkins, Harvard English Studies 16 (Cambridge, MA: Harvard Univ. Press, 1991), 85-113. Copyright 1991 by the President and Fellows of Harvard College and reprinted with permission of the publisher.

that compose a single genre, the drafts that lead to a published text that is a member of a genre, and by the ideological implications that result from different genres that combine, contrast, challenge, and oppose one another. The processes of generic change are locatable not merely within written genres but between written and oral genres, verbal and nonverbal genres (art, music, architecture). A definition of genre by a film theorist, Rick Altman, can perhaps provide a beginning for understanding these processes:

> In assessing theories of genre, critics have often labeled them according to a particular theory's most salient features or the type of activity to which it devotes its most concentrated attention. Paul Hernadi, for example, recognizes four general classes of genre theory: expressive, pragmatic, structural, and mimetic. In his extremely influential introduction to *The Fantastic*, Tzvetan Todorov opposes historical to theoretical genres, as well as elementary genres to their complex counterparts. Others, like Fredric Jameson, have followed French semiotics in distinguishing between semantic and syntactic approaches to the genre. While there is anything but general agreement on the exact frontier separating semantic from syntactic views, we can as a whole distinguish between generic definitions which depend on a list of common traits, attitudes, characters, shots, locations, sets, and the like—thus stressing the semantic elements which make up the genre—and definitions which play up instead certain constitutive relationships between undesignated and variable placeholders—relationships which might be called the genre's fundamental syntax. The semantic approach thus stresses the genre's building blocks, while the syntactic view privileges the structures into which they are arranged.[2]

Such a theory attends to the introduction and change of basic semantic elements, for example, from opera to swing and from folk music to rock. Altman points to the changing relationship between the construction of a film and its implications for viewers of particular communities. In their theories of genre the historian and the theorist are at one in analyzing the "semantic elements and syntactic bonds."

This tentative definition relates constituents of a film to the aim or aims of a generic structure. A further discussion of genre would plot the changes resulting from adding, subtracting, or renaming constituents or ends. For example, the novel develops by drawing upon constituents from eighteenth-century genres such as chapbook narratives, newspapers, religious autobiographies, confessions, histories, and romances. The aims of this genre have been amply discussed and critics have demonstrated the significance of genre study in charting this change in literary history.[3] I note parenthetically that technological inventions such as printing, engraving, and photography can help initiate new genres and alter old ones.

Once a new way of writing produces several examples, a basis exists for writers to identify it further by imitation and for critics by naming and analyzing it. This is done by distinguishing this kind of writing from those from which it has drawn constituents that have combined into a distinct identity or genre. Until some agreements exist about a genre's distinctness, its identity remains in doubt and its denomination puzzling, for example, *Finnegans Wake*. Even when some agreement exists, no text is free from the possibility that it can belong to more than one genre. Members of a genre add, vary, modify, or abandon constituents so that the genre is modified by additional instances. This is especially apparent in the oppositional writings of feminists, Marxists, and African Americans who deliberately seek to oppose patriarchal, bourgeois, or white writings in order to reform the genre system without abandoning a theory of genres.

Altman's theory about writing a history of the American musical emphasizes the shuttling or changes of constituents among the examples of such films, although his reliance upon formal features limits the range of his prospective definition. But he does realize that film genres can become stabilized for economic and other reasons, and that such genres become governed by predictable formulas. This is the case with written texts as well; the modern romance can of course become governed by a conventionalized relation between constituents and aims. But it is also possible that some romances can initiate significant changes.

Critics and theorists such as Northrop Frye, Alastair Fowler, Rosalie Colie, and Barbara Lewalski have demonstrated that debates about the fixity of literary genre classifications took place in the Renaissance. But it is only recently that genre has been recognized as revealing a historical process that provides a valuable, practical, and theoretical understanding of the changes, gaps, incompletions, and transformations that take place in the writing of literary history and other histories.[4] I wish in this essay to analyze how some contemporary critics and theorists explain change, continuity, and difference in generic discourses used in the history of philosophy, in the history of ideas, in literary history. Such critics do not uniformly agree on the operation of genres, but they take it for granted in analyzing change.

A genre theory about the writing of history, history of philosophy, or literary history must confront at the very least the question whether genre is discipline-controlled or nation-controlled or both. Is a history of philosophy a history of philosophical problems in Greek, French, German, and English philosophy? If a history of philosophy is situation-based, do the problems change when considered in different language communities? Since medieval romance crosses territorial boundaries and several languages whereas modern romances in English are confined to Britain and the United States, does the romance genre remain historically situated or does it shift when the reading community shifts? These questions only begin to touch the function of genre in literary history; genres are cultural formations and their relation to cultural forces should perhaps begin with an inquiry into their critical and theoretical reemergence.

Why at this time have generic theories once again become important? In recent years a huge number of little known texts written by women, by African Americans, and other minorities have been recovered. They reveal the inadequate "data bases" for constructing genres in the past. We now know that critics and theorists have disregarded texts such as slave narratives, domestic journals, feminist autobiographies, and confessions and kept them outside the range of literary study. Such genres did not fit a conception of education aimed at preparing white males for advancing in social and economic hierarchies. The need now is to educate people to understand that received genres, the so-called mass culture genres such as Westerns and detective stories and new ones such as advertising or television sitcoms, affect their thinking, feeling, and knowledge. Reemergence of genre criticism and theory results from the need for feminist and African American and sympathetic critics to demonstrate the prejudices hidden or obvious in received texts. Such critics undermine the assumptions of objectivity of received critical and theoretical genres. Moreover, writings that deal with interrelations between literary and nonliterary genres or between genres of different disciplines—literary history and art history, literary criticism and psychoanalytical criticism and practice—have led critics and theorists to a reconsideration of genre as a unified kind.

There are other more general reasons for studying the generic history of past writings. A generic history involves the study of genres that include and exclude constituents; but it also involves the inclusion and exclusion of genres themselves. In this respect it makes readers conscious of the functions of repression and renewal in our society. A generic history stresses both the need for classification and the need to realize the limits of any monolithic classification. Classifications are multidimensional; thus every text within a genre can also be a member of another genre. This in no way denies identity to a genre or a text within a genre. It means that such identity requires for its analysis a knowledge of a generic past and its distinction from related coexistent genres. Such analyses are characterized in contemporary critical discourse by such terms as "appropriation," "dominance," "power," "ideology," "politics." The reemergence of genre criticism and theory thus corresponds to the multifaceted study of identity as a social process. That different readers may disagree about a text's genre is neither contradictory nor surprising. It merely indicates that a genre is combinatory, not monolithic.

Terms like "tradition," "discipline," "subject," "self-awareness" direct the inquiries of genre criticism to the constituents of a text and their multiple relations to political and social aims. The genre criticism I describe, therefore, focuses upon problems of change: in studying the genre of tragedy it seeks to explain the changes in characters, class, economic authority, and oppositional status, from *The Merchant of Venice* to *The London Merchant*, from period texts identified as modernist to those identified as postmodernist. In such cases genre critics self-consciously question their own practices with a view to recasting them. When ballads become part of another genre called ballad opera, what consequences ensue? What literary and social practices are altered? And for what end?

Genre criticism, as I propose it, challenges the received view of historical change. Change remains problematic because we are only beginning to recognize the importance of genre theory in formulating its problems. Genre theory provides formulations for change by stipulating constituents of a text within a genre. Thus it becomes possible to note the particulars of a change and what these imply in relation to aims. Moreover, by recognizing the interrelation of texts from different genres, one can note the shifting directions of texts. This is the case when feminists introduce autobiographical discourses into theoretical discussions, thus removing claims made about objectivity. Genres indicate change when they more up or down the hierarchy of genres. They indicate change when they keep the terms of discourse but change the meaning of the terms. Generic boundaries change when diverse genres such as songs, narratives, critical essays become collected in a genre like the miscellany or periodical paper or magazine, and the generic constituents are changed by further inclusion. I want to argue that genre theory becomes the enabling basis for discussing any part-whole relationship.

Semioticians like Maria Corti and Yuri Lotman think of genre as a cultural classification system in which all written texts form part of one or more genre systems, and that these help construct the large system which shapes, characterizes, and defines a culture. My essay is much more restricted. Part I offers examples of genre constructions of the history of philosophy and intellectual history. Part II poses some new alternatives to the generic procedures offered in part I. Part III discusses cultural change in oppositional literary genres.

I

In his essay "The Historiography of Philosophy: Four Genres," Richard Rorty offers a generic approach to the writing of the history of philosophy as discipline-bound.[5] He begins with the genres "rational reconstruction," "historical reconstruction," *Geistesgeschichte,* and doxography. Each of these has its characteristic aims and procedures. Rorty discusses each genre in terms of the practices that have specific effects upon the modern reader. He writes: "The main reason we want historical knowledge of what ... dead philosophers and scientists would have said to each other is that it helps us to recognize that there have been different forms of intellectual life than ours" (51). As the result of recognizing what is necessary and what merely contingent and dependent on our own arrangements, we as readers have a key to self-awareness. We want also to assure ourselves "that there has been rational progress in the course of recorded history—that we differ from our ancestors on grounds which our ancestors could be led to accept" (51). Rational reconstruction, historical reconstruction, and *Geistesgeschichte* have their self-justifications; doxography, according to Rorty, has no such justification, since it assumes that all great philosophers in a history of philosophy were addressing "continuing concerns."

In describing the task of rational reconstruction, historical reconstruction, and *Geistesgeschichte*—as analysis of a past problem in philosophy, as a construction of the historical environment that made such problems possible, and as a study of the history of an idea or ideas as developed by Wilhelm Dilthey and A. O. Lovejoy—Rorty identifies a philosophical genre by a dominant subject matter. It is important to note that Rorty's view of genre does not rest on a body of constituents that undergo change. Genres are discussed as confined to particular tasks and such tasks are treated as though they remain the same. Still, Rorty's procedure is comparative and underlines the way in which histories of philosophy differ from histories of science. In this respect his historical genres quite rightly demonstrate that histories of philosophy require for their practice a comparison with other kinds of historical genres.

Genres are constructions and constructions operate with and against each other. Genres help define each other; they serve Rorty to demonstrate that genres of the history of philosophy are pertinent to establishing our self-awareness. But we must not assume that all genres of the history of philosophy are useful. Doxography, which refers in Rorty's context to the praise of philosophical orthodoxies and illustrates his ironic attitude to them, becomes divorced from an analysis of philosophical problems in terms of current issues.[6] Rorty urges its abandonment because such histories "impose a problematic on a canon drawn up without reference to that problematic, or, conversely, . . . impose a canon on a problematic constructed without reference to that canon" (62). Such histories lack self-justification and the self-awareness such justification produces. A generic text, then, can be identified as adequate or inadequate in relation to its aims and practices.

Rorty writes of the three usable genres that "any given book in the history of philosophy will, of course, be a mixture of these three genres. But usually one or another motive dominates, since there are three distinct tasks to be performed. The distinctness of these tasks is important and not to be broken down" (68). Nevertheless, each genre can include elements of the others. Such intertextuality leads Rorty to posit the notion of a dominant generic motive—each genre is identified by a dominant motive governed by its aim. Each genre gives rigor to one or more of the others by "keeping in mind the possibility that our self-justifying conversation is with creatures of our own phantasy rather than with historical personages" (71).

Rorty does not, however, inquire into the generic problem posed by identifying Descartes's *Meditations* with religious and poetic meditations. Does the book belong to two genres? It could not in Rorty's system. It may, however, fall within a new useful genre which Rorty names "intellectual history."

> I should like to use the term "intellectual history" for a much richer and more diffuse genre—one which falls outside this triad [rational reconstruction, historical reconstruction, and *Geistesgeschichte*]. In my sense, intellectual history consists of descriptions of what the intellectuals were up to at a given time, and of their interaction with the rest of society—descriptions which, for the most part, bracket the question of what activities which intellectuals were conducting. Intellectual history can ignore certain problems which must be settled in order to write the history of a discipline—questions about which people count as scientists, which as poets, which as philosophers, etc. Descriptions of the sort I have in mind may occur in treatises called something like "Intellectual life in fifteenth-century Bologna," but they may

also occur in the odd chapter or paragraph of political or social or economic or diplomatic histories, or indeed in the odd chapter or paragraph of histories of philosophy (of any of the four genres distinguished above). Such treatises, chapters, and paragraphs produce, when read and pondered by someone interested in a certain spatio-temporal region, a sense of what it was like to be an intellectual in that region—what sort of books one read, what sorts of things one had to worry about, what choices one had of vocabularies, hopes, friends, enemies, and careers. (68)

This genre opens philosophy to nondisciplinary analyses and inquiries about the moral tendencies of intellectual life. It revises the notion that history of philosophy must be confined to purely philosophical texts. It provides, therefore, a puzzling problem in the practice of the history of philosophy. It suggests that the very discipline of philosophy needs to be refigured, that the practice of this genre can lead to a reconception of the discipline to which it refers.

Rorty's essay points to several pertinent generic problems: one is that his useful genres are necessary to define each other and to provide a comprehensive history of philosophy. The second is that though each genre is self-contained, it nevertheless includes intrusions from related genres. The third is that some genres need to be abandoned because they cease to function effectively. Rorty writes about a single discipline and implies that its useful genres are discipline-determined, are ways of formulating the tasks that characterize the history of philosophy.

But the genre of intellectual history is not discipline-determined. Rather, in Rorty's terms it "is the raw material for the historiography of philosophy—or, to vary the metaphor, the ground out of which histories of philosophy grow" (70). It serves as ground for the other three useful genres and at the same time is equal to them because it plays "the same dialectical role with respect to *Geistesgeschichte* as historical reconstruction plays to rational reconstruction" (71). Rorty's intellectual history is thus a genre that applies to history of society or literature as well as to history of philosophy, and thus is not discipline-determined; it can, however, also be considered discipline-determined in relation to *Geistesgeschichte*. "Intellectual history," in Rorty's explanation, functions as a ground for his genres in the history of philosophy and is, itself, one of these genres. It thus undermines the rigidity and self-containedness that Rorty attributed to his useful genres. Several points should be made about the consequences of his use of intellectual history as a genre. The first is that as a "diffuse" genre, it indicates that genres can be more or less diffuse, can contain few or many constituents. Genre can, as intellectual history does, call a "discipline" into question; it can undermine the assumptions that govern philosophy. Genres can function as ground and as constructs derived from the ground. If this creates a conceptual problem concerning genre as process and product, it also raises questions about how to define the task of a genre.

Rorty's intellectual history crosses disciplinary lines and calls into question the discipline-determined history that his essay assumes. But some of the generic difficulties that intellectual history raises for him are also discoverable in the uses that the historian Donald R. Kelley makes of this genre. He treats it as a revision and extension of Lovejoy's "history of ideas":

> In the first place, I think, the history of ideas should represent itself as (according to recent convention) "intellectual history," if only to lay to rest the ghosts of antiquated idealism and to set aside, at least for historical purposes, the imperialist aspirations and invidious claims of philosophy to be a "rigorous science" (in the phrase of Husserl). Intellectual history is not "doing philosophy" (any more than it is doing literary criticism) retrospectively; it is doing a kind, or several kinds, of historical interpretation, in which philosophy and literature figure not as controlling methods but as human creations suggesting the conditions of historical understanding.[7]

For Kelley, intellectual history is a genre or group of genres that "suggest" the conditions of historical understanding, not a genre that studies social or political history. Since Kelley is discussing history, he denies that either philosophy or literature controls intellectual history. The kinds of interpretations that intellectual history produces merely rely upon philosophy and literature to suggest the conditions of historical interpretations. But whereas Rorty discusses the tasks of the kinds or genres of interpretation, Kelley is intent on tracing the transition from a history of ideas to intellectual history. What he undertakes is an explanation of generic change: the transformation of history of ideas. This transformation results from a criticism of Lovejoy's idealism and an extension of what he preached rather than practiced. Kelley writes that Lovejoy attended

> not only to concepts and rational arguments but also to the other layers of linguistic meaning—and indeed this is the justification for applying to the rhetorical as well as to philosophical traditions in historical interpreta-

tion, since rhetoric, and its extensions in modern literary criticism, reveals the resources, structures, and perhaps cultural memories preserved by language (topoi, tropes, metaphors, constructions, analogies, connections, etc.), popular as well as literary, beyond, or beneath, the reaches of logical formulation, or at least of narrowly rational argument and "reasoned history." (20)

Lovejoy's history of ideas was a study of change that included varied kinds of philosophical and literary discourses, interpretations of elite and nonelite views of the past. But it neglected any study of the genres with which it dealt. The history of the great chain of being can be found as a topos in philosophical treatises, novels, poems, dramas, but Lovejoy does not consider how sermons, lyrics, tragedies, for example, affected the interpretation. Kelley recognizes that intellectual history includes the use of history of philosophy and literary-critical analyses, but he contrasts the practice of this history not with that of history of science or architecture, but with theory of history: "Intellectual history has its own aims, values, and questions to pose about the human condition; and these cannot ultimately be honored and pursued on the level of theory, which, distracted by the conversations of neighboring disciplines, tends to neglect the practical problems of its own historical craft" (24-25).

It is one of the puzzling problems in analyzing the writing of a genre such as intellectual history that thoughtful and careful writers such as Rorty and Kelley insist on making temporary into permanent stability. Although both writers are cognizant of generic boundary crossings, they avoid any generic theory that can buttress the practices they describe.

Without attempting to offer such a theory here, I suggest that a genre theory can deal with temporary stability. To begin with, a genre requires a group of texts that have some trait in common at any one time so that they can be distinguished from other groups. A genre cannot be defined by its own terms. It needs at least one other genre from which it can be distinguished. Call a genre a family of texts, a communal group of texts, a consortium of texts. Whatever they are called, such texts are dynamic. Their semantic elements are *intra*-active within the genre and *inter*active with members of other genres. Genres can be broad or narrow; they can distinguish literary from nonliterary texts, and parody from irony. When Aristotle distinguished tragedy from epic or when critics distinguish the medieval mystery play from the morality play they indicate the presence of some generic repertoire. Moreover, genre is historical in that its texts exist over time, no matter how short. The stability of a genre is always tentative because different instances or examples within a genre can alter its aim. Thus the novel, for example, has one type of semantic-syntactic construction in *Joseph Andrews* and another in *Pride and Prejudice.*

I mention these practices of genre to stress that genre members, that is, individual texts in a genre, cannot be identical and that subgenres are initiated or combined to tie groups of texts more closely together to achieve more precise stability. Thus tragedy includes tragicomedy or domestic tragedy. The genre "history" in the seventeenth century is distinguished from types of romance. In the eighteenth century the terms "life history," "biography," and "confession" become connected with the novel.

II

The introduction of a genre like intellectual history is obviously combinatorial—a combination of varied discourses that cross generic boundaries. It is an ad hoc effort to make historical writing pertinent to the aims with which we identify our lives. But the combinatorial relations are evident not merely in constructions of "intellectual history" but in the multiple discourses of all writing and speaking, and in the varied contexts of socialization that characterize human experience—no identity without some difference, no change without some continuity. These clichés need to be replaced by what might be called a combinatory consciousness—a theory of genre in which identity is not unity but groups of constituents that can reject unity or coherence as readily as affirm it.

Italo Calvino in *Six Memos for the Next Millennium* offers a statement of the combinatory situation as an aspect of human experience:

> I have come to the end of this apologia for the novel as a vast net. Someone might object that the more the work tends toward the multiplication of possibilities, the further it departs from that unicum which is the *self* of the writer, his inner sincerity and the discovery of his own truth. But I would answer: Who are we, who is each one of us, if not a combinatoria of experiences, information, books we have read, things imagined? Each life is an encyclopedia, a library, an inventory of objects, a series of styles, and everything can be constantly shuffled and reordered in every way conceivable.[8]

Novels are combinations of varied features that include "a multiplicity of subjects, voices, and views of the world, on the model of what Mikhail Bakhtin has called 'dialogic' or 'polyphonic' or 'carnivalesque,' tracing its antecedents from Plato through Rabelais to Dostoevsky" (117). Calvino notes that novels like Robert Musil's *The Man without Qualities* seek to include all possible relations and thus remain incomplete by their very nature. And he refers to another type of novel that corresponds to "what in philosophy is nonsystematic thought, which proceeds by aphorisms, by sudden, discontinuous flashes of light" (118). These varied genres of the novel are for him instances of combinations that lead the reader to possibilities beyond the text. One might say of genre that its aim ought to be, in Calvino's view, to move beyond known relationships, to move beyond any established boundary to the challenge of the unknown.

The very notion that "everything can be constantly shuffled and reordered in every way conceivable" would seem to argue for far more fluidity than a genre theory can accommodate. But Calvino's image of selves as combinatoria of experiences indicates that this genre is constructed by relations within its encyclopedia and by its interrelation with other genres at any one time.

Calvino makes reference to Bakhtin's genre theory of multiple discourses in the novel. Such discourses are examples of the different levels within a novel and of the contradictory ideologies that result from them. It is important to note, too, that Calvino's description of contemporary identity is exactly that. Implicit in his description is a historical dimension of what a life was and what it is. Genre makes it possible to contrast what representations of a society were and what they are. But it also indicates that members of the genre novel, for example, can be defined at the same time in terms of national identity in one society and in terms of generic change that crosses national boundaries.

Every boundary crossing inevitably substitutes another boundary. The issue is whether the premise of combinatorial genres offers a more comprehensive explanation than the addition of a genre such as "intellectual history." An example of a combinatorial genre that supports Calvino's views is Hélène Cixous's essay "From the Scene of the Unconscious to the Scene of History," for it is an autobiographical essay and a study of generic differentiation in the writing of her fiction and drama. The essay is not written as a theoretical inquiry into genre or literary history; it is a description of two kinds of writing which she has practiced. But it posits a conception of genre that is based on her combinatory experiences as a woman. Her fictions are controlled by her feminine absorption of language, rhythms, family, and historical experiences.

Her writing of drama, however, is different in kind because it depends upon actors—male and female—to complete her play.

What she implies is that her fictions are so controlled by her personal experience in writing that they cannot be generalized, whereas her dramas are collaborative, requiring men and women to complete them. Her essay suggests the possibility that genre can be understood in terms of subjectivity and otherness. Genres thus become forms of otherness in which constituents of prior texts—dialogue, bodily representations, scene, and characters—intrude upon the writer's subjectivity and invoke collaboration with others. In this respect genre would explain why some writers like Joyce experiment with many genres and others, like Cixous, restrict themselves to very few. Since such generic limitations occur in writers living at the same time, it is apparent that generic selection becomes an act of mediating between one's self-awareness and the historical otherness that one wishes to resist, affirm, transform, or explore. Here is Cixous:

> I have never dared create a real male character in fiction. Why? Because I write with the body, and I am a woman, and a man is a man, and I know nothing of his *jouissance*. And a man without body and without pleasure, I can't do that. So what about men in drama?
>
> The theater is not the scene of sexual pleasure. Romeo and Juliet love each other but do not make love. They sing love. In the theater it's the heart that sings, the breast that opens up, one sees the heart rend. The human heart has no sex. The heart feels in the same way in a man's breast as in a woman's. That does not mean that characters are demi-creatures who stop at the belt. No, our creatures lack nothing, not penises, not breasts, not kidneys, not bellies. But I don't have to write all that. The actor, the actress give us the whole body that we don't have to invent. And everything is lived and everything is true. This is the present that theater makes to the author: incarnation. It permits the male author to create women who will not be feigned, and the woman author is granted the chance to create perfectly constituted men! . . .
>
> The discovery of theatrical time is essential for someone who, like me, has written fiction during a long period of time. My texts are tapestries, and they weave themselves in a horizontal manner: what is given to these texts is the chance to take their time to make sense, and sometimes to send meaning quite far off in an afterthought. The Book has all its time and even eternity. The reader can drop the book, come back to it, close it forever, read it in one night or in a year, there is an absolute liberty which is also a limit, in the reading of the text.

> In the theater, impossible. Drama writes itself out in a "vertical" manner. Enter Hamlet: and you don't have a minute, you have ten seconds, thirty seconds for everything to write itself out and make itself understood. The theater is impatience. The theater shouts: Hurry! Hurry. Shakespeare's plays are so great because they are carried away by impatience. Cleopatra is impatience incarnated. . . .
>
> The theater is an eternal yet extremely mortal genre. Those who live it know that it is *going to end*. One lives its life, its death immediately. Passion and ethics come from this. The author also must accept his mortality, more than ever, in several ways. First, the author encounters his limits: he is not God, he is only a demigod. That means that he writes a demi-oeuvre. He writes something and then he awaits his other as a soul awaits its body. He waits for the other part of the theater to come to him, the part that will be given by the actors.[9]

In this passage, Cixous begins with an autobiographical statement of how she writes and what her exclusions are. She then goes on to make generalizations about theatrical performance, and establishes a philosophical distinction between fictional time and dramatic time. Her fictional writing becomes "horizontal." It is linear and leisurely. To this she opposes her "vertical" writing: abrupt, imperative, hasty, bustling. The last section is in the third person, a statement about the ontology of theatrical performance.

Cixous's description of the differences between the two genres is personal not theoretical: "in the domain of women nothing can be theorized" (11). But it does represent an analysis of two genres that can apply to Lispector and other women writers. One view of drama and fiction is that these can be divided into more specific genres such as comedy and tragedy, epic and novel, these into still more refined genres (or subgenres) like tragicomedy or domestic tragedy. Cixous is not interested in charting the relation between the frequent social changes and generic transformations. Her concern is with the relation of her female subjectivity as it requires or denies the need of collaborators for artistic (generic) expression. Fiction for her derives from her womanly self, but drama means giving birth to the other—to men and history. In the theater, "the actor, the actress give us the whole body that we don't have to invent."

In her play about Cambodia, she writes about others than herself who are of herself: "Because it is not me, because it is me, because it is the world different from myself that teaches me myself, my difference, that makes me feel my/its difference" (17). The two genres of fiction and drama become forms of self-exploration. But not only of self-exploration. For the writing about Cambodia makes it possible to realize that there are forces of religion that resist history's capture of the self despite life in refugee camps and in exile where the children "who were born in the camps and have never known anything but the fences of the camp, learn eternal dance" (17).

I began by noting the reemergence of genre theory in recent times and provided literary and social reasons for this generic change. I offered a tentative definition of genre as used in film criticism, indicating its relation to literary study, especially to historical study. I then indicated the social formations involved in genre and their relation to historical change. And to illustrate the extensive use of genre theory, I used one example from the history of philosophy and another from the history of ideas. In both examples I sought to inquire into generic explanations of change in a genre called "intellectual history" that was employed by both writers. Here I argued that the two versions of a genre raised questions that a comprehensive genre theory would have to answer. I then offered my suggestions for a comprehensive literary history based on genres and used examples from Calvino's criticism to support my combinatorial theory. Last, I used Cixous's explanation of two genres to illustrate the innovative possibilities of a combinatorial history. My aims have been to demonstrate the inevitability of some type of generic distinctions in the writing of history and to examine some representative generic practices as they enhance or ignore our understanding of historical change.

Genre criticism and theory undergo change in terms of their aims and practices. But all generic practices deal with wholes, with entities, and genre thus remains a basis for analyzing identities and differences. Entities, after all, need not be unified or centered or fixed. (I use the term "entity" to avoid the holism implicit in the term "wholes.") Critics who seek specificity, but claim that they do not find it in genre criticism rely on conceptions of genre that are no longer practiced or defended. If one considers the current practices I have described, then it is apparent that genres are collections of texts each of which has specificities that relate it intertextually to other genres.

Cixous's text is both private and public. Fiction written from the gendered body and drama written from this same body do not produce the same effects. Drama requires other bodies to fulfill it and thus leads to a different kind of fulfillment for the writer, the actor, and the audience. Genre practice, therefore, can be related to the self and to combinations that relate history to conscious and unconscious constituents of autobiography and criticism.

III

Combinations in no way imply harmony. The constituents of a genre can come in conflict, as Hamlet's discourse of revenge conflicts with his later discourse of peace and fate. Such clashes are only one of the generic interrelations that can occur in a text. One can observe the elevation or domination of one genre by another when, for example, ballads become part of the ballad opera or when, in *A Portrait of the Artist*, a dialogue on aesthetics provides the grounds for understanding the narrative structure.

If we grant that a genre is a construction by writer and reader, then it follows that readers interpret the genre differently at the same time or at different times. What genre theory contributes to this phenomenon in literary history is that at any one time in any one country there are genres that have longer durability than others and that prevent any chronological period from being generically unified.

The genre of literary history is an embracing name for those genres that construct approaches to works identified as literary, whatever "literary" may include at any particular time. A "history" includes many ways of thinking about the past outlined in my discussion of Rorty's and Kelley's essays. But I should note that Rorty's rejection of the historical genre he calls doxography indicates that one can be against certain kinds of historical genres. I wish in this section to concentrate on those genres of literary history that can be identified as oppositional. That is, they work within the framework of received genres, but invert the constituents and the aims.

Before turning to such oppositional genres, however, I wish briefly to comment on one type of generic histories, namely, histories of a genre like the elegy, satire, novel, criticism. Such histories assume that the genre's constituents and aims change over time. But such changes are always contingent on some constituents remaining unchanged. This conception of genre is governed by Wittgenstein's family resemblance hypothesis or by the assumed contractual relation between writer and reader. This history is often challenged on the ground that a genre like "romance" or "novel" has no continuity other than the name. One reply to this criticism occurs in Jean Radford's introduction to her volume *The Progress of Romance*. She writes: "In so far as genres are contracts between a writer and his/her readers, these contracts, and the conventions which go with them, obviously differ according to the conditions of class, ideology and literacy in different social formations."[10] Radford is fully aware of Raymond Williams's claim that genres such as "tragedy" have no historical relations other than the name. She defends the validity of "romance" as a generically pertinent inquiry by arguing that historical transformations provide an understanding of the interaction between literary and social history. Such transformations, when theorized, provide the continuity that Williams denies.

> These theoretical arguments about the continuities or discontinuities of romance or tragedy (indeed of history itself) are necessary but not perhaps sufficient. It is in the detailed historical accounts of the *transformations* of codes and conventions that these questions will be clarified. For if generic forms are, as I argued earlier, signals in a *social* contract between writers and readers, changes in these conventions will be regulated by transformations at other levels of social relationships. Thus for cultural historians, the study of genres may provide a mediation between literary history and social history—one which enables us to break out of the "splendid isolation" in which traditional histories of literature are confined.
>
> Put another way, to see modern romances as genealogical upstarts, or the bastardised offspring of originally noble forbears, is to reproduce a fantasy of the decline-and-fall type, but does *not* help to explain the evolution of cultural forms. But we can instead ask why the romance has moved from being about a male subject to being about a feminine one; or in what way the tests and trials faced by the hero of medieval romance differ from the obstacles and trials through which the heroine of contemporary romance must typically pass to achieve her object; or how it is that the "magic" which in earlier romances rescues the hero from false Grails becomes in *Jane Eyre* a supernatural voice which unites her with her "true" destiny; and why that magic/supernatural/Providential force is in today's romance represented as coming from *within:* as the magic and omnipotent power of sexual desire. A structural and semantic reading of these changing codes necessarily engages with questions of gender, ideology and change. (9-10)

Radford states that changes in the individual examples of a genre "regulated by transformations at other levels of social relationships" lead her to look to the writings of cultural historians for whom "the study of genres may provide a mediation between literary history and social history—one which enables us to break out of the 'splendid isolation' in which traditional histories of literature are confined." Radford's point is that the two genres, literary history and intellectual history, are, in respect to dealing with popular and canonical texts as transformations, intertwined. Each prioritizes its own discipline and thus can be named as belonging to either genre. It is with particular jointures such as these that an interdisciplinary genre develops. Radford's generic procedures constitute a challenge to Kelley's insistence that intellectual history confronts historical, not literary problems. The problems that Radford poses are indeed historical problems, but they are also literary.

Radford notes that since generic forms are "signals in a *social* contract between writers and readers, changes in these conventions will be regulated by transformations at other levels of social relationships." Other Marxists have found genre theory immensely useful in drawing attention to changes in the constituents of literary forms. They convert the Wordsworthian premise of a contract between author and reader, in which the author agrees to answer given expectations of a form, to a "social" contract governed by class or by a relation between producer and consumer. The contract theory is generic because it claims that readers of a particular genre assume that a novel or poem that they are reading will resemble previous instances of the genre. But such views of reader-text relationships tend to refer to texts of the same time; they have little support in assuming that the text of a medieval romance creates contractual relations for a Barbara Cartland romance. Radford is aware of this; still, she overlooks the difficulties in a generic hypothesis based on the contractual metaphor. Her reliance on textual transformations, however, shows genre as a dynamic and changing phenomenon.

Obviously, texts conceal as well as reveal to readers aspects relevant to their constituents or aims. These may be ideological exclusions governed by class or social prejudice or some larger category such as "late capitalism." Such exclusions are deconstructed or exposed in other genres that focus upon the concealed constituents. The literary history of a genre like romance draws attention to its status as a high literary form at one time and as an object of mass cultural consumption at another. These shifts in social level are interwoven with changes in what is called literature, in the audiences to which works are addressed, and in the aims of such writing.

This phenomenon of change in an oppositional genre is apparent in the history of feminist autobiography. Sidonie Smith, in *A Poetics of Women's Autobiography,* argues for generic practices that refigure patriarchal autobiography. She finds that the feminist autobiographer needs "to liberate herself from the ideology of traditional autobiography and to liberate autobiography from the ideology of essentialist selfhood through which it has historically been constituted."[11] If feminists are to write their own autobiographies rather than try to fit them to the male-dominated genre, they must write against the genre "by shifting generic boundaries so that there is neither margin nor center. For as she [the autobiographer] experiments with alternative languages of self and storytelling, she testifies to the collapse of the myth of presence with its conviction of a unitary self" (59).

Smith indicts the autobiographical genre for its construction of male boundaries, and her revisionary procedure is to recast the constituents of the genre so that they become decentered, fragmentary, polyphonic, and feminine. This imaginative vision rests on the transformation of some of the constituents of the genre. Smith reconstitutes the features of the genre in order to have it represent the pursuit of the female autobiographer's own desires. Her aim is to shatter the portrait of herself she sees hanging in the textual frames of patriarchy, and to create the conscious and unconscious of her sex by claiming the legitimacy and authority of another subjectivity. With that subjectivity, says Smith, may come a new "system of values, a new kind of language and narrative form, perhaps even a new discourse, an alternative to the ideology of gender." One hopes that this is the case, but one misses the procedures that would, as in the work of Radford, provide a theory of transformation leading to a new system of values, language, discourse, and genre. This view of the future history of a genre is an expression of utopian desire. It should be contrasted with other feminist views of autobiography that focus on the historicity of generic change. For example, Rita Felski writes:

> The autobiographical writing inspired by the women's movement differs, however, from the traditional autobiography of bourgeois individualism, which presents itself as the record of an unusual but exemplary life. Precisely because of this uniqueness, the eighteenth-century autobiography claims a universal significance. Feminist confession, by contrast, is less concerned with unique individuality or notions of essential humanity than with delineating the specific problems and experiences which bind women together. It thus tends to emphasize the ordinary events of a protagonist's life, their typicality in relation to a notion of communal identity.[12]

Felski shares with Smith the need for a different language and prefers the name "confession" to that of autobiography. She does so because she wishes to stress the historical differences she attributes to feminist genres. Felski is aware that in the writing of confessions women do not abandon all the constituents of a genre that men use, but they combine them to express the notion of communal identity.

I do not wish to discuss the agreements or disagreements that occur among feminist critics and between feminist and nonfeminist critics. Rather

I wish to note that feminists engage in refiguring autobiography as a genre. Such refiguring is connected with inquiries into "communal identity" through combinatory events and discourses.

This type of generic history plays a minor role, if any, in literary histories of a period or some other slice of time. Such histories are often entitled *The Age of...*, or are named after movements such as romanticism or modernism. These literary histories discuss common themes or ideas within a country or in several countries; they attempt to locate common traits that are not genre-bound. Such works can study styles in different countries and disciplines such as history of the baroque or rococo, but they ignore genres in order to emphasize similarities among the diverse kinds of writing.

There are other literary histories that are not generic and that are allied to histories of movements and periods. These are histories of ideas such as the great chain of being or imagination or organic unity or histories of rhetorical features such as irony or allegory. All such histories, whether by a single author or groups of authors, are characterized by an absence of generic contextualization. Themes and ideas in such histories are extracted from their genres and become idealized objects. They lose their particularity, which is embedded in the genres in which they appear.

A generic history of a period or movement would discuss the varied constituents of the different genres and the procedures by which they set forth the divisive aspects of a period as well as its continuities. It would relate received genres to new ones. It would point to the literary and social changes implied in the phenomenon that certain genres cease to be written but start up again at a later date. An example is sonnet sequences, absent in the eighteenth century and resumed by Wordsworth at the beginning of the next century. Generic histories can deal with particular genres—the drama is one example—that come to be prohibited by educational institutions, government, church, or patron. Generic histories would consider the literary and social implications of the return to and revision of older forms, for example, biographies of the nineteenth century or translations from older works that are incorporated in newly written poems by later poets, as for example Pound's *Cantos*. Such procedures raise questions about generic inclusions that involve what we call plagiarism and provide examples of legal problems in literary history.

Histories of movements are all too often written without an awareness of how they move. By seeking to achieve coherence, critics neglect both the procedures by which movements begin or conclude and the generically varied texts that compose a movement. So, too, the attempts to relate the practices of a period to its critical premises overlook the fact that a chronological period combines texts produced much earlier, such as those of Homer, Virgil, Shakespeare, and Milton. A period is not a unified time. The works of Shakespeare and Milton, for example, live as effective presences in later periods. However much their presences are reinterpreted, they create problems in the assimilation to and identification with later examples of their genres.

It should also be noted that to attempt to connect literary history with theory of the period is to assume that theory and practice are synchronic. But works innovated in a period often have no theory to explain them. Theories that exist—whether mimetic or contemplative—are applicable to texts and genres previously written, not to innovations.

In an attempt to write a theory applicable to contemporary black writings, Henry Louis Gates Jr., one of the most astute of our African American critics, outlines a project for a genre called black literary theory. He knows that such a project cannot ignore the problems set by literary theory regardless of who proposes them. He therefore suggests restating "white" principles of criticism in the language of black critics to create a black theory genre that will address the "integrity" of the black tradition. But the very notion of a tradition implies that the genres of poetry, novel, criticism, and theory form its constituents. Such a generic theory addressed to an interpretation of the black language of black texts would still be distinguished only by comparison to white critical genres. White generic criticism would, therefore, propose the very basis for what a literary theory might be. And this is self-evident in Gates's plan to translate white theory into black idiom:

> *renaming* principles of criticism where appropriate, but especially *naming* indigenous black principles of criticism and applying these to explicate our own texts. It is incumbent upon us to protect the integrity of our tradition by bringing to bear upon its criticism any tool of sensitivity to language that is appropriate. And what do I mean by "appropriate"? Simply this: *any* tool that enables the critic to explain the complex workings of the language of a text is an "appropriate" tool. For it is language, the black language of black texts, which expresses the distinctive quality of our literary tradition.[13]

Gates is aware that renaming is one of the procedures of change. It is understandable that he should wish to dissociate his theory from that of critics who belong to and represent—consciously or not—the attitudes of societies that oppressed his people. To transform the theoretical genre by changing the language in which it is expressed is one way to redraw theory so that it applies to a specific group of texts. In this procedure, genre prompts black writers and critics to analyze the social and political transformations resulting from special language uses.

But Edouard Glissant, the Caribbean critic, declares that genre theory cannot accommodate the needs of newly independent countries because it is too rigid; he proposes instead a criticism that he identifies as nongeneric because it is uncentered, disordered, and replete with diverse styles and discourses.[14] Glissant desires texts that provide an insight into the uncertainties and dislocations as well as the pleasures of the newly won independence. His text is not merely opposed to earlier genres. It is an effort at constructing genres that represent not a racial but a national and social identity.

For him, genres that appear in Caribbean countries and in Western countries do not function in the same way. In the West genre criticism based on multiplicity, combinatory aspects of experience, its complexities, contradictions, and fragmentariness is identified with the breakup of unified identity. In Glissant's view, the combinatory procedures make a new national identity possible, though he might very well deny that this procedure is generic. In my argument for a combinatory genre concept, I find that Glissant argues for the kind of criticism I have been urging: the theory of combinatory genres is itself an oppositional view of previous generic theories.

In my concentration on generic change in literary history, I have deliberately ignored questions of method. The particular kind of literary history is often identified by the method of the discipline it relies on—psychoanalysis, phenomenology, Marxism, formalism, reader response, and so on. Such history can also be identified by its dialectical, pluralistic, or organic hypotheses in organizing the constituents of the texts in studies. Generic constraints, however, impose historical changes on the methods employed. The dialectical method of dialogue differs from dialectical method in tragedy of different periods. In this respect the ideological implications a Marxist criticism imposes on the novel *Lord Jim* are constrained by the received implications of a biographical narrative. A psychoanalytic study of a novel, for example, is itself a member of a genre. In its narration of psychoanalytic assumptions, in its analysis of rhetorical constituents including varied discourses, it remains tied to the cultural implications of some of the cultural continuities that belong to its recent generic past.

I have been arguing that genres and their members are combinatory procedures that provide the most effective procedure for dealing with change in literary history. I have described three examples of literary history that oppose received generic practice and that offer revisionary procedures. These procedures are generic even when they deny the usefulness of genre. I have sought to show that a theory of genre can account for literary change more adequately than histories based on themes, ideas, periods, and movements. This theory accepts the assumption of a combinatory consciousness. It argues that texts, especially those by experimental authors, are combinatory entities that challenge us to grasp our multitudinous experiences with their possibilities of irreconcilable values. We need a new literary history, and I believe that a genre theory can provide it.

NOTES

1. Mikhail Bakhtin, *The Dialogic Imagination: Four Essays,* ed. Michael Holquist, trans. Caryl Emerson and Holquist (Austin: Univ. of Texas Press, 1981), and *Speech Genres and Other Late Essays,* ed. Caryl Emerson and Michael Holquist, trans. Vern W. McGee (Austin: Univ. of Texas Press, 1986); Alexander J. Butrym, ed., *Essays on the Essay: Redefining the Genre* (Athens: Univ. of Georgia Press, 1989); Gian Biagio Conte, *The Rhetoric of Imitation: Genre and Poetic Memory in Virgil and Other Latin Poets* (Ithaca, NY: Cornell Univ. Press, 1986); Stuart Curran, *Poetic Form and British Romanticism* (New York: Oxford Univ. Press, 1986); Heather Dubrow, *Genre* (London: Methuen, 1982); Alastair Fowler, *Kinds of Literature: An Introduction to the Theory of Genres and Modes* (Cambridge, MA: Harvard Univ. Press, 1982), and "The Future of Genre Theory: Functions and Constructional Types," in *The Future of Literary Theory,* ed. Ralph Cohen (New York: Routledge, 1989), 291-303; Linda Hutcheon, *A Theory of Parody* (New York: Methuen, 1985); Fredric Jameson, *The Political Unconscious: Narrative as a Socially Symbolic Act* (Ithaca, NY: Cornell Univ. Press, 1981); Arnold Krupat, *The Voice in the Margin: Native American Literature and the Canon* (Berkeley: Univ. of California Press, 1989); Susan Lohafer and Jo Ellyn Clarey, eds., *Short Story Theory at a Crossroads* (Baton Rouge: Louisiana State Univ. Press, 1989); Michael McKeon, *The Origins of the English Novel 1600-1740* (Baltimore: Johns Hopkins Univ. Press, 1987); Franco Moretti, *Signs Taken for Wonders: Essays in the Sociology of Literary Forms,* trans. Susan Fischer, David Forgacs, and David Miller (London: Verso, 1983), and *The Way of the World: The Bildungsroman in European Culture* (London: Verso, 1987); Gary Saul Morson, *The Boundaries of Genre: Dostoevsky's Diary of a Writer and the Traditions of Literary Utopia* (Austin: Univ. of Texas Press, 1981); Richard Rorty, "The Historiography of Philosophy: Four Genres," in *Philosophy in History,* ed. Rorty, J. B. Schneewind, and Quentin Skinner (Cambridge: Cambridge Univ. Press, 1984), 49-75, hereafter cited in text; Adena Rosmarin, *The Power of Genre* (Minneapolis: Univ. of Minnesota Press, 1985); Jean-Marie Schaeffer, "Literary Genres and Textual Genericity," in Cohen, *The Future of Literary Theory,* 167-87; J. W. Smeed, *The Theophrastian "Character"* (Oxford: Clarendon Press,

1986); Leonard Tennenhouse, *Power on Display: The Politics of Shakespeare's Genres* (New York: Methuen, 1986). These few references cannot begin to convey the extent and subtlety of generic theory and practice at the present time.

2. Rick Altman, *The American Film Musical* (Bloomington: Indiana Univ. Press, 1987), 95. This definition, based on speech act theory and on insights from some of the genre critics mentioned in the quotation, indicates that some types of generic theory can be interdisciplinary.

3. J. Paul Hunter, *Occasional Form* (Baltimore: Johns Hopkins Univ. Press, 1975); McKeon, *The Origins of the English Novel*; Lennard J. Davis, *Factual Fictions: The Origins of the English Novel* (New York: Columbia Univ. Press, 1983).

4. Ralph Cohen, "History and Genre" and "Reply to Dominick La Capra and Richard Harvey Brown," *New Literary History* 17, no. 2 (1986): 203-18 and 229-32; included in the present volume.

5. Discussions of Descartes's *Meditations* as a genre can be found in Amélie Oksenberg Rorty, "Experiments in Philosophical Genre: Descartes' *Meditations*," *Critical Inquiry* 9, no. 3 (1983): 545-64; a revision of this essay entitled "The Structure of Descartes' *Meditations*" appeared in *Essays on Descartes' "Meditations,"* ed. A. O. Rorty (Berkeley: Univ. of California Press, 1986), 1-20. Bradley Rubidge, in "Descartes's *Meditations* and Devotional Meditations," *Journal of the History of Ideas* 51, no. 1 (1990): 27-49, offers a critique of Rorty's views.

6. Traditionally, "doxography" refers to compilations of texts from early Greek philosophers.

7. Donald R. Kelley, "What Is Happening to the History of Ideas?," *Journal of the History of Ideas* 51, no. 1 (1990): 3-25, on 18; hereafter cited in text.

8. Italo Calvino, *Six Memos for the Next Millennium* (Cambridge, MA: Harvard Univ. Press, 1988), 124; hereafter cited in text.

9. Hélène Cixous, "From the Scene of the Unconscious to the Scene of History," in Cohen, *The Future of Literary Theory*, 15-16; hereafter cited in text. Critiques of Cixous's feminist positions but not the genre views that she published in 1989 are found in Toril Moi, *Sexual/Textual Politics: Feminist Literary Theory* (London: Methuen, 1985), 102-27; and in Janet Todd, *Feminist Literary History* (New York: Routledge, 1988), 55-59.

10. Jean Radford, *The Progress of Romance: The Politics of Popular Fiction* (New York: Routledge, 1986), 8; hereafter cited in text.

11. Sidonie Smith, *A Poetics of Women's Autobiography: Marginality and the Fictions of Self-Representation* (Bloomington: Indiana Univ. Press, 1987), 58; hereafter cited in text. Recent studies of autobiography are very numerous. Bibliographies can be found in the notes to Smith's text and in the notes to the essays in *Life/Lines: Theorizing Women's Autobiography*, ed. Bella Brodzki and Celeste Schenck (Ithaca, NY: Cornell Univ. Press, 1988). Earlier bibliographies can be found in James Olney, ed., *Autobiography: Essays Theoretical and Critical* (Princeton, NJ: Princeton Univ. Press, 1980).

12. Rita Felski, *Beyond Feminist Aesthetics: Feminist Literature and Social Change* (Cambridge, MA: Harvard Univ. Press, 1989), 94.

13. Henry Louis Gates Jr., "Authority, (White) Power, and the (Black) Critic; or, It's All Greek to Me," in Cohen, *The Future of Literary Theory,* 335.

14. Edouard Glissant, *Caribbean Discourse: Selected Essays* (Charlottesville: Univ. Press of Virginia, 1989).

What Are Genres?

Genres exist in nonverbal activities no less than in verbal. There are history paintings, portrait paintings, abstract paintings, as there are kinds of architecture and music genres. But if we wish to describe or explain or interpret these genres we use language—descriptive explanations and interpretation are themselves genres. I make this acknowledgment in order to indicate the range of this paper: I limit myself to our statements about speech and written genres. Since this is the first paper to be presented at this conference on genre, I want to assess the situation of genre criticism and theory as the participants at this conference have developed it. My summaries of key issues may be incomplete, fragmentary, but I hope not incorrect. The aim of this paper is to describe where we stand with regard to our views on genres, and what are the implications of these views.

All the writers on genre agree that to some extent, as Carolyn R. Miller states, "classification is necessary to language and learning." She sets as her goal, however, a study not of all language or learning, but of rhetorical discourses. Recognizing that rhetorical discourses have been identified in various ways, she enumerates them by references to audience, to modes of thinking, and to formal similarities. She grants that "classifications and distinctions based on form and substance have told us much about sentimentalism, women's liberation and doctrinal movements."[1] But she finds that calling these by the term "genre" is not helpful. She seeks a definition that will apply to all verbal situations—writing genres and speech genres—a definition that will address the construction of individual texts—that is, to genre members—as well as discourses about such texts. Genre, she points out, does not lend itself to taxonomy, for genres change, evolve, and decay; the number of genres

---

This essay is published here for the first time. It was delivered September 11, 1998, to a conference held at Colgate University entitled "Genre Theory at the Millennium," sponsored by Colgate University and Hamilton College.

current in any society is indeterminate and depends upon the complexity and diversity of the society.

Rhetorical genres are typified human situations that are recognized by the audience because these situations recur in human affairs. She wishes to establish a theory that applies to homely as well as sophisticated writings: to "the letter of recommendation, the user manual, the progress report, the ransom note, the lecture, and the white paper, as well as the eulogy, the apologia" (27). Each of these is characterized by a generic form that shapes the response of the readers and/or listeners as they are led from one part of the text to another. Carolyn is committed to genre as characterized by a form and substance (form and content), and she sees these as providing a hierarchical relationship: "It is through this hierarchical combination of form and substance that symbolic structures take on pragmatic force and become interpretable actions; when fused, the substantive and formal components can acquire meaning in context. A complex hierarchy of such relationships is necessary for constructing meaning" (32-34).

In this theory, genre is rule-governed: its constitutive rules tell us "how to fuse form and substance to make meaning and regulative rules that tell us how the fusion itself is to be interpreted within its contexts" (35). Such a theory is intended to establish the ways a society acts together. In addition to referring to a conventional category of discourse based on typification of rhetorical action, meaningful rhetorical action is the result of rules. Also, "a genre is a rhetorical means for mediating private intentions and social exigence" (37). It connects the private with the public, the singular with the recurrent.

Carolyn's essay is an important effort to systematize our various views of genre. By treating genres as governed by constitutive and regulative rules she gives coherence to our discussion of rhetorical analyses of human behavior. Her theory of genres is hierarchical: genres move from what might be called simple genres to more complex ones, and she astutely recognizes that the texts that are members of a genre can themselves become the basis for genres. In this way she suggests how genres are innovated. Moreover I should note that her paper provides a careful criticism of the writings on genre by rhetoricians.

But her procedures for establishing a system of genre raise some puzzling problems. If genres are rule-governed (though not fixed), what are the processes by which genre members change, evolve, and decay? Can one describe a text as rule-governed without attending to its nonruled aspects? Rule-governed assumptions need to distinguish between kinds of such government: the rules governing a genre need to be distinguished from the number as well as kinds of rules for a sermon.

Carolyn does not discuss poetry or fiction in her essay and this may be due—I cannot be sure about this—to an assumption about the special nature of literary language, an assumption the New Critics advanced. But as Igor Shaitanov makes clear in his essay "The Concept of the Generic Word: Bakhtin and the Russian Formalists," both the formalists and Bakhtin derived their genre theories from a broader conception of language than that of rhetorical discourses.[2] Bakhtin's discussion of such genres applies to all language uses. Human utterances are not based on recurrent behavior but on recurrent language uses of all types: "We usually take them from *other utterances,* and mainly from utterances that are kindred to ours in genre, that is, in theme, composition, or style. Consequently, we choose words according to their generic specifications."[3] The basis for genre usage, therefore, is recurrent or similar language use rather than recurrent situations leading to language. Yet despite the difference of generic behavior in these two approaches, both agree on the social character of linguistic behavior.

Anne Freadman agrees with Carolyn Miller's concern for classification, but her view of constitutive rules depends on specific "like" (recurrent) features and "not like" features. A genre class is marked off from other genres by contrast with them:

> Starting from the class of all texts, or discourse, the not-statement is the first move establishing a generic classification. Indeed, it is the first move establishing the very postulate of genre. Nevertheless, typical genre descriptions take the form: "like ... but not. ..." The "like" part of the generic description establishes the domain of pertinent comparisons; the "not" part establishes a boundary, not in the sense of limitation, or a limit on possibilities, but in the sense of locating "this kind" of text in a space, and vis-à-vis other kinds. The not-statement gives this kind a place among other places.[4]

A single not-statement, however, cannot define a genre; the definition "arises as (or 'from') a series of contrasts which position 'this' kind in amongst other adjacent kinds of texts" (54). But are "like" and "not like" statements genres, since description is always of a particular kind? Descriptions of different genres obviously invoke different "like" and "not like" statements.

Anne includes in "not statements" nonverbal procedures: type fonts, ticket colors, boxes in newspapers. She writes, "Just as two kinds of typeface are used in dictionaries and encyclopedias to distinguish 'word' and 'explanation' within the entry, and paragraphing and columns to distinguish entries, so do these sorts of typographical techniques provide ways of saying 'not that, but this' in other kinds of printed objects" (55-56). These typographical devices function as "like" and "not like" statements. Anne's examples are ingenious, but to convert a system of nonverbal signs into a verbal classifying system is moving an "unlike" system to a "like" one. The process leads her to suggest that "classifying might always be *re*classifying" (56).

The extension of genres to nonverbal mechanical procedures distinguishes her view from that of our other participants. Although a number of them would agree with Carolyn Miller in extending genre to rhetorical verbal discourses (it is not clear whether she includes literary texts), such discourses constitute systems that permit change. Typographical devices don't form systems equivalent to language. But paintings, music, and architecture do reveal systems of construction; moreover, the term "genre" referred to a particular kind of painting long before it came to refer to verbal kinds. For Anne, objects, activities, and behaviors can be understood in terms of a "filing system" with "like" and "not like" distinctions that define genres. But this implies that codes are languages and this seems a category confusion.

But in applying her insightful view to genres in literature, film, television, everyday behavior, Anne advances important directions of genre. In attending to the feature of place, she astutely sees it as tied to genre. She notes that the genres of literature have been traditionally distinguished by high and low, elite and popular, even if some of her contemporaries now reject this hierarchical approach. She identifies high genres with class and power and imagery of light against which she sets urban landscapes, hovels, and villages. She is cognizant of the maxim that the poor will inherit the earth and that the low can sometimes see themselves as high. Where a text occurs is germane to its generic function. Still, typical spaces of the novel are governed less by high and low than by the "essentially horizontal axis of the inner and the outer," the private spaces of personal sentiment and that of the city, country, world.

Anne points out that genre theory operated in the systems of classification used in libraries and that these necessarily involved considerations of space. "Some kinds of texts occur necessarily, or always, in kinds of places, between participants defined by their social roles" (57). The ruling of a judge in a court or the interview in a doctor's office. Slotting programs into a television program—prime time, late night—are examples of the place and time that precede the specifically internal features of a given genre chosen to occupy the slot.

The way in which setting or place operates in literature is evident in the excerpt from Heather Dubrow's new book. Referring to romance and pastoral, she writes that "the deprivation and recuperation of dwelling places is as central to them as *nostos,* the classical motif of homecoming, is to epic; for all that these genres are apparently more concerned with amorphous landscapes than houses, they offer precedents and potentialities for engaging with the very issues about the loss and recovery of housing . . . as well as with larger issues about that complex concept 'home.'"[5]

Given these generic procedures we can revise our definition to say that *a genre is group (or class) of texts distinguished from other groups by their internal interaction and shared social purpose and by their intertextual relation to other genres.* Still, in order for critics to identify genres as kinds they need to know what does not count as a genre. When Anne Freadman sets out her theory of contrastive distinctions which make it possible to identify the distinctiveness of a genre, she also needs to distinguish not-genres from genres. She does this by establishing two kinds of not-genres. One is "ceremonials," the other is "commentary." Ceremonies are like genres that situate genres, the rules for setting a game, and Anne suggests that each ceremonial device is a genre. Another way of describing ceremonials is as framing devices, a literal example of which is the framing and placing of paintings.

The purpose of this distinction seems to be to separate types of distancing behavior like ritual, games, or initiations of action from the acts or genres which they encompass. But one wonders whether this is an adequate way in which to distinguish certain times and places or whether one is better served by a procedure like Carolyn Miller's that involves establishing a hierarchy of complexity among genres.

The denial of "commentary" as a genre is based on the assumption that commentary reveals its own genre rather than that on which it comments (this is a subtle and provocative argument, and I want to note here the subtlety of insights and arguments in Anne's essay). Nevertheless, to deny generic identification to the kinds of readers' responses to genres other than their own is to avoid confronting the problem of generic intervention and to deny to some verbal entities what one attributes to others. Anne promises a resolution of this problem and I hope we shall have it.

But this is the kind of problem that Mary Gerhart and Alvin Melvin Russell pose in "The Genre Bidisciplinary Dialogue."[6] The genre they posit is a dialogue between two very different disciplines: Darwinian biology and evangelical religion. But such a dialogue involves a number of preparatory genres: choosing the disciplines, selecting participants, agreeing upon a subject. The possibilities of resolution seem remote on the basis of generic analysis offered. We must remember that the philosophical dialogue such as Hume practiced has long since dwindled as a form, as Michael Prince argued in *Philosophical Dialogue in the British Enlightenment*.[7] The first question, therefore, is: Are there bidisciplinary dialogues and how do we account for them at the present time? If no such dialogues exist, can we describe such a dialogue as a hope rather than a practice?

If we have disciplines that intersect but offer no intertextual possibilities, do we have a nongeneric interrelation? A Darwinian view of the origin of the human life and a religious view? Are two views of the same situation within a discipline more likely to have some elements or components in common than the interaction of two totally different genres with different assumptions about knowledge and its acquisition?

Genres, as many of us know, are innovated, developed, and disappear and often are revived. This is the case of the sonnet that thrived in Shakespeare's time and continued as a used form up to Milton's time. But in the first half of the eighteenth century no major writer wrote sonnets. In the second half of the eighteenth century it was revived and Wordsworth and the following generation of poets wrote sonnets in profusion. The dialogue has not undergone such a revival. One of the inquiries genre theory needs to undertake is how to account for such changes.

There are many changes which genres undergo and which genre members undergo. For instance, fables told as moral tales for children become political tales in a totalitarian country. *Huckleberry Finn* has come under racial censorship when placed in libraries of some black communities. Members of a genre, though sharing one or more markers, are also different from one another. A genre theory must account for these differences as well as for similarities, especially if a given genre has a long life with new members being added.

What a theory of genre does or can do is to consider whether such terms refer to kinds that are recurrent or to words or images that are incidental but not irrelevant to the interaction of parts. When critics treat gender or class do they not necessarily redefine a genre? Still, to add additional elements to a genre, for example, to insert autobiographical statements about one's education in a theoretical essay, does not make the essay autobiography; rather it makes theory nonobjective. Genre requires distinctions within the member texts that compose it. A genre requires analysis of the difference among the texts that compose a genre.

If we wish to assess where genre theory is today, we might consider how this study has advanced since Heather Dubrow's 1982 informative survey entitled *Genre*.[8] Heather discusses many of the issues with which we deal: She draws attention to genres as possessing rules, though some genres exert more control than others. Because she is historically oriented she is not concerned with the constitutive or regulative role of rules. She recognizes the importance of convention in genre which she sees as types of continuity that make change apparent; for her form also leads to reform. She discusses generic choice and she offers as a metaphor for genre the human personality.

Heather's historical review of genre theories is ignored by most contemporary theorists of genre although her discussion of the Russian formalists is pursued in revisionary detail by Shaitanov. Heather finds it difficult to arrive at a definition of individual genres and of a genre itself because "the concept encompasses so many different literary qualities" (7). Thus our major alteration in treating genre, by some of us, is its deliberate extension beyond "literature." The second major change is our rejection of Heather's conception of genre as resembling human personality:

> A genre closely resembles a human personality in the way it may incorporate elements from many other personality types while still conforming to one basic type itself: someone whose fundamental configuration is obsessive may include elements of the depressive, much as a genre that is primarily epic may also participate in romance and pastoral.... Genres resemble human personalities, too, in their complex relationships with those around them. They are, as we have often observed, shaped both by learning from and by rebelling against their literary parents, those earlier forms from which they develop. (117)

These are pertinent comparisons, but both Miller and Freadman and Charles Bazerman would reject the comparison. For these critics classification in human experience subordinates "personality" to genre theory; indeed, generic terms make it explicable.

The historical shifts that have led to this revisionism of genre make it desirable to consider the historical changes that apply to the term. "Genre," taken from the French, entered English vocabulary late in the eighteenth century. The source is Latin *gens* which refers to a class, a number of linked families connected by common consent; it also refers to offspring, to descendants, to tribe, people, district, country, nation. Its origin, therefore, insists on its linkage to family or to large social units such as district or clan or country. I stress this etymological emphasis because it makes clear that "genre" is a collective noun. It is not a reference to a single text but to a group of texts. Whatever is denominated a "genre" is a group of writings, speech, or behavior. In addition, etymology makes clear that the source term moves from originating family to group of families and clans to country and nation. "Genre" in other words is a term that can refer to small and to large groups, to social and to political groups. The term itself is a collection of histories.

The history of what we now call "genre," however, did not begin when this name was applied in English to particular texts. The term that preceded it was "kinds," and this has a much more extensive etymological history than "genre." "Kind" was related to "kin" and it, too, indicates a group that moves from familial relation to an increasingly comprehensive reference to human beings and animals that possess distinguishable attributes. "Kinds" referred not merely to writings but to all kinds of groups. This collective concept is obvious in Aristotle's discussion of tragedy, in which he refers to plays by Aeschylus, Sophocles, Euripides, and others. For him tragedy is but one procedure among other mimetic processes. And it is characterized by a particular mixture of its elements or components: "So tragedy as a whole will necessarily have six elements, the possession of which makes tragedy qualitatively distinct [from other literary kinds]: they are plot, the mimesis of character, verbal expression, the mimesis of intellect, spectacle or song-writing."[9]

It is important to note that classification for the great libraries from the time of the Alexandrian library to the present invoked classification of all possible works and that its aim was use or ease of retrieval. In this respect, the current attempt to extend the theory of genre to all aspects of behavior is a return to comprehensiveness that characterized its library function.

By the eighteenth century "kinds" had become a rigid classification, especially when applied to literary works; by the end of the century the new term "genre" began to be used, probably to stress a less rigid application than the term "kinds." "Genre" was part of the new vocabulary of literary texts stressing its "creative" qualities and connecting the kinds with genesis, genius, and imagination. The *OED* points out that at this time "genre"—though related to kind and sort—also had a specific literary meaning: "A particular style or category of works of art, esp. a type of literary work, characterized by a particular form, style or purpose."

However inadequate this trivial definition is in explaining the introduction of the term "genre" into English usage, it points to a recurrence, a literary type. It attributes to "genre" a specialized version of "type" distinguishing it from other types and kinds. Genres then become disconnected from Samuel Johnson's view of "literary history" as a history of writing (of "letters"). It referred to a special kind of writing—"literary" writing.

In the twentieth century the reservations about the writing of "history" including "literary history" have grown so prevalent that David Richter can refer to this phenomenon as "the annihilation of history." But literary history is a collective name for a series of genres, and what David is addressing is the history of a particular kind of literary writing: the Gothic, "the criticism of Gothic texts from the period of its first vogue and in contemporary popular culture."[10] He discusses "three specimen approaches" that represent what he calls "the variety of ways of evading historiography that modern critical theories encourage" (4).

The three types of historical avoidance in treating the Gothic novel are (1) treating the Gothic novel as a set of conventions; (2) treating the Gothic novel as Feminist Charter; (3) treating the Gothic novel as a form of myth. Richter's inquiry is important for genre criticism because it addresses the problem: what kind of generic claim does a critical text make and what supporting evidence does the claim provide? Is Eve Kosofsky Sedgwick's book *The Coherence of Gothic Conventions* an attempt to write a history of the Gothic novel or is it merely an attempt to describe the rules she takes to be characteristic of this type of writing? If she is merely describing rules, then genre critics would argue that she is not only failing to develop a genre but that she has not attempted to fully describe a genre. Rules in themselves do not constitute a genre; as Miller argues, there must be a satisfactory fusion of substance and form "that could serve as substance to higher level forms and contexts" (38). In other words, the Sedgwick volume is not generic, not because it is failed history but because its conception of rules is inadequate to provide the generic coherence intended.

Richter's second example of the avoidance of history in Gothic criticism is the discussion by Sandra Gilbert and Susan Gubar in *The Madwoman in the Attic*. This work, which "instituted a revolution in feminist criticism," "imposes an essentially Gothic myth upon all female creativity" (6). The myth of the female artist and its changes to all female writing. Richter argues that the history of the female writer is not sequential as Gilbert and Gubar claim but that "the strategies of denial, rage, and withdrawal are all *simultaneously* available to and were used by nineteenth-century women authors" (8). Richter objects to their narrative because it flattens out history.

Here we do have a version of literary history, but Richter's objection to it is that as Gothic history it lacks distinctiveness so that the Gothic type of female writing is insufficiently differentiated. For him it is a failed genre because there is inadequate consideration of all the elements in recurrent rhetorical situations. But is this history of female writing to be analyzed as "literary history" or as an innovative genre called "Female literary history"? If this is the case, is the innovation precisely based on recurrent types of writing strategies? Are the distinctions demanded by Richter irrelevant to the kind of recurrence sought by Gubar and Gilbert?

Finally the third type of avoidance of history writing occurs when "the Gothic is approached as the bearer of an essence or the carrier of a myth" (9). As a result, "the genre becomes timeless: each instance of the Gothic is simply a different manifestation of its eternal form" (9). Although Richter finds that such works, especially William Patrick Day's *In the Circles of Fear and Desire,* make insightful comments about features of Gothic novels, Day cannot "explain why the Gothic novel grew up in the latter part of the eighteenth century" (11). Richter points out the herculean labors involved in fitting varied texts into the myth of the Gothic. Richter is right to note that it deliberately avoids history, and it obviously also avoids a genre system that is pragmatic. But is a myth supposed to be a pragmatic history?

Although this mythic writing avoids history and genre, it nevertheless offers valuable insights that connect with both; there are filiations and even elements that can serve as intertextual relations. But the textual elements are related essentially; they are not subject to change, only to variations of the same. This is not the case with the innovation of a genre. At this point it is appropriate once again to revise the definition of genre: *a genre is a group (or class) or groups of texts historically composed of elements (or components) in interaction toward some general purpose containing intertextual filiations, the whole forming an entity that can become a subgenre or can be the source of new genres.*

The innovation of a genre can derive from one or more "parent" genres. Such innovations derive from the social pressures within a society resulting from technological changes or social, political, or economic needs. E-mail and hypertext are examples of technological advances and *testimonies* is an example of social needs. Testimonies is a genre derived from autobiographical narratives, memoirs, and journals. It is the specialized version of a life-shattering experience, a text that bears witness to the viciousness of human beings and to the society that condones it. Testimonies is a memorial and a warning, and it has filiations to contemporary genres of photographs of mass murders and torture victims. I quote one definition of this new genre:

> By *testimonio* I mean a novel or novella-length narrative in book or pamphlet (that is, printed as opposed to acoustic) form, told in the first person by a narrator who is also a real protagonist or witness of the events he or she recounts, and whose unit of narration is usually a "life" or a significant life experience. *Testimonio* may include, but is not subsumed under, any of the following categories, some of which are conventionally considered literature, others not: autobiography, autobiographical novel, oral history, memoir, confession, diary, interview, eyewitness report, life history, *novela-testimonio*, nonfiction novel, or "factographic literature." . . . The situation of narration in *testimonio* has to involve an urgency to communicate, a problem of repression, poverty, subalternity, imprisonment, struggle for survival, and so on.[11]

Testimonio is a genre because numerous such texts exist from the Second World War, they have a specific identity, they share generic markers and have intertextual features to other genres, are complete entities, and serve social ends. This genre is so obviously historical that it raises the more general question of the kinds of historicity that genres possess. A genre, being composed of numerous texts over time, is inevitably historical. Member texts add or lose components (elements) and there are changes in its filiation with other texts and in its generic marker.

How some of these changes work is described by Lee Clark Mitchell in his study of the Western. He remarks:

> One of this book's two premises, in fact, is that any popular text engages immediately pressing issues — issues that become less pressing in time. With each generation, a genre's plots, narrative emphases, stylistic pressures, even scenic values have less in common with earlier versions of that genre than with competing genres, all striving to resolve the same contemporary anxieties. Yet the second premise is just as crucial and controverts the first: that from the beginning the Western has fretted over the construction of masculinity, whether in terms of gender (women), maturation (sons), honor (restraint), or self-transformation (the West itself).[12]

Members of the genre Westerns, Mitchell argues, become in time more identified with non-Western genres than with earlier members of the genre. Zane Gray's Westerns have more in common with Scott Fitzgerald's "Gatsby" than with Cooper's Leatherstocking Tales. The initial filiations diminish in time. The assumption therefore is not of generic continuity but that generic intertexture undergoes change. Thus the original functions of components such as character or plot or style (diction) become differently combined and constructed. That each member of a genre differs in some measure from others is obvious. But Mitchell points to an antithetical characteristic of genre that prevents it from being historically progressive or regressive or even cyclical. He writes: "The second premise is just as crucial and controverts the first [premise of change]," namely, "from the beginning the Western has fretted over the construction of masculinity," whether in terms of gender, maturation, honor, or self-transformation. There is, in other words, another level of genre in which the Western becomes a species of the cultural genre of patriarchy or masculinity.

The analysis of history in terms of the members of a genre suggests two further contributions. The first has to do with the continuity of a genre. Continuity in the interaction of some of its components, despite changes in others, is what gives stability to a genre. These result from rules or conventions or markers that survive. Stability, however, functions as a conserving as well as conservative function. The resistance to genre is often the result of this ideological remainder, but generic change serves as a counter to its stability. It is this paradoxical situation that gives genre its openness as well as its ideological ambiguity. Generic identification is at times as ambiguous as its ideology. One reason for this is that variation within a genre can so transform the components as to lose the specificity that belongs to the genre. The notion of stability implies a range within which stability resides. It is, therefore, necessary to distinguish the changes within a genre from the change of one genre into another or the creation of one genre from another, a change of style. This is the problem that June Howard addresses in her book *Form and History in American Literary Naturalism,* the shift in American literature that led from realism to naturalism.[13] This is a challenging generic problem: to explain how one style form—realism—led to such constitutive changes that the issue of belonging to realism became problematic.

June argues that there were specific social and economic changes in the society that led writers to develop a new style. But this generalization, as David Richter pointed out, cannot explain the innovation of a particular movement, since such change affected a whole society. June is aware of this problem because she argues that naturalism is *not* merely a change in some of the elements of realism, but is a constitutive change. The elements of naturalism, its purposes and componential interactions, are related to, but are distinct from, realism. The two styles have filiations, but not identical roots, for naturalism has its source in the writings of Zola.

Is her version of generic change sufficiently detailed to be persuasive? Was there a tradition in writing that could serve to explain naturalism more aptly than realism? Naturalism as a style seems more related to yellow journalism and to historical muckraking than to the high style of Howell's or James's realism. The social conditions that account for naturalism can account equally well for a journalistic and history writing tradition that developed with it. Whatever my reservations, June Howard is quite right to relate genre to style and movements. Genre critics have only just begun to track changes in writing and I recommend the study of the change of letter writing from private to public in Frans De Bruyn's *The Literary Genres of Edmund Burke*.[14]

It is, finally, appropriate to ask about the relation of genre to the individual text, the genre member. There are two essays that deal with analysis of individual novels. These are Robyn R. Warhol's "Double Gender, Double Genre in *Jane Eyre* and *Villette*"[15] and Peter J. Rabinowitz's "'Reader, I Blew Him Away': Convention and Transgression in Sue Grafton."[16]

Robyn's essay is based on the critical-interpretive genre that espouses the reconciliation of opposites—in her argument, the combination of feminist narratology and the features of Gothic and realist styles (that she calls "genres"). By feminist issues of narratology, Robyn means "how a Victorian woman novelist exploits possibilities for doubleness that narratology's categories can bring into the foreground" (858). The generic issues are not connected with the definition of narratology, but with the claim that a tension "exists in these novels between the realism and Gothic romance. I will argue that the two genres are not so much in competition as in continuous oscillation with each other, serving to double each other at crucial moments of both narratives" (858).

What Robyn has to say about the two novels is governed by her commitment to feminist literary criticism and to her generic assumption about style mixture. In dealing with the novels, her approach can be interpreted as generic intervention. When a critic interprets the genre novel, she inevitably searches for structural support for her knowledge. However carefully she seeks to reveal what the novel seeks to do, her concessions are limited by her own generic commitment as a critic. There are, of course, many possibilities for misinterpretation and mistakes, wrong information, inadequate or incomplete arguments, and other examples that are not the consequences of interpretation. But a generic approach is distinctive by drawing attention to the critic's invasive function, and the inevitable limitation that each invasion brings.

Robyn's essay provokes a question about generic identification of texts that belong to more than one genre such as Horace's *Ars poetica* and Lucretius's *De rerum natura,* and satires that are genres composed of contrasting components. Does knowledge of such works compel us to rethink what interpretation involves? Such rethinking creates space for modifying the rules for reading and interpreting. But not only dual genres lead to modification; interpretation as a genre is also modified by the different fictions one invades. Interpretation as a generic member participates in the changes that I discussed above without losing its stability as a genre.

The problem of interpretation as a genre is what Peter Rabinowitz confronts. His inquiry deals with the question, "To what extent are generic narrative patterns a prison house that confines the scope of women's action? Specifically, I want to stake out the intersection between convention and transgression with an eye toward discovering how far Grafton has in fact succeeded in resisting the traditions she is playing with, and what this can tell us about genre more generally" (327). Grafton's *"A" is for Alibi* is a detective novel in the hard-boiled tradition of Hammett and Chandler, but it deliberately transgresses this tradition by making the detective a woman and by "sympathetic narratives of the ways in which women are brutalized by men" (328). Peter argues that this novel contains parodies of some of the conventions found in the detective novel in order to expose and explode their violent misogyny. Its convention of disclosure is but a "front for a covert narrative of concealment, as the formula masks violent misogyny by disguising it as a generalized and gender-neutral form of justice" (331).

What genre criticism does, according to Peter, is to identify the rule-governed conventions of a genre and inquire into the uses to which they have been put and the language in which they are expressed. Criticism can position itself either by resisting and ridiculing such rules or by acknowledging their validity and cultural significance. He recognizes that criticism is a genre of its own in spite of the fact that it restates some of the rules of the work it criticizes. From the reader's perspective, genres can be seen as interpretive procedures used to unlock literary structures. The importance of Peter's essay is that it formulates the generic basis of interpretation. In doing so, he clearly relates literary interpretation to general generic behavior.

Peter develops reader's rules which he identifies as rules of notice, of configuration, and of coherence. Rules of configuration and the rules of coherence seem to be constitutive to interpretation. Peter is aware that different readers read differently, and that their procedures are not firmly fixed; but he believes that most interpreters share his view. For example, readers of hard-boiled novels "interpret them according to a familiar set of pre-existing rules" (334).

Peter is tentative about the operation of rules, and he concedes that what he called transgressions of conventions could also be interpreted as concessions to them. His conclusion is that we need to consider "genres not only as features but also as strategies" (341). But the strategies of a particular text are not applicable to all texts in a given genre. A theory of genre compels us to consider the consequences of generic intervention and filiation. It recovers what was overlooked and discovers what was never found.

What these strategies might be are determined in the definition of genre which we have proposed. *A genre is a group (or groups) of texts historically characterized by components in interaction toward some general purpose containing features that are intertextual, the whole forming an identity that can become a subgenre or can be the source of new genres. Genres occur in every language and many cross national borders. They are procedures for organizing knowledge, and for communicating it. They express our thoughts, feelings, and actions with regard to that knowledge.*

As Charles Bazerman, whose extensive survey of the role of genre in various studies has helped advance the inquiries into genre, puts it: "Together these studies in various fields suggest that the typification of discourses into various types is a fundamental process in the formation of our sense of where we are, what we are doing, and how we can do it. Genre appears to be a constitutive mechanism in the formation, maintenance, and enactment of society, culture, psychology, imagination, consciousness, personality, and knowledge, interactive with all the other processes which shape our lives."[17]

In pursuit of generic understanding this paper has addressed the following questions: Are all writings generic? Are interpretations generic? Are there nonverbal texts that are generic? Since a genre is a class or group of individual texts, how are they related to each other? What types of interaction occur in these texts? Are texts members of one genre or can they be multigeneric? How are members of one genre related to those of other genres? Why are genres inevitably historical? How and why are genres innovated? What kinds of changes do genres undergo? What accounts for generic stability? Why do genres become ideologically ambiguous over time? Why is it important for us to ask generic questions? And why do the answers matter?

I think these are some of the questions this conference was convoked to answer.

NOTES

1. Carolyn R. Miller, "Genre as Social Action," in *Genre and the New Rhetoric,* ed. Aviva Freedman and Peter Medway (London: Taylor & Francis, 1994), 27; hereafter cited in text.

2. Igor Shaitanov, "The Concept of the Generic Word: Bakhtin and the Russian Formalists," in *Face to Face: Bakhtin in Russia and the West,* ed. Carol Adlam, Rachel Falconer, Vitalii Makhlin, and Alastair Renfrew (Sheffield: Sheffield Academic Press, 1997), 233-53.

3. M. M. Bakhtin, "The Problem of Speech Genres," in *Speech Genres and Other Late Essays,* trans. Vern W. McGee, ed. Caryl Emerson and Michael Holquist (Austin: Univ. of Texas Press, 1986), 87; Bakhtin's emphasis.

4. Anne Freadman, "Anyone for Tennis?," in Freedman and Medway, *Genre and the New Rhetoric,* 51-52; hereafter cited in text.

5. Heather Dubrow, *Shakespeare and Domestic Loss: Forms of Deprivation, Mourning, and Recuperation* (Cambridge: Cambridge Univ. Press, 1999), 98-99.

6. See Mary Gerhart and Allan Melvin Russell, "The Genre Bidisciplinary Dialogue," in *New Maps for Old Explorations in Science and Religion* (New York: Bloomsbury, 2001).

7. Michael Prince, *Philosophical Dialogue in the British Enlightenment: Theology, Aesthetics and the Novel* (Cambridge: Cambridge Univ. Press, 1996).

8. Heather Dubrow, *Genre* (London: Methuen, 1982); hereafter cited in text.

9. Aristotle, *Poetics* 1450a.

10. David H. Richter, *The Progress of Romance: Literary Historiography and the Gothic Novel* (Columbus: Ohio State Univ. Press, 1996), 4; hereafter cited in text.

11. John Beverley, "The Margin at the Center: On *Testimonio* (Testimonial Narrative)," *Modern Fiction Studies* 35, no. 1 (1989): 12-13.

12. Lee Clark Mitchell, *Westerns: Making the Man in Fiction and Film* (Chicago: Univ. of Chicago Press, 1996), 4.

13. June Howard, *Form and History in American Literary Naturalism* (Chapel Hill: Univ. of North Carolina Press, 1985).

14. Frans De Bruyn, *The Literary Genres of Edmund Burke: The Political Uses of Literary Form* (Oxford: Oxford Univ. Press, 1996).

15. Robyn R. Warhol, "Double Gender, Double Genre in *Jane Eyre* and *Villette,*" *SEL* 36, no. 4 (1996): 857-75; hereafter cited in text.

16. Peter J. Rabinowitz, "'Reader, I Blew Him Away': Convention and Transgression in Sue Grafton," in *Famous Last Words: Changes in Gender and Narrative Closure*, ed. Allison Booth (Charlottesville: Univ. of Virginia Press, 1993), 326-44; hereafter cited in text.

17. Charles Bazerman, "Social Forms as Habitats for Action," *Journal of the Interdisciplinary Crossroads* 1, no. 2 (2003): 123-42. A version of this essay was delivered to a session on "theorizing genre" at the 1994 meeting of the Modern Language Association. The session was organized by Michael Prince; participants included Charles Bazerman, Hayden White, Linda Kauffman, and Ralph Cohen.

PART II
LITERARY CHANGE AS GENERIC HISTORY

Innovation and Variation
Literary Change and Georgic Poetry

The study of literary history inevitably involves the study of literary change, and any explanation of change must distinguish among the types of change that are possible. These include changes within the work of a single writer, changes among different writers who share common ends, like the Scriblerus group (this can include, as well, changes in what are called "schools," "movements," and "periods"), changes in the forms of genres, changes in style, changes in critical interpretation. It is apparent that the term "change" identified with these many different literary situations—and they are not all that one can name—needs to be limited and other terms introduced to make the discussion manageable.

I. THE PROBLEM OF CHANGE

Perhaps the most elementary distinction is one that must precede interpretation of individual works—and has indeed preceded the application of interpretation to literary study. It is the recognition that history must be segmented in order to be comprehensible. Such segments are not arbitrary divisions, but presuppose some rationale such as importance or consequentiality, some natural divisions (infancy, childhood, etc.), or some common stylistic features that can account for the kind and sequence of changes.[1] Whatever the rationale, it is possible to note within any explanation the beginning of a

---

This essay was originally published in *Literature and History: Papers Read at a Clark Library Seminar, March 3, 1973*, by Ralph Cohen and Murray Krieger (Los Angeles: The William Andrews Clark Memorial Library, University of California, Los Angeles, 1974), 1-42, and is reprinted with permission of the publisher. A version of this paper was published in *Neohelicon* 1-2 (1975): 149-82.

change as well as the continuation of this change. The beginning of a change I call "innovation," its continuity, development, and extension I identify as "variation."

If we grant, therefore, that no matter how scholars deal with literary history, they impose at least these two types of change, the problem is, "How do we distinguish innovation from variation?" How do we distinguish between changes that initiate new styles, periods, movements from those which merely expand upon or extend the received conventions? All poems are, by definition, different in some respects from one another. If we confine our problem to poems within a common form like the eclogue or georgic, and select the seventeenth and eighteenth centuries as the time for our inquiry, we note a major change in the interrelation of georgic to pastoral. The didactic poem, treated by Sidney with considerable reservations about its function as poetry, became in the second half of the seventeenth century one of the major poetic forms.

The change in the idea of poetry and poetic practice was enacted by writers; this was an empirical phenomenon recognized by contemporary and subsequent critics. What is remarkable is the increased production of poems in a form previously minimized or neglected. Can there be a procedure for indicating why and how this occurs, a procedure for detecting and identifying innovation?

By putting the question in this way, I seek to avoid entanglement in the critical arguments about the problems of tradition and influence. Any attempt to explain change inevitably touches on inherited conventions and direct relation to earlier writers. But tradition and influence—no matter how one deals with them—are subsumed under the more general question of innovation and variation. At what point does a writer so alter a tradition as to begin a new development? How can one distinguish between merely varying a tradition, so that concepts are not changed, and innovating within it so that poetic features become indicative of new ways of conceiving experience?

For this, one criterion is the new relations of poetic features to poetic ends: the speaker assumes a new role, or the rhetorical devices are given new functions, new subjects are introduced, and so forth. With regard to the georgic poem, for example, new perceptual techniques are introduced and new subjects are pursued. The georgic poem not only reveals new functions for poetic features so that these become, in time, new conventions, but the form as a whole urges on its readers a new way of responding. Not only is rationalistic and commercial imagery introduced, not only is perception of nature made primary, but these innovations socialize a form that had up to that time been emblematic.

The georgic form becomes a literary genre for exploring man's experience, and it leads to prose works such as the novel and periodical essays that embody the exploratory variety of the new georgic. This aspect of innovation cannot be pursued here, but the relation between innovation and originality can be indicated. Within a genre, innovative developments are inevitably original; they introduce new subjects or new functions for old features. Innovations are "original" in the sense that they are new; they should be distinguished from artistically valuable instances of originality. The example of *Windsor Forest* modeled upon *Coopers Hill* demonstrates that a variant of an innovation can be artistically original in its use of inherited conventions, and, indeed, can use them in ways undeveloped in the form that sets the new model.

I do not argue that innovation within a genre implies that all features of the genre undergo change. I accept the premise that a literary form is composed of features—rhetorical, metrical, narrative, etc.—that either lead to or imply an aim or end, but the features are related in terms of hierarchical importance. The iambic pentameter couplet used in "To Penshurst" and *Coopers Hill*, is functionally more prominent in the later than in the earlier poem. It is necessary for aspects of a form to be repeated—whether directly or in terms of family resemblances—if it is to be considered a member of a genre. Thus innovative features do not make a form unrecognizable. The argument that genres are altered by their place in the hierarchy of forms will become apparent, but, more importantly, the role of kinds or genres at any moment in literary history is determined by this relationship.

Here I can merely point out that, since the Renaissance, all generic innovations occur despite the availability of older uses. Virgil and Lucretius are repeatedly reprinted and translated in the seventeenth century, and innovations in georgic poetry occur in spite of these models being available for comparison. So, too, Jonson, Waller, Marvell are available to readers who can recognize the difference between imitation (as variation) and innovation. In this essay I use Denham as the model for innovation in georgic poetry. This is because John Dennis, Pope, and Johnson refer to him as an innovator. For Johnson, Denham is taken as the author of the form; Waller is taken as the author of the smoothness of, the new use of, the couplet. But although innovations that become models for subsequent writers are the achievement of individuals, they do not arise from the self-contained privacy of the poet's mind but from that mind responding to the experiences that engage it. Waller, Denham, Milton are poets of a revolutionary period, and although they were not on the same sides of the Civil War, they all recognized in art the divergent and even contradictory tensions that ultimately brought on the Civil War. In answer to the question, therefore, "How do we distinguish innovation from variation?" the first criterion is that the poets and, subsequently, the contemporaneous critics that comment upon them *identify* the innovations.

II. INNOVATION, FUNCTION, AND CONVENTION

When Samuel Johnson wrote the life of Sir John Denham, he declared that *Coopers Hill* was a new "species of composition" in English literature:

> *Cooper's Hill* [sic] is the work that confers upon him the rank and dignity of an original author. He seems to have been, at least among us, the author of a species of composition that may be denominated *local poetry,* of which the fundamental subject is some particular landscape, to be poetically described, with the addition of such embellishments as may be supplied by historical retrospection or incidental meditation.
>
> To trace a new scheme of poetry, has in itself a very high claim to praise, and its praise is yet more when it is apparently copied by Garth and Pope; after whose names little will be gained by an enumeration of smaller poets, that have left scarcely a corner of the island not dignified either by rhyme or blank verse.[2]

The poem gave Denham the rank of an "original author," the "author of a species of composition." To the extent that one literary work is different from any other, it is unique; yet works can be and need to be grouped together. Whenever this is done, it will inevitably be observed that some works introduce new ways of organizing and expressing thoughts in poetry, thereby initiating the possibility of new groupings. Johnson identified *Coopers Hill* as such a poem and selected as its novel literary features the description of a landscape "with the addition" of two kinds of "embellishments": "historical retrospection or incidental meditation."

The selection of these features proved, for Johnson, the basis of a "new scheme of poetry." They were, for him, new features. But Denham himself saw the poem as a georgic, as an innovation within the received form. And this view was shared by Pope and John Dennis. The latter identified the purpose of *Coopers Hill* as a form of persuasion or instruction:

And as the Admirable Poet took Occasion before, from the View of St. *Anne's* Hill, to give the most important Instruction that can be given to this Island, upon a Religious Account; *viz.* That we should banish Persecution, and an ill-grounded Zeal, from among us; he takes an Opportunity now, from showing the Prince and the People assembled upon that memorable Occasion, to conclude this Poem, with the most important Instruction, that, upon a Civil Account, can be given, either to Prince or People, *viz.* That the Prince should avoid intrenching upon Liberty, and the People upon Prerogative; and thus he has in this short, but admirable Poem, given those Instructions, both to the Prince, the Church, and the People, which, being observ'd, must make the Prince Powerful and Glorious, the Church Great and Venerable, and the People a Flourishing and a Happy People; and which, being neglected, must bring universal Misery upon the Nation.[3]

There can be no doubt that Dennis saw the poem as a georgic, a poem for which Virgil's *Georgics* were the model.

But the kind to which *Coopers Hill* belongs has also been identified as a topographical poem for which "To Penshurst" was the model, as an antecedent of the "greater romantic lyric," as a pastoral as well as a georgic poem.[4] The solution to this problem of classification is not a matter of pluralistic choice; it is rather dependent upon a theory of change and innovation. Without an explanation that accounts for the difference between changes that are variants of a type (norm) and those that alter the type (norm), no resolution can be made between classifications that select descriptions and historical retrospection as governing features in contrast to those that prefer references to a country house as primary.

And the issue cannot be resolved by proposing an analysis of *Coopers Hill,* for such analysis presupposes a decision about the innovative or variational category into which it is to be fitted.

To refer to a "norm" within a genre is to presuppose that the georgic of Virgil, of Jonson, and of Denham constituted a type of verse different from, for example, the lyric or the drama. In this most extended sense, the variants within the class are irrelevant because two different classes or family groups of poetry are being distinguished. But if one sought to distinguish the historical differences within the class of georgic poems, it would then be important to establish a series of "norms" or "types" of georgic. In recognizing innovations that create a new type of georgic, one can refer, as I have, to contemporary critics who give reasons for assuming a new type: new subject matter, new forms of transition, new relations among nature, history, and morality.

But a second argument can be advanced in interpretative terms; not only are new features introduced for new ends, but old features function in new ways by implying resistance to or rejection of former usages. Such rejections are a consequence of discovering or exploring poetic expression for new concepts of experience. Man's relation to man, nature, and God lead to new poetic expressions and means of organization. These conceptual changes form the basis for a new "type" within the genre as well as for new roles for former genres.

This procedure can be noted in *Coopers Hill*. It begins as a perceptual poem: the speaker mounts Cooper's Hill and from it surveys distant St. Paul's as well as the nearby hills and dales, relating acts and events pertinent to these places. Concluding his reflections on Windsor Castle, he turns to St. Anne's Hill:

> Here should my wonder dwell, & here my praise,
> But my fixt thoughts my wandring eye betrays,
> Viewing a neighbouring hill, whose top of late
> A Chappel crown'd, till in the Common Fate,
> The adjoyning Abby fell: (may no such storm
> Fall on our times, where ruine must reform.)[5] (111-16)

The question whether this practice of a survey leading to historical reflections is a Virgilian technique being adapted to Denham's purposes, or some new implication of the poet's view of his environment, cannot be answered by a reading which does not interpret the technique as a response to or departure from preceding poetry. The way the speaker proceeds in his transitions, repetitively organizing responses to hills which contrast with each other—the great heritage of Windsor Castle and the destruction of Chertsey Abbey by Henry VIII—cannot in itself explain whether the poem is suggesting a new approach to the encomiastic procedures of "To Penshurst" or is using these as features for a quite different end.

The basis for such a decision rests upon understanding whether repetition in preceding georgic poems functioned to establish God's harmony by contrast and harmonious extent or whether repetition and survey functioned to make nature an emblem for man-made works. This decision rests on the "type" of georgic that it seems most reasonably to fit. But unless one is aware that the different types imply different concepts of experience, there will be no adequate procedure for distinguishing consequential from inconsequential change within a genre. The multiplication of genres into country-house poems, descriptive poems, loco-descriptive poems, hill poems merely confounds the analysis of literary works because they provide no defensible basis for classification. Ultimately, on this ground, every poem is its own genre.[6]

What is required is a theory of innovation and variation which makes classification possible; if one relates the idea of "function" to concepts of experience, to relations within the poem, to effects upon the reader, and to relations among literary forms, one can avoid the circular argument based merely on "function" within the poem. If it is claimed that one knows how a poem functions only by interpretation and that the process of interpretation is based on tacit assumptions about function, then surely we have an example of the hermeneutic circle. But statements about interpretation do not rest merely upon statements about internal functions. Such statements about identification of generic features operate on a quite different level from those about poetic functions. Statements about interrelation of forms, about the relation of forms to nonliterary experience, deal with analyses of classification systems; the interpretation of features within any specific poem takes account of the poet's private and shared expression of experience, how parts relate to the whole. Concepts of forms, therefore, can be arrived at by comparison of classification systems and are not dependent upon interpretation within a work. But even such interpretation, when it is understood as historically dependent upon earlier works, can provide a basis for distinguishing between innovation and variation. Conceptual changes are noted by the fact that poetic features which were recessive or backgrounded or even nonexistent in the previous type are now dominant or foregrounded.

Coopers Hill alludes to Edmund Waller's poem "Upon His Majesty's repairing of Pauls": "*Pauls*, the late theme of such a Muse whose flight / Has bravely reach't and soar'd above thy height" (19-20). But Denham's perceptual use of St. Paul's introduces a spatial concept foreign to Waller's poem. It also alludes to Virgil's first *Georgic,* in which the crops are described as overwhelmed by storms and floods of uncontrolled nature.

> Often, too, there appears in the sky a mighty column of waters, and clouds mustered from on high roll up a murky tempest of black showers: down falls the lofty heaven, and with its deluge of rain washes away the gladsome crops and the labours of oxen. The dykes fill, the deep-channelled rivers swell and roar, and the sea steams in its heaving friths.[7]

Coopers Hill incorporates this allusion in a political comparison:

> When a calme River rais'd with sudden raines,
> Or Snowes dissolv'd o'reflowes th'adjoyning Plaines,
> The Husbandmen with high rais'd bankes secure
> Their greedy hopes, and this he can endure.
> But if with Bays, and Dammes they strive to force,
> His channell to a new, or narrow course,
> No longer then within his bankes he dwels,
> First to a Torrent, then a Deluge swels;
> Stronger, and fiercer by restraint, he roares,
> And knowes no bound, but makes his powers his shores:
> Thus Kings by grasping more then they can hold,
> First made their Subjects by oppressions bold,
> And popular sway by forcing Kings to give
> More, then was fit for Subjects to receive,
> Ranne to the same extreame; and one excesse
> Made both, by stirring to be greater, lesse. (1642; 333-48)

The manner in which these allusions are to be interpreted depends upon the relation the critic makes between them and the poems to which they refer. But this relation can only be defined in terms of the poet's concept of imitation, of relating past to present—in general, some form of variation of a past work or some attempt to innovate upon it. The most perplexing problems about the use of classical allusions in seventeenth- and eighteenth-century poems stem from the failure on the part of critics to recognize that the difficulty is not a matter of interpreting the poem but rather of assuming a theory that distinguishes conventional uses of allusion from others that are innovative, thus identifying allusive procedures as belonging to one group of poems rather than another.

I have deliberately used the term "conventional" in order to point up the hidden historical assumptions that inevitably exist in interpretative criticism, even among the most able critics. In a valuable article on the eclogue tradition, Paul Alpers remarks in a discussion of Spenser's April eclogue that though "the tone is elevated, Spenser, like Virgil, extends rather than transforms the mode: throughout the eclogue he stays in touch with homely expressions and pretty descriptions." This implies that an extension of a mode can be achieved by varying but not transforming a feature like diction. Yet in a discussion of the December eclogue he remarks upon a fundamental transformation of the Virgilian eclogue: "The idea that there is a proportion between man and nature is basic to Renaissance pastoral and represents a fundamental point of difference between it and ancient pastoral, where life in nature is an ethical alternative, one possibility for the good life. In Renaissance pastoral, with its Christian perspective, man's life has an inherent relation to nature."[8] Unless I mistake these remarks, there is a fundamental difference between Renaissance and Virgilian pastoral in man's relation to nature, yet this fundamental difference does not lead to transformation of the mode, merely extension of it. The question about analysis of a form that has a history requires distinctions between changes that are "extensions" and changes that are "transformations."

The concept of a "convention," for example, requires an understanding of the manner in which it functions in earlier poems in order for it to be assessed as "extending" rather than "innovating" a procedure. It will not do to explain, for example, as Earl Wasserman does—and he is our best critic of this poem—that the "ambience of this doctrine of *concordia discors*"[9] is drawn from Cicero and St. Augustine as well as Davenant, because it is the innovative or variant use that is necessary to be established if the interpretation is to be supported. To see all uses as variants of an "ambience" is to reduce literary study to no more than individual examples. Poetic conventions exist only in poems; they must, therefore, always be identified with a particular use or function. Consider the description of Penshurst in "To Penshurst" and that of Windsor Castle in *Coopers Hill*:

> Thou art not, *Penshurst,* built to envious show,
>   Of touch, or marble; nor canst boast a row
> Of polish'd pillars, or a roofe of gold:
>   Thou hast no lantherne, whereof tales are told;
> Or stayre, or courts; but stand'st an ancient pile,
>   And these grudg'd at, art reverenc'd the while.[10] (1–6)

and

> So *Windsor,* humble in it selfe, seemes proud
> To be the Base of that Majesticke load.
> Than which no hill a nobler burthen beares,
> But Atlas onely, that supports the spheres.
> Nature this mount so fitly did advance,
> We might conclude, that nothing is by chance,
> So plac't, as if she did on purpose raise
> The Hill, to rob the builder of his praise. (1642; 65-72)

Both structures are harmoniously related to the place in which they stand; both are objects of reverence. In "To Penshurst" the structure becomes an emblem of the natural harmony of the grounds and the Sidney family. In *Coopers Hill* Windsor Castle is but one part of a contrasting relationship with Chertsey Abbey, a structure ruined by Henry VIII. It is, moreover, seen as a response to nature's creation of Windsor Hill on which it stands so that the hidden force in nature becomes the dominant feature in this use of the convention.

The failure to distinguish between variants and innovation in a convention, in allusions, in the manner of proceeding, in the classifying of a poem in a genre—and, I would add, in such matters as the semantic and rhetorical dimensions of a poem—results in interpretative difficulties. All these features have a history, but it is a history that exists only in poems. The use of a convention or an allusion or a way of proceeding must be understood, therefore, as interacting with other works. Whether it is a variant or an innovation of a convention, cluster of ideas, or genre, the nature of this interaction forms the basis for divisions in literary study.

The only interaction leading to change that has been studied to any extent is that of the writer with himself: the study of drafts or revisions. These second thoughts or second "sights" are among the simplest of changes because they take place while other unrevised features remain constant. Such studies become the basis for our knowledge of a writer's range of choices as they affect his and our version of his stability and change. They provide an interpretative guide to his grammar and vocabulary, and they make it possible for us to distinguish procedures which are consistent with and thus variants of his earlier practices from those which are innovative, introducing conceptual changes through poetic transformations.

Denham's revisions of the 1642 *Coopers Hill* were published in 1655 and 1668. These sophisticated variations function consistently with the unchanged portions. They do not alter the structure of the poem, but they do extend some scenes and provide a model for the couplet. In 1642 Denham wrote, comparing his verse to the Thames:

> O could my verse freely and smoothly flow,
> As thy pure flood, heav'n should no longer know
> Her old *Eridanus,* thy purer streame
> Should bathe the gods, and be the Poëts Theame. (219-22)

He revised this in 1655:

> O could I flow like thee, and make thy stream
> My great example, as it is my theme!

> Though deep, yet clear, though gentle, yet not dull,
> Strong without rage, without ore-flowing full. (189-92)

The bold metonymy of the revision—"O could I flow like thee" for "O could my verse freely and smoothly flow"—referring to his inspiration as well as his verse, becomes an image of man naturalized, the moving stream being that to which the poet is compared. The unfolding of the image proceeds by indication of harmonious features that mingle natural with personified terms. This interrelationship by its repetitive pattern—"Though . . . yet, though . . . yet not"—establishes those concessions which make for harmony; that is, harmony conceived of as a balance between opposite or contrasting qualities, and in the following line—". . . without . . . , without . . ."—instead of concessions there are rejections by which strength and completion can still be seen as harmonious norms.

Denham's revisions run from 1642 (there were drafts that preceded the initial publication) to 1668, and the later revisions are improvements in the handling of the couplet. We can conceive of the revisions as helping Denham to fulfill more successfully the innovative concept that *Coopers Hill* represented. The "Thames couplets" did effect what the earlier ones did not quite achieve: the revelation of the reciprocal relation between man and nature governed by a harmony based on contraries the source of which was an underlying power. To have fashioned the couplet that expressed these ideas in its structure was a significant achievement, as Dryden and Johnson noted.[11]

To make this point more general, the innovation of the first "Thames couplets" was consistent with the retrospective and spatial features; what the revised couplets provided was an original way of phrasing the same experience. It should, therefore, be apparent that "innovation," as I use it, in no way implies a value term. I noted above that "originality" could be a descriptive as well as evaluative term, and the "Thames couplets" are an example of innovation as evaluation in verse form. The revised lines provided a model for poets who exploited in variant ways the possibilities both of the couplet and of that new georgic scheme that Denham created. So much so, in fact, that Swift declared:

> Nor let my Votaries show their Skill
> In apeing Lines from *Cooper's Hill;*
> For know I cannot bear to hear,
> The Mimickry of *deep yet clear.*[12]

III. THE RELATION OF TECHNIQUE TO CONCEPTS

I have argued that innovation is marked by the attempt to alter the poetic techniques characteristic of a form, to suggest that the manner of conceiving a poetic relationship is no longer tenable. To put the issue in terms of the language of problem solving, the poet finds that the problems posed in the form need reordering. This is what takes place at the opening of *Coopers Hill:*

> Sure there are Poets which did never dream
> Upon *Parnassus,* nor did tast the stream
> Of *Helicon,* we therefore may suppose
> Those made not Poets, but the Poets those,
> And as Courts make not Kings, but Kings the Court,
> So where the Muses & their train resort,
> *Parnassus* stands; if I can be to thee
> A Poet, thou *Parnassus* art to me.
> Nor wonder, if (advantag'd in my flight,
> By taking wing from thy auspicious height)
> Through untrac't ways, and aery paths I fly,
> More boundless in my Fancy than my eie. (1-12)

The literalizing of Parnassus and Helicon by converting them to the actualities of the writing of poetry—where poetry is written there Parnassus is—reveals the demythologizing procedure of the poem. It plunges at once into the denial of the conventional place of the muses and the river Helicon, by making these imaginative places in the environment of the writing of poetry. Now this alteration of mythological to an actual place, Cooper's Hill, near Denham's childhood home, is based on a perceptual rather than allegorical or emblematic scheme. The eye is related to the "Fancy" as the hill is related to the body. To see the prospect from Cooper's Hill, the body must climb it; the imagination is dependent upon the actual height to which it can rise. The relation of Windsor Hill to Windsor Castle, of Runnymede to the Magna Charta, of the river to its banks—of the literal place to its possibilities—is defined by the kind of acts associated with it.

This perceptual procedure is expressed in poetic techniques that are innovative in dealing with man's relation to nature in the georgic poem. For example, the introduction of the prospect view, the technique by which distance is measured by reference to selected places, becomes a way of "contracting" or diminishing space, and in doing so, provides a basis for contracting time.

> My eye, which swift as thought contracts the space
> That lies between, and first salutes the place
> Crown'd with that sacred pile, so vast, so high,
> That whether 'tis a part of Earth, or sky,
> Uncertain seems, and may be thought a proud
> Aspiring mountain, or descending cloud,
> *Pauls,* the late theme of such a Muse whose flight
> Has bravely reach't and soar'd above thy height. (13-20)

The prospect view, as it attends to a specific place, leads to meditation or historical retrospection. The poetic feature of moving from place to time takes several variant expressions. The feature can be followed by moral reflections so that place is identified with events and these are seen in eternal time. Or they can be followed by historical retrospection in which past events are seen to offer present spectators the possibilities of the future.

The observation of external details followed by reflection formed the basis for a new kind of poetic responsiveness. Early in the eighteenth century William Wollaston wrote that reflection and thinking were the two principal methods of perception: "The more frequent or intense the acts of advertence and reflexion are, the more consciousness there is, and the stronger is the *perception.*" And he went on to relate advertence, or attention, to sights and events in their temporal procedures.

> ... all perceptions are produced in time: time passes by moments: there can be but one moment present at once: and therefore all present perception considerd without any relation to what is past, or future, may be lookd upon as momentaneous only.... But in reflexion there is a repetition of what is past, and an anticipation of that which is apprehended as yet to come: there is a *connexion* of past and future, which by this are brought into the sum, and superadded to the present or momentaneous perceptions.[13]

In quoting Wollaston, I mean to suggest a further criterion for the recognition of innovation: the manner in which philosophers and critics draw attention to a new kind of consciousness analogous to that which the reading of the poem evokes. The organizing techniques of prospect view, specific place, and historical or moral reflection operate in the poem like a survey, moving from one scene to the other, the transition being associative rather than logical. When, for example, Denham concludes the London description with an exclamation of hope for peace and contentment, he continues his survey with Windsor Hill:

> Oh happiness of sweet retir'd content!
> To be at once secure, and innocent.
> *Windsor* the next (where *Mars* with *Venus* dwells.
> Beauty with strength) above the Valley swells
> Into my eye, and doth it self present
> With such an easie and unforc't ascent,
> That no stupendious precipice denies
> Access, no horror turns away our eyes:
> But such a Rise, as doth at once invite
> A pleasure, and a reverence from the sight. (37-46)

On the most obvious level the survey technique insists on the visible variety; this variety is distinguishable not only through hills and plains, but also through a series of repetitions of hills: Cooper's Hill, Windsor Hill, St. Anne's Hill. The latter become a basis for the contradictory possibilities of man's use of nature, the physical variety being analogically seen in terms of regal possibilities. The function of repetitive similarity and contrasting variety is to insist on a perceptual relationship which didactically forces the reader to choose among the possibilities. The manner in which this persuasion operates is to suggest an underlying absolute which is the true binding power of God.

The perceptual survey presupposes a journey—visual and imaginative. It is a journey which the poet announces as innovative: "Through untrac't ways, and aery paths I fly, / More boundless in my Fancy than my eie." This relation between the speaker's eye and his imagination, in which the latter is "more boundless" than the former, nevertheless is tied to the bounds of Cooper's Hill. When his fixed thoughts settle on the heroic kings of Windsor Castle, his "wandring eye" betrays his thoughts, and he observes the ruins caused by Henry VIII's tyrannical behavior. The desire to rest on moral wonder and praise is counteracted by the need to examine the contrary actualities that have also left their visible traces. The contrary forces that have tugged at the speaker, the need for memory to be stimulated, not lulled, demand the continuity and variety of the journey. As Denham wrote in *The Progress of Learning*, the expulsion of Adam had to be remembered, if the offense was not to be forgotten. Memory arose out of disobedience:

> Had Memory been lost with Innocence,
> We had not known the Sentence nor th' Offence:
> Twas his chief Punishment to keep in store
> The sad remembrance what he was before.[14] (7-10)

The journey remains, in Denham, unfinished, and it is a reflection of the kind of anxieties that confront the reader. The innovative quality is not the journey, but the perceptual features of the journey which thrust political and moral implications upon the reader. If one compares the ending of the 1642 version with those of the 1655-68 versions, the dependence upon the reader as participant becomes clear.

The first version insists on the need for restraint on the part of king and subject and urges the need to submit to restraint or law. But after the death of Charles I, this inner law was no longer an injunction that could persuade subjects or king to act with control, and the conclusion is the image of a river rampant. This image, which was originally followed by an injunction for king and subjects to restrain themselves, now concludes the poem.

> No longer then within his banks he dwells,
> First to a Torrent, then a Deluge swells:
> Stronger, and fiercer by restraint he roars,
> And knows no bound, but makes his power his shores. (355-58)

Thus the revised poem concludes more anxiously open-ended than the earlier version, the didactic persuasion being superseded by the frightening deluge and its moral implications.

The innovative strategies of poetical organization have their sources in the naturalizing of mythology and allegory, and, in doing so, they suggest the secret power, the "law," the underlying but unknown force that God exercises in governing the world. That "nature" which makes possible the order in variety, which man must seek in himself if he is not to be governed by excess, is a concept that Denham introduced in other works as well. In *The Progress of Learning* (1668) Denham wrote that the necessary purpose of knowledge is to flow back to God, for then it is always under proper control.

> So Learning which from Reasons Fountain springs,
> Back to the sourse, some secret Channel brings.
> 'Tis happy when our Streams of Knowledge flow
> To fill their banks, but not to overthrow. (221-24)

The river image had occurred not merely at the conclusion of *Coopers Hill* but in the London section where the "secret vein" led only to continued loss:

> While luxury, and wealth, like war and peace,
> Are each the others ruine, and increase;

> As Rivers lost in Seas some secret vein
> Thence reconveighs, there to be lost again. (33-36)

The contrast between secret veins or channels that lead to God and those that lead to chaos reinforces the technique of alternatives. The surface scenes that reveal contradictions can be reconciled by underlying beliefs, for the variety and contrast have their source in and a commitment to God whose work they are.

These innovative features are reworkings of procedures found in Virgil's *Georgics* and in the poetry of Denham's predecessors and contemporaries. Since I have already mentioned Jonson and Waller, I wish to turn to Denham's use of the *Georgics*. The *Georgics* are didactic poems in which political sentiments are either directly expressed or expounded in myths or allegories. But the political or moral sentiments do not arise from the perception or survey of nature. They arise, rather, in man's attempt to work with nature—to plant, to grow vines, tend crops, keep bees: acts of living that require man to manage nature, and although he succeeds at times, he also fails when nature resists his control or his management. Thus in the *Georgics* the husbandmen seek to fulfill nature's possibilities; Denham's speaker recognizes that nature's contraries are reconcilable by God's unknown law. The perceptual pattern of the contraries involves the imaginative journey—a journey that in its variants can become the pilgrim's progress, spiritual journey, or the experiential journey—but no such journey defines the *Georgics*.

The speaker's perception of place in *Coopers Hill* provided a moving version of the environment; the river and the secret channels are part of the necessary conception of a world in motion. Places call forth the events associated with them because the present is confronted with alternatives met previously in the past. Virgil dealt with the contrary forces of nature by seeing them in the present or by offering them as myths. His view is based on beliefs or myths as teaching; Denham's on the substitution of history for myths or remembered knowledge. For Virgil, moreover, the *Georgics* was the second venture in treating man and nature. The first, his *Eclogues,* dealt with nature as the environment for celebration, mourning, competitive play, self-derision, and misfortune.

Virgil, therefore, has a range of relations that is missing from Denham's poem; his eclogues are to his georgics as play or ceremony is to work and effort. But at the time of Denham's innovative experimentation, this Virgilian order no longer existed. I do not deny that the Virgilian sequence of pastoral, georgic, and epic existed for Denham and that Pope imitated it. What I *do* deny is that pastoral and georgic or their poetic features had the same meaning or function for Pope as they had for Virgil. The two forms had a different kinship to one another. I have indicated some of the transformations in the georgic renewal—the perceptual view contracting space and time, the naturalizing of man as an aspect of nature, the extension of consciousness through reflection, the identification of place with the function of historical memory as a moral guide, the recognition of variety within repetitive features of nature, and the underlying force of God's creativity by which contraries move to resolution by restraint. These become aspects of a transformed didacticism; their innovative direction alters the conventions and techniques of the songs and poems that are part of the eclogue or pastoral tradition.

Contemporary critics have not always been attentive to the fact that pastoral and georgic were different in their ends—the first a lyric and the second a didactic form. The reason for this has been the neglect of the interrelation of forms. But innovation cannot be understood by application merely to a single literary form like the georgic because forms themselves are interrelated in dealing with the varied possibilities of experience in poetry. The georgic becomes, for the eighteenth century, a more important and more practiced form than the pastoral, and the manner in which this occurs reveals itself in the altered use of traditional features during the innovative period. R. S. Crane was one of the few critics who recognized the theoretical problems of such interrelations:

> From a historical point of view, the most significant shifts in literary ends are clearly those to which the historian can refer—as their necessary or probable consequences—the greatest number or variety of other changes in the kinds of materials writers chose to exploit and in the kinds of devices of construction, characterization, thought, imagery, diction, prosody, or representation they invented or revived for the purpose. Generally speaking, it may be assumed—again not as a dogma but a rough guide in interpretation—that a widespread shift on the part of the ablest writers from the cultivation of mimetic to the cultivation of didactic forms (such as occurred after the middle of the seventeenth century) is likely to have more far-reaching results of the kinds mentioned than a shift from serious forms to comic in drama or fiction, and that a shift of the latter sort is likely to be considerably more consequential than one involving only such formal differences.[15]

Crane saw innovative changes as "more consequential" than variations. And he was correct. But he needed criteria to distinguish innovation from variations, and innovations of a Denham or Milton or Marvell from the variations of a Pope or Thomson. As part of the innovative procedures, what Crane called the change from imitative to didactic forms, the traditional pastoral form underwent alteration and finally became extremely limited in its possibilities. The innovative techniques to express the new perceptual and religious dilemmas are found not only in Denham but also in Milton's *A Masque presented in Ludlow Castle* (1634) and *Lycidas*, published in 1638, four years before the initial publication of *Coopers Hill*.

Among the most important of these challenges is Milton's handling of the relation of place and figure to perception in the traditional disguise character. The Attendant Spirit and Comus both become shepherds: the problem is to distinguish virtue from vice through the disguise. The *Masque* is a journey like the perceptual journey in *Coopers Hill*, but one in which the secret forces of good, both of the upper world (the Attendant Spirit) and the underworld (Sabrina), arrive to support young virtue. Both Milton and Denham turn to individual restraint and virtue as traits that help master the contrary possibilities offered by nature.

Milton's management of *Lycidas*, for example, also reveals an innovative effort to resist or transform the received conventions. His remarkable handling of gentle nature and of such destructive forces as occasioned the drowning of Edward King reveals the technique of contraries resoluble in resurrection. The echoes of this technique reverberated through eighteenth-century georgic poems. The lowest of forms became capable of articulating the highest insights; it led to the abandonment of the pastoral as a form of play describing actual situations. Instead, it was reserved for the idealized play of the Golden Age or for satiric treatment of shepherds and their pursuits. The actualities of pastoral became part of the reformed georgic.

IV. ROLE CHANGES OF PASTORAL AND GEORGIC

Innovations within a genre are identified by (1) the altered functions of literary conventions, themes, characters, language, and imagery to express new conceptions; (2) the retrospective grouping of works in a single class by contemporaneous critics; (3) the coeval exploration by philosophers and critics of the kind of consciousness the new poetry is expressing; and (4) finally, the altered relation of other forms to the innovative ones. Just as new concepts call forth some features to reveal them, so, too, only some genres at any one time undergo innovative revisions. Critics have repeatedly drawn attention to the fact that *Paradise Lost* was the last successful English epic, and while the georgic poem developed, the sonnet languished.

Innovation is not a procedure confined to one poet, and, in identifying the variations that follow upon innovations, one has a span of time in which the hierarchy of literary forms undergoes a change. An example of this is the manner in which the pastoral undergoes a change in relation to the georgic. The Virgilian pastoral was, in the late sixteenth century, a lyrical form of considerable importance, whereas the Virgilian georgic was considered a very minor form indeed. But, by the beginning of the eighteenth century, this pastoral had been reduced to idealized emptiness, often parodied and ridiculed, whereas the georgic became the more practiced form, the one for which important themes and subjects were reserved.

When George Puttenham in *The Arte of English Poesie* (1589) wrote of the eclogue, he did so with a knowledge of the discussions of the form. He treated it as an allegorical poem whose purpose was not to imitate rustic life but "under the vaile of homely persons and in rude speeches to insinuate and glaunce at greater matters, and such as perchance had not bene safe to have beene disclosed in any other sort." Reference was made to the georgic poem not specifically mentioned in a paragraph entitled "the forme wherein honest and profitable artes and sciences were treated."[16] Sir Philip Sidney listed the *Georgics* under "matters Philosophicall" and left open the question whether writers of this kind "properly be Poets."[17] Eclogues or pastorals belong to genuine poetry, and they can treat serious themes frankly, allegorically, or ironically. But at midcentury René Rapin (1659, trans. 1684) wrote a treatise on pastoral song in which he denied that Virgil's Pollio (fourth eclogue) was a fit subject for pastoral and pointed out that the manners of shepherds should "be represented according to the *Genius* of the *golden Age.*"[18] The subject matter of the pastoral was being narrowed and its characters removed from the actualities of the existence they had in Theocritus and Virgil. Fontenelle further limited the scope of the pastoral, seeking to disengage it from shepherds' actual concerns.

Fontenelle claimed that the advantage of poetry consisted in being relevant, "in representing to us in a lively manner the things that concern us, and in striking strongly a heart which is pleased with being moved."[19] The things that concerned his readers were not the actualities of pastoral life, but rather the satisfaction of their most rewarding passions—laziness and love—

without permitting them to become obsessive. Pastorals used the idealization of nature and the character of shepherds only because these seemed the most likely representatives of the middle way of passions.

> This considered, it is not to be admired why the pictures which are drawn of a pastoral life have always something so very smiling in them, and indulge our fancies more than the pompous description of a splendid court, and of all the magnificence that can shine there. A court gives us no idea but of toilsome and constrained pleasures. For, as we have observed, the idea is all in all. Could the scene of this quiet life, with no other business but love, be placed anywhere but in the country, so that no goats nor sheep should be brought in, I fancy it would be never the worse, for the goats and sheep add nothing to its felicity; but as the scene must lie either in the country or in towns, it seems more reasonable to choose the first.[20]

The stabilization of this view of the pastoral takes place with Pope, whose *Discourse on Pastoral* was based on the essays by Rapin and Fontenelle. Pope saw pastoral as the image of the Golden Age, and he was aware that poets must "use some illusion to render a Pastoral delightful; and this consists in exposing the best side only of a shepherd's life, and in concealing its miseries."[21] His pastorals must be understood in the hierarchy of his work as representing those situations which have no relation to the life as described in *Windsor Forest* or in the satires, imitations, and epistles. But it does reveal the manner in which an innovative change becomes a variant of a received position. And, in contradistinction, Virgil's *Georgics* became in the words of Addison, "the most complete, elaborate and finished piece of all antiquity."[22]

V. REASON-GIVING AND HISTORICAL EXPLANATION

Having presented the arguments for innovative techniques and their variations within a genre, having discussed how these function and how the forms themselves undergo shifts in the hierarchy of forms, I wish to conclude by turning to the kinds of explanations that are given for innovation.

Innovative changes are conceptual, and their concepts are analyzable in the techniques used to express them. I have above (in III) analyzed some of the relations between techniques and concepts, but other critics have put forward alternative explanations that merit consideration. John Chalker has written: "The most significant factor in the development of English Georgic poetry was the correspondence between the situations of pre-Augustan

[Rome] and post-Restoration England, and it is certainly true that that correspondence is of great importance and is deeply felt. Imitation begins on the thematic and develops to a formal level. But with Pope, and even more Thomson, it becomes clear that, although imitation of the *Georgics* was first inspired by historical factors, its continuation involved much wider sympathies between eighteenth-century writers and Virgil."[23] This explanation of innovation, while seeking to account for the prominence of the English georgic as a form in the late seventeenth century, presents numerous difficulties. In the first place, Denham's model of the georgic was published before the Restoration. Secondly, the prominence of the Virgilian georgic was matched by that of the Horatian odes and satires, and these were so well known at the beginning of the century that Ben Jonson was called the "English Horace." There is no procedure that John Chalker offers that identifies the georgic form as a characteristically post-Civil War form. And on this must rest the special artistic correspondence. Will it serve to argue that imitation of Virgil first existed on the thematic level when the themes of Virgil's *Georgics*, whether planting or beekeeping, have no place in the poems of Denham, Pope, or Thomson? Explanations which rely upon historical parallels cannot assume that imitation which begins thematically leads to formal changes without having some hypotheses about either change or continuity of formal features.

Maren-Sofie Røstvig, whose valuable study *The Happy Man* is well known, is far more circumspect in her critical explanation, recognizing the need to attend to history as continuity rather than as spots of time. Tracing the *beatus ille* tradition in the seventeenth century, she quite properly notes that the tradition "was seldom rendered accurately, since in most cases it came to be coloured by the prevailing mood of each succeeding generation."[24] Referring to the period during which Denham revised his poem, she points to the second metamorphosis that the "classical Happy Husbandman" underwent.

> The second metamorphosis occurred in the fifth and sixth decades of the seventeenth century, at a time when civil dissent forced a large part of the nation to court retirement out of sheer necessity. This fact, together with the pronounced influence of Neoplatonic and of mystic or semi-mystic thought at exactly this point, must be considered responsible for the transformation of the neo-Stoic Serene Contemplator into an ecstatic Hortulan Saint. While the neo-Stoic poets had added the motif of solitary contemplation to the classical *beatus ille* motifs, the Neoplatonic poets of the mid-century added two further themes: the Biblical theme of the Earthly Paradise

(or the classical motif of the Golden Age), and the partly Hermetic, partly Neoplatonic theme of Nature as a divine hieroglyph which, when properly studied, bespeaks a secret, spiritual connection with the Deity.[25]

Professor Røstvig is tracing the history of a classical topos in the seventeenth century, and she is cognizant of change that is imitative as against change as metamorphosis. But the changes apply to all forms in which the "Happy Husbandman" appears, and the relation of theme to form never becomes clear. Moreover, one of the difficulties with a historical explanation like "civil dissent" is that it can apply to all types of literature and can, therefore, not be used to explain why a work takes the form it does.

The question of why the georgic becomes innovative at midcentury can be answered in three ways: (1) the religious-scientific discourse and argument; (2) the historical situation; (3) the kinds of problems poets writing georgics set themselves to solve. The seventeenth-century religious controversies do not need to be documented, but it is useful to draw attention to the literary techniques derivable from the merger of religion and science.

Using the 1646 essay by John Wilkins, *A Discourse concerning the Beauty of Providence,* as a representative text, we can see that certain poetic features are consistent with and, indeed, can be derived from religious arguments. Wilkins declared that God's presence was available not merely through revelation, but through man's contemplation of the objects in nature. He pointed out that "in the works of *Nature,* where there are many common things of excellent beauty, which for their *littlenesse* do not fall under our *sence;* they that have experimented the use of *Microscopes,* can tell, how in the parts of the most minute creatures, there may be discerned such gildings and embroideries, and such curious varietie as another would scarce beleive."[26]

This argument for the identification of God's presence in a variety of objects forms the basis for the apparent, but only apparent, randomness of observed detail. It finds poetic expression in the techniques that point to the different aspects of the same objects—variation in repetition—and similar aspects of different objects. This procedure becomes, in works that do not deal with nature, an example of Augustan wit and subtle discrimination. The observations of Wilkins provide an explanation for the gradual inclusion, in subsequent variations of georgic poems, of ordinary domestic objects that come to be part of the catalogs and the inclusive harmonies.

Wilkins was thoroughly aware of the view of nature that he called "the *dark side* of Providence,"[27] but he urged that man disregard the obvious disorder and contrariety of nature, since man was unable in such instances to fathom God's ways: "'Tis our safest way then to conclude that all matters are for the best, *beautiful in their times,* though to us they may seem full of disorder and contrariety."[28]

The relation of science to nature in this account is analogous to the relation between Cooper's Hill and the perception of the surrounding environment: one makes it possible for the other to take place. Our knowledge is enlarged by science in realms unnoticed by the naked eye. And this argument is developed further in John Ray's *The Wisdom of God in the Creation.* Ray not only refers to Wilkins's argument, but makes overt the art-nature relationship: "I might draw an Argument of the admirable Art and Skill of the Creator and Composer of them, from the incredible Smallness of some of those natural and enlivened Machines, the Bodies of Animals."[29] Ray explicitly argues that we ought "let us ourselves examine Things as we have opportunity, and converse with Nature as well as Books."[30]

The conversation with nature that Ray advocated extended beyond the realm of mere observation of the harmony of God's design in the smallest natural object; it suggested that man consider his own smallness in regard to the heavens—the sun, moon, and stars. To praise God for noticing man was the function of all who loved God. The immensity of nature as well as its smallness—the sublimity of the first and beauty of the second—were alike the consequences of observation. The details of landscape were, therefore, to be understood as marked by attention to minute details and to the immensity of the heavens.

Ray's argument, with its appeal for a new view of natural history based on observation, for a need to "converse with Nature," drew attention to the language of metaphor. His argument, indeed, urged a scientific basis for classifying objects in nature, and it helped to explain the use of scientific terminology and classification in this poetry. It indicated, too, the evident limitation of man's ability to see all of nature's possibilities, thus reinforcing the techniques of limitation which form one of the key themes of this poetry. It insisted on the pattern of contemplation following upon observation, emphasizing that opposites such as insects smaller than the eye could see and the extensive heavens above revealed the immensity of God's variety and his bounty, benevolence, and power. And because God's power operated in such diverse objects, there was present the justification of a metonymic language in which references to the whole, like "nature," could refer to particular objects and situations.

The scientific-religious controversies made clear the relation of themes to techniques in the renewal of the georgic. But innovation in the georgic also resulted from an effort by poets to deal with problems resulting from the historical situation. Thomas S. Kuhn in his discussion of the changes in science points out that there were, beginning with the seventeenth century, norms for scientific problem solving and that the norms, or paradigms, changed as a result of "the persistent failure of the puzzles of normal science to come out as they should."[31] Such failures resulted in anxiety and insecurity among scientists and led to periods of "crisis." Robert A. Nisbet, in discussing sociological change, writes: "A given way of behaving tends to persist as long as circumstances permit. Then, as [W. I.] Thomas points out, the way of behaving ceases to be possible, as the result of some intrusion, some difficulty which is the consequence of event or impact, and a period of crisis ensues.... It is impossible for me to think of any empirical study of change in contemporary social science—change of political, economic, ethnic, rural, urban, or other type of social behavior—in which the element that Thomas called crisis is not clearly present."[32]

The innovative poems I have been discussing have as one of their major themes the resolution of anxiety. The voyage in the *Masque* is fraught with danger, the Lady is subject to temptations, and the brothers almost neglect to free their sister. The theme of *Lycidas* begins with the shepherd-singer referring to himself as plucking the unripe berries, as being compelled to an act that analogically is like the untimely drowning of Edward King. And the shepherd's lament is a series of questions about responsibility for death, about the aim of life or the role of poetry in life, about man's faith and its rewards—questions that suggest the immensity of the anxiety and crisis that the singer is himself undergoing. The anxiety characteristic of *Coopers Hill* is locatable in the imagery of contraries and in the recognition that man's relation to nature depends on his exercise of restraint and his willingness to fulfill its possibilities.

The sense of crisis is apparent in the organization of these poems as well as in some of their rhetorical features. Consider the use of the fictive narrative of the stag hunt and its contrast with the perceptual and didactic responses to the surrounding environment in *Coopers Hill*.

There is a shift in the poem from an observing and commenting speaker addressing the reader to a speaker who sympathizes with and tells a story from the point of view of the hunted stag.

> And as a Hero, whom his baser foes
> In troops surround, now these assails, now those,
> Though prodigal of life, disdains to die
> By common hands; but if he can descry
> Some nobler foes approach, to him he calls,
> And begs his Fate, and then contented falls. (313-18)

The narrative heightens the didactic statements by creating the example of the animal willing to submit to his killing by the king. The procedure is that of a moralized tale and it becomes a model for the sentimentalizing of situations, even though in later eighteenth-century writers the sentimentalizing of animals is achieved by opposing killing rather than by showing the animals' readiness to die.

The mixture of narrative and precepts serves, also, to point up the distinction between an imitated action and one spoken in the poet's voice. The precepts and the historical references to persons, places, and events function in terms of statement and example. The poems for which *Coopers Hill* becomes a model have, therefore, two related kinds of truth-value, which support or undermine one another. One is fictive and the other referential, and such mixtures are in sharp contrast to the fictive truths of songs or pastorals. The georgics were always recognized as poems that presented mixed truth-values (in Virgil these were myths and advice). Addison made this clear in his essay when he wrote: "No rules, therefore, that relate to Pastoral, can any way affect the Georgics, since they fall under that class of poetry which consists in giving plain and direct instructions to the reader."[33]

The mixture of types of truth can be understood as solutions to particular poetic problems. The poets sought to continue the tradition of nature as emblem while insisting on its scientific validity. They recognized God's presence and power in nature's harmony on a religious or metaphysical level; on the descriptive level they recognized a universe often disharmonious and threatening. They introduced the clashing present in nature with reflection on the unchanging patterns of nature. Nature became the ground for comparing the known with the unknown, present sight with insight into the past. Denham sought to convert direct praise of political action into indirect persuasion. His resolution involved the perception of nature as necessarily political and moral. Milton sought to convert pagan conventions by transforming them into preludes of Christian resurrection. Both poets in rejecting the classical solutions for pastoral and georgic were seeking to extend the bounds of poetical experience. The perceptual view of nature, and all the techniques this entailed, provided a basis for resolving this problem by offering God's nature as a model for resolving opposites.

The techniques and methods I have discussed must be seen as returning to the classics—especially Virgil and Horace—to select such features as the retreat passages, the fortunate husbandman, and the raging river in order to support views reinterpreting these phenomena. For instead of showing the contrasting forces as examples of nature's or of fate's action, they suggest that the opposites were part of God's larger harmony, thus making possible the excusing or transmuting of what appeared like unresolvable contrarieties.

In this respect, the literary historians who discuss the late seventeenth and eighteenth centuries have failed to understand what the return to the classics meant for these poets, assuming that they were seeking to identify themselves with the classical writers. But the nature of their poetry was to break with the variant procedures and seek innovative explanations. The turn to certain aspects of classical poetry was to provide a norm against which to innovate. Literary historians who wish to place the classical tradition in "context" require a theory of change, of variation and innovation, if "context" is to have validity as an interpretative principle.

I have undertaken in this essay to explore some of the problems of change in terms of variation and innovation. I have argued that to distinguish between the norm of variation and the rejection of this norm is to provide a basis for divisions in literary history. Such divisions are not only necessary for giving order to history, but for interpreting individual poems within this order. If my aim has been achieved, then I have succeeded in proposing more adequate ways of writing literary history and the explanations that help define it.

VI. AFTERWORDS: QUERIES AND AFFIRMATIONS

Q. Is "innovation" the result of evolutionary change or the result of some type of discontinuity?

A. Thomas Kuhn and Robert Nisbet argue that "revolutions" in science "cannot be deduced from, be understood in terms of, the kinds of minor, adaptational, more or less cumulative change.... A 'scientific revolution' transforms the scientific imagination and leads to a transformation indeed of the whole world of the scientist."[34] Robert Nisbet applies this view to "major changes" in society, arguing for the recognition of discontinuity.

I have applied the term "innovation" to conceptual changes that underlie the altered hierarchy of poems, their features, and the function of these features. But it should be noted that the altered hierarchy of forms is identifiable in two ways: (1) poets give new functions to forms that have previously been minimized or avoided (and avoid or minimize others); (2) contemporaneous critics identify the hierarchy by indicating the altered status of forms. Since literary forms are always interrelated with each other, what takes place is an altered conception and function of all synchronic forms.

Are these the result of gradual variations? Prior to innovative change, poets and critics make efforts to introduce unexpected themes and procedures within the customary functions: thus the so-called forgeries of James Macpherson and Thomas Chatterton, the attempt to place medieval ballads within the Augustan tradition, Gray's use of elegy and ode to widen the possibilities of Augustan subject matter and form. But these do not "lead" to innovative change except in the sense that they exemplify the limits within which writers are able, at this time, to explore the possibilities of the perceptual, reflective, and naturalistic concepts that are "givens."

Of course, a body of past poems is always present to keep the poets cognizant of past practices, to keep an element of stability before them. The poems of Virgil, Horace, Chaucer, Spenser, Shakespeare, Milton, and others were available in the eighteenth century, and they represent forms whose functions are reexamined in terms of the present. But they embody alternative ways of writing poetry and using poetic forms; they are quarries, elements of which are selected in each period to support the conceptual changes that take place. Does a conceptual change apply to all features and functions within a poem? Denham's perceptual, additive procedures of organization do not prevent him from including emblematic passages. What takes place is a shift in the governing principles of the poem, a reordering of the hierarchy of features and their function. Moreover, innovative procedures do not apply to all literary forms. Post-Restoration tragedy becomes more rigid than earlier tragedy, just as pastoral loses its coherence as a form. Nor is it necessary to assume that all poems exhibit innovative procedures—only that these become models for the major poetic works as well as for an overwhelming body of poems.

Q. Is scientific change applicable to literary change?
A. Scientific change is identifiable by repeatable experiments, and to this ex-

tent can be recognized and charted. Literary innovation, in the sense that I have argued for it, is identifiable within a theory of the interrelation of forms and of the interrelations of any single form within a hierarchy of functions. Such changes are recognized by critics and practiced by poets, though they have not previously been explained in this manner. I would wish to argue that explanations of change need to be compared and tested with regard to literary works, and that alternative explanations must be alternative explanations of innovation and variation. Innovative literary change involves a conceptual change, but this takes place by an alteration of the features previously found in the supplanted concept. To this extent the model of scientific change is not applicable.

Q. Do you find any order in the variations that occur between innovations?

A. If we assume that one innovation occurred at about the time of the English Revolution and another at the end of the eighteenth century, then the question refers to the poetry written within this segment of time. "Innovation" is the term I use to explain the shift in the hierarchy of poems, features, and functions in order to convey a changed conception of knowing and experiencing. These result in altered conceptions of what poetry is, how it is organized, and how features function. The changes involve shifts in emphasis of forms—georgic, pastoral, epigram, etc.—and shifts in the way in which all forms tend toward the didactic. Since innovations arise as a result of prior variations no longer sufficing, we can expect that aspects of form—like blank verse, types of imagery, the nature of character—will be experimented with within the earlier concept before the change takes place. Prior to innovation, efforts are made to bring within the established concept ways of thinking and feeling that seem no longer variations of the original innovative concept. After innovation, the writers who follow upon the innovators tend to expand, to vary, to explore the possibilities of the new concept. The pastoral, for example, becomes subject to extensive debate and alteration. Pope uses the form to idealize the past whereas Gay adapts it to satire. Others argue its irrelevance to the time. The subject matter of georgic is expanded by Pope and Thomson to include ways of treating religion, science, and nature.

The answer to the question is that variations can be grouped together to permit narrower generalizations that, at the least, reveal three stages: expansion, stabilization, unsuitable accommodation. Of course, the smaller the unit, the more distinctions one can introduce into the groupings that are variations.

Q. Doesn't the view of a period as explained by "innovation" and "variation" become reductive? Doesn't it eliminate the variety of poems within a given time span?

A. The notion of "variety" of poems within a period usually refers to the opposing political tendencies in the poems; to the extensive forms that are used, whether epigram, ode, elegy, georgic, epic, and so forth; to the different metrical forms; to the different treatments of common subject matter, etc. The hypothesis of "innovation" and "variation" does not deny this variety; in fact, its purpose is to make variety understandable by indicating what it is, why and how it occurs. Conceptual change can underlie the most wide-ranging subject matter or metrical forms because it explains why these function differently—why poets present the conflict as an antithetical form, or why political themes are presented in naturalistic imagery, or why odes and elegies are structured additively to imply knowledge gained sequentially.

It is possible for critics to construct generalizations about uses of subject matter or literary forms or tendencies, but these will still depend on hypotheses about the beginning and end of a tendency or movement, and will, therefore, inevitably involve the critic in some theory of "innovation" and "variation." What I present is, I hope, a valid procedure for dealing with a necessary part of literary study.

Q. Doesn't "innovation" apply to all literary works, since every poem is unique? Isn't the distinction a fruitless one?

A. The argument for "uniqueness" must presuppose similarity, otherwise there would be no differentness. "Uniqueness" is a consequence of certain interrelations, some of which must be familiar in order for uniqueness to occur. Surely, the letters of the alphabet, the words themselves, sentence forms, verse forms, even the themes are not, nor can they all be, unique. To talk of a poem as "unique" is to imply that certain features lead to such an impression of the whole. The question, then, rests on unexamined assumptions about differentness and similarity, on unexamined assumptions about "innovation" and "variation." Only as these unexamined assumptions become the object of analysis, as in this paper, does it become possible to make adequate distinctions about "uniqueness."

Q. How do premises of "innovation" and "variation" help us interpret the individual work?

A. The distinctions that I seek to introduce are part of a theory of literary history and interpretation. The argument has been that interpretation rests on identifying the implications of meaning and the function of features toward a given end. But meaning and function are normally arrived at by reference to "convention," "tradition," "influence"—by some hypothesis of past practice. Any such hypothesis assumes a theory of how convention or tradition operates, and it is this assumption that I am analyzing, offering a procedure for more accurate interpretation. As I indicated, this procedure is not circular. The hypothesis which suggests interrelations of forms is not arrived at by part-whole relationships within a poem, but by how forms function as a group in a society. Statements about interrelation of forms, about the relation of forms to nonliterary experience, deal with analysis of classification systems. The understanding of such systems becomes then the precondition for interpretation; it is not determined by interpretation of specific poems.

Q. How does a discussion of "innovation" and "variation" help us grasp the value of a poem?

A. I have suggested that this hypothesis deals with the way poems relate to each other. In this sense it is necessary for interpretation. But is the *value* of a specific poem dependent on its relation to other poems? This is not the occasion to enter into a discussion of value, but I should point out that the question, "Is this a good poem?" can mean is it good of its kind, is it good in terms of the exploitation of its possibilities by the poet, is it good in the sense that it adheres to some absolute values? To determine the goodness of a "kind" or genre requires the historical knowledge of the function of features that I have indicated. This applies, too, to the comparison with other poems (and their possibilities) by the same poet. As for the hypothesis of some absolute "good," I can only say that the concept of innovation and variation calls the meaning of this question into doubt.

NOTES

1. Recent discussions of literary change in the eighteenth century can be found in W. J. Bate, *From Classic to Romantic* (Cambridge, MA: Harvard Univ. Press, 1946); Ralph Cohen, ed., "Literary and Artistic Change in the Eighteenth Century," special issue, *Eighteenth-Century Studies* 2 (Autumn 1968); Raymond Williams, *The Country and the City* (New York: Oxford Univ. Press, 1973); Paul Korshin, ed., *Studies in Change and Revolution, 1640-1800*, (London: Scolar Press, 1972); Maren-Sofie Røstvig, *The Happy Man*, 2 vols. (Oslo: Norwegian Universities Press, 1962, 1971); Harold Bloom,

The Anxiety of Influence (New York: Oxford Univ. Press, 1973); Josephine Miles, *Poetry and Change* (Berkeley: Univ. of California Press, 1974). Recent discussions of scientific change have derived from the works of Karl Popper and from Thomas S. Kuhn's *The Structure of Scientific Revolutions* (1962; Chicago: Univ. of Chicago Press, 1970). Important criticism of Kuhn's position can be found in Imre Lakatos and Alan Musgrave, eds., *Criticism and the Growth of Knowledge* (Cambridge: Cambridge Univ. Press, 1970); and in Stephen E. Toulmin, *Human Understanding* (Princeton, NJ: Princeton Univ. Press, 1972), 1:41-132.

2. Samuel Johnson, *Lives of the English Poets*, ed. G. B. Hill (Oxford: Clarendon Press, 1905), 1:77.

3. John Dennis, "Remarks upon Mr. Pope's Translation of Homer" (1717), in *The Critical Works of John Dennis*, ed. E. N. Hooker (Baltimore: Johns Hopkins Univ. Press, 1943), 2:137.

4. See "Introduction to *The Forrest*," in *The Complete Poetry of Ben Jonson*, ed. W. B. Hunter Jr. (New York: New York Univ. Press, 1963), 75; M. H. Abrams, "Structure and Style in the Greater Romantic Lyric," in *Romanticism and Consciousness*, ed. Harold Bloom (New York: Norton, 1970), 207-12; H. E. Toliver, *Pastoral Forms and Attitudes* (Berkeley: Univ. of California Press, 1971), 212; "Introduction to *Coopers Hill*," in *Expans'd Hieroglyphicks, A Critical Edition of Sir John Denham's Coopers Hill*, ed. Brendan O Hehir (Berkeley: Univ. of California Press, 1969), 12-13.

5. All quotations from *Coopers Hill* are from the 1668 edition of the poem (unless otherwise specified) in *Expans'd Hieroglyphicks*, ed. Brendan O Hehir.

6. For a discussion of the country-house poem as a genre, see Alastair Fowler, "The 'Better Marks' of Jonson's *To Penshurst*," *Review of English Studies* 24 (1973): 266-82; and Charles Molesworth, "Property and Virtue: The Genre of the Country-House Poem in the Seventeenth Century," *Genre* 1 (1968): 141-57. For an older view of *Coopers Hill* as local poetry, different from the georgic, see Dwight L. Durling, *Georgic Tradition in English Poetry* (New York: Columbia Univ. Press, 1935), 193. For discussions of genre, see E. D. Hirsch Jr., *Validity in Interpretation* (New Haven, CT: Yale Univ. Press, 1967); and Paul Hernadi, *Beyond Genre* (Ithaca, NY: Cornell Univ. Press, 1972).

7. *Virgil*, trans. H. Rushton Fairclough (London: Heinemann, 1932), 103.

8. Paul Alpers, "The Eclogue Tradition and the Nature of Pastoral," *College English* 34 (1972): 352-71.

9. Earl Wasserman, "Denham: *Cooper's Hill*," in *The Subtler Language* (1959; Baltimore: Johns Hopkins Univ. Press, 1968), 57.

10. Jonson, *The Complete Poetry*, ed. Hunter, 77-78.

11. Dryden is quoted in *The Poetical Works of Sir John Denham*, ed. T. H. Banks (New Haven, CT: Yale Univ. Press, 1928), 29; for Johnson, see *Lives*, ed. Hill, 1:78-79.

12. Swift, "Apollo's Edict," in *The Poems of Jonathan Swift*, ed. H. Williams (Oxford: Clarendon Press, 1958), 1:271.

13. William Wollaston, *The Religion of Nature Delineated* (London: printed by Samuel Palmer, 1726), 32.

14. Denham, *The Poetical Works,* ed. Banks. All quotations from Denham's poems other than *Coopers Hill* are from this edition.

15. R. S. Crane, *Critical and Historical Principles of Literary History* (Chicago: Univ. of Chicago Press, 1971), 41-42.

16. George Puttenham, *The Arte of English Poesie,* in *Elizabethan Critical Essays,* ed. G. Gregory Smith, 2 vols. (Oxford: Clarendon Press, 1904), 2:40, 46.

17. Sir Philip Sidney, *An Apologie for Poetrie,* in Smith, *Elizabethan Critical Essays,* 1:158-59.

18. René Rapin, *De Carmine Pastorali,* ed. J. E. Congleton, *Series Two: Essays on Poetry,* Augustan Reprint Society (Ann Arbor, MI, 1947), 33.

19. Fontenelle, *Of Pastorals* (1688; trans. 1695, Peter Motteux), in *The Continental Model: Selected French Critical Essays of the Seventeenth Century in English Translation,* ed. Scott Elledge and Donald Schier (Minneapolis: Univ. of Minnesota Press, 1960), 347.

20. Fontenelle, *Of Pastorals,* 345.

21. Alexander Pope, *A Discourse on Pastoral Poetry* (1709), in *The Poems of Alexander Pope,* ed. John Butt (New Haven, CT: Yale Univ. Press, 1963), 120.

22. Joseph Addison, "An Essay on Virgil's Georgics" (1697), in *The Works of Joseph Addison,* ed. T. Tickell (London, 1804), 5:454.

23. John Chalker, *The English Georgic: A Study in the Development of a Form* (London: Routledge, 1969), 209. In the introduction, Mr. Chalker remarks that Virgil's *Georgics* proved popular in the eighteenth century because "on the one hand it promotes awareness of the instability of civilized values, and on the other the ethic of work, and of the need to build patiently by mastering the fundamental resources of life" (15). Howard D. Weinbrot, in "History, Horace and Augustus Caesar," *Eighteenth-Century Studies* 7 (1974): 391-414, draws attention to some of the confusions of modern critics in their comparisons of eighteenth-century England with the Rome of Augustus Caesar.

24. Røstvig, *The Happy Man,* 1:313.

25. Røstvig, *The Happy Man,* 1:314.

26. John Wilkins, *A Discourse concerning the Beauty of Providence* (London, 1649), 49-50.

27. Wilkins, *A Discourse,* 72.

28. Wilkins, *A Discourse,* 89.

29. John Ray, *The Wisdom of God in the Creation* (London, 1701), 185.

30. Ray, *The Wisdom of God,* 192.

31. Kuhn, *Structure of Scientific Revolutions,* 68.

32. Robert A. Nisbet, *Social Change and History: Aspects of the Western Theory of Development* (New York: Oxford Univ. Press, 1969), 282-83.

33. Addison, "Essay on Virgil's Georgics," 5:446.

34. Robert A. Nisbet, "Introduction: The Problem of Social Change," in *Social Change,* ed. Nisbet (Oxford: Basil Blackwell, 1972), 20.

Historical Knowledge and Literary Understanding

My argument shall be that the historical study of literature is a necessary condition for any literary analysis. As critics and scholars, we invoke historical assumptions in our practice, our methods, and our theory. The problem, therefore, is to present a conception of historical knowledge and literary understanding that will acknowledge this phenomenon and make practice consonant with it. And to do this, one must begin by recognizing the historical nature of literary study. In this essay I shall be using examples from my own work in progress—a study of literary change from Milton to Keats—and although I present conclusions, they are not meant to be conclusive.

A "literary" work—and I leave the term *literary* undefined—is a member of at least three historical classes and the object of investigation of a fourth. First, every literary work is a form or genre. If we conceive of genre as possessing a subject matter, as a means of ordering a subject matter, as a manner of presenting the ordering, we can define genre in terms of lyric, drama, or narrative and note the subgenres within each. In the very process of composing an ode, for example, the writer is committed to historical possibilities: to compose a Pindaric ode or an irregular variant; to compose a great ode or a lesser ode; to use the given variations of appropriate diction or to add, supplement, invent others; to invoke certain received or new rhetorical methods for shifts in associating his subject matter; to adapt the poem to conventional ends of praise or narrative or example, and so forth. The point to be observed here is that a writer's composition is based on historical precedents which

---

This essay was originally published in *Papers on Language and Literature* 14, no. 3 (1978): 227-48, copyright 1978 by the Board of Trustees, Southern Illinois University at Edwardsville, and is reprinted with permission of the publisher. A version of the paper was read at a 1978 symposium, "Historical Knowledge and Literary Understanding," held at the University of Iowa.

offer the sources for a particular generic construction. The constructional view of genre as historically mixed is a reaffirmation of its origins. Genres originated, according to Francis Cairns, from actual social discourse. "The genres are as old as organized societies; they are also universal. Within all human lives there are a number of important recurrent situations which, as societies develop, come to call for regular responses, both in words and in actions. Because literature, which in early society means poetry, concerns itself with these situations, it is natural that renderings and descriptions of these responses should become the staple subject-matter of literature."[1] Genres have their sources in the conventions of cultural behavior, and they continue as responses to and shapers of such behavior. The concept of genre needs, therefore, to be understood as a combination of discourse or rhetorical conventions, subject matters (themes), poetical and social ends, and their changes.

Here it might be noted that in oral societies where critics can find no generic heritage there exist two modes of reconstitution. First, the *Iliad* and *Odyssey* are seen by Aristotle and the rhetoricians, for example, as comprehensive genres from which can be extrapolated all other genres, and second, by analogy with contemporary narratives—such as provided by American Indian communities—earlier oral genres can be explored.

Past genres offer the writer a group of possibilities which include previous variations and alterations of rhetorical features and their modes of combination. I do not, however, mean to overlook the problematic aspects of genre choice. It is precisely because of the combinatory nature of genre that certain kinds of poems, for example, are closely allied in groups and become members of a larger unit such as lyric. Thus, the poem of praise, the canzone, the elegy, the song, the sonnet, the pastoral, possess shared features combined for different ends at different times, but these are all part of the lyric. So, too, autobiographical narrative, journal, prayer, proverb, and authorial intervention are joined in *Robinson Crusoe,* and letters, journal, narrative, and authorial intervention are joined in *Pamela*—the genre itself being distinguished from mere letters or biography or spiritual autobiography to form a genre called novel which can be subsumed under narrative. Such procedures are historical not merely because they happen at a particular time but because the formal features function with particular cultural implications.

If a literary work is historical because it belongs to a genre, it is also historical because it is a member of at least two other temporally defined systems, neither of which is generic: it is part of a writer's total work, his oeuvre, part of his literary identity in whatever genre he composes, and it is, at the same time, part of the order of all other literary and verbal works synchronous with it. Thus "Lycidas" is a member of a subgenre called pastoral elegy, a part of Milton's oeuvre, and one of the total number of works composed in the years preceding the Civil War.

The nature of the historical existence of a literary work is thus defined by the convergence of at least three systematic procedures: the genre, the oeuvre, and the synchronic hierarchy. I call such a work "historical" because by definition (1) it is a cultural alteration of an inherited form; (2) it is the expression of a historical being; and (3) it is a member of a chronologically identifiable literary norm.

Besides the three, there is a fourth systematic procedure of which every literary work is a part: the transaction between it and the reader. A reader belongs to a historical ambience, and his literary hypotheses derive from interactions with a norm of which he himself cannot be fully conscious. Not fully conscious because, however self-aware he may be, he is living in the midst of a norm that can only be adequately perceived after it has been supplanted. The interpreter can overlook but he cannot deny that the work has a generic past identified by rhetorically inherited devices; whatever analysis he undertakes will presuppose—with his awareness or not—that there exists a relationship historically developed among particular conventions of construction and language. To identify a writer's figure or figures in the carpet, the interpreter must commit himself to some hypothesis about identity, about repetition, about the relation of the self to artistic expression. And a cultural definition is a necessary part of this literary self. Insofar as the literary work is interrelated with other contemporary works, the critic presupposes some shared norm defined by specific periods of time, specific movements, currents, or generations, however loosely the time boundaries may be conceived. In what sense can my description of genre, oeuvre, norm, author, and interpreter be called "knowledge"? It is certainly not scientific "knowledge" in the sense of fact, experiment, and verification. But is it "historical knowledge"?

If "historical knowledge" can be defined as the interpreter's reconstitution of an event, document, or situation by reference to the frame in which it occurred, then what I identify as the necessary conditions for analysis is "historical knowledge." I use the term *necessary condition* because literary analysis, regardless of how it is undertaken, requires as one methodological procedure a hypothesis that is historically determined. The critic, whether he undertakes to analyze a past work or one written by a contemporary, makes assumptions about the nature of a literary work, about its linguistic and nonlinguistic features, about the relation of parts to whole or this work to others, about subject matter and aims that are the result of current knowledge. Moreover, historical knowledge—defined in terms of constructive procedures on the part of an author, constitutive procedures on the part of a critic—is necessary because regardless of what features are considered transhistorical or ahistorical, the establishing of such similarities can only be made by demonstrating that it exists with and can only be defined by differences between works. And such differences are explainable only by historical procedures of construction and interpretation. Thus historical knowledge is logically "necessary."

I argue that every literary work possesses a historical frame of genre, oeuvre, and norm, and that no explanation which ignores these can prove sufficient. I note here the distinction between "necessary" and "sufficient." Historical knowledge is necessary, but it is not sufficient. If generic features are historically selected and function artistically and culturally in particular combinations, their nature as a language system requires a theory of language. So, too, the author's figure or figures require some hypotheses about the nature of literary identity and how it functions. This can include, then, some theory of language repression or some interrelation of language to nonlinguistic signs or some psychological theory of an individual's imaginative patterns. The norm generalizations require assumptions about nonconscious modes of combination and their moral implications, some hypotheses about the relation of quantitative data to qualitative distinctions, for example, that satire becomes a comprehensive form in a period and that such forms are related to social, political, and other behavior.

Critics may disagree about any specific description of genre, but this merely means that this knowledge, like all historical knowledge, rests upon canons of contemporary evidence and is open to debate and refutation. But that the conditions are historical seems inherent in the nature of composition, for the work includes a selection and revision of earlier generic features recombined with new ones, the literary identity of a writer at a particular moment in time, and the inevitable interrelation of this work with others composing the literary hierarchy. Clearly, this view of historical conditions of analysis entails a definition of the literary work as a combination of rhetorical or expressive features, subject matters, dictional styles, and aims.

Since the "historical knowledge" I refer to applies to literary features, expressions, interrelations, is it not possible to conceive of historical knowledge in nonliterary contexts? What of the licensing act of 1737 which ended Fielding's career as a dramatist? Surely this political act had literary consequences. I do not wish to deny the impact of external pressures on literary works—that censorship can make writers turn to allegorical forms or adhere to established combinations of social realism. I merely note that the argument begins with a literary work and some of its formal features and moves to a social cause. If historical acts like legislation or political maneuvers can affect literary forms or subject matter, it is necessary to note that "historical knowledge" can also apply to fictive behavior that becomes a model for social behavior. Thus what is "fictive" can become a historical description, as "quixotism" and "quixotic" apply to a way of acting in society. This is the situation of Pamela's secret writing that changes public attitudes to class and virtue in the novel and instructs readers of the novel to accept and to pursue such values.

Pamela is a common enough story of the pursuit of a maid by her master. It is told by Pamela, first in letters to her parents and then, after her abduction, in a journal that she writes in private and conceals from her pursuer. Her writing defines her to herself and strengthens her resolve because it has the power of making a contract with herself. Her letters and journal are written in privacy and constitute a reflection upon her actions and a procedure for remembering herself and her actions in endangered situations. The important fact is that Mr. B., her master, sets himself to spy upon her letters and then upon her journal. The spying is an invasion of privacy, an attempt to read the secret thoughts of another, and in so doing, to plot her undoing. Pamela's private journal, her efforts to keep it from Mr. B., imply her recognition that for him to see it is to rape her mind, a prelude to the rape of her body. She sews the journal into her undergarments, creating a symbolic relation between uncovering the journal and uncovering her self. Writing is thus seen as an intimate extension of her body, of her privacy. Reading the journals becomes identified with invasion of her body: "I went to my closet, and there I sat me down, and could not bear the thoughts of giving up my papers. Besides, I must all undress me, in a manner, to untack them."[2]

But the submission of the documents to Mr. B. has the most interesting consequences. He is persuaded by Pamela's journal to treat her as an equal, not a maid, and he proposes marriage. And one of the great gifts he gives her after marriage is a poem. Writing has changed an upper-class vulgarian into a poet of nature. His poem is about the beauty that flowers and women give each to the other: "For flow'rs and women are allied; / Both, nature's glory, and her pride!"[3] In achieving poetic sensibility, he has found the universalizing language of nature to justify Pamela's class elevation. And her journal becomes a document to change the social views of his recalcitrant sister.

Notice that the structure of *Pamela* is such that the readers of the journal set a model for the readers of the novel. There is, therefore, a cyclical procedure in which the fictional readers, Mr. B. and his sister and others, set the model for the readers external to the fiction. Thus the private situation is made public because writing itself and the reading of writing are assumed to control and alter responses. But not merely this. Reading is made into a commercial matter; when the impulses of readers can be trusted, invasion becomes invitation. The reader is not alone; he becomes part of a community of readers. Richardson even concludes his book with a series of propositions that he wants his readers to remember.

Although I have analyzed *Pamela* as an example of a literary work providing a model for social behavior, I wish also to draw attention to it in terms of book production. Pamela is both the author and distributor of her text—an individual entrepreneur who profits in economic (as well as social) terms by her enterprise. She distributes—in the manner of a lending library operator—the book she has written, and thus illustrates the kind of books that can serve to support the system of social classes while indicating how, within such a system, it is possible to win social mobility.

If I turn now to the more limited view of historical knowledge as a necessary condition for adequate literary understanding, I attend to the types of inquiry necessary to examine such conditions. These are implicit in my definition of genre as a mixed or combinatory form, with the combinations requiring an understanding of nonverbal as well as verbal procedures. Such an understanding will inevitably lead to questions of the following kind: Why does a literary work use its elements as it does? Why does the work present features from its own and other generic possibilities? In what sense are the aims or aim present, implied, or, at best, only partly given? How do these procedures apply to a poem? What kinds of specific questions do they answer? What kind of historical knowledge do they reveal? I give *Il Penseroso* as an example.

Il Penseroso

Hence vain deluding Joys,
    The brood of Folly without father bred.
How little you bestead,
    Or fill the fixed mind with all your toys;

Dwell in some idle brain,
   And fancies fond with gaudy shapes possess,
As thick and numberless
   As the gay motes that people the sunbeams,
Or likest hovering dreams,
   The fickle pensioners of Morpheus' train.
But hail thou Goddess, sage and holy,
Hail, divinest Melancholy,
Whose saintly visage is too bright
To hit the sense of human sight;
And therefore to our weaker view,
O'erlaid with black, staid Wisdom's hue.
Black, but such as in esteem,
Prince Memnon's sister might beseem,
Or that starred Ethiope queen that strove
To set her beauty's praise above
The sea nymphs, and their powers offended.
Yet thou art higher far descended;
Thee bright-haired Vesta long of yore
To solitary Saturn bore;
His daughter she (in Saturn's reign
Such mixture was not held a stain).
Oft in glimmering bowers and glades
He met her, and in secret shades
Of woody Ida's inmost grove,
While yet there was no fear of Jove.
Come pensive nun, devout and pure,
Sober, steadfast, and demure,
All in a robe of darkest grain,
Flowing with majestic train,
And sable stole of cypress lawn
Over thy decent shoulders drawn.
Come, but keep thy wonted state,
With even step and musing gait,
And looks commercing with the skies,
Thy rapt soul sitting in thine eyes:
There held in holy passion still,
Forget thyself to marble, till
With a sad leaden downward cast,
Thou fix them on the earth as fast.
And join with thee calm Peace and Quiet,

> Spare Fast, that oft with gods doth diet,
> And hears the Muses in a ring
> Aye round about Jove's altar sing.
> And add to these retired Leisure,
> That in trim gardens takes his pleasure;
> But first, and chiefest, with thee bring,
> Him that yon soars on golden wing,
> Guiding the fiery-wheeled throne,
> The cherub Contemplation;
> And the mute Silence hist along
> 'Less Philomel will deign a song,
> In her sweetest, saddest plight,
> Smoothing the rugged brow of night,
> While Cynthia checks her dragon yoke
> Gently o'er th' accustomed oak;
> Sweet bird that shunn'st the noise of folly,
> Most musical, most melancholy!
> Thee chantress oft the woods among,
> I woo to hear thy evensong;
> And missing thee, I walk unseen
> On the dry smooth-shaven green,
> To behold the wandering moon,
> Riding near her highest noon,
> Like one that had been led astray
> Through the Heaven's wide pathless way;
> And oft as if her head she bowed,
> Stooping through a fleecy cloud.

At the most elementary lexical level, the mythological references to "Morpheus, "Prince Memnon's sister" (Herrera), "that starred Ethiope Queen" (Cassiopeia), "Vesta" (virgin daughter of Saturn), "Saturn," "woody Ida's inmost groves" (Mt. Ida, where Saturn reigned in the Golden Age) require historical knowledge to be identified, but such lexical knowledge does not provide literary understanding. For this understanding to take place it is necessary to conceive of *Il Penseroso* as a genre functioning to create a lyric in praise of a goddess, Melancholy. In this situation the features of invocation, of the genesis of a goddess, of the relation of the goddess to her family and to the poet—all of these are joined to features of another subgenre of lyric—the eclogue or pastoral. For the eclogue is a poem in which two singers compete on a given theme, in this particular case, of companion poems, the pleasures of joy and the pleasures of melancholy. The eclogue can deal with the relation between the singer and the cycles of the day as it does in some of Virgil's *Eclogues,* and the eclogue is seen as a fragmentary work, possessing some of the possibilities of relating contemporary political and social events to highly artificial contests. In recognizing the variations that Milton introduces into the lyric genre of the poem of praise, it is important to note that subgenres—the pastoral elegy, the hymn, the funeral elegy, the meditation—form a group of interrelated lyrics the particular identity of each being altered by the particular historical moment in which they occur. Puttenham, notes Barbara Lewalski, "identified hymns praising the gods as the 'highest and stateliest' kind of epideictic lyric, followed by 'ballades of praise called *Encomia*' and also historical poems, which were appropriate especially to princes and great men who 'most resembled the gods by excellencie of function, and . . . by more then humane and ordinarie vertues.'"[4]

But the literary understanding is governed by Milton's selective use of the combination of genres, for he begins each of his companion poems with an imprecation, a ten-line division, reflecting in *Il Penseroso* the "vain deluding joys"—the gaudy and idle joys—followed by an invocation to Melancholy, an affirmation of the symbol of melancholy pleasure. Now the structure of the poem is to be understood by observing the connection of the expressive features of the genre and how they are joined. For the rejection-affirmation is a pattern of Milton's verse: the initial disruption of the universe came from a rebellion of the angels, and melancholy is related to this disruption by the memory of a past not to be restored in this life. Thus melancholy provides the contemplative means by which the individual can remember his ideal past. The rejection of false pleasures leads directly to an invocation to melancholy, and the invocation leads to a genesis passage detailing the birth of Melancholy. Genesis constitutes for Milton a typology of all future life, and not only is *Paradise Lost* a poem of the genesis of man and his expulsion from paradise, but the adherence to original principles, to genesis, is the basis of Christ's triumph over Satan just as the rejection of God's prohibition is the grounds for man's fall. Samson's fall is the result of his disobeying his pact with God, and *Samson Agonistes* is a play narrating the genesis of Samson's power and its betrayal. The genesis element which explains the organization of this part of Milton's structure in *Il Penseroso* relates it to Milton's combinatory procedures.

The genesis is followed by an invocation to the Christianized goddess to walk the earth with her allegorical train—Peace, Quiet, Spare Fast, retired

Leisure, the cherub Contemplation. The allegorical family belongs with Milton's view of the family group as the expressive feature essential to convey the harmonious community. The triadic godhead, the loyal band of angels, Adam and Eve before the fall, even the cohorts loyal to Satan form a community (though one of evil). But the family possesses a leader and demands discipline—they constitute the fortunate few.

The generic features that Milton selected for *Il Penseroso* permitted him to transform a pagan goddess into a Christian saint and to relate heavenly allegorical behavior to the poet's activity on earth. His selectivity, cognizant as it was of prior uses, introduced a typology for the contemplative man, attending to learning, communing with nature, and religious retirement as associated activities. In this manner, the poem indicated the relation between virtue and retirement, between movement and the dreams of the past. But if one consults *Areopagitica,* some of the incidental features of the poem become clarified:

> It was from out the rind of one apple tasted, that the knowledge of good and evil, as two twins cleaving together, leaped forth into the world. And perhaps this is that doom which Adam fell into of knowing good and evil, that is to say of knowing good by evil. . . . I cannot praise a fugitive and cloistered virtue, unexercised and unbreathed, that never sallies out and sees her adversary, but slinks out of the race, where that immortal garland is to be run for, not without dust and heat. Assuredly we bring not innocence into the world, we bring impurity much rather; that which purifies us is trial, and trial is by what is contrary.[5]

The rejection-affirmation pattern can be seen as existing together in the post-Edenic world. Rejection is thus an affirmative action, upholding purity and virtue. If we conceive of satire as purification by rejection, if we recognize in *Pamela* purification by rejection, we can move from the particular version of rejection-affirmation in *Il Penseroso* to a pattern that extends over a long chronological period ending in the late eighteenth century. If we recognize in *Il Penseroso* cyclical natural time—the movement of the day and the movement of man from birth to death—and supernatural time, we can identify the genesis pattern as belonging to both. And whereas in the poem the ordering of the speaker's experience is sequential—place leading to activities of learning or of reciprocity with nature—we can recognize in *Pamela* the sequence of events resulting in her need to use writing as a basis for remembering. There is a relation—as Johnson observed in his "Life of Denham"—between a particular poetic landscape and "the addition of such embellishments as may be supplied by historical retrospection or incidental meditation."

My strategy here is to lead into the concept of period norm by illustrating that works over a considerable period of time are not merely interrelated, but that their individual combinations reveal analogous or similar implications of construction. These implications can be seen retrospectively in the particular kind of genres that most practiced—as the georgic, satire, and epistle in the eighteenth century or the varieties of lyric in the period immediately following. The selection of such forms is not easily explained, either in terms of individual writers or the communities of writers. But the interpreter's recognition of a generic hierarchy is necessary to explain why satiric and georgic poems, for example, become comprehensive forms that can include features from most other types not previously associated with them.

A period norm must take account of the different political implications of literary works at any one time, just as it needs to deal with linguistic functions rather than with words or sentences as such. In doing so, it seems possible to urge a distinction that can best be made by the hypothesis of a work as a combination. This definition permits a distinction between how these features are joined and between the overt statements of subject or the historically identifiable rhetorical devices. Thus, for example, the subject of *Robinson Crusoe* is the rejection of his father's advice and his going to sea, which leads to his shipwreck, his stay on the island, and his eventual return to England. But the manner of joining the rejection-affirmation pattern is serial and sequential, connected with the process of learning about himself and about the world. Thus the process by which he comes to true belief is a crisis illness, and his subsequent good fortune is then attributed to his religious redemption. It is the pattern or method of experiencing as a basis for knowing that functions as norm. The way of experiencing is connected with commerce, with individual experience, with re-creating the idea of sea house and country house in an uninhabited island, with the maintenance of writing and craft for self-identification, historical recollection, and personal justification despite isolation, and with isolation as a stimulus for virtue.

The distinction between the nonconscious norm of the writer and his overt subject matter serves to explain why works that support Walpole and those that attack him can, nevertheless, be part of the same norm. They belong to the norm in the sense that the critic is providing an explanation of the underlying principles of combination. I have identified the sequential procedure of construction and illustrated how this has social, religious, moral, and artistic implications. The subject of travel from one's own land to another and then returning, of movement from the country to the city and back—all such movement has an underlying consistency by which place leads to reflections on past or future time, past and present actions. The underlying pattern is to provide the individual with a sense of the risk involved in his choice of alternatives that are implicitly political and social. It appears in the retirement images recurrent in the poetry of the eighteenth century, and I quote two examples, one from *The Rape of the Lock* and the other from Gray's *Elegy:*

> Yet am not I the first mistaken Maid,
> By Love of *Courts* to num'rous Ills betray'd.
> Oh had I rather un-admir'd remain'd
> In some lone Isle, or distant *Northern* Land;
> Where the gilt *Chariot* never marks the Way,
> Where none learn *Ombre,* none e'er taste Bohea!
> There kept my Charms conceal'd from mortal Eye,
> Like Roses that in Desarts bloom and die. (4.151-58)

> Full many a gem of purest ray serene
> The dark unfathomed caves of ocean bear:
> Full many a flower is born to blush unseen
> And waste its sweetness on the desert air. (53-56)

The first, occurring as it does in a mock epic, ironically uses the image of beauty concealed in the empty vastness of nature as an example of unnatural behavior. It is preceded by a series of negations that imply the affirmation of retirement as a value. Yet, though the structure of the image is consistent with the rejection of risks, the irony makes it clear that Belinda, by polarizing her choices—social betrayal or social isolation—is to be seen as a woman whom we ought to treat with ambiguous sympathy and humor.

The passage from the *Elegy* directly addresses the "Proud," urging that they not condemn the poor for lacking proper memorials. "Their lot forbade" them from moving into the public arenas. The inevitable rejection involved in their state leads to an affirmation that is an acceptance. The narrator is at a distance from the gem in the ocean cave as he is from the "unseen" flower in the desert. The relation of gem to ocean and flower to desert implies a durability and value, a goodness, without the opportunity to use this goodness, as well as a freedom from wickedness. Since these are possible disadvantages as well as possible advantages, what is at issue is the justification for avoiding risk, the acceptance of a world that God has made. In this respect, it is possible to argue that Gray's acceptance of both the poor and powerful is governed by an inherent belief that God's secret hand is best acknowledged by not taking unnecessary risks, in contrast to Milton's belief that man's behavior in taking risks is his demonstration of his trust in God, or Pope's that some risks ought not to be taken too seriously. What has changed in Gray's variation of the norm is man's distancing from God and his consequent fear of altering what is given. Thus the norm accommodates love and resignation because within the context of virtue the risks of bloodshed contain an irretrievable moral ambiguity. So, too, the failure to take risks contains an ambiguity that can only be overcome by love.

What would be a norm model for variation and supersession? Variations proceed by formalizing combinatory procedures so that it is often the case that originating works are not the model examples of the norm though some of its features may become models, as the Thames couplets in Denham's *Coopers Hill*. It is precisely because works are convergences of genre, oeuvre, and hierarchy that variations compel poets to seek new ways for expressing old thoughts. These procedures invoke features from older forms to make certain values acceptable—as, for example, the use of romance ending in *Joseph Andrews* and *Tom Jones* in order to maintain the fantasy of secret reward for human decency. The norm is questioned by the manner in which literary combinations move to include in their references social classes that seem ignored—as in the *Elegy*. This is exemplified in the use of combinatory features to invert values—as in *The Beggar's Opera*, where the alteration of folk songs to thieves' songs, the idea of commerce as reciprocity, where the underlying pattern of rejection of conventional life becomes a parodic affirmation of the very values that are rejected. The norm exists side by side with works that have been parts of earlier norms. What takes place at first is the adapting of works to new combinations such as the adaptations of Shakespeare and Horace and Pope's reworking of Donne's satires. Or beginnings can be observed by writers like Dryden or Wordsworth who seek to follow older models and then abandon them for a different idiom. Norm competitors are introduced to suggest either class values or political values that have been rejected: thus Percy's *Reliques* introduces medieval ballads that stress conflict within the family and between lord and leader. So, too, Ossian's poems are introduced as norm alternatives by James McPherson, who hesitated to identify himself as a poetic rebel seeking to introduce new rhetorical modes and subject matters. Such poems in their metrical patterns offer alternatives to the model of the concession-confirmation couplet construction in the famous lines of Denham's poem:

> O could I flow like thee, and make thy stream
> My great example, as it is my theme!
> Though deep, yet clear, though gentle yet not dull,
> Strong without rage, without o'er-flowing full. (189-92)

Norm variation, in contrast to norm alternatives, results from extensions of norm combinations to include features that call the norm values into question: this is done by converting variety into polarities, by falsifying the normal procedures for knowing by withholding information or introducing supernatural events, by introducing combinations based on sources of value previously prohibited or inhibited.

The variations are, on one level of explanation, the result of the poet writing out of personal and social pressures. But at another level they are the result of the eighteenth-century writer's effort to include in his poem features that his contemporaries neglected without abandoning the received method of composing. By this means the function of poetic combination as a moral and epistemological procedure for dealing with the immediate past results in extensions that no longer coincide with the earlier versions of norm value. Thus Goldsmith's couplets in *The Deserted Village* remain consistent with the norm, but his village types have been ejected, compelled to move, so that the poem is an elegy to a past time, not a study of available choices. In this respect the family as the community of trust is subordinated in Sheridan's *The School for Scandal* to the family as a commercial entity in which even trust is identified in commercial terms.

The procedure of variation can be seen as leading to the supersession of the norm, to the shift in function of form features. It can be illustrated by referring to two poems on melancholy that return to Milton's theme. In Warton's *The Pleasures of Melancholy,* modeled on Milton's poem, the norm hypothesis of sequential development that exists as a method for providing knowledge and recognizing the kind of possibilities man and nature offer is also undermined. By converting reciprocal relations into polarities, by extending the variations, Warton establishes combinations of features that function to undo the moral implications of the norm. Compare, indeed, the retirement figure of the Russian exile with Milton's contemplative hermit. Milton's lines are:

> And may at last my weary age
> Find out the peaceful hermitage,
> The hairy gown and mossy cell,
> Where I may sit and rightly spell
> Of every star that Heaven doth shew,
> And every herb that sips the dew;
> Till old experience do attain
> To something like prophetic strain.
> These pleasures, Melancholy, give,
> And I with thee will choose to live. (167–76)

Warton reads as follows:

> What are the splendors of the gaudy court,
> Its tinsel trappings, and its pageant pomps?
> To me far happier seems the banish'd lord,
> Amid Siberia's unrejoicing wilds
> Who pines all lonesome, in the chambers hoar
> Of some high castle shut, whose windows dim
> In distant ken discover trackless plains,
> Where Winter ever whirls his icy car;
> While still repeated objects of his view,
> The gloomy battlements, and ivied spires,
> That crown the solitary dome, arise;
> While from the topmost turret the slow clock,
> Far heard along th' inhospitable wastes,
> With sad-returning chime awakes new grief;
> Ev'n he far happier seems than is the proud,
> The potent Satrap, whom he left behind
> 'Mid Moscow's golden palaces, to drown
> In ease and luxury the laughing hours. (226–43)

Rejection that results in isolation and estrangement becomes a form of pleasure; injustice becomes a form of justice. If the question arises as to the transposition of the norm, the recognition of its conversion into a new organizing structure, we can look at Keats's *Ode on Melancholy*. There the first stanza begins with a parody of eighteenth-century poems of melancholy, concluding with the lines that reject the serial, sequential approach to melancholy of the prior norm: "For shade to shade will come too drowsily, / And drown the wakeful anguish of the soul" (9–10).

This stanza, combined with the other two, rehearses the rejection-affirmation pattern of the previous norm, except that the first stanza parodies it and the second, which is an affirmation, treats it comically. For what is affirmed is the suddenness, not the seriality of melancholy: it falls "Sudden from Heaven like a weeping cloud." The melancholy fit is then described as "glutting" and "feeding" itself on a series of perceptions, playfully fulfilling itself or gorging itself on transient beauty or rewarding "rich" anger. The conjunction of delight with melancholy is an affirmation that undoes the combination of consistently sad and meditative pleasures as the characterization of melancholy. If Milton's poem began as an imprecation, a rejection of abstract joys, Keats's first stanza begins as interrupted discourse—"No, no, go not to Lethe . . ."—that continues through the second stanza. The final stanza, signaled by a change in the speaker's form of address, offers a totally new version of melancholy. Not only have genesis and genealogy disappeared from the poem, but the relation of pleasure to melancholy has been transformed. The pleasures of melancholy led to religious and sensitive musings in the poems of Milton and Warton. In *Ode on Melancholy* pleasure must be sacrificed to attain melancholy, not sacrificed by discipline or self-control but sacrificed by engaging in the most sensuous human activities: "Veiled Melancholy" can be seen "of none save him whose strenuous tongue / Can burst Joy's grape against his palate fine" (27-28).

Melancholy can be achieved only at the expense of losing the most intense sensuous pleasures that make life desirable. Thus the attaining of melancholy is a warrant that one has lived intensely at the same time that such intense living is over. The moral ambiguity of melancholy, its severance from religious contemplation, the construction of an imaginative remembered world for that of a supernatural one—all these indicate that the subject of melancholy is embedded in different combinations of selected generic features. It offers a norm—if this poem is typical—whose moral finds transcendence to be a consequence of the intensely natural. The works of other Romantics do not accept Keats's mode of transcendence but they do identify, as he does, transcendence with imagination.

Even if it should be remarked that rejection-affirmation are examples of binary opposites that are inherent responses of the human mind, it would serve only to confirm the necessity for historical knowledge as necessary for literary understanding of particular expressions of it. For these are consequences of specific historical poetic choices.

My examples of genre, oeuvre, and norm as "historical knowledge" have necessarily been selective, though I trust they are representative. What I wish now to argue is that critics who reject my view of the literary work as historical event are obliged, of necessity, to introduce some type of historical argument as essential to their own version of literary understanding. At the outset of this essay I referred to critics who argued that a literary work is a self-contained language—in contradistinction to my definition of it as a mixed language system (natural and literary language). Barbara H. Smith, for example, defines a poem as a fictive utterance that "consists entirely of a linguistic structure"[6] which is historically indeterminate. Nevertheless, she finds it necessary to identify literary understanding (interpretation) with historical knowledge: "The poet, in composing the poem, will have made certain assumptions regarding his audience, specifically that they are members of a shared linguistic and cultural community, and thus able and willing to abide by relevant linguistic, cultural, and indeed literary conventions. To the degree that our interpretations of a poem are ignorant of those assumptions or violate these conventions, *we are not that poem's audience,* and whatever use we may be making of it, we are not responding to it as what it is."[7]

I draw attention to the dilemmas in which such a critic is involved when she invokes such terms as "audience," "community," and "literary conventions" to define historical knowledge as a necessary condition for interpretation. That an author makes assumptions regarding his audience is self-evident. But these assumptions rest on his view of the transaction of his work with readers. There is no reason to assume that an author must fulfill his readers' expectations rather than defeat them, thus leading readers to new kinds of expectations. In fact, both of these processes usually occur, and they are to be identified by the selection of generic features and the functions they serve in combination.

That an audience may represent one or more cultural communities is surely apparent in diverse critical controversies since the Renaissance. But is it appropriate to assume that the cultural community determines (an author "abides by") cultural and literary conventions? It is precisely the nature of a writer's oeuvre that it alters literary conventions by its variations from received practices. Without denying that a work has implications that it shares with its community, the explanation of an author's generic selection and combination are functional within a work and can never be dictated merely by past practice.

I have no desire to quarrel with Professor Smith's view of the nature of literary discourse; I merely wish to show that she requires in her view of literary understanding assumptions about historical knowledge as a given.

Her difficulties arise by seeking to identify the sources of this knowledge with the responders to it, depriving the author of his relation to past works and those of his own time.

The serious difficulties of treating historical knowledge in this way become apparent in her identification of literary conventions. For she provides no guide either for critical construction of norms or for explaining how conventions arise and disappear. One of the critics who shares Barbara Smith's view of the literary work as a unified linguistic whole, Michael Riffaterre, argues cogently for literary norms as descriptive systems. He grants that descriptive systems change and he sees each literary work as a coherent descriptive subsystem.[8] But because he wishes to argue for a literary work as a linguistic system of a distinctive kind, separated from natural language systems, he refuses to consider the relation between linguistic features and the social sources they imply or derive from. Any literary linguistic system thus remains self-reflexive and is, indeed, reducible to a single metaphor. Historical knowledge thus becomes equated with purely linguistic conventions that are transmitted without the interference of any other kind of knowledge.

This creates a dilemma, for the "norm" that is discovered is the result of a modern critic offering hypotheses upon past language systems. Any such hypothesis is historical in that it aims to reconstruct past linguistic systems, but its view of such systems eliminates the possibility that the past system can question the hypothesis itself. And a historical hypothesis that does not take account of the actual linguistic variations within a work—of the mixtures of natural and literary language—can only serve to cast doubt upon its own usefulness.

I hope my procedure in this section of the essay is clear. I am not examining the literary theories of the different scholars to whom I refer. I merely wish to demonstrate that they introduce into their theories aspects of historical knowledge as necessary conditions for literary understanding. In doing so, they present various hypotheses and assertions about how this knowledge is discoverable or recoverable. I wish to inquire into the adequacy of their procedures for attaining the very knowledge they consider essential.

Even deconstructionist criticism, with its reference to centuries of Western metaphysics, necessarily entails historical hypotheses. J. Hillis Miller, for example, in describing literary understanding as a recognition of the parasite-host relation, acknowledges that this relation is a matter of temporal sequence. In each of the major texts the relation undergoes reexpression that results from the cultural role of the author in his moment in history: "That poem [*The Triumph of Life*], in its turn, or Shelley's work generally, is present within the work of Hardy or Yeats or Stevens and forms part of a sequence in the major texts of Romantic 'nihilism' including Nietzsche, Freud, Heidegger, and Blanchot, in a perpetual re-expression of the relation of host and parasite which forms itself again today in current criticism."[9]

This perpetual reexpression of a theme by different authors necessarily implies the historical nature of the different kinds of formulations given by the critic to these expressions. Even though deconstructionists do not write in terms of genres or wholes, the very use of rhetorical features and their changing function must be explained. It is one thing to argue that critical interpretations call their own premises into question, but quite another to overlook the very premises that are to be questioned.

The critics to whom I have been referring do not make interpretative or form changes central to their analysis, and yet it seems to me they are obliged to posit the literary work as recoverable in part through historical knowledge as literary understanding. But what of the critics who begin with the hypothesis that the literary work needs to be reconstituted as a historical and literary object? Do they not take for granted a knowledge of generic features, oeuvre, and norm as a necessary condition for historical understanding? Surely my own essay has literary forebears, and I believe the following critics provide some of the historical antecedents for the theoretical principles that I propose. I begin with R. S. Crane's discussion of a "narrative history of forms." He points out that in such a study the crucial problem is "the discrimination of the various artistic ends pursued by writers from time to time and the organization of these differences into significant lines of change."[10] The critic tries as carefully as possible to discover the problems of particular writers at different times—their changes in forms, materials, and techniques—that explain their works as "multiple historical relations" and as "unique artistic wholes."[11] Crane's view of constructional principles is extremely helpful in defining necessary historical inquiries. So, too, his emphasis on forms, materials, and techniques makes possible important distinctions. In another vocabulary and out of different theoretical concerns there are contemporary critics who consider literary works in terms of semiotic systems. Yuri Lotman argues, for example, that a literary work is composed of rhetorical, metrical, thematic, and other subsystems while being a system itself. And the text is itself part of a larger system which he calls "culture." In his terms, every literary code contains a typology of literary texts that specifies what the various kinds of literature are, what identifies each of them, what differentiates each from the other.[12]

Both theories are important because of their systematic nature and because they define the constitution of texts as historical activities. They do, however, entail hypotheses about the literary work that violate the consistency of their historical procedures. Crane, despite his defense of diverse constructional principles, is at one with Lotman in conceiving of the literary text as an "artistic" whole. This view presupposes a consistency of systems or functions that is unnecessarily rigid in explaining the diverse rhetorical procedures and their combinations. The aims of a literary work need not be seen as single, and the proposals I have made for examining generic features, oeuvre figures, and period norm are an attempt to release the rigid conceptions of "literariness" to which these theories subscribe. Because of this subscription, they lack procedures for explaining the interrelation of forms and the construction of norms. Thus even they lack adequate constraints for defining historical knowledge.

I began by arguing for historical knowledge as a necessary condition for literary understanding; I proceeded by giving a series of examples of how such knowledge is located by a contemporary critic; I then argued that even critics who were, on one count or another, nonhistorical or antihistorical nevertheless recognized the need for historical knowledge as necessary (though not sufficient) for literary understanding; and I concluded by presenting two antecedents of the position I am urging.

The critical works that I have mentioned belong to writing genres called loosely "criticism" and "theory." These are combinations just as poems are combinations, and statements about the necessity of historical knowledge are one of the kinds of argument that combine with others to form such works. These critical works relate historical hypotheses to those of literary language, the definition of a literary work, the phenomenological, Freudian, hermeneutical, and other claims for interpretation.

Do the criteria for historical knowledge apply to technological changes in the production of books—from writing to print and from expensive to inexpensive means of production? Do the criteria indicate the relation between work and readers? I have referred to the problem of book production and distribution in my discussion of *Pamela,* and I can note here that such production affects the status of writers—as it did Pamela—and it affects the handling of subject matter. My example, therefore, indicates both how the author's figure or figures in the carpet are intertwined with such productivity and distribution problems. But, further, I would point out that generic choices and combinations are determined by what a writer wishes to do with his received choices. So, too, as the critic constitutes a norm, he must take account of the writer's effort to conform by varying viewed practices or to oppose by rejecting received modes of combination. Technological changes of production and distribution are causes for change in the selection of generic features, in the subject matter and techniques a writer introduces, and in the manner in which literary works become interrelated with each other (and with works from other arts).

I have confined myself to demonstrating that historical knowledge is a necessary condition for literary understanding, but I have defined the latter term only by example. In my usage, "literary understanding" refers to statements a reader makes, pertinent to describing his "literary" (however defined) transaction with a work or works and all the interrelations and processes these undergo. Such understanding, indeed, any discussion of a literary work, has, as its ultimate end, the belief that literary study is important to society. Thus, any literary explanation is ultimately connected with the role of literary works in a society. Even if it is only to draw readers away from their own everyday concerns or to realize the ahistorical character of writing, such aims are social and, since they change as the social goals change, historical.

In selecting those statements pertinent to historical knowledge as a necessary condition for literary understanding, I have been indicating at least one characteristic of the modern interpreter and thus have offered some evidence for the identification of our critical norm, namely, the false dichotomy between historical and ahistorical explanation. What I have been demonstrating is that they necessarily entail each other. But in my own procedures I have provided a theoretical explanation of why this occurs: that literary genres are combinations of diverse rhetorical features, subject matters, and aims. Thus by illustrating how I proceed, I have rejected the use of terms such as "novel," "criticism," and "theory" as though these are not interrelated forms. But the very description of what one does when he practices "criticism" or "theory" makes clear that these "genres" cannot be defined in traditional ways; that, indeed, for the theory I am positing, the very vocabulary of criticism has to be identified with what scholars do when they offer instances of literary understanding.

The ambivalences that I have described in the works of contemporary critics arise from the phenomenon that we live as historical beings who are creating the very norm which provides assumptions for the analysis of past norms. Despite such ambivalences, however, critics do have, with regard to historical knowledge, an area of agreement. Regardless of what kind of literary scholarship they engage in, they include, as a feature of their work, historical knowledge as a condition for literary understanding.

NOTES

1. Francis Cairns, *Generic Composition in Greek and Roman Poetry* (Edinburgh: Edinburgh Univ. Press, 1972), 34.
2. Samuel Richardson, *Pamela* (New York: W. W. Norton, 1958), 246.
3. Richardson, *Pamela*, 256.
4. Barbara Lewalski, *Donne's Anniversaries and the Poetry of Praise: The Creation of a Symbolic Mode* (Princeton, NJ: Princeton Univ. Press, 1973), 19.
5. *Areopagitica*, in *John Milton: Complete Poems and Major Prose*, ed. Merritt Y. Hughes (New York: Odyssey Press, 1957), 728.
6. Barbara Herrnstein Smith, "Poetry as Fiction," *New Literary History* 2, no. 2 (1971): 273.
7. Smith, "Poetry as Fiction," 279.
8. Michael Riffaterre, "The Stylistic Approach to Literary History," *New Literary History* 2, no. 1 (1970): 40.
9. J. Hillis Miller, "The Critic as Host," *Critical Inquiry* 3, no. 3 (1977): 447.
10. R. S. Crane, *Critical and Historical Principles of Literary History* (1967; rpt. Chicago: Univ. of Chicago Press, 1971), 38.
11. Crane, *Critical and Historical Principles*, 46.
12. See Yu. M. Lotman and B. A. Uspensky, "On the Semiotic Mechanism of Culture," and Lotman and A. M. Piatigorsky, "Text and Function," *New Literary History* 9, no. 2 (1978): 211-32 and 233-44; Lotman et al., "Theses on the Semiotic Study of Cultures (as Applied to Slavic Texts)," in *Structure of Texts and Semiotics of Culture*, ed. J. van der Eng and M. Grygar (The Hague: Mouton, 1973); and Lotman, *The Structure of the Artistic Text*, trans. Ronald Vroon (Ann Arbor: Michigan Slavic Contributions, 1977).

Some Thoughts on the Problems of Literary Change 1750-1800

I. THE NATURE OF CONTINUITY AND DISCONTINUITY

Literary change is intertwined with problems of individual change and social change. Human beings undergo physiological as well as cultural changes just as societies undergo institutional, political, religious, and technological changes. Although in our time concern with all types of change has become common because of the increased rapidity of social and technological changes, the desire, even need, to understand change in the Western world has a long philosophical history, as can be seen from the remarks of Heraclitus and Parmenides.

To confine one's inquiry to a very limited segment of time and to confine it to a body of writings that we call "literary" is drastically to limit the inquiry into change. But even though the inquiry is so limited, it reveals the nature of many of the general issues inherent in any pursuit of the nature of change.

To begin with, any kind of change implies continuity.[1] To discuss "change," there must be a person, entity, situation, concept, system which undergoes alteration but still retains some continuity with that which is altered. If we refer to the transformation from childhood to adolescence, we refer to certain physiological changes in a human being, but there remain characteristics of the individual that permit us to refer to change in terms of a continuing identity. There are critics who use the term "change" in a quite different way. When Raymond Williams says of Blake's "London" that it provides "a new way of seeing the human and social order as a whole,"[2] he is suggesting that this way of writing poetry is conceptually different from that practiced by preceding poets. It is a "change" that is discontinuous and can be seen as a "change" only in terms of the embracing category of urban or city poetry. But

---

This essay was originally published in *Dispositio* 4, nos. 11-12 (1979): 145-62, and is reprinted with permission of the publisher.

in this case an embracing category which can be seen as continuous in some respects is necessary if we are to make sense of "change."

There is a well-known passage in *The Rape of the Lock* that describes the transformation of three seal rings. They become, in turn, a buckle, a whistle, and, finally, a bodkin. Each of these serves somewhat different functions, but the nonchanging entity is the metal that is given diverse shapes.

> Now meet thy Fate, incens'd *Belinda* cry'd,
> And drew a deadly *Bodkin* from her Side.
> (The same, his ancient Personage to deck,
> Her great great Grandsire wore about his Neck
> In three *Seal-Rings;* which after, melted down,
> Form'd a vast *Buckle* for his Widow's Gown:
> Her infant Grandame's *Whistle* next it grew,
> The *Bells* she gingled, and the *Whistle* blew;
> Then in a *Bodkin* grac'd her Mother's Hairs,
> Which long she wore, and now *Belinda* wears.) [5.87-96]

The bodkin can provide a basis for understanding "change" as a series of variations within a given concept. If we place this in literary terms, we shall find that we can study nature imagery within a number of poems over many years and find that it possesses certain features such as separation of vehicle and tenor, the use of a particular vocabulary, the use of spatial terms in an extended or linear manner. But for subsequent writers the vehicle and tenor "are wrought in a parallel process out of the same material";[3] poets read meanings into the landscape, dramatize the spiritual "through the use of the faint, the shifting, the least tangible and most mysterious parts of nature" (111), and use other such features that result in a nature imagery different in function and concept from the earlier practice.

I have, of course, been paraphrasing William Wimsatt's essay on "The Structure of Romantic Nature Imagery," but my aim has been to show that the discussion of imagery requires the hypothesis that a group of writers represent a norm, a way of imaging, and that this group is followed by another that composes images in terms of another norm.

The examination of image making in poems is not confined to one genre—the lyric—or, as some critics would prefer, to lyric-like forms or genres such as the sonnet, the ode, the elegy, the "conversational poem." To trace changes in imagery requires an examination of all the varieties of poems that are written at any one time, through an empirical procedure that may yet be available by means of computer studies. But even these studies would require a hypothesis about poems and their changes. Poems are members of a genre, and a genre has not only a synchronic but a diachronic history. The change that a genre undergoes is no more than a possible variation of a lyric in subject, lexical and syntactical features, ends, and effects aimed at readers. If we examine Milton's "Lycidas" and Shelley's "Adonais," or other variants of the lyric dealing with solitude, whether of Pope, Thomson, Wordsworth, or Shelley, we find that a genre possesses a number of features which characterize its structure and effects. Some of these are necessary for the identity of a genre to be sustained. Is it reasonable to argue that the Romantic lyric has its own structure without conceding that it must also possess earlier features of its genre and other genres?

There are two different kinds of change involved here, and these intertwinings have been responsible for the knotty problems that have resulted. Every literary work is an instance of a genre, and to this extent it always possesses a number of features of past works. On the other hand, every literary work is synchronous with a number of other works composed or interrelated in accordance with some common principles. There is, therefore, a constant tension in making a work part of a norm, a variant of common principles of ordering, language, and the philosophical implications that underlie them, and in making it a member of a genre which resists the adherence to any one norm. Every work is involved in this tension.

II. SOME CURRENT TREATMENTS OF CHANGE 1750-1800

I shall return to the discussion of "norms" and periods in section III; here I wish to examine several contemporary explanations of change during the years 1750-1800. Every literary critic is aware that changes take place, changes of subject matter, of ideas, changes of vocabulary and of the meanings of words within a given vocabulary, changes within genres, changes within periods and of periods. The explanations critics offer, however, can be seen as evolutionary—that is, as antecedents leading to a conclusion; as revolutionary—that is, as changes which break with the past by introducing new perceptions and conceptions; as disjunctive and cyclical—that is, as breaks with the past that are or are not recurrent.

Explanations for the time segment 1750-1800 that are evolutionary have as their model Meyer H. Abrams's essay "Structure and Style in the Greater Romantic Lyric." Mr. Abrams's argument is that the "greater Romantic lyric" displaced "what neo-classical critics had called 'the greater ode'... as the favored form for the long lyric poem."[4] But its origin was the loco-descriptive poem, especially John Denham's *Coopers Hill*. It also had antecedents in seventeenth-century meditative verse. At the end of the eighteenth century, the loco-descriptive poem was lyricized by the sonnet and thus led to the greater Romantic lyric as practiced by Coleridge.

The assumption about antecedents is that different genres seem to convert into one another, that is, that a georgic poem can be transformed into a lyric. What sort of evolutionary concept can be used to explain that a form—governed, as Mr. Abrams grants, by epistemological premises—can be converted into a different form and then rejected? For as he indicates, Coleridge rejected Locke's dualism, the elementarism that "conceives all wholes to be a combination of discrete parts, whether material atoms or mental 'ideas'" (545). And as a result of this rejection and the affirmation of a theory of organicism, Coleridge adopted a theory of poetry that led to "a change in his practice of the form" (550).

Mr. Abrams wisely relates the structure of a poem to certain underlying epistemological views, but his difficulty lies in explaining how one form can lead to another. If works are wholes, it becomes necessary to insist that disjunctions or differences involve continuity. How else is it possible to explain that rejection of certain types of lyric was also a rejection of certain kinds of georgic and that, despite such rejection, the lyric descended from (had as its "antecedent"), and thus retained, certain features of a non-lyric? In this model of change there is concealed a genuine difficulty with what a literary text is and with the continuity in which to place two different kinds of change—that which results from a genre and that which results from a norm for Romantic lyric poems.

The difficulty with antecedents in any theory that accepts conceptual or revolutionary change is to explain why such anticipations do *not* lead to a new concept. Such antecedents must then be seen as accidental or artistically unsatisfactory or disjunctive. René Wellek's argument, for example, that any "new age" or period has antecedents, implies that norms of one period survive in the next. But also, every new period has anticipations. Still, such anticipations have to be considered as conjunctive—as part of the norm—or disjunctive or discontinuous with the norm. René Wellek puts it this way: "If there were no preparations, anticipations, and undercurrents in the eighteenth century which could be described as pre-romantic, we would have to make the assumption that Wordsworth and Coleridge fell from heaven and that the neoclassical age was unperturbedly solid, unified, and coherent in a way no age has ever been before or since."[5] For René Wellek the underground tendencies strengthen and collect but do not lead to Romanticism: "The great poets of the English romantic movement constitute a fairly coherent group, with the same view of poetry and the same conception of imagination, the same view of nature and mind. They share also a poetic style, a use of imagery, symbolism, and myth, which is quite distinct from anything that had been practiced by the eighteenth century, and which was felt by their contemporaries to be obscure and almost unintelligible" (178).

There is a certain ambiguity, if not contradiction, in the views of change that are presented in the two quotations from the same article. Preparations, anticipations, undercurrents prepare for something, but if what they prepare for is "quite distinct from anything that had been practiced by the eighteenth century," then the anticipations must be disjunctive. Since René Wellek believes in a literary work as multiply layered, he may very well believe that ideas may have a continuity uncontaminated by the "style" in which they are expressed. But this would then imply a theory of change in which style, imagery, symbolism, and myth introduce revolutionary changes in a part of the work whereas other parts still exist without these changes. Such a view of multiple norms, it should be noted, does not explain how any particular work would come to embody contrary norms. If one argues for norms, then anticipations belong to one norm, but imply another nonexistent norm. One must grant that some features of a work are less adequate than others, but this does not mean that they refer to some subsequent norm. Their inadequacy is defined by their failure within the norm.

One is led from these attempts at evolutionary or cumulative explanations of change to consider explanations that are based on revolutionary changes, on sudden disjunctions. The essay that has won greatest currency in describing this period as disjunctive is Northrop Frye's "Towards Defining an Age of Sensibility." Refusing to see 1750-1800 as a period which is part of other periods—either the end of the Augustan age or the pre-Romantic beginnings of the Romantic age—he argues for the independence of this period as a unit in itself. It is neither a conclusion of nor a preparation for another period. It exists independently. The disjunction in periods is accomplished by postulating continuity in the composition of poetry but discontinuity in attitudes to it. According to Mr. Frye, there exist two discontinuous kinds of composition as well as two discontinuous views of literature: literature as process and literature as product. "In the history of literature we become aware, not only of periods, but of a recurrent opposition of two views of literature. These two views are the Aristotelian and the Longinian, the aesthetic and the psychological, the view of literature as product and the view of literature as process."[6] The duality is a given, and it operates successively, not simultaneously. Northrop Frye subtly derives features from process poetry that have become the hallmark of the "age of sensibility," but "process" and "product" poetry are terms that signal "a recurrent opposition." Since this opposition is the result of an "interest" (314) in one aspect of composition rather than another, the explanation of change does not seem to involve anticipations or antecedents. It does not, in fact, involve explanations of why poetic interests should change as they do. All ages of product or process poetry are instances of a typological consistency, but why a process age should become one of product is explained by an inevitable recurrence. In pointing to the change from the age of sensibility to Romanticism, Mr. Frye remarks: "With the 1800 edition of *Lyrical Ballads,* secondary imagination and recollection in tranquility took over English poetry and dominated it until the end of the nineteenth century" (318). But even he acknowledges that aspects of product poetry are to be found in a process period: "the Romantics tended to see the poem as the *product* of the creative imagination, thus reverting in at least one respect to the Augustan attitude" (315).

Although Mr. Frye is extremely subtle in deriving literary traits from attitudes to writing and relating these in turn to view's of nature and history, he resists the view that periods, for example, need to be studied in terms of beginnings and endings. What his explanations offer are the characteristic features of a way of writing at a particular time. How such characteristics develop is a given; that some features of opposing ways of writing exist in different periods is acknowledged, but they are insignificant in defining the period. Those features which are not disjunctive with the previous way of writing are not central to his explanatory aims.

Mr. Frye's disjunctions exist within a system that posits a continuing dialectic of disjunctions. But such a critical procedure need not be confined to process and product. It can lead to other dichotomies that characterize periods—reason and emotion, beauty and sublimity, rationalism and the marvelous. Wallace Jackson explains the years 1750-1800 as characterized by two revolutions, not one. The first was a radical interest in the marvelous; the second defined the marvelous within the probable. "Between the years 1750 and 1800 two revolutions in English poetry not at all irrelevant to each other occurred. The first, with which I associate chiefly the poets Collins, Gray, and the brothers Joseph and Thomas Warton, was largely encouraged and supported by a body of literary criticism that began to appear at mid-century. For both the poets and the critics, the touchstone of their movement was a decidedly more radical interest in the poetic marvelous than had been tolerated by the literary Augustans."[7]

These poets sought to delineate the passions, the furies and beneficent deities of the human mind. They sought "a newly marvelous subject" founded on the probabilities of human nature and justified by past literature. But they did not create a poetry of "direct and immediate contemporary reference." The "second revolution was created by Blake and Wordsworth within the framework of lyric poetry. . . . They redefined the marvelous within the probable and suggested the sublimity of the ordinary aspects of human experience. It is fitting, therefore, to view both new poets within the contours of eighteenth-century literary history, for the urgencies that summoned them cannot be estimated without reference to the renaissance of mid-century" (6).

"Revolution" and "renaissance" are exaggerated terms for the change that Mr. Jackson describes. He acknowledges that the humanist tradition survives in this period. He acknowledges, too, that the changes which these revolutions introduce are matters of degree and evolution: "In this period the dominant creative energies have been transferred from that always lightly fortified bastion we know as English Augustanism; if such energies slowly coalesce into the untidy form or forms of Romanticism they yet retain something of what they were" (8).

We can see here some of the difficulties in explaining change when distinctions are not made between changes within a system or period and changes of a system. The changes within a period are not revolutionary but are variations, alterations of what are generally accepted though not necessarily consciously accepted premises for the writing of poems or prose. A critic needs, therefore, to note the range of possible variations that can take place lest his language imply changes far more radical than those which took place. The language of energy and power tends to avoid the necessary relation between structural features and thematic continuity or discontinuity. Indeed, what is at issue is the nature of a literary text as a social statement or action. The explanation of thematic change requires some systematic statement of the relation between these and artistic structure.

In calling upon critical theory of the 1750s and 1760s for support, Wallace Jackson argues for the revolution in literary theory similar to that in poetry. But P. W. K. Stone insists that no such revolution occurred, at least with regard to the theory of composition. The latter half of the eighteenth century was a continuation of the earlier half. It was the Romantic critics, he claims, who created a revolution in poetic theory: "There is one department of poetic theory, a fundamentally important one, in which the Romantics did produce a radically new set of ideas. Their notions about the writing of poetry are indeed so much at variance with any hitherto entertained that they might almost be said to have invented a new conception of the art. It is notable that Wordsworth and Coleridge, and their fellow poets and critics, themselves asserted that in their lifetime a new sort of poetry had begun to be written on new principles."[8]

All the critics I have thus far discussed agree that a literary change took place at about 1800, but their explanations of this change show no such agreement. Explanations are always made within a system, within the critic's boundaries pertinent to subject matter and methods. In explaining literary change within the time segment 1750-1800, some critics limit themselves by referring to those traits they consider characteristic, assuming that works or traits that are continuous are insignificant for period description. For them, discontinuity becomes the basis for explanation, a discontinuity in the attitude to composition or a rejection of an earlier way of writing for personal or other reasons.

In drawing attention to the primacy of "characteristic" features, these critics imply a hierarchy of explanations. What is "characteristic" becomes for them the most significant aspect of writing whereas other features that are continuous are seen as undistinctive in explaining change. The critics who propose explanations in terms of "anticipations" or "antecedents" find such individual poetic traits discontinuous with a norm, whether the "norm" refers to imagery, to "sensibility," or to a period. But such "antecedents" also create explanatory problems. Insofar as the Romantic period is considered a conceptual norm change, no antecedent which is part of a prior norm can lead to it.

III. PROBLEMS, PERIODS, AND NORMS

Although several of the critics discussed have avoided analyzing change in terms of a "system," it is apparent that they do imply generalizations about a hierarchy of explanations, about continuity and discontinuity. But there are others for whom the notion of a literary system is a given and who describe continuity and change in systematic terms. That there are different kinds of systems within literature can be taken for granted. A poem is a system or network of relations, but insofar as a text is always an instance of genre, it is part of this larger system. Thus the study of change and continuity can deal with large segments of time as well as with very narrow ones of no more than fifty years.

Changes always take place within time limits, and these are specified by the critic and are based on the works that constitute his study. But how broad ought the explanatory hypotheses to be? Any discussion of literary change can be confined to a literary system or can proceed by relating nonliterary activities to literary. There is no doubt that the closing of the theaters affects the kind of writing that is done, that censorship suppresses as well as leads to certain forms of expression, that some forms of writing are deliberately aimed at expounding and praising the values of the state. I wish in this short essay to confine myself to changes within a literary system that can be explained by it.

In this respect it will appear that explanations of change must presuppose continuity and discontinuity and must expound the diverse interactions between them. Such interactions begin with the concept of the literary work as a multiply layered system, containing within it varieties of diction, rhetorical and lexical features from other forms, and manners of ordering this diversity for particular ends. Such works are related to all others in any moment in history either in Eliot's sense of composing a huge system in time for great works, or in Lotman's sense that any particular time provides a network that includes all kinds of writing. The kind of explanation that the critic will employ will depend upon his definition of a literary work and the temporal system in which it is placed.

It is appropriate therefore to extend our discussion to critics who treat changes as systematic phenomena and who, in doing so, specify the nature of the system they propose. R. S. Crane, in outlining the procedures governing change in literary history based on the principles of artistic synthesis, declares:

> The collective enterprise of historians in this mode would consequently have as its ultimate purpose the writing of a narrative-causal history of the various literary arts in terms of four things: (1) the successive shifts in the artistic or formal ends which writers at different times and in different places have pursued, (2) the successive changes in the materials through which the different ends were realized, (3) the successive discoveries of more effective or at least new devices and techniques for the achievement of the different

forms in the different materials, and (4) the successive actualizations of all these changing possibilities in the production of artistically valuable or historically significant works in the different arts with which the history deals. . . . It is the distinguishing assumption, however, of the kind of history we are now considering that complete historical intelligibility demands not only the inclusion of all three elements but the recognition that the first is necessarily prior in importance (though not always prior in the historian's order of inquiry) to the other two, since in the actual construction of literary works of a given kind the latter either depend upon it as a principle or are fully explicable, in all their peculiarities as combined in particular works, only by reference to it. It is appropriate therefore to describe this mode of literary history as the narrative history of forms.[9]

This exposition of the narrative history of forms is based on explaining the kind of changes that take place. But it is apparent that although Crane draws attention to changes from didactic to lyric forms, for example, his study of change does not, systematically, distinguish between changes within a system and changes of a system. Indeed, although Crane's system is comprehensive and thoughtful, it leaves open the question of collective explanation or period explanation of changes. He is astute in recognizing that variety exists at any one time, but he concedes that large collective factors in literary production and appreciation "are not easy to discuss by means of the analytical procedures we have been considering" (112).

There is another aspect of this exposition of change that needs to be considered. Since constructional problems are central to this analysis of change, the nature of the work to be constructed needs to be specified since his definition of the work will determine the kinds of constructional problems he finds. For Northrop Frye constructional problems are derived from a view of the nature of literature and for William Wimsatt structure is determined by certain epistemological concepts governing the poet's (nonconscious) relation to his subject matter. Of course, explanations are judged in terms of our standards of evidence, argument (the persuasiveness of the evidence), and adequacy (the appropriateness of evidence to the situation).

If change in writing is to be explained, and writing is done in genres, then change must inevitably account for simultaneity of continuity and difference. And if change involves such simultaneity, how extensive is this simultaneous phenomenon? Crane's theory confines itself to individual problem solving, and the problem of a period hypothesis for change is left open. But a history in terms of the "problems faced by writers in the process of making poems, dramas, or narratives of different kinds" (37) cannot be delimited by the problems the writers knew they were facing, especially since later commentators recognize "problems" of which the writers were not conscious. Even if different historians discover different ends, it is apparent that, to some extent, every work has its own way of reaching its ends. The historian must, therefore, posit certain ends which are analogous or variations of one another and he must distinguish between these and those which are conceptually different. The most the critic can do "is to make clear whether the novelty was the result, in a given case, of a revolutionary rejection of the past or of a more or less thoroughgoing adaptation of traditional materials to new ends and uses. There will consequently always remain a margin of chance or mystery after the historian has done his best" (77).

But even the systematic procedures for explaining continuity and change cannot be adequately unfolded without the critic's presupposing what a literary work is, since this hypothesis governs the problems he discovers and the aims or ends he specifies. For example, if one believes that a work is a concrete whole which has as one of its principles of construction "a particular manner of representation (as narrative or dramatic)" (12), then he will find that change takes place in terms of this manner. If one believes, however, that any manner of representation is a hierarchy of manners of representation, then he will see change as taking place within the hierarchy as well as between hierarchies.

Critics who refer to "periods" do not always refer to the same period concept. For some it is identified by common forms, for others by characteristic poetic procedures, for still others by characteristic themes or dominant literary figures. To understand period changes is to presuppose that periods exist and that there are changes within a period that are different in kind from changes of a period. What type of evolutionary or revolutionary change does a period imply?

To answer this inquiry it is necessary to assume that a period is a temporal segment which has some coherence. And yet, by definition, every work in a period brings with it features of prior periods. Each work, even of the same genre, is different to some extent—however slight—from every other. And what of works from past periods that are models for the period like Milton's *Il Penseroso* and *L'Allegro* or Spenser's *Faerie Queene* or Shakespeare's plays as well as Homer's epics? In the face of such diversity—as well as the obvious diversity resulting from different political persuasions and different value judgments—can there be any coherence?

A systematic explanation for a period and for period change was offered by Jan Mukarovsky, the Prague critic, and his views have been developed and revised by René Wellek. Mukarovsky declares that "a real norm" exists "when we have a publicly acknowledged goal with respect to which value is perceived as existing independently of the will of an individual and his subjective decisions. In other words, it must exist as a fact of the so-called collective awareness."[10] He is cognizant that groups within a community have different goals, and he posits the view that "the co-existence and competition of numerous parallel aesthetic norms" (42) occur. These are accepted by the community as forming a hierarchy, and the aesthetic hierarchy has a complex relation to social hierarchies in society (49ff).

The collective awareness on which Mukarovsky bases his period norms implies that the readers and writers of a period are the ones who identify it. This procedure, which seeks to make period definitions historically independent of the modern reader, has some serious drawbacks. Readers and writers while living within a period cannot see its boundaries, for in whatever part of a period they find themselves, they cannot know the next period which is the one that forms its boundary. A period, moreover, deals not only with conflicting types of awareness, but with types of nonawareness. If we are to consider a period in all its complexity, then we must consider subject matter that is suppressed or prohibited, forms that are known but neglected—such as the sonnet up to the last two decades of the eighteenth century or the epic poem in the nineteenth—preferences for some types of imagery rather than others, and so forth.

René Wellek agrees with Mukarovsky that different norms exist within a period, although he rejects the homology between aesthetic works and social hierarchies. A period, he declares, "is no metaphysical entity nor an arbitrary cross-section, but rather a time section dominated by a system of literary norms whose introduction, spread, diversification, integration and disappearance can be traced. . . . We must extract it [this system of norms] from history itself: we have to discover it there in reality."[11] But if this is the case, what purpose does the notion of "period" serve? Why not a history of the different and changing norms? In fact, this is precisely the argument offered by Claudio Guillén: "If we conceive of the diachronic object of periodization as being multiple in the first place, it is then not so difficult to accept the idea of multiple periodization, either in terms of dynamic, dialectical periods or of separate 'durations,' 'currents,' processes, and other terms comparably diachronic in character."[12]

"[This] alternative," writes Guillén, "relies on the use of a noninterpretative chronology.... It stresses essentially the confrontation, within such chronological units, of a plurality of durations, movements, ... and other temporal processes" (469). If in any historical segment there are confrontations, diverse movements, and currents—and Wellek grants this—does not the assumption of a unified norm or system of norms reduce this diversity and make it subordinate to a false unity? Does not a period procedure falsify the different kinds of historical time that works represent at any moment in history so that a period gives simultaneity to works that derive from different times or "periods"? To cite an example, Shakespeare and Milton and Coleridge and Arnold and Eliot coexist in the modern period although their works are constructed in terms of different period norms. Doesn't a period concept erase the different temporal histories of its texts? Doesn't it arbitrarily impose an a priori dichotomy such as "process" and "product" or some other embracing generalization?

IV. TENTATIVE PROPOSALS FOR A SOLUTION

These questions lead to a more challenging one: What purpose does periodization serve in the study of literary history? The one phenomenon on which critics who write about the time segment 1750-1800 agree is that a major change in the composition of poetry and the principles of criticism took place at the end of the eighteenth century and the beginning of the nineteenth. It was a change that rejected eighteenth-century poetic procedures, psychological and epistemological hypotheses, and thematic conceptions and exemplified an organic structuring or ordering of poetry, different aesthetic functions of its features, a relation of these features to epistemological and psychological hypotheses about imagination and nature, and a new mythic use of thematic materials.

But did these changes govern all works, all the major works, of a movement? The period answer of multiple norms becomes one with the diversity of movements or schools, except that a period change presupposes a rejection of a mode of structuring and its philosophical and psychological premises. There are, however, some period hypotheses that can serve to clarify, to provide a basis for, redoing literary history.

A literary period is a time segment in which literary texts are composed, interpreted, distributed, and received. But within the time segment, works composed in the past live in the present as models, ideals, competitors.

Such texts can be increased during the time segment as medieval ballads are brought into prominence in 1765, or they can become dominant ideals as in the idolatry—in contrast to the prior admiration—of Shakespeare's plays that began with Garrick. The purpose of conceiving of a period in these terms is to grant that as time segments, periods permit a variety of changes consistent with so-called norms. Periods as time segments have beginnings, middles, and ends. But what constitutes the basis for consistency within a period? Different instances of genre within a period system indicate not only what is included but what can be included but is excluded. A period, therefore, while time centered, includes features and works from other periods or times and combines past with present time, past artistic features and forms with present. Underlying this combination, therefore, is a conception of literary structures that, in their very ordering, imply combinations, associations, interrelations specific to a body of works.

Another hypothesis has to be introduced if a period hypothesis is to have validity in explaining change. Namely, genres are social in origin and in their development and are, thus, historically defined in their very ordering. Not only are instances of genre exemplifications of time conceptions; they are also conceptions of the individual in relation to language, to diction, to meter, to themes and myths that serve communicative ends. There are, indeed, differences in the works of a period, but these differences fall within the range of accommodatable change. Every period, therefore, contains features that reappear in others, but within each period they are related to the concepts governing the network of texts.

An example of this procedure is to be found in the work of Eric Rothstein, who describes certain patterns of fiction writing throughout the eighteenth century. He sets forth three principles—breadth, freedom from manipulation, and particulateness—and declares that these principles "flourished widely in various genres before 1750, but shrunk in range as the century wore on." In the latter part of the century the novel revealed "a system of order depending more on causality (linear plot), less on analogical panorama. When the characters no longer had a plenitude to interpret, the system of inquiry changed, with the factitious mysteries of Gothic novels the last attempt to maintain it. The new modes and methods of reading permanently displaced the old, never again endemic, even in the age of sweeping works like *Middlemarch, Vanity Fair,* and the later novels of Dickens."[13]

The principles governing a period system imply that beginnings and endings are identifiable but vague. The art historian Meyer Schapiro finds a similar vagueness in art history: "Since development is gradual and uneven, periodizing must be vague in its boundaries. The types of art which seem distinct in the particular works cited in defining the types become less distinct when we try to specify the earliest and latest examples of the types."[14] And Thomas Kuhn, the historian of science, finds the ending of a paradigm period a time of crisis and confusion of method and problem solving.[15] But literary beginnings and endings can be differentiated. Beginnings are marked by rejections of early formal features and their underlying premises, a practice that leads to parodying them, to including and transcending them, to positing them and offering alternatives to them. The major works of a period are not usually those which begin it, but rather those which amplify the modes of organization, provide subtle analysis of the works of the past by retranslating them, by indicating how prior genres can become dominant and can be expanded to include new features and new forms. The novel, for example, derives from biography, from the periodical essay, from the romance, from the picaresque novel, from epistolary correspondence, but in developing a narrative with selections from these features, it serves to mingle fictional narrative with nonfictional statements in order to explore the dilemma of the individual who undermines moral or public values while wishing to live by them. The relation between the novel and satire illustrates the attacks upon corrupt values while seeking to imply that true ones can be recognized at once.

Why do periods end? Although this is a question that cannot be answered exclusively in literary terms, some literary explanations can be proposed. The organizing or ordering principles of composition within a period lead to self-parody, contradictions within the principles themselves. If we recognize that the principle of the detached observer describing different views of nature is based on Lockean views of knowledge as successive and fragmentary, then it will be apparent as the period develops that differences of description call common human nature into question. When differences of response rather than similarities of response become the basis for understanding, the detached observer becomes an unusable fiction and sequential seeing or ordering requires some organic hypothesis lest knowledge be purely subjective and noncommunicative.

The very extensive additions of "sensibility" that Thomas Warton lists in *The Pleasures of Melancholy* reveal that he is writing within the premise of

Lockean ordering, but that his additions lead to parody of the principle. The resort to magic and the marvelous in Gothic novels is still another example of attempts to accommodate individual disorder or tyranny within the norm. Individual behavior in *The Castle of Otranto,* for example, is punished by supernatural order, but the principle of effects as a form of God's presence and power is continuous.

In fact, the distinction between "product" and "process" can be seen as falsely dichotomous if we recognize that the couplet is a completed fragment and is not inconsistent with oracular procedures of composition. The repetitiveness of the couplet has, as one of its functions, to give the impression of completion in works that remain under repeated revision such as *The Rape of the Lock.* And in prose *A Tale of a Tub* is an example of the "process" writing inevitably mixed with illusions of "product." The range of variation within a period is extensive, and the boundaries within which this range operates have been little studied. But Josephine Miles has demonstrated that quantitative changes in vocabulary and sentence structure can provide a basis for period vocabulary. This basis is not without continuity, though the changes in the same word would have to be identified. But the method does provide a basis for period lexicons as they establish continuity and change. She writes:

> The chief vocabulary of English poetry at any one time reveals persistent strands, recent losses, incipient gains. Chief words waver and die away from the work of one poet and of many, perhaps return again for a few but in the main subside, while at the same time new words appear in major emphasis, tentatively or in large bursts of assurance. The stock of words is, one supposes, open-ended; yet simplicity and common usage have reason, and as some words in the most common stock in prose start to fade, we may not unwisely seek their successors from the common stock again.
>
> Structural proportionings too develop and decline in certain lines of agreement, as if choice of sentence structure were based not only on whim, subject matter, mystery of ear, but also on needed functions in the time: crisp assertiveness in one era, complex subordinations in another, qualifying assumptions in another, none ever in complete control of the literary language, but each often dominating for a while as if to set clear certain relations, in certain vocabularies, and in certain sound patterns.[16]

The loco-descriptive poem to which Meyer Abrams referred did contain a distanced spectator and descriptive and meditative passages, but these were connected to provide a relation between itemized past and present, between nature as a model of modification and compromise. The structure implied a

SOME THOUGHTS ON THE PROBLEMS OF LITERARY CHANGE

naturalizing of the myth of writing, of Helicon, as it suggested the need to modify the myth of kingly power. The features of this type of poem do not lead to the greater Romantic lyric but are included in it to be rejected. Alteration by rejection constitutes a recognition of prior functional uses and the rejection of these functions.

An example of the disjunctive approach to change is Raymond Williams's analysis of William Blake's "London." His view is that Blake's poem breaks radically with poetic (or period) norms of the eighteenth century by a new perception of the city: "a making of new connections, in the whole order of the city and of the human system it concentrates and embodies" (148-49). Blake began, writes Mr. Williams, by seeing the city in his poem in terms of the eighteenth-century norm and then, "suddenly, within this, he sees the capital in a new way" (148). Here is Mr. Williams's analysis:

> It was in this still eighteenth-century sense that Blake, himself a craftsman and a Londoner, saw the capital city:
>
>> I wander thro' each charter'd street,
>> Near where the charter'd Thames does flow . . .
>
> He had originally written "dirty" street and "dirty" Thames, and these would have been evident enough; but what he adds is the perception of "chartering": the organisation of a city in terms of trade. Suddenly, within this, he sees the capital in a new way: not the riot, the noise or the monstrous wen of earlier and contemporary observation; but an organisation, a systematic state of mind:
>
>> . . . And mark in every face I meet
>> Marks of weakness, marks of woe.
>>
>> In every cry of every Man
>> In every Infant's cry of fear,
>> In every voice, in every ban,
>> The mind-forg'd manacles I hear.
>
> The cries, the fears and the bans would all have been evident, but Blake now generalises them to an imposed and yet self-imposed organised repression: "the mind-forg'd manacles." What he then sees, dramatically, are the submerged connections of this capital system:
>
>> How the Chimney-sweeper's cry
>> Every black'ning Church appalls;

LITERARY CHANGE AS GENERIC HISTORY

> And the hapless Soldier's sigh
> Runs in blood down Palace walls.
>
> But most thro' midnight streets I hear
> How the youthful Harlot's curse
> Blasts the new born Infant's tear
> And blights with plagues the Marriage hearse.

This is very far from the traditional way of seeing innocence in the country, vice in the city. The innocence and the vice are in and of the city, in its factual and spiritual relations. The palace which impressively symbolises power has to be seen as running with blood: the real but suppressed relationship is made visible, as also in the conventions of church and marriage against the reality of those who suffered and were despised and outcast. It is not just an observation of, say, the chimney-sweepers; before Blake wrote there had been vigorous and partly successful campaigns against the appalling conditions of the chimney-sweeping children. It is a making of new connections, in the whole order of the city and of the human system it concentrates and embodies. This forcing into consciousness of the suppressed connections is then a new way of seeing the human and social order as a whole. It is, as it happens, a precise prevision of the essential literary methods and purposes of Dickens.

It is worth stressing this in Blake, since although he inherits many eighteenth-century pastoral images, in his whole work he transforms them to elements of a general condition. The simplifying contrast between country and city is then decisively transcended. (148-49)

Now these remarks are important in three ways: they stress the continuity of eighteenth-century attitudes which are transformed by externalizing what had been suppressed, they insist on discontinuity by the suddenness of the insight, they insist on a new systematic way of seeing. These remarks are contributions to an understanding of the nature of the change, but insofar as they describe change within a literary system, they need to be adapted to the very ways in which received features are rejected. The hymn meter, often identified with children's songs in the earlier period, becomes in the violence of the language an attack on and rejection of a call to peace. The childlike repetitions—"mark," "marks," "in every"—stand in opposition to the very "blasting" of the child. The wandering, seeing, and hearing speaker who in eighteenth-century poetry is distanced from nature, here stands condemned as the mere observer.

The recognition of change, therefore, is not merely a re-seeing of a subject matter, but a remaking of poetic structure, of poetic ordering. This remaking begins a period by reversing most of the functions served by the prior structure. And this reversal includes the speaker, the metrical pattern, the assumed functions of the hymn, the themes of birth and family, the very language which was formerly identified with accommodation and falsification.

Explorations of literary continuity and change are confined to the boundaries of the system the critic proposes. With reference to history Michel Foucault puts it this way: "What is significant is that history does not consider an event without defining the series to which it belongs, without specifying the method of analysis used, without seeking out the regularity of phenomena and the probable limits of their occurrence, without enquiring about variations, inflexions and the slope of the curve, without desiring to know the conditions on which these depend."[17]

Granted all these specifications, the discourse of the modern critic arises from adherence to a movement or a school or a period which is itself unfinished, incomplete. The critic, therefore, despite such cautionary remarks as Foucault's, needs to begin by postulating his own premises, but especially his view of how a literary text is constituted and how such constitution is inevitably tied to premises of change and continuity. Every study of literary texts must grapple with this problem. It has been the aim of this paper to offer some clarifications.

NOTES

1. Anthony Smith, *Social Change* (London: Longman, 1976), 7.

2. Raymond Williams, *The Country and the City* (New York: Oxford Univ. Press, 1973), 149; hereafter cited in text.

3. William Wimsatt, "The Structure of Romantic Nature Imagery," in *The Verbal Icon* (Lexington: Univ. of Kentucky Press, 1954), 109; hereafter cited in text.

4. Meyer H. Abrams, "Structure and Style in the Greater Romantic Lyric," in *From Sensibility to Romanticism,* ed. Frederick W. Hilles and Harold Bloom (New York: Oxford Univ. Press, 1965), 528; hereafter cited in text.

5. René Wellek, "The Concept of Romanticism in Literary History," in *Concepts of Criticism,* ed. Stephen G. Nichols Jr. (New Haven, CT: Yale Univ. Press, 1963), 159, see also 184; hereafter cited in text.

6. Northrop Frye, "Towards Defining an Age of Sensibility," in *Eighteenth-Century English Literature: Modern Essays in Criticism,* ed. James Clifford (1956; New York: Oxford Univ. Press, 1959), 312; hereafter cited in text.

7. Wallace Jackson, *The Probable and the Marvelous: Blake, Wordsworth, and the*

Eighteenth-Century Critical Tradition (Athens: Univ. of Georgia Press, 1978), 3; hereafter cited in text.

8. P. W. K. Stone, *The Art of Poetry, 1750-1820: Theories of Poetic Composition and Style in the Late Neo-Classic and Early Romantic Periods* (London: Routledge, 1967), 3.

9. R. S. Crane, *Critical and Historical Principles of Literary History* (1967; rpt. Chicago: Univ. of Chicago Press, 1971), 37-38; hereafter cited in text.

10. Jan Mukarovsky, *Aesthetic Function, Norm and Value as Social Facts,* trans. Mark E. Suino (Ann Arbor: Department of Slavic Languages and Literature, Univ. of Michigan, 1970), 25; hereafter cited in text.

11. René Wellek, "Periods and Movements in Literary History," in *English Institute Annual 1940* (New York: Columbia Univ. Press, 1941), 89-90. See also Wellek's "Period in Literature," in *Dictionary of World Literature,* ed. Joseph T. Shipley (New York: Philosophical Library, 1953).

12. Claudio Guillén, "Second Thoughts on Literary Periods," in *Literature as System: Essays toward the Theory of Literary History* (Princeton, NJ: Princeton Univ. Press, 1971), 464; hereafter cited in text.

13. Eric Rothstein, *Systems of Order and Inquiry in Later Eighteenth-Century Fiction* (Berkeley: Univ. of California Press, 1975), 243-44.

14. Meyer Schapiro, H. W. Janson, and E. H. Gombrich, "Criteria of Periodization in the History of European Art," in "A Symposium on Periods," special issue, *New Literary History* 1, no. 2 (1970): 113.

15. Thomas Kuhn, *The Structure of Scientific Revolutions,* 2nd ed. (Chicago: Univ. of Chicago Press, 1970), chaps. 7 and 8. See also his postscript in which he defends his position on paradigms. Attacks on this position have been made by Stephen Toulmin, in *Human Understanding: The Collective Use and Evolution of Concepts* (Princeton, NJ: Princeton Univ. Press, 1972), and by other philosophers of science.

16. Josephine Miles, *Poetry and Change: Donne, Milton, Wordsworth, and the Equilibrium of the Present* (Berkeley: Univ. of California Press, 1974), 35-36.

17. Michel Foucault, "The Discourse on Language," in *The Archaeology of Knowledge and the Discourse on Language* (New York: Harper and Row, 1972), 230.

Literary History and Literary Theory

Although I shall address myself to literary history and literary theory, because this relation is central to our time, this is not the traditional relation that, for centuries, interested scholars. The traditional contrast established by Aristotle was between *history* and *poetry*. He distinguished between them by declaring that "poetry is something more philosophic and of graver import than history, since its statements are of the nature rather of universals, whereas those of history are singulars. By a universal statement I mean one as to what such or such a kind of man will probably or necessarily say or do—which is the aim of poetry, though it affixes proper names to the characters; by a singular statement, one as to what, say, Alcibiades did or had done to him."[1] His distinction was between universals and singulars, between probabilities and particularities, and the inquiry was pursued into the nineteenth century when the distinction no longer was taken for granted.

It should be noted, however, that as G. Giovannini remarked, "In every age poetry has gravitated toward history and historiography toward poetic fiction as in a type of Hellenistic history imitating tragedy . . . medieval rhyming chronicles, and modern histories that read like fictions (e.g., C. Bowen's *John Adams*)."[2] The gravitational pull here is between fact and fiction, that is, between the factual material that a poem can possess and the techniques identified as literary that histories reveal. Indeed, one group of historians in our time, by conceiving of history as narrative, argue that it is to be understood as literature. I quote Hayden White: "History as a discipline is in bad shape today because it has lost sight of its origins in the literary imagination. In the interest of appearing scientific and objective, it has repressed and denied to itself its own greatest source of strength and renewal. By drawing historiography back once more to an intimate connection with its literary basis, we will be not only putting ourselves on guard against merely ideological distor-

---

This essay is published here for the first time. It was delivered April 29, 1982, to a seminar held at the Center for 20th Century Studies, University of Wisconsin-Milwaukee.

tions, we will be arriving at that 'theory' of history without which it cannot pass for a 'discipline' at all."[3] For such historians, the truth-value of history is always coupled with ideology, with "fictionalization" as explanation, so that the difference between "universal" and "singular" is minimized because it is a distinction between two types of fictive narrativizing.

The very question of history and theory, therefore, can be seen as arising from the identification of history with narrative and theory with commentary, and of poetry with theory and theory with poetry. For Aristotle theory and poetry shared the universalizing function and were thus opposed to history. A modern philosopher puts the relation between theory and history this way: "Narrative form as it is exhibited in both history and fiction is particularly important as a rival to theoretical explanation or understanding. Theory makes possible the explanation of an occurrence only by describing it in such a way that the description is logically related to a systematic set of generalizations or laws."[4] Hayden White and Richard Reinitz and others see narrative as a form in which the historian produces his work; they see history as a "literary artifact" or as a text that can be treated as a literary artifact. But narratives, according to literary theorists, are to be found in epics, dramas, novels, biographies, autobiographies, and other forms of writing. History, therefore, to the extent that it involves a connected sequence of events in discourse is related to a family of quite diverse kinds of writing.

One might want to ask of historians who write of "narrative form" what this "form" might be, since in literary texts "narrative" is a term that characterizes an abstraction. The narrative of Fowles's *The French Lieutenant's Woman* is a novel, and it was reworked into a film. The narrative is recognizable, but the *forms* of novel and film are quite disparate. "Narrative form" is an abstraction from form rather than any specific kind of writing.

Although "history" is often used to refer to past *actions* and *societies,* some of their artifacts in the form of architecture and paintings still exist in the present, but their explanation or interpretation is to be found only in *writing* or words. It is this writing—or discourses—to which historians like White refer when they call "history" a narrative.

To the extent that history is an interpretation, description, and explanation of *nonverbal* events, it involves a verbal translation. But insofar as history involves the interpretation of words, of written documents, it is inevitably intertwined, it is intertextually involved, with the writings it interprets and corrects. Of course, literary history can apply to more than these texts and their interrelations; it can apply to the production, publication, distribution, and reception of these texts. And in these respects it can involve actions that form the basis for intellectual or cultural history. A history of the Bloomsbury group would include some reference to the Hogarth Press and its role, just as a history of contemporary Russian literature would have to include some explanation of governmental censorship.

In order to deal clearly with the interrelations of literary history and of literary theory, it is desirable that we acknowledge them to be genres of writing, like letters or memoirs or laws. I suggest that we consider literary history as a genre, and that we consider literary theory as a genre as well. If one asks what it means to consider literary history and literary theory genres, I reply that a genre is a class of writing, the members of which all share a number of features for a common end, whether it be the production of generalizations or the interconnection of texts in time to illustrate continuities and change.

What, I may be asked, is gained by this generic move? The first thing to note is that this recognition eliminates any *necessary* privileging of a form. It also makes history and theory candidates for intertextuality, that is, they can include aspects of each other. Moreover, as forms of writing they transpose into their own traditions (genre) the writings to which they refer. As instances of creativity, they reinscribe elements from one genre into another. It makes any text, history or theory, part of a tradition of such texts and thus part of a diachronic as well as synchronic chain. This generic move gives to literary theories, as well as literary histories, a temporal existence, or beginnings and endings. It also makes such writing examples of entities, of wholes, such that the writing of history or the writing of theory involves a selection of formal features, of subject matters, of ends. Such wholes are pluridimensional discourses, and as histories and theories they can supplement, complement, and even contradict one another.

Now it is apparent, and I don't believe I have to argue the case, that the production of any *instance* of a genre stems from a history of possibilities and from a language that is acculturated. It is composed by a writer at a particular time (Barthes suggests this kind of history), and is read by a reader at another (Jauss has argued for this history). Any text is so constituted that it is part of these several systems. As genres, therefore, literary history and literary theory have different temporal existences and have, at different times, different interconnections. This accounts for the varied relations between history, poetry, and theory. If theory is identified with poetry because of its universality at one time, it is separated from poetry at another when "poetry" becomes historical. Literary history and literary theory, therefore, are conditioned and constituted differently at different times. And although history has always been distinguished from theory by nature of its particularity, it has had connections with theory in this very procedure. A generic approach makes it possible to both distinguish and relate them.

At present, for example, theory shares with history the need to descend to particulars, to select data in accordance with some aim, to provide explanations for the connections it makes. A theoretical work such as Genette's *Narrative Discourse* uses Proust's *Remembrance of Things Past* as a basis for illustration and interpretation. It is thus constituted by features from theory as well as from this novel and from the "classical novel" while adhering to its generic aim of providing a theory for certain aspects of narrative. In setting up a narrative theory with the aim of providing a "scientific" vocabulary, Genette reveals his intertextual alliance with a "scientific" discourse. At the same time he is also aware of the historical transitoriness of his theorizing. He writes:

> Therefore I think, and hope, that all this technology—prolepses, analepses, the iterative, focalizations, paralipses, the metadiegetic, etc.—surely barbaric to the lovers of belles letters, tomorrow will seem positively rustic, and will go to join other packaging, the detritus of Poetics; let us only hope that it will not be abandoned without having had some transitory usefulness. Occam, already uneasy about the progress of intellectual pollution, forbade us ever needlessly to invent creatures of reason—today we would say theoretical objects. I would be annoyed with myself if I fell short of this rule, but it seems to me that at least some of the literary forms designated and defined here call for further investigations, which for obvious reasons were not more than touched on in this work. So I hope to have furnished the theory of literature and the history of literature with some objects of study that are no doubt minor, but a little trimmer than the traditional entities, such as "the novel" or "poetry."[5]

A generic procedure such as I am recommending takes for granted the historical nature of genres and the transience of some of its features and the transhistorical continuity of others. I draw your attention to Genette's statement "I hope to have furnished the theory of literature and the history of literature with some objects of study." His book addresses itself to literary theory and to literary history, though in it the second is subordinated to the first. But the theoretician no less than the historian operates from his existence in the present, and if the historian interprets the past as it leads (however disjunctively and nonprogressively) to the present, the theorist offers generalizations that are aimed to apply beyond the present. As Genette very modestly puts it, his contribution will, he hopes, prove a little "trimmer" than the traditional entities. But if this is an effort toward a more scientific terminology, it is not intended to be, nor is it a story about the past. Genette's *Narrative Discourse* includes analyses of Proust's text as a test case for the usefulness of his narrative theory, but the theory is not meant as history of past works and their interconnections.

Literary history offers a particular ordering, explaining, interpreting, narrating of texts or passages of texts in time. It explores their interrelations to make them understandable and justifiable for modern scholarship or reading. In this respect it is continuous with the aims of history as posited by Nietzsche in the nineteenth century. For him, the production of history was to be judged with reference to its nourishment, liberation, and preservation of contemporary life. Whose "life" and what kind of "liberation" was not very clear, but the different kinds of history were directed to these aims. He found in his own age a surfeit of history in the schools and in the thought of his age. He sought, therefore, to reconceive the nature of history so that it could be turned from "what is alien and past," from a conception of history that was distant from the needs of his contemporaries, to one that was appropriate to them and that they could achieve by "reflecting on their genuine needs."[6] The three different constituent principles Nietzsche found in history he identified as *monumental, antiquarian,* and *critical:* "History belongs to the living man in three respects: it belongs to him so far as he is active and striving, so far as he preserves and admires, and so far as he suffers and is in need of liberation. To this triplicity of relations correspond three kinds of history: so far as they can be distinguished, a *monumental,* an *antiquarian,* and a *critical* kind of history" (14).

Nietzsche was very shrewd in recognizing that history as writing was constituted by a selectivity of actions and explanations. Each of these had advantages and disadvantages. *Monumental* history was the study of the rare and the great of the past. But this great-man version of ordering has its disadvantages: "Whenever the monumental vision of the past *rules* over the other ways of looking at the past, I mean the antiquarian and the critical, the past itself suffers *damage:* very great portions of the past are forgotten and despised, and flow away like a grey uninterrupted flood, and only single embellished facts stand out as islands" (17). *Antiquarian* history gives a sense of reverence to everyday details. Its disadvantage is in its veneration of anything past: "The antiquarian sense of a man, of an urban community, of a whole people always has an extremely limited field of vision; by far the most is not seen at all, and the little that is seen is seen too closely and in isolation; it cannot apply a standard and therefore takes everything to be equally important and therefore each individual thing to be too important" (20). *Critical* history is that which criticizes and condemns the past. But such a deconstruction of the past is not without its dangers.

> At best we may bring about a conflict between our inherited, innate nature and our knowledge, as well as a battle between a strict new discipline and ancient education and breeding; we implant a new habit, a new instinct, a second nature so that the first nature withers away. It is an attempt, as it were, *a posteriori* to give oneself a past from which one would like to be descended in opposition to the past from which one is descended:—always a dangerous attempt because it is so difficult to find a limit in denying the past and because second natures are mostly feebler than the first. (22)

I have attended to Nietzsche's three types of history and their advantages and disadvantages for "life" because I wish to draw from them three inferences about the relation of literary history to literary theory. The kind of "life" that the genre of history referred to is not the idea of "life" as developed in theory. That which is implicit in one genre (history) becomes explicit and thus characteristic of another genre (theory). The valuing of items of the everyday in history has its counterpart in theories that value, for their own views of "life," the texts that convey the interests of particular social or political groups or classes; and that history which is a criticism of the past forms the basis for a theory that is skeptical of texts and language. Of the literary theories practiced in our time, it is necessary to point out that they are the consequences of histories, of the histories of prophetic books of Blake, of the historic voices of women and blacks, of the histories of texts that demonstrated ambiguities, concealed assumptions, hidden negations.

The kinds of *history* that Nietzsche analyzes by showing their underlying or implicit ordering principles become in contemporary literary theory overt principles of theory. What is implicit in history becomes explicit in theory. Thus *monumental* history becomes the theory of strong poets who respond to their strong poetic fathers. It is not necessary to argue that Harold Bloom derived his theory from Nietzsche or Carlyle. It is necessary to point out that if a history of poetry is governed by the interrelations of major poets, then the theorist will concern himself with the grounds that govern this selection. For Bloom the selection of such poets is connected with the sources of religion and prophecy, and the aim of his poetic theory is to return readers to the religious nature of poetic expression—or the theory of the great tradition by Leavis.

What Nietzsche described as *antiquarian* history has become in contemporary literary theory a veneration of the consciousness-raising of a particular group or class—whether women or blacks or Chicanos or gays or the proletariat. This theory has as its aim the instauration and maintenance of a particular group awareness through literature, and the fact that many of the works they include in their literary tradition have been considered minor or unworthy of study is taken as indicative of a prejudice against, and suppression of, the group itself.

Nietzsche's *critical* history involved the shattering and dissolving of past views. According to Nietzsche, the historian accomplished his end by dragging a view "to the bar of judgment, interrogating it meticulously and finally condemning it; every past, however, is worth condemning—for that is how matters happen to stand with human affairs: human violence and weakness have always contributed to shaping them" (21-22). The modern deconstructionist view as expressed by Paul de Man seeks to lead readers to doubt the reliability of language, to doubt the assuredness of historical narration. His aim, as he indicated in *Blindness and Insight,* was to rewrite literary history as an endless series of meanings in which truth and falsehood are intertwined: "If we no longer take for granted that a literary text can be reduced to a finite meaning or set of meanings, but see the act of reading as an endless process in which truth and falsehood are inextricably intertwined, then the prevailing schemes used in literary history (generally derived from genetic models) are no longer applicable."[7]

Nietzsche's reference to "life" has been supplanted in contemporary theory by the "life" of classes and groups. The aim of theories—and this is especially pertinent to those antiquarian theories I have described—is to advance the interest of society in terms of a view of how such a society is constituted. This is especially true of Marxist literary theorists. One type of Marxist—Walter Benjamin, for example—in considering the cultural treasures of the past, remarks that these "owe their existence not only to the efforts of the great minds and talents who have created them, but also to the anonymous toil of their contemporaries. There is no document of civilization which is not at the same time a document of barbarism."[8] History is seen methodologically as tainted, and dialectically in a continuing process that advances and contaminates the future, and will continue to do so until we reach a classless society. When a version of this view is applied by Fredric Jameson to a feature of literary history—for example, Henry James's "point of view"—we get the following explanation:

> The fiction of the individual subject—so-called bourgeois individualism— had of course, always been a key functional element in the bourgeois cultural revolution, the reprogramming of individuals to the "freedom" and equality of sheer market equivalence. As this fiction becomes ever more difficult to sustain (or, to use the somewhat mythic terminology of the Frankfurt School, as the old "autonomy" of the bourgeois subject is increasingly lost under the effects of disintegration and fetishization), more desperate myths of the self are generated, many of which are still with us today. Jamesian point of view, which comes into being as a protest and a defense against reification, ends up furnishing a powerful ideological instrument in the perpetuation of an increasingly subjectivized and psychologized world.[9]

The theoretical concept governing this explanation is that of "reification," a process in which social forms "are systematically broken up in order to be reconstructed more efficiently . . . ; but in which, at the same time, these now isolated broken bits and pieces of the older unities acquire a certain autonomy of their own" (63). Jameson believes that the history of forms reflects this process, and James's "point of view" is an example of it. This version of history takes for granted that the point of view must be an ideological instrument "in the perpetuation of an increasingly subjectivized and psychologized world."

Such an explanation is wedded to a hypothesis of change in which reconstruction and fragmentation are identified as disintegration. But "point of view" was no mere broken bit of construction; as a procedure in organizing a fiction it sensitized the reader to increasing industrialization and exploitation. And, in another sense, it led to works like *The Waste Land* with their artistic orchestration of myths through the fragments by which they were constructed.

The movement from principles implicit in history to those explicit in theory, from the concept of "life" for all to "life" for a group or class within society, leads me to the inference that the two genres are interactive in still another sense—in the modifications of theory and practice and the modification of history as narrative. In reviewing Jameson's historical homology between decline in society and fragmentation in point of view, I see his theorizing as speculative, as an effort to draw attention to the kind of theorizing that can be done about artistic features of a novel. But it also reveals the fact that Jameson is not interested in considering his hypothesis in terms of James's plays or his nonfictional essays or his development from the early novels to the later ones. The difficulty with such theorizing is that it is made, as Genette remarked above, to be replaced, though perhaps it may reveal some slim contribution to a more adequate theory.

I have been stressing some of the aspects involved in the production of literary history and literary theory. I began by pointing to the various historical relations that philosophers found between history and theory. In some instances history was related to poetry and opposed to theory. In contemporary thought, history has, in the work of some historians, once again come close to poetry as narrative form and in this respect it is once again opposed to theory. But although history in its particularity is always contrasted with theory in terms of generalizations, history requires conceptual assumptions with regard to the selecting of a subject, with regard to underlying principles of connection and explanation, with regard to its writing—whether it is a commentary, a mixture of science and interpretation, a narrative. So, too, theory requires the use of some historical materials. These include historical examples for testing the theory, the inevitable use of imagery, the dependence on prior instances of literary theory as models.

Because of these interrelations I have identified the relation between literary history and literary theory as genres of writing, and thus made them both instances of historical actions. My aim in doing this is to remove any notion that history or theory is a privileged form. By considering literary history and literary theory as genres, it is possible to trace their languages and their linkages, and I gave Genette's *Narrative Theory* as one such example. I then proceeded to several types of history as outlined by Nietzsche in order to classify a number of additional interconnections between history and theory.

It seems appropriate, therefore, to turn now to a statement about the literary historian in which his work is not characterized by the kinds of interrelations I have suggested, in order to contrast it with the position I have taken. A typical statement about the procedures of the literary historian reads as follows:

> For him the poem is essentially a historical phenomenon, arising out of conditions of thought and experience that may differ in countless ways from modern conditions, and that therefore require to be studied if the poem is to yield up its full meaning. He attempts to set the poem once again in its original context in time, reconstructing the circumstances of its composition and public reception, pointing out its connection with the artistic and intellectual assumptions of its age, and thus restoring as fully as he can the aspect it would have worn for a contemporary reader.[10]

The text, it should be noted, is a historical phenomenon because it arose out of past conditions of thought and experience. I have indicated above that statements of this kind may indeed help to explain the subject matter of a work, but they do not consider the selection of a genre and the nature of the genre as historical. In this respect such historical statements overlook the very *form* of a text as historical. The desire to reconstruct the circumstances of a text's composition and reception is certainly an attempt to place it within the assumptions of its age, but Nietzsche, White, and others who have written about historical reception have just argued that no history can be written without an ordering or controlling hypothesis which governs the history. Whatever kinds of history the historian adheres to, he inevitably introduces theoretical assumptions about periods, primary and secondary writers, the grounds of norms and the grounds governing changes of norms or movements.

There seem to me a number of other objections to this conventional way of conceiving of literary history. The first is that past conditions of thought and experience must be studied by distinguishing that which remains continuous from that which is discontinuous. No work is wholly and fully continuous, just as no work can reveal its "full" meaning, since meaning is the result of a transaction between reader and text, and this undergoes repeated change. This version of "literary history" takes no account of the different receptions of a text shaping how the modern critic will interpret it. It is not sufficient to suggest that the historical critic "regards the past of the poem as implicit in its present" because that past which he finds in the present is a consequence of considering other aspects of its past as non-present, as strange or "other." A second inadequacy has to do with reconstructing "the circumstances of its composition." The kind of questions that I have suggested as historically appropriate have to do with the selection of a particular genre and the reasons for such a selection. Why drama should be a dominant form in the Elizabethan period and satire in the early eighteenth century are not going to be revealed by a study of the writer's drafts or influences. Indeed, the example about "point of view" that I quoted above can serve as an illustration of formal features that are historically dictated, however dissatisfied we may be with Jameson's explanation of "history."

A text is certainly connected with the "artistic and intellectual assumptions of its age," but any age possesses contradictory assumptions and those that have continued from past ages. A conception of literary history, for example, that does not take for granted the living presence of the works of Milton and Shakespeare in the eighteenth century and of the living presence of the works of Homer, Horace, and Virgil will have an inadequate sense of the intellectual and artistic assumptions of the age. What is at issue, then, is a concept of an "age." For the mere chronological period gives no proper indication of the different time schemes an age possesses, nor does it indicate why these time schemes are connected in one way in the eighteenth century and another in the nineteenth.

A version of literary history that proposes to restore the poem to "the aspect it would have worn for the contemporary reader" ignores the fact that contemporary readers did not have one response—as witness the reception of Richardson's *Pamela*. Underlying this misconception is a theoretical assumption about the nature of a text, the claim being that it controls the response rather than providing a basis for transaction. But this theoretical assumption of literary history also assumes that the text is of its time, whereas it is a combination of different temporal states resulting from the continuity and discontinuity of its structural components. In Bakhtin's view of novelistic discourse, for example, he argues that the language is stratified and heteroglot (a combination): "Thus at any given moment of its historical existence, language is heteroglot from top to bottom: it represents the co-existence of socio-ideological contradictions between the present and the past, between differing epochs of the past, between different socio-ideological groups in the present, between tendencies, schools, circles and so forth, all given a bodily form. These 'languages' of heteroglossia intersect each other in a variety of ways, forming new socially typifying 'languages.'"[11] Bakhtin's discussion of the social nature of language is historical in a manner that the conventional view cannot manage. This is because literary history in his sense functions to describe and interpret a process as well as a product.

In this version of literary history, the nature of change becomes a dominant problem. The social nature of forms changes; the features of forms, the interpretations of forms, the functions of language, the norms of writing—all undergo change, and change can only be discussed, of course, in terms of certain continuities. The historical nature of literary change is seldom discussed, and when Michel Foucault in *The Order of Things* develops his view of epistemes, he notes that the changes from one episteme to another remain, as yet, an unsolved problem.

If we consider one statement about change by R. S. Crane, it will appear at once that his premises, his theoretical premises, are not based on a view of the individual text as containing its own negations but on changes in the realm of explicit features. The principles, which determine the variety and interrelation of the propositions the historian has to make, are the general factors implicit in any concrete instance of change, of whatever sort, in nature or human affairs. These are: (1) an initial situation from which the change proceeds; (2) a final situation in which the first situation eventuates and which contrasts with the first in kind, quality, or amount; (3) a continuing matter which undergoes change and of which both end terms can be predicated; and (4) a moving cause, or convergence of moving causes, capable of bringing about the particular change defined by the other variables.[12]

Crane's view of change is a procedure without ideology and without the presence of the interpreter, and it depicts a literary history that moves without committing itself to any kind of historical involvement in the kind of, or need for, readers. As such, its evaluative or valuing principles, its organizing principles, sanction the order that the changes undo. In fact, one of the aspects of the writing of literary history is that in any particular instance the history possesses features which look back (continuity) and forward (discontinuity) and reveal in its practice the extension and negation of the genre to which it belongs. Herbert Marcuse, to whom I give the last word, puts it this way (and he shares this view with Benjamin):

> There is no work of art which does not break its affirmative stance by the "power of the negative," which does not, in its very structure, evoke the words, the images, the music of another reality, of another order repelled by the existing one and yet alive in memory and anticipation, alive in what happens to men and women, and in their rebellion against it. Where this tension between affirmation and negation, between pleasure and sorrow, higher and material culture no longer prevails, where the work no longer sustains the dialectical unity of what is and what can (and ought to) be, art has lost its truth, has lost itself. And precisely in the aesthetic form are this tension, and the critical, negating, transcending qualities of bourgeois art— its antibourgeois qualities.[13]

NOTES

1. Aristotle, *Poetics* 9.1451b1.

2. G. Giovannini, "History and Poetry," in *Encyclopedia of Poetry and Poetics*, ed. Alex Preminger (Princeton, NJ: Princeton Univ. Press, 1965), 351.

3. Hayden White, "The Historical Text as Literary Artifact," in *The Writing of History: Literary Form and Historical Understanding*, ed. Robert H. Canary and Henry Kozicki (Madison: Univ. of Wisconsin Press, 1978), 62.

4. Louis O. Mink, "Narrative Form as a Cognitive Instrument," in Canary and Kozicki, *The Writing of History*, 131-32.

5. Gérard Genette, Afterword to *Narrative Discourse: An Essay in Method*, trans. Jane E. Lewin (Ithaca, NY: Cornell Univ. Press, 1980), 263-64.

6. Friedrich Nietzsche, *On the Advantage and Disadvantage of History for Life*, trans. Peter Preuss (Indianapolis, IN: Hackett, 1980), 64; hereafter cited in text.

7. Paul de Man, *Blindness and Insight: Essays in the Rhetoric of Contemporary Criticism* (Minneapolis: Univ. of Minnesota Press, 1971), ix.

8. Walter Benjamin, "Theses on the Philosophy of History," in *Illuminations*, ed. Hannah Arendt, trans. Harry Zohn (New York: Schocken, 1969), 256.

9. Fredric Jameson, *The Political Unconscious: Narrative as a Socially Symbolic Act* (Ithaca, NY: Cornell Univ. Press, 1981), 221; hereafter cited in text.

10. "Criticism," in Preminger, *Encyclopedia of Poetry and Poetics*, 167.

11. M. M. Bakhtin, "Discourse in the Novel," in *The Dialogic Imagination*, ed. Michael Holquist, trans. Caryl Emerson and Holquist (Austin: Univ. of Texas Press, 1981), 291.

12. R. S. Crane, *Critical and Historical Principles of Literary History* (Chicago: Univ. of Chicago Press, 1967), 33.

13. Herbert Marcuse, *Counterrevolution and Revolt* (London: Allen Lane, 1972), 92-93.

A Propaedeutic for Literary Change

I wish in this short paper to touch on three aspects of literary change: (1) the nature of change; (2) the kinds of change; (3) explanations of change. I do not wish to debate the meanings of the term "literary," and I shall, therefore, assume that what is "literary" is what authors, critics, theorists have identified at the same time or at different times as "literary." The fact that such authorities may disagree about the significance of "literary" will in no way affect the inquiry I propose. My aim is to offer a propaedutic for a study of literary change.

I. THE NATURE OF LITERARY CHANGE

Any discussion of literary change implies that there is a stable entity which can be divisible into parts. If a part of this entity changes, the gestalt can still be recognized; there remains a continuity which is necessary for change to take place. Change is opposed to the concept of changelessness on the one hand and differentness on the other. Changelessness undergoes no alteration of its parts. Differentness (and this applies to at least two events, situations, texts, etc.) refers to unrelated instances. Robert Nisbet puts it this way: "Change is a succession of differences in time in a persisting identity"; and he goes on to say that "only when the succession of differences in time may be seen to relate to some object, entity or being the identity of which persists through all the successive differences, can change be said to have occurred."[1] Nisbet is referring to social change, and differences in time are necessary for change in society to take place. But if, for example, one discusses changes in

---

This essay was originally published in *Society for Critical Exchange Reports* 13 (1983): 1-23, and was reprinted, with guest editor's preface and seven commentaries, in *Critical Exchange* 13 (Spring 1983): 1-17. It is reprinted here with permission of the publisher. The prefaces and commentaries in *Critical Exchange* are available at http://societyforcritical exchange.org.

the meaning of the word "wit" in the *Essay on Criticism,* the idea of time is of trivial importance: change of meaning here is not governed by time but by context. Different contexts, different meanings. This steers us at once to further discriminations. Semantic change need not imply change of concept. In fact, it indicates the variations that fall within the range of a single word. It is quite another case to consider period change or style change in which concepts undergo alteration despite the continuity that persists among parts of elements of a period or a "style." To relate literary change to concepts of thought and feeling or to forms of authorial and reader consciousness is to realize that literary change is connected with larger frameworks of change in nature and in man. Change is one of the ways in which we describe natural events: a seed "becomes" a seedling, a caterpillar "becomes" a butterfly; water "becomes" (changes into) steam. These are changes of shape with underlying identities. In the first two examples, we have a progress in which the change is seen to be inherent in the seed or in the stages of growth. In the third, the transformation retains the same chemical properties though these have turned from liquid to gas. Thus, the study of change in all these cases involves frameworks from botany or entomology or chemistry.

Consider the problem of identity and form change in mythological stories. Zeus, Hera, and other Greek gods and goddesses are constantly changing shape. Such form change, whatever its aim, is governed by a consciousness of the god's power and the god's knowledge that whether he becomes a bird or a beast, he can return to his original form. In other words, the language, soul, or spirit retains an identity. In literary texts, transformations of shape that retain identity are common. We can see this clearly in Apuleius's story written in the second century AD of Lucius, who is transformed into an ass though he continues to think in the language of a human being: "though I was no longer Lucius, and to all appearances a complete ass, a mere beast of burden, I still retained my mental faculties."[2] Or consider the famous twentieth-century story which begins "As Gregor Samsa awoke one morning from uneasy dreams he found himself transformed in his bed into a giant insect."[3] Gregor's shape has changed but he continues to think in human language and to be concerned about his human affairs.

My point is that change can be seen only against continuity, and in literary study, continuity can be studied only against or in contrast to change. The reason for this is that each literary text is always different from all others—no matter how slight the difference. However, the term "text" will not serve me in accounting for the kinds of change that I propose to discuss. What is needed is to redefine every literary "text" as a member of a genre. In doing so, it is possible to find that every text includes some elements from its generic past and others that relate to its synchronic present. Every text thus can be understood as multidimensional, possessing elements which constitute it as a member of one or more genres and which relate it to other texts in different genres.

I realize that numerous contemporary critics and theorists consider received generic classifications discredited, and I share their opinion. But I find no need to identify genre with such received categories (those that Maria Corti identifies) as "abstract, atemporal," didactic, or those that are "historic, diachronic, inductive."[4] Maria Corti's semiotic approach is to relate genres to the "universe of senders and addressees" and to concern herself with the problems of the transformation of genres. Other theorists, like Tzvetan Todorov and Mikhail Bakhtin, have also redefined "genre" without accepting the older and defunct classifications. After all, terms like "trace," "discourse," "absence" have been redefined, and there is no reason to assume that "genre" need be excluded from this process, especially since, as a critical formulation, it makes accessible an understanding of literary change.

In this new sense, genre can be understood as a family term, constituted by elements or parts such as meter, character, types of rhetoric, and discourse to produce certain effects. These elements can, of course, appear in different genres, each genre being identified by the nature of their combination and the effects produced. It is not surprising that genres differ in comprehensiveness and scale. A proverb can be part of a tragedy or comedy or a book of proverbs; a tragedy that is considered a performance genre by one critic may be considered a poem by another. The Pentateuch may be considered a sacred narrative at one time and a secular narrative at another. My point is that "writing" is identified in generic terms and that there exists no such phenomenon as "writing" which escapes forms or genres. This in no way is meant to imply that a text belongs only to one genre. *An Essay on Criticism,* for example, is obviously both a didactic poem and a critical text. Even an author may recognize that his text can be interpreted as belonging to more than one genre. Henry Fielding calls *Joseph Andrews* "a comic romance," which he defines as a "comic epic poem in prose; differing from comedy, as the serious epic from tragedy: its action being more extended and comprehensive; containing a much larger circle of incidents, and introducing a greater variety of characters."[5] Relying on epic, comedy, and romance, this definition indicates that for Fielding the work possessed elements from all three genres that were combined in imitation of *Don Quixote.*

Without proceeding to a theory of genre, it may be appropriate to note that because genre has some continuity of elements and effects, it provides a basis for locating which elements have been changed or added or omitted. The term "genre" indicates the kind of changes it can deal with. The term has its source in the Latin "genus," which refers to "kind" or "sort" or "species" or "class." Its root terms are "genere," "gignere"—to beget and (in the passive) to be born. "Genre" can refer to a member of a class or a whole class; it can refer to how a class is constituted (the varied members); it can refer to a changing process, or to the members of a class as definite and unchanging, a product. It has the same root as "gender" and, in being related to gender, indicates the naturalistic distinctions that are implied. Genres have many elements in common but they do have distinct ends that change according to the historical situation.

If we consider the kind of changes that are generic, we note changes within a genre and changes between genres. Maria Corti puts it this way: "A genre may be transformed by itself from the inside by a change in the function of one of its constitutive elements, following which the traits that are secondary in one era become primary in another; the genre reproduces like a microsystem those functional variations that generate the very movement of literature" (133-34); and again: "a genre is also transformed by changes in the other genres in the literary system, which means that there cannot be a history of a genre in isolation; on the contrary, every phenomenon of correlation and influence must be considered" (134).

Any attempt to discuss change in a genre system, however, cannot avoid explanatory models from history or politics or anthropology or some other field in which change is a factor. But the subject matter of literature complicates the uses of any model. In any period there are texts from the past that are treated as present and living works, there are genres that have been disregarded or are minimally practiced, and there are genres that are dominant and those that are considered minor or short forms. Those that are part of the living literature form a hierarchy. The concepts that govern such a hierarchy will explain both the nature of the hierarchy and the values attributed to it. Thus, every text is an intersection of at least two systems: a diachronic generic system and a synchronic, hierarchical one.

Such systems are constructed by critics to explain continuities and discontinuities in relating particular works or groups of works to the kinds of changes that are posited. Are changes made consciously by authors or formulated by critics? To put the question in this way is to pose a separation that need not be honored. Since every text shares elements with others and introduces new elements, the issue of change is not properly discriminated by such differences. Changes may be no more than variations of underlying period concepts of organization, philosophy, or language, and there is no necessary relation between a new genre and a new concept. A new genre such as the novel in the eighteenth century may conform to the concepts underlying the received genres, may, indeed, be no more than a variation of them. On the other hand, it is possible for Wordsworth correctly to claim that his rejection of eighteenth-century poetic language and the concepts of modification and epistemology underlying it leads to a new kind of poetic language and artistic vision.

The consciousness of change may apply to the individual writer, but the description of beginnings and endings of periods or movements are formulated after the fact by critics and scholars. These are fictions that depend on the critic's view of what texts constitute a period and why he wishes to divide ongoing time in this particular manner. I shall return to these problems in my discussion of the explanations of change, but it is necessary to note here that the subject matters selected for change—as, for example, changing attitudes to women or the changing role of the father—can be derived from disciplines other than literature. In this sense, some inquiries into change result from knowledge of change developed in other areas such as psychoanalysis or linguistics or history. The pursuit of inquiries into literary change, therefore, has an element of the unpredictable, and, indeed, the multiplicity of instances that would be considered literary changes have yet to be charted.

Since change inevitably involves a relation with continuity, it will follow that discontinuities will entail the persistence of some larger entity. If there is a change in the diction of poetry, what persists is the relation of diction to thought or to poetic structure or to a speaker. If a particular genre like the sonnet is not written over a period of time, what persists is the relation of this omission to a poetic hierarchy or to the lyric poems that are written. And if a period ends and a new period begins, what persists is a hypothesis (or a theory) about the process of periodization or about the persistence of some elements or the discontinuity of others from one period to another.

The nature of literary change is thus a study of alterations which can only be understood in terms of the persistence of nonaltered elements of frameworks which provide an identity. Literary change is always connected with or characterized by concepts of knowledge, language, and structure that define some changes as variations of these and others as contradicting, rejecting, or overturning them. Change is then a form of adaptation or of "revolution." But it is the nature of literary structures that change and persistence are present together. The kinds of relations between them account for the kinds of changes critics identify.

II. KINDS OF CHANGE

The kinds of change mentioned by critics are so varied that it seems difficult to organize them into coherent groups. Indeed, discussions of change occur in almost all texts, although there seems little theoretical awareness of the problems involved. I shall focus on changes within a text (an instance of a genre), changes that apply to groups of texts (within one or more genres), and changes that are the result of the impact of nonliterary institutions and actions upon literary texts.

Within a single text we note the changes that take place in its production. This can involve a study of work sheets or revisions in which the changes are examined in terms of certain persistent elements. Such study may serve to reveal the adaptations appropriate to support or supplement or expand concepts governing a genre. Or it may indicate the network of elements from different genres with which a work is being connected. Whether in work sheets or in print, the revisions will be seen as trivial, as adapted to received concepts, or as resistant to them.

In this respect a generic theory will make it necessary to provide a revisionary vocabulary of generic change. If satires that are exemplary are seen by Dryden as heroic poems, this conceptual change is the result of redefining satire by including heroic elements in it. When Meyer Abrams describes the "greater Romantic lyric" as a development of the georgic descriptive poem, he must provide a series of revisionary or developmental procedures that can "transform" one kind of poem into another. And this must be a matter of the ratio of change to persistence of elements. The kind of change that an individual text undergoes can involve the placement of a sermon, for example, into the text of a novel—as in *Tristram Shandy*. The insertion of one genre into another so that the whole becomes a part implies the comprehensiveness of genres and may indicate the nature of a generic hierarchy. But can one genre be transformed into another? Can a sonnet be transformed into the greater Romantic lyric? Does the epic become transformed into the novel?

The transformation image in botany or chemistry presupposes that change is either an evolution of an identity or the retention of an identity in different form. In order to explain literary transformation as a change, for example, the critic needs to argue that the greater Romantic lyric is inherent in the georgic descriptive poem or that it is a member of the same family of genres. It might be possible to argue, for example, that the ten-line stanza that Keats developed for his odes is a variant of the sonnet form—a quatrain and a sestet instead of two quatrains and a sestet. But then one would have to argue that the sonnet and Keats's odes compose a family that displaces rather than transforms the georgic descriptive poem. Whatever similarities of imagery or rhetorical procedures the genres share, these are connections, not evolutionary developments.

Among the kinds of changes in literature are those that involve parody or burlesque of non-comic genres. In such conversions there may be an opposition or an attack upon the values attributed to the original text. But parodies often aim to draw attention to the values of the original by indicating the pleasures that can be taken in it. This is often the case with ballad parodies.

I have suggested that genre study seems to me the most adequate procedure for discussing change, but many of my colleagues prefer to consider texts as composed of words or sentences and consider genres as units resulting from these initial combinations. For such critics literary change becomes a consequence of changes in a linguistic code. Hayden White, basing his discussion of change in literary history upon Roman Jakobson's sixfold model of the literary field, remarks that changes in the linguistic code "will in turn be reflected in changes in both the cognitive content of literary works (the messages) and the modes of contact (genres) in which messages are transmitted and received."[6] In this view the changes in language determine the kind of genres most appropriate for the changed messages: In a given period and place in history, the system of encodation and decodation permits the transmission of certain kinds of messages regarding one context and not others; and it will favor those genres adequate to the establishment of contacts between different points in the whole communication system represented by language in general. Significant periods of literary change will thus be signaled by changes in the linguistic code; changes in the code will in turn be reflected in changes in both the cognitive content of literary works (the messages) and the modes of contact (genres) in which messages are transmitted and received. Changes in the code, finally, can be conceived to be reflective of changes in the historico-natural context in which a given language game is being played.

Now this is an important hypothesis regarding the relation of "language" to genre. And it begins with the assumption that since language is a literary component shared by "the context, the audience, the artist, and the work alike," any statements about literary change must be related to "the more general field of linguistic transformation" (White 106). What we have here is the claim that literary texts are read in language and written in language and that the system of encodation and decodation define the transmission or prohibition of messages.

Such a hypothesis seems to me to misconstrue the relation between language and genre. Although genres are language structures, they are not reducible to language nor are they merely reflections of changes in the language code. Because every text is an instance of a genre (at least one), genre as a structure always includes features that have continuity with the past—whether these are compositional or metrical or thematic, etc.—and features that are innovative. Genre by this definition is constituted by linguistic codes that are inconsistent in their implications; moreover, the reading by scholars of any past work involves the imposition of their own linguistic code upon one of the past.

But in another sense, such a view of change overlooks the control a literary genre exercises upon the codes appropriate to it at any historical moment. The primacy of tragedy and comedy or of kinds of lyric poetry alters the conception of the codes appropriate to each genre. The choice of genre becomes not a linguistic act but a social one which determines the linguistic. If one takes a ballad like "The Ballad of Jane Shore" and converts it into a tragedy, the historical situation of the genre dictates that the characters will have to be elevated and the subject related to affairs of state. When a novel is converted into a film, it is self-evident that the visual imagery will dictate the possibilities of verbal transformation.

Consider one other valuable analysis of literary change, that of Michael Riffaterre. He finds that language forms a descriptive system "built of nouns, adjectives, ready-made sentences, clichés; stereotyped figures, arranged around a kernel word that fits a mental model of the reality represented by that word."[7] Such systems function differently in different genres and at different times. Now Michael Riffaterre wishes to stress the language system current at a particular time, and, indeed, he wisely urges its value in contributing to a more adequate study of historical analysis and change: "Style analysis should contribute to thematology in future by including all descriptive systems in these compilations arranged according to type, indicating their generic and chronological distribution" (52).

Such a hypothesis of descriptive systems is transgeneric. It may be found in whatever genres are current at a particular time. But can we accept this version of continuity and change of a descriptive system within a genre without knowing its role in the structure of a genre? Do such systems arise exclusive of the genres in which they are found in order to fit some abstract mental model of reality? Does it not seem more likely that such systems would arise culturally as extrapolations from generic explanations? That such systems exist as abstractions providing only some similarities in any specific instance?

In order to describe the kinds of changes that exist among groups of genres, the critic must posit such abstract entities as norms, epistemes, periods, individual and period "styles," "modes of writing," etc. With regard to change, these groupings imply a systematic approach to literary study; they aim to locate similarities among diverse individual texts and to explain the changes that—as a group—such texts undergo. (Of course, the identification of texts as "literary" or "literature" belongs with inquiries about changes governing the nature of literary study.)

If we wish to discuss changes among "norms" or "periods," it will be apparent that the definition of what these are must precede any analysis of change pertinent to them. When Mukarovsky defined a norm "as a publicly acknowledged goal with respect to which value is perceived as existing independently of an individual and his subjective decisions," he relied on a "so-called collective awareness."[8] He realized there are not only competing norms, but that norms are constantly being undermined. The relation between norm continuity and discontinuity becomes too elusive to pursue and thus the beginnings and endings of norms, the numbers and kinds of works and elements involved, become resistant to systematization. A much simpler procedure for dealing with norm change is offered by Thomas Kuhn, the historian of science. He tracks the beginning and ending of a scientific paradigm by referring to common institutional procedures used in educating scientists, to a practical institutional "norm."

Any application of Kuhnian "normal science" to literary study has to substitute concepts of generic expectations or common problem solving for institutional practice. But because, in literary study, these are always multiple, the notion of a unified "norm" seems unusable. As for multiple norms, these seem to pose problems about their discontinuance.

Periods no less than norms are critical abstractions or fictions, and any attempt to explain period change must do so within a framework of persistence between periods. Does a period consist of "literary" texts written within a particular time span or of literary texts available in a time span or of those that writers and readers find valuable? In any time period there are texts composed in earlier times; are these to be considered part of the "period"? It is difficult to avoid the view that texts which form part of a canon regardless of when they were composed do indeed form part of a period. This means that a period is multitemporal as well as multidimensional; the literary texts of a period so understood will then be governed by concepts of different chronological time. A change of period will thus have to make reference to different rates of change and to different relations among genres.

Because critics introduce period change in order to explain large-scale or revolutionary changes, or changes of literary hierarchies, they tend to neglect the continuities. The strategy is understandable, but it cannot lead to an adequate study of conceptual change. Some literary unit like genre is necessary to include continuity in any discussion of change. Debates over the length of time of periods or over the existence of periods—whether there is an Age of Sensibility or whether it is no more than the concluding thirty years of a neoclassical period or whether we have entered a postmodern period following modernism or are in the concluding phase of modernism—are misplaced because such determinations are not part of any theory of change, only ad hoc claims for evidence that is slanted to support one's hypothesis. They are fictions that function to explain particular changes; they do not explain the need, function, and aim of such changes.

When discussions of periods are displaced by discussions of receptions of literary texts, types of change become primary. But even if we attribute "receptions" to critics who express their views in writing (in contrast to readers about whom the critic can only speculate), the usefulness of such reception depends on the kinds of explanations offered.

III. EXPLANATIONS OF CHANGE

Although I have divided my discussion into "the nature of change," "the kinds of change," and "explanations of change," I have done so merely for strategic purposes: to open different aspects of the question of literary change. It is apparent that I have not hesitated to cross boundaries and move among the three areas despite my emphasis on a particular one. Description and explanation are obviously intertwined even though Michel Foucault in *The Order of Things,* for example, tries to keep them separate and to resist methodological explanations in the empirical sciences:

[T]he role of instruments, techniques, institutions, events, ideologies, and interests is very much in evidence; but one does not know how an articulation so complex and so diverse in composition actually operates. It seemed to me that it would not be prudent for the moment to force a solution I felt incapable, I admit, of offering: the traditional explanations—spirit of the time, technological or social changes, influences of various kinds—struck me for the most part as being more magical than effective. In this work, then, I left the problem of causes to one side; I chose instead to confine myself to describing the transformations themselves, thinking that this would be an indispensable step if, one day, a theory of scientific change and epistemological causality was to be constructed.[9]

He exaggerates his modesty, but his reference to "spirit of the time, technological or social changes, influences of various kinds" seems to be quite distant from other contemporary explanations of literary change. These explanations begin with concepts of a literary text: a text which is a multi-dimensional system will inevitably possess some elements that are changing more rapidly than others. In fact, the changes will be recognized only in terms of continuities. Different rates of change will, of course, also apply to membership in a hierarchy of genres. I have offered as an explanation of this the notion that every literary text is inevitably different from any other in the same genre. Let me add here that these differences operate within a series of temporary possibilities.

So too, technological or social changes need not be disregarded. The closing of theaters certainly provides a reason for not writing dramas, just as the insistence by government on the writing of "social realism" threatens punishment to those who disregard this policy. Such social pressures, at the very least, explain the neglect of certain kinds of writing even if they do not explain those that are written. But the notion of "explanation" is at issue here, for if Foucault conceives of explanation in terms of causes, he will expect relations that historians will rarely be able to provide. Explanations in literary study are always made in terms of the aims of the explainer. To ask why a genre like the novel was introduced in the eighteenth century is to take for granted that the novel is a genre and that its novelty is a chance occurrence or the result of a series of writings that are intertextual with it. The term "introduction," therefore, conceals within it evolutionary or developmental categories which involve ratios of continuity and change or randomness or both.

At which point is the "cause" to be discovered? Does it not imply an originating moment when the particular originating work is not yet identified? Is it *Robinson Crusoe* or *Moll Flanders* or *Pamela* or *Joseph Andrews?* If the critic puts aside the notion of "cause" and substitutes probable reasoning or reason giving, he will introduce reasons about generic differentiations, about the relation of such differentiations to social attitudes, about the relation of this genre to a synchronic system, about the shifts in function to the elements that compose the genre.

Sociologists and anthropologists who discuss social change tend to use three explanatory procedures: evolution, revolution, and randomness. Social change thus is the result of certain developmental or evolutionary procedures. Evolution need not mean a movement from a lower to a higher stage but to a series of successive stages not unlike the charting of individual growth by Erik Erikson. Such developments are connected to particular social structures and the kinds of changes are identified as adaptations or adjustments. Those changes which result in reorganizations of the structure are revolutionary changes. As for randomness, it is an attempt to leave open the introductions of unexpected pressures—whether legal, military, etc.—upon the structure.

Explanations of literary change are often related to and sometimes dependent upon moral, social, political, and psychological concepts. The most elementary procedure here is to make literature reflective of such changes: a social or political change is posited and literature is claimed to mirror it. More sophisticated critics grant that literary language constitutes its world and they recognize that what they have to explain is a change in the manner of literary construction. One of the ways in which this is done is to argue that changes in the external world result in changes in the psyche. Thus literary texts by revealing changes in consciousness reveal changes in the external world. This is Fredric Jameson's procedure: "An objective fragmentation of the so-called outside world is matched and accompanied by a fragmentation of the psyche which reinforces its effects. Such fragmentation, reification, but also production, of new semi-autonomous objects and activities, is clearly the objective precondition for the emergence of genres such as landscape, in which the viewing of an otherwise (or at least a traditionally) meaningless object—nature without people—comes to seem a self-justifying activity."[10]

The correlation is not merely reflective, for it involves the production "of new semi-autonomous objects and activities." But the difficulty with this type of explanation is that by insisting on reification and fragmentation, it becomes the procedure it describes. It neglects the relation of continuity and the concepts that underlie it so that the relation of landscape poetry to pastoral and georgic forms from which it comes is suppressed or overlooked. And the role of nature as place as well as the connection of place to property and politics is misconstrued.

Since changes are of different kinds, it is obvious that explanations of them will be of different kinds. I mean by this that although all explanations will have to refer to evidence to support their claims and will need to specify the changes to which they refer, some changes are directly social while others are only remotely so. Some literary change is the result of imposing censorship where none previously existed, or the imposition of an index or a canon that undergoes change as a result of institutional decisions. So, too, the vocabulary of literary criticism becomes social at one time and scientific at another. The social vocabulary of "refinement" and "decorum" and "correctness" is clearly related to social behavior, that of "scientific," "evolutionary," or "developmental" much less so.

What do explanations of literary change explain? Any explanation will describe the kind of change that has taken place and will offer some historical clues for it. But no explanation by a modern critic of a past change avoids distortion. What we can do is to control the distortion by introducing generic elements stipulated by others from earlier times. Such continuities are not so much fused horizons as they are possibilities from which choices are made. But history is sometimes treated as though an element of past writing is always essentially the same, and the differences in time are trivial. When Paul de Man argues that the language of criticism and literature is permanently "unreliable"—"the most unreliable language in terms of which man names and modifies himself"—he stresses the continuity, the persistent function of language.

If we wish to explain literary change, can we avoid the changing attitudes toward poetic language? And, of course, it will be remarked, can we avoid the changing attitudes toward genre? A theory of literary change should be able to explain such changes, but what is needed for such an explanation is a unit of analysis that will permit all such inquiries. I think that genre as I have been using it can serve such a purpose. And it can serve because a genre is a social as well as literary unit; thus it is subject to the acculturating processes of language and of symbolic behavior. If we accept the view that any example of a genre is a combination of elements, then only some of these undergo change; for, otherwise, how would it still retain membership in a class? Therefore, we can argue that every literary text is constituted by elements that are in opposition or tension because they are identified, at the very least, with different time schemes and the intersection of diachronic and synchronic systems.

This phenomenon makes clear why beginnings and endings of periods can only be tentative and uncertain. In fact, the more extensive the change to be explained, the more useful a system which will control the explanation. It is always tempting to posit an essential continuity such as the oedipal conflict between strong poets of different times while minimizing or ignoring other explanatory procedures. But if it is granted that genre exercises control in constituting a text, no explanation can neglect its function.

The theories of literary changes that I have been discussing fall within the group of related genres called literary history, literary criticism, or literary theory. Those critics who find only differences of degree—and not always these—between the languages of criticism and poetry insist on the fictive constructs of both. For them, explanation is inevitably about themselves because a literary genre theory is as self-reflexive as poetry. If one argues that all writing is genre-bound, then a theory of change will deal not only with the nature and kinds of change but with the explanatory functions of each genre.

Theory and criticism are important today in the hierarchy of genres because they function as explanations of other genres and of themselves in a society in which orality is competing with writing. At such a period in the history of culture, efforts are made to consider explanation as forms of pleasure and as instances of fictive construction. Thus, historical, critical, and theoretical genres are seen as being reconstituted by their own processes of explanation. And the boundaries that separated these genres from those that were traditionally constituted as fictions are in process of erosion. A theory of literary change will explain that such a shift in the generic hierarchy and in the reconceptualizing of genres is a form of resistance to and subversion of received assumptions and practices of explanation. But not all are subverted, and I have suggested that generic procedures may well lead us to the consciousness of literary change that we seek.

NOTES

1. Robert A. Nisbet, "Introduction: The Problem of Social Change," in *Social Change,* ed. Nisbet (New York: Harper and Row, 1972), 1, 2.

2. Apuleius, *The Transformation of Lucius, Otherwise Known as "The Golden Ass,"* trans. Robert Graves (New York: Farrar, Strauss and Giroux, 1951), 72.

3. Franz Kafka, "The Metamorphosis," in *The Basic Kafka,* with an introduction by Erich Heller (New York: Pocket Books, 1979), 1.

4. Maria Corti, *An Introduction to Literary Semiotics,* trans. Margherita Bogat and

Allen Mandelbaum (Bloomington: Univ. of Indiana Press, 1978), 115; hereafter cited in text.

5. Henry Fielding, "Author's Preface to *Joseph Andrews*," in *Joseph Andrews and Shamela*, ed. Martin Battestin (Boston: Houghton Mifflin, 1961), 7.

6. Hayden White, "The Problem of Change in Literary History," *New Literary History* 7, no. 1 (1975): 107; hereafter cited in text.

7. Michael Riffaterre, "The Stylistic Approach to Literary History," *New Literary History* 2, no. 1 (1970): 40; hereafter cited in text.

8. Jan Mukarovsky, *Aesthetic Function, Norm and Value,* trans. Mark E. Suino (Ann Arbor: Univ. of Michigan, 1970), 25.

9. Michel Foucault, "Foreword to the English Edition," in *The Order of Things: An Archaeology of the Human Sciences* (New York: Random House, 1970), xiii.

10. Fredric Jameson, *The Political Unconscious: Narrative as a Socially Symbolic Act* (Ithaca, NY: Cornell Univ. Press, 1981), 229.

Generic History as New Literary History

It gives me great pleasure to return to the University of Konstanz because it is here that Hans Robert Jauss elaborated his theories of aesthetic reception and hermeneutical analysis, and it is here that Wolfgang Iser propounded his theories of the act and process of reading and of functional history. For more than a decade the three of us have collaborated in presenting to scholars the values of literary theory and its importance for the study of literature. I take this occasion to acknowledge their important contributions not only to *New Literary History* but to the study of literature in the Western world.

They are among the few contemporary critics who have concerned themselves with literary history aside from the followers of Prague structuralism and Marxism. Most contemporary theorists have turned from history as succession and interrelation of texts to analyses of discursive formations, psychoanalytical interpretations, contradictions, or systematic structure of the individual text. Insofar as the reading and interpretation of the individual text constitute a respect for and inquiry into its identity, its communicative and expressive aspects, this procedure is understandable. Living in societies which minimize individual identity and maximize systematic anonymity, such teaching and reading represent a resistance to institutional and bureaucratic norms. Such concern for the scholar's and theorist's independence would seem ample justification for ignoring questions about the relation of the past to the present.

But those of us who see the present as in part the past cannot ignore the contradictions, controversies, continuities that such a hypothesis entails. It compels us to recognize, as Professor Iser does, that literary history changes in terms of its different functions for readers, critics, and theorists. It compels

---

This paper is published here for the first time. It was delivered June 14, 1985, to an academic audience at the University of Konstanz, Baden-Württemberg, Germany.

us to recognize, as Professor Jauss does, that literary and social receptions are intertwined, that any contemporary response is a fusion of horizon between a present reader and a past text.

Whatever literary history is taken to be, and although there are many agreements about it among the three of us, each provides his own construct which differs from that of the others. But I think we should agree that such history is central to literary study because only by it do we understand present literature, present theory, present criticism. René Wellek has stated that it is "inconceivable" to write "literary theory without criticism or history, or criticism without theory and history, or history without theory and criticism."[1] I believe he is right but I believe, too, that he may not have understood the sense in which he was right. For on the face of it such a statement is unhistorical. It does not indicate why at this time one should assume that different kinds of writing about literature entail each other and it does not indicate why literary histories were so prevalent in the nineteenth century and relatively infrequent today. What I find unhistorical about it, too, is the assumption that intertextuality between history, theory, and criticism has always existed.

What, then, do I find right about this statement; with what do I agree? I agree with the assumption that any kind of writing about literature is combinatory (a combination of elements from varied genres) and that such combinations are historical in the sense that they include different elements at different times. Literary history can include not only elements from criticism and theory, but poems, biographical data, economic statements about publishing and distribution. This leads me to my first point about literary history: that it is a kind of writing, a genre. Now the idea of genre that I wish to offer is historical because it is a theoretical construct for a particular purpose and because the purpose changes as the numbers of examples change.

We do not have a term for an individual member of a genre so that a novel, for example, refers to a single work as well as to a class. This creates some difficulty in understanding that the class is composed of members, of individual novels, each of which tends to alter the genre "novel" until the genre itself seems inapplicable in establishing distinctions that seem useful to a theorist. I wish merely to add this consequence of my remarks on genre: if elements from different genres are embedded in any text, then the decision about the genre or genres to which it belongs is made by the critic, theorist, or historian. His choice of construct, his conception of genre is a historical event. Thus Aristotle's generic discussion of tragedy not only establishes its constituents and their most effective use, but deals with the ends of tragedy in terms of communal health. Classification is thus used to establish different artistic ends based on comprehensiveness as a criterion. Northrop Frye uses genre as a basis for interpretation. Even when Derrida rejects the use of genre, he does so by assuming that genre is some classificatory "law" and opposes it because he believes genre insists on fixed boundaries.

I use these examples to illustrate that genre theorists are themselves historical, that is, they undergo change in consequence of the different examples that constitute a class of such theories. I stress this view of history in order to argue that although each theorist develops his own construct, such constructs are inevitably tied to continuities of a class and to discontinuities or disruptions within the class. The roads into which the individual examples lead us can be dead ends or they can lead us to new frontiers or merely unexplored places among the older roads. Each historical and theoretical construct is, as we know, connected with aims that the writer wishes to achieve—aims that are literary and social. In this paper I set out some examples of a genre theory that I apply to literary history.

My aim in conceiving of genre in this way is to inquire into the nature of literary and social change, to understand how change proceeds in order to give us some knowledge of and perhaps some authority over the process. If there is no essential trait in the study of a literary genre, there are traits or elements that are more enduring than others. Many theorists believe that "genre" as a class is sufficiently stable so that we, as readers, respond to the clues which we recognize in any new work and at least begin to interpret it in terms of past members of the class. Even in Ezra Pound's cry "Make it New" and in Shklovsky's statement that the technique of art is to defamiliarize texts, we note the assumption that newness is based on oldness and defamiliarization is based on a theory of genre that emphasizes the familiar.

This is less a paradox than a principle, an accepted principle in dealing with social change: no differentness without familiarity, no change without some persistence and continuity. The expectations one has, therefore, can only be fulfilled or defeated if one has a readiness for the unexpected. With this readiness the reader or critic does not complete but does engage a text. A generic history opens for us a series of questions, the answers to which undo any total systematic approach to history or literary history. I do not deny the usefulness of a generic or other limited system, only the assumption that we can at present, on the basis of our knowledge, offer any comprehensive and inclusive system that encompasses every literary relation.

My first example deals with the question of generic elevation. Some genres are considered unliterary, inappropriate—for whatever reason—to be considered "literary" at one time or another. Thus Gibbon's *History* was considered belletristic or literary in the eighteenth century but not literary for critics like F. R. Leavis and Cleanth Brooks in the twentieth. Slave narratives, women's journal writing, children's stories, were not considered "literary" by most American critics of the first half of this century, but are now considered "literary" by social and gender critics. The literary historian and theorist is faced with the question, "How does a genre which is considered unliterary come to be considered 'literary' or worthy of study?" Put more technically, how do they enter the literary canon? We shall see that in order to answer this question it is necessary to inquire into historical and theoretical assumptions of critics and authors. And no answers will prove useful without examples that initiate or confront them.

My examples are taken from English balladry—oral and broadside ballads. I hope that the use of ballads will permit you to follow the examples by considering them in your German context. The ballad, though known as a genre from the Middle Ages, was never studied as the epic or tragedy. Rather, although sung by the common people inside and outside their homes, the ballads were themselves outside the realm of serious study. But at the beginning of the eighteenth century—in 1711—there was published for the first time a critique of two ballads—"Chevy Chase" and "Two Children in the Wood"—written by Joseph Addison for his *Spectator*, a periodical paper. Why did this attempt to elevate the ballad as proper for literary study occur at this time? The example of such a critique was unusual even though Addison argued that he was not importing new criteria of judgments but merely showing that the ballads conformed to the sophisticated tenets of criticism. In other words this example was seen by his opponents as a mismatch between the ballad and the epic. The example did not fit the critical principles. Either the criticism of Addison was inadequate or totally different criteria needed to be applied.

What led Addison to make this choice? His explanation was that the grand tour—the singing of ballads in different countries—confirmed to him the universal artistic quality of ballads. He wrote: "When I travelled, I took a particular Delight in hearing the Songs and Fables that are come from Father to Son, and are most in Vogue among the common People of the Countries through which I passed; for it is impossible that any thing should be universally tasted and approved by a Multitude, tho' they are only the Rabble of a Nation, which hath not in it some peculiar Aptness to please and gratifie the

Mind of Man. Human Nature is the same in all reasonable Creatures; and whatever falls in with it, will meet with Admirers amongst Readers of all Qualities and Conditions."[2]

But such an explanation does not account for the formal "critik" of the ballad, matching "Chevy Chase" with Virgil's *Aeneid*. In Addison's quotation there are at least three historical-theoretical issues that need to be untangled. The first deals with the relation of genres to each other at a historical moment: the generic and social ambience that converts pleasure into literary pleasure. The second deals with matching the historical continuity and universality of the low form with the artistic quality of classical models. The third deals with a historical analogy comparing the transactions involved in social travel and commerce with those involved in sophisticated responses to low ballads.

Genres cannot be studied by themselves. Since genres are combinatory, they can only be understood in their relation to each other. Thus the periodical essay in which Addison wrote his "critik" of "Chevy Chase" was itself an example of a new genre, a miscellany, a combination of genres: letters, critical essays, stories, narratives that were formal and informal. In other words Addison's critical essays appeared in conjunction with other genres. In all of these, natural sentiment and simplicity of thought functioned as a criterion of literature. Natural sentiment was for him a given in human nature, and it thus permitted him to link the ballad with the epic.

Addison sought to demonstrate that the ballad "Chevy Chase" was an epic and that it possessed the sentiments, thoughts, heroes, and actions of a heroic poem. He sought to show "that the Sentiments in that Ballad are extremely Natural and Poetical, and full of the majestick Simplicity which we admire in the greatest of the ancient Poets: For which Reason I shall quote several Passages of it, in which the Thought is altogether the same with what we meet in several Passages of the *Aeneid;* not that I would infer from thence, that the Poet (whoever he was) proposed to himself any Imitation of those Passages, but that he was directed to them in general, by the same Kind of Poetical Genius, and by the same Copyings after Nature" (*Spectator* 74).

Addison's comparison of "Chevy Chase" with the *Aeneid* implied that an anonymous ballad of the people was part of a great English literary tradition. His claim was nationalistic, and the process by which this was managed can be identified in generic matching: the matching of a low generic form with one of the highest—the epic or heroic poem—in order to make them level— to attribute to the lower the same literary and social status of the higher. This matching was achieved by comparing the English "Chevy Chase" with

Virgil's Latin. But more was involved, as Addison's quotation makes clear. The anonymous author of the ballad was like Virgil in not possessing critical knowledge of epic composition; by relying on "nature" and his own talent he achieved what the rules specified. Addison thus claimed for the anonymous ballad author what his contemporaries claimed for Virgil. For example, in 1711, the year of Addison's essay, Alexander Pope expressed this point about Virgil in *An Essay on Criticism:*

> When first young *Maro* in his boundless Mind
> A Work t' outlast Immortal *Rome* he design'd,
> Perhaps he seem'd *above* the Critick's Law,
> And but from *Nature's Fountains* scorn'd to draw:
> But when t'examine ev'ry Part he came,
> *Nature* and *Homer* were, he found, the *same:*
> Convinc'd, amaz'd, he checks the bold Design,
> And Rules as strict his labour'd Work confine,
> As if the *Stagyrite* o'erlook'd each Line. (130-38)

The issue here is more than the relation of particular examples to a theoretical assumption—that any good composition falls within the critically established principles of its genre whether the author intended the genre or not. Addison obviously knew that critics did disagree about individual examples. He remarked upon those critics who mocked the epic device of cataloguing in "Chevy Chase": "your little Buffoon Readers (who have seen that Passage ridiculed in *Hudibras*) will not be able to take the Beauty of it" (*Spectator* 74). What is at issue is the limiting range of examples that a critical generalization entails.

We can grant that any theory which is exemplified by practical examples can result in disagreement about whether the examples fall within it; can we assume that theoretical explanation serves as anything more than a strategic and circular device? That it pertains only to those examples which formed the basis for it? If we conceive of theory as a genre, the aim of which is to systematize certain literary relations, must not the theory be in constant alteration, like any genre, as it is used to apply to different examples? Do we not mislead ourselves by talking of theory and criticism as fixed entities rather than kinds of writing? As a kind of genre the theory specifies its own tentativeness, and each successive theorist engages the theory as he engages a poem. A theory thus understood cannot with any accuracy specify its limits of applicability to future texts, cannot specify when its applicability ceases. The historical shifts in the writing of theories are no less apparent than in that of ballads. The elevation of theories like the elevation of ballads is subject to analysis—and in the same manner.

Addison's strategy was to elevate the low and unliterary ballad genre by claiming its thoughts and sentiments to be universal. It was thus possible for him to elevate as well the makers and continuators of the ballad, the common people, into the realm of reliable literary judgment by linking their taste with that of the educated. In fact, this political and literary strategy was aimed at attacking the writing of the metaphysical poets of whom Addison chose Abraham Cowley as the vicious model, calling their writing "Gothic," a term that implied for him the un-British character of such writing and that brought with it the implication of forced conceits as disunifying and inharmonious, as opposed to the simple and natural beauty and sentiment of the ancient writers: "*Homer, Virgil,* or *Milton,* so far as the Language of their Poems is understood, will please a Reader of plain common Sense, who would neither relish nor comprehend an Epigram of *Martial,* or a Poem of *Cowley:* So, on the contrary, an ordinary Song or Ballad that is the Delight of the common People, cannot fail to please all such Readers as are not unqualified for the Entertainment by their Affectation or Ignorance; and the Reason is plain, because the same Paintings of Nature which recommend it to the most ordinary Reader, will appear beautiful to the most refined" (*Spectator* 70).

This passage illustrates what we all know, namely, that a historical construct defends certain kinds of literary works by attacking or resisting others. Addison's attack on metaphysical poetry, on a poetry of conceits whether of Martial or Cowley, is countered by his approbation of an ordinary song or ballad. His choice of these low forms makes clear the importance of hierarchical generic distinctions for his argument. Genre classification permits him to argue against the narrowness of the received classifications; and such argument also permits his writing to imply—whether he intends to or not—that the theory needs to be revised to include what it has excluded. Historically, then, the theory seems to be involved in a contradiction: its revision involves the inclusion of what it was constructed to exclude. Every generic instance used to exemplify a theory distends and even distances the theory. There is a point, therefore, at which a theory ceases to be useful; at such a time other theories are proposed. Unless examples illustrating a theory are understood generically, that is, unless they are seen as ballads elevated to epic poems, as satires elevated by Dryden to heroic poems, as novels elevated by Fielding to comic epics, unless we recognize the historical strategies of the critic in using theory we cannot observe and will not understand the gradual abandonment of theory as a consequence of its including or confronting examples that undermine it. As the ballad, as satire, as the novel begin to be identified as "epics" or heroic poems the concept of heroic poetry becomes a basis for its own disuse because the examples included within it render it ineffective in making the distinctions for which it originally served.

Addison's example is but part of the generic changes in English writing that were taking place at the beginning of the eighteenth century, and Addison permits us to see how changes in the general literary hierarchy were analogous to explanations of social change. In the essay immediately preceding that on Chevy Chase, he discussed the new place that was being occupied by the merchant class. The rising status of this class, therefore, served as a subtext for the rising status of the ballad; raising its literary status was a social act no less than a literary one. It was a strategy of analogical association.

Addison's political and economic essay (*Spectator* 69) began: "There is no Place in the Town which I so much love to frequent as the *Royal-Exchange.*" The term "exchange" referred to fair and equitable trading transactions, and the "exchange" was the place in which transactions involving distant countries were arranged by merchants who remained at home. Addison praised the nationalistic extension of Britain's economic power, the harmony of private and public interest between his own more advanced country and those less advanced. Merchants bring into their own country whatever is wanting and carry out whatever is superfluous. "Nature," he wrote, "seems to have taken a particular Care to disseminate her Blessings among the different Regions of the World, with an Eye to this mutual Intercourse and Traffick among Mankind, that the Natives of the several Parts of the Globe might have a kind of Dependance upon one another, and be united together by their common Interest" (*Spectator* 69).

Addison described commercial behavior in the imagery of moral and political benevolence; he used the language of commercial reciprocity to invoke a harmony between distant wealthy nations, between Britons and "Mohametans," Britons and "inhabitants of the frozen Zone." He touted the merchant as one of the most useful members "in a Commonwealth," although previously merchants had occupied no position of importance in English society.

Just as he praised the elevation of the merchant because of the private and public harmony he achieved between his own and other countries, so, too, Addison pointed to the actual elevation of the ballad because it harmonized the sentiment and taste of the rabble and the best critics: "If this Song had been written in the *Gothic* Manner, which is the Delight of all our little Wits, whether Writers or Readers, it would not have hit the Taste of so many Ages, and have pleased the Readers of all Ranks and Conditions" (*Spectator* 74). The universality of the ballad was based on that aspect of human nature which revealed an "essential and inherent Perfection of Simplicity of Thought" (*Spectator* 70).

But assumptions about simplicity of thought were not shared by many of Addison's fellow critics. Neither was the elevation of the ballad nor its nationalistic function. John Dennis objected to Addison's assumption about universality of judgment between uneducated and educated human beings, and he argued further that one ought not to separate simplicity of thought from simplicity of expression, since it was art that joined them. Addison's readiness to justify the thought of a ballad in spite of "a despicable Simplicity in the Verse" confirmed the validity of Dennis's attack. In fact, the reception of Addison's essays on the ballad was marked by numerous parodies by contemporaries. These were unimpressed by the inadequacies of an argument that sought to apply contemporary critical criteria of a heroic poem to ballads that dealt with a local battle or a betrayal of family obligation.

It is necessary to acknowledge, therefore, that Addison's effort to elevate popular ballads into the domain of the highest literary genre by matching them with the classical epics had no critical support; in fact, his arguments were effectively refuted. It created no followers. But refutation of criticism is often irrelevant if a genre engages poets, dramatists, and novelists. For the incorporation of ballads into the literary hierarchy was achieved, even if they were not considered epics.

The critical arguments about the ballad as epic had no supporters and, indeed, the arguments were not able to be implemented by the examples of many other ballads. Nevertheless, Addison's theoretical and critical essays sought to establish a nationalistic literary tradition by illustrating the primitive artistry of these old poems and to oppose the current vogue of metaphysical poetry. Since he did not achieve his aim of ballad elevation, how was it achieved? It was accomplished by poets, dramatists, novelists who brought ballads into the established literary genres, brought them from the streets into the theater. It was accomplished with the help even of the parodists.

There arose a series of parodies and attacks on Addison's view of the ballads and their role in literature. His claim was thus disavowed, but it lived in its oppositions. A historical view need not be triumphant to be continued. It exists insofar as it is entertained as a possibility that needs refutation. This can explain the fact that Addison as a critic merited replies; it does not account for the triumph of ballads as a literary genre.

Here it is necessary to insist further on the value of a generic approach to history. For what happened in the years following Addison's essays was the introduction of ballads into the writing of established genres. Nicholas Rowe converted the ballad of Jane Shore into *The Tragedy of Jane Shore* in 1714; ballads were collected in 1723; *The Beggar's Opera* introduced ballads into a new comic form in 1728; George Lillo wrote a ballad opera in 1730 and converted "The Ballad of George Barnwel" into a tragedy, *The London Merchant,* in 1731. There were numerous ballad operas performed between 1731 and 1760.

The importation of ballads into other genres or as the basis for other genres is a significant aspect of literary history. Tragedy, for example, considered in the eighteenth century one of the highest genres, gave the status of subject matter to ballads that formed the basis for a dramatic narrative. In this procedure, moreover, the ballad story became a constituent of tragedy. When poets essayed the ballad, they provided it with a legitimate status it did not previously have. The consequence is that, historically, poems and tragedies and other literary texts can function as critical illustrations. They demonstrate by their production that ballads do form part of the current literary hierarchy. Thus without generic analysis, this new function would go unrecognized by critics and readers.

Before the ballad became a recognized genre in its own right with a theoretical rationale for its independence—and it did so in 1765 in Percy's *Reliques of Ancient English Poetry*—it became a part of established genres, or was converted into established genres, or was parodied and ridiculed as a literary form.

If we are writing a literary history of the rise of English ballad to literary status, it is necessary to explain not only the criticism of Addison and its failure to attract adherents but the byways and discontinuities the ballad underwent—such as Sir Philip Sidney's praise of "Chevy Chase" and the occasional translation of a ballad. Even before Addison wrote his essays there appeared in the third edition of Dryden's *Second Miscellany* (1702) "The Ancient and Most Famous Ballad of Chevy Chase, With the Translation of it into Latin by the Command of the Bishop of London." This strategy of conversion was to demonstrate the literary quality of a popular ballad by translating it into the language of the learned. Translation in this instance became a critical act that lent some authority to the literary possibilities of the ballad. It was an early and singular effort of what was to become widespread demonstrations of the ballad as a literary genre.

In our time theoretical writing has shown similar transformations. Theorists like Harold Bloom and the late Paul de Man and intellectual historians like Hayden White and Dominick LaCapra consider theoretical writing a form of fiction, and seek to erase the boundaries between genres of history, theory, criticism, and other narratives. But rather than erasure perhaps we might note the tentativeness with which boundaries can be remapped rather than removed.

I wish to trace some of the remapping of the boundaries of the ballad and other genres in the early eighteenth century to illustrate the strategies of generic accommodation in altering the consciousness of sophisticated readers and audience so that they accept the social, political, and literary implications of the ballad and other unliterary forms as literary. The first example is the new genre called ballad opera. This genre ingests a number of ballads, puts new words to their music, and makes them part of a comic or serious drama. The ballads are moved from the streets to the stage and their elevation is identified by becoming part of a formal performance. In *The Beggar's Opera,* for example, the incorporation of ballads into the comic drama enacts the same leveling that Addison sought in comparing the ballad with the epic. Here the leveling makes the ballad part of comedy; in other ballad operas it becomes part of domestic drama. The ballads of *The Beggar's Opera* are converted to social commentary just as the actions of the criminals and prostitutes are a satiric conversion of the actions of the upper classes. This ballad opera satirizes the narratives of social history, showing the merchant as a self-interested exploiter so that the Addisonian image of the benevolent merchant is mocked by a counterimage in a different genre. And at the same time, Addison's aim to elevate the ballad is achieved by an incorporation that was mock-epic.

Critics and theorists sometimes ask: "Which comes first in the elevation and change of the ballad genre—the social and economic conditions or the literary revisions?" The answer that I have given is that such a question of origins is misconceived. And it is misconceived not because origins are, as we have been persuaded, multiple but because explanation and condition are not comparable, only explanations and explanations of conditions are. In trying to explain, to shape, to control our actions and the events in our society, we write in various genres. We can understand that what is the surface text in one genre (Addison's commercial essay) becomes a subtext for another genre (his critical essay). One of the aims in Gay's joining the ballad to comedy is to level the behavior of the low (ballad) and the high (comedy), to suggest that the merchant mediators are the exploiters and betrayers, the makers of fake harmonies.

The Beggar's Opera demonstrates the possibility of the ballad as a literary form and at the same time mixes and levels popular and polite genres. I have been emphasizing the social analogy of the ballad opera as a combinative genre; I wish now to add that the combination is held together by a concept of fictionality. The romance ending, the assurance that no serious consequence is intended by the social analogy, defuses the political power of *The Beggar's Opera*. The characters thus remain within the domain of the unpunished and the unserious. The conclusion, by making justice an act of romance, retreats from the seriousness of justice that is bought and sold.

The historian who deals with ballad inclusion will connect the ballad opera with the novel, recognizing that both these new species of writing involve characters and events that appear in ballads. He will attempt to explain the successive use of ballads in the opera and the successive use of incidents in the novel as indicative of sequential experience and observation. The combination of elements results in a different linkage of genres from that in the previous century. And the connection of ballad with tragedy indicates the widespread shift that takes place even in the constituents of long established forms. Such a shift creates a new importance for common characters and in doing so indicates an indictment of those classes that corrupt and exploit them. Such changes are not to be understood as revolutionary, but they show that new genres can bring to the consciousness of readers and viewers what was previously hidden or accepted or submerged.

Three years after *The Beggar's Opera,* the seventeenth-century "Ballad of George Barnwel" was rewritten by George Lillo as a tragedy, *The London Merchant.* In the ballad, an apprentice seduced by a prostitute robs his merchant master and eventually murders his rich uncle. When the prostitute throws him out, he peaches on her and she is apprehended and hanged. He escapes to Poland and is hanged for a murder he claims he did not commit. The rewriting of this criminal, confessional first-person ballad into a tragedy constitutes a reinterpretation of the characters and events; the absent character of the merchant in the ballad becomes the model figure of the tragedy. Characters unmentioned become physical presences, places undescribed become identified on the stage.

The reinterpretation of the ballad raises no question of authenticity or of historical accuracy. History in the tragedy serves a generic not a factual purpose: the time of the play is the Elizabethan period which makes it possible to consider the untitled merchant as a contemporary of Antonio, *The Merchant of Venice*. This use of history is not connected with any reality principle but with a political strategy to elevate the role of the merchant. The tragedy, by rewriting the ballad, merges it with its own genre. The ballad disappears as a ballad, unlike the procedure in *The Beggar's Opera* where it retains its ballad form though not its words. But as a result of its incorporation into tragedy, the ballad is raised and the concept of tragedy lowered.

Lillo's choice of the ballad (and, parenthetically, other plays of his, *The Country Burial, Fatal Curiosity,* and *Arden of Faversham,* were also based on ballads) committed him to retention of the protagonists—a merchant's apprentice and a prostitute. But these were traditionally and critically unfit to be the figures of a tragedy, which at this time dealt with affairs of state in the hands of kings, princes, and aristocrats. What Lillo did, therefore, was to portray the merchant as concerned with and peripherally involved with affairs of state. Addressing one of his apprentices, the merchant declares:

> you may learn how honest merchants, as such, may sometimes contribute to the safety of their country as they do at all times to its happiness; that if hereafter you should be tempted to any action that has the appearance of vice or meanness in it, upon reflecting on the dignity of our profession, you may with honest scorn reject whatever is unworthy of it.[3]

Although every critic who has written about *The London Merchant* has noted the merchant's morality and his increased importance in the tragedy, none have attended to the historical question of Lillo's use of the ballad. Only if we realize that Lillo considered the ballad narrative worthy of elevation can we understand why he sought to extend (and in extending to lower) the aim of tragedy. Lillo introduced protagonists from common life because he found their lives no less capable of tragedy than those of kings and princes. *The London Merchant* is, in its way, a tragedy about power that is rooted in corruption and criminality. Lillo's own explanation for his introduction of low protagonists was that such common people constituted most of the audience. These were, therefore, more likely to be more affected by what they themselves could experience than by what princes could. However inadequate this argument may be, Lillo used it to change the nature of the tragic effect. For him, the end of tragedy became "the exciting of the passions, in order to the correcting such of them as are criminal, either in their nature or through their excess" (*The London Merchant,* "Dedication," iii). The aim of tragedy was to stifle criminality, and thus tragedy became a justification of the legal basis of the state. The concern for legality and the observance of legality made a case for equality before the law for merchant and aristocrat and common man. Subtextually, this strategy indicted the irresponsible aristocrats who seduced women and brought inequality into the state.

Although I cannot in this paper set out in detail all the strategies of generic linkages, I do wish to mention the difference between strategies that merely vary a norm and those that overturn it, between strategies that operate within a concept and those that supersede it. Lillo claims merely to extend the received concept of Aristotelian tragedy. But I find that the changes he introduced conceptually changed the genre. His project linked tragedy to genres from which it had previously been separated; his change of protagonists included classes previously considered unfit for tragedy; his change of the effect of tragedy from the purgation of emotions through pity and terror to the exciting of passions in order to correct those that are criminal altered its social and literary aims. Tragedy became connected with stories about criminals and treatises of law. Ballads dealing with criminals and murder became the basis for high art. Nevertheless, tragedy retained some of the features of the genre such as limited time or a single action. As a result of retaining some of these received elements in combination with the new, the tragedy led to contradictions in its structure—to anachronistic behavior and a forced summary of behavior that falsified human action. "The Ballad of George Barnwel," which unfolds in weeks—perhaps even months—is rewritten so that the same action takes place within a matter of two days.

For a critic or historian to disregard the relation of the ballad to tragedy in interpreting *The London Merchant* is to ignore the complicated process of generic and historical change and the fact that the tragedy is an interpretation. In our time when it is customary to assume that interpretation is a genre called literary criticism or literary theory or some combination of these with history, we misconceive how, in the eighteenth century, comedies reinterpreted romances, tragedies reinterpreted ballads. We misconceive how one genre was rewritten in another, how one genre came to reinterpret another. The types of interrelation and their social and political consequences reveal the conflicts and intersections among the various genres. I have deliberately avoided discussing examples of interactions between verbal and nonverbal genres, the latter including painting, drawing, gardening. In preparing a history of literature I believe the need to understand the functions of verbal genres and their changes should precede any larger project.

It should, indeed, be apparent now that attempts to formulate norms for discussing literary history are useful only if they illustrate the kinds of changes within the genres of a given period or time span. Discussions of historical norms without recognition of the different rates of change and the varied interactions of genres can provide only inadequate explanations.

When the ballads were made part of formal literature in 1765, Thomas Percy published them with some ballads by contemporary writers. And the first ballad in the collection was the ballad of "Chevy Chase." Percy remarked that Addison in his "excellent critique" "is mistaken with regard to the antiquity of the common-received copy; for this, if one may judge from the style, cannot be older than the time of Elizabeth, and was probably written after the elogium of Sir Philip Sidney: perhaps in consequence of it. I flatter myself, I have here recovered the genuine antique poem; the true original song, which appeared rude even in the time of Sir Philip, and caused him to lament, that it was so evil-apparelled in the rugged garb of antiquity."[4]

One of the important issues here is the question of authenticity, a critical problem that had not previously been raised with regard to the ballads. To consider authenticity a critical problem there had to develop—and I have shown the nonevolutionary process involved—a respect for the past as different from the present, yet worthy of preservation.

Still, the concept of "authenticity" should not be interpreted in our terms. Percy sought to establish the ballads as a literary genre in order to illustrate the evolution of English poetry. He published contemporary poems with them to demonstrate the "highest beauties" that poetry had achieved in his time. Thus the ballads as legitimate genres were needed to demonstrate the value of the "modern." But because his audiences might be repelled by some of the language of the ballads, Percy's notion of authenticity permitted revisions to suit the needs of his audience: "His object was to please both the judicious antiquary, and the reader of taste; and he hath endeavoured to gratify both without offending either" (*Reliques*, "The Preface," 29).

Even as Percy gave the ballads literary legitimation, he placed them in combination with contemporary poetry to demonstrate their failure to reach the highest poetical beauties. Their revision for moral or social reasons still seemed a desirable procedure to him and to contemporary critics. But by returning them to the Middle Ages, Percy at least restored to the earlier period an awareness of generic possibilities.

I have sought in this paper to provide an example of a generic literary history. I have suggested that for me genres are combinatory, that we must distinguish between genre as the term for a class and as the term for an individual text. A text can belong to one or more genres; the decision is made by the critic historian. Histories are human constructs and historians choose the texts that compose them. Such choices always have aims and these are social, political, economic, and literary. I have tried to explain why historians need a genre theory if they choose to explain continuity and change in literary texts. The justification of one's choice should be part of any historical explanation. I have defended mine on the grounds of the concern for change in a time such as ours.

I have argued that we must conceive of genre as a class in which examples lead us to change our construct. Constructs without examples are empty, with examples are limited. As a construct or generalization becomes more extended, it becomes more and more likely to be inapplicable. Constructs are limited systems held tentatively, and we alter them because they cease to be useful as explanatory tools. In this respect, theoretical claims are often less effective than the interpretative or explanatory function that is implied in poems, tragedies, and novels. Addison served as a case in point. The elevation of ballads was more effectively demonstrated by noncritical writing than by his critical tenets. It was the use of literary genres that demonstrated the literary possibilities of the ballads. This was done by new generic strategies and by introducing new generic linkages in a traditional genre like tragedy. If what I have shown is persuasive, then this generic history is a new literary history.

NOTES

1. René Wellek, "Literary Theory, Criticism, and History," in *Theory of Literature*, by René Wellek and Austin Warren (New York: Harcourt Brace Jovanovich, 1949), 39.

2. Joseph Addison, *Spectator* 70; papers hereafter cited in text.

3. George Lillo, *The London Merchant: or, The History of George Barnwell* (London, 1731), I.i.16-22; hereafter cited in text.

4. Thomas Percy, "The Ancient Ballad of Chevy-Chase," *Reliques of Ancient English Poetry,* Series the First (Edinburgh: James Nichol, 1858), 1:1; hereafter cited in text.

The Generation of Conceptual Changes in Literary Study

Since a centennial is an opportunity to look backward and forward, I have chosen a subject that I feel is appropriate to the occasion: the generation of conceptual changes in literary study. The kind of changes I refer to are what Foucault called epistemic changes, what Meyer Abrams has characterized as a change from a pragmatic to an organic orientation, what the anthropologist Clifford Geertz calls "an alteration of the principles of mapping. Something is happening to the way we think about the way we think."[1] The conceptual change I refer to is what Brian McHale and other postmodern critics claim is a change from modernist epistemology to postmodern ontology. In referring to a "conceptual change," to a way of thinking, I do not confine myself to literary study. Unless one assumes that thinking in literature is different in kind from other kinds of verbal thinking (and I do not), conceptual change must refer to all genres.

Procedures to initiate change involved the production of varied, often opposing, theoretical discourses from different disciplines. These indicated how, in different countries, these discourses offered options for the rethinking of formal interpretations by indicating what these could become incidental to discussions, for example, of the reception of interpretations, discussions of the nature of reading, discussions of the relation of literary signs to other sign systems. Not only did the journal [*New Literary History*] introduce multiple discourses about theory and about the relation of literary study to other disciplines and their impact on literary studies, it conducted sessions at the MLA on these subjects. I cannot claim that *New Literary History* was the sole reason for a shift in critical consciousness, but when it was founded there was no *Critical Inquiry,* no *Diacritics,* no *Clio,* no *Cultural Critique* or *Social Text.* And

---

This essay is published for the first time. It was delivered January 1988 to an academic symposium at the University of Minnesota, in recognition of the university's centennial celebration.

when *Critical Inquiry* was to be founded Sheldon Sacks wrote to say that he was modeling his journal upon some of the features of *New Literary History*. One more statistic is needed to indicate that a conceptual change has taken place, with critical theory taking a prominent place in the academic curriculum. When the journal was founded there were no courses in literary theory in any major university in this country. Now there is no major university without them.

But the basis of the conceptual change or the change in consciousness of theory in history of art, history, and literature cannot be adequately explained in these one-sided terms. There had to be a dissatisfaction with the conventional study—and this was widespread, as indicated by student resistance and unrest. There needed to be an audience prepared to purchase the journal, for it had three years to demonstrate that it fulfilled a need. The University [of Virginia] was not prepared to finance a journal that brought neither profit nor recognition. Moreover, there were in France, Germany, Italy, and the Soviet Union those who had developed programs in theory that were largely unknown in the United States. The journal, therefore, sought to overcome the resistance to theory by presenting the findings of international scholars. No conceptual change takes place without continuing resistance so that a description of conceptual change has to acknowledge retention of older procedures—interpretative and historical—by scholars who argue for their value.

I want to turn now to particular texts in order to argue that the term "conceptual change," no less than the term "paradigm change," refers to multiple discourses. I have said that *New Literary History* presented multiple discourses though they all were theoretical. But it is apparent that such discourses were not necessarily harmonious or complementary. Not only are there various and even contrasting feminist discourses, but many of these are incompatible with Marxist discourses. What takes place within a conceptual change, therefore, is the democratization of differences among phenomenological, psychoanalytic, Marxist, feminist critics, a sanctioning of pluralism or perspectivism. On the one hand, John Drakakis, a Marxist, argues that "methodologies which naively favour plural 'approaches' or a multiplicity of 'readings' generated from within the essentialist individual critical consciousness" are examples of "unbridled subjectivity" and "are wholly inadequate as responses to the challenges now proposed by theoretically informed modes of criticism."[2] On the other hand, Alasdair MacIntyre suggests that there are at least three *continuing* and *enduring* traditions confirming perspectives or partiality.

THE GENERATION OF CONCEPTUAL CHANGES IN LITERARY STUDY

One is that we have to overcome partiality in all cases; the second is that we cannot now overcome partiality in all cases; and the third is that partiality can never be overcome.

Once a conceptual change is effected, the various discourses that supported it become divided about the nature of this variety. But one is compelled, in accounting for conceptual change, to do more than point out that agreement on the *notion* of theory is not agreement on *particular kinds of theory*. What becomes pertinent then is to consider which features of theoretical discourse provide the basis for conceptual change. I have drawn attention to the presentation of various theoretical models. Clifford Geertz provides two further grounds for assuming such a change: generic blurring and the incorporation into theory of a new or borrowed vocabulary. Geertz notes that there has been an enormous amount of genre mixing in social science, as in intellectual life generally, and this blurring of kinds is continuing. There are, he writes,

> scientific discussions looking like belles lettres *morceaux* (Lewis Thomas, Loren Eiseley), baroque fantasies presented as deadpan empirical observations (Borges, Barthelme), histories that consist of equations and tables or law court testimony (Fogel and Engerman, Le Roi Ladurie), documentaries that read like true confessions (Mailer), parables posing as ethnographies (Castaneda), theoretical treatises set out as travelogues (Levi-Strauss), . . . methodological polemics got up as personal memoirs (James Watson). Nabokov's *Pale Fire,* that impossible object made of poetry and fiction, footnotes and images from the clinic, seems very much of the time; one waits only for quantum theory in verse or biography in algebra. (20)

The second point that Geertz makes is that "analogies drawn from the humanities are coming to play the kind of role in sociological understanding that analogies drawn from the crafts and technology have long played in physical understanding" (19). The analogies he refers to are game, drama, and text. Geertz is writing about social thought and its refiguration. He believes that the conceptual change he is noting is "in our notion not so much of what knowledge is but of what it is we want to know" (34). The blurring of genres and the introduction of humanistic analogies into social thought thus alter the way social scientists think about their discipline and it is this change which merits "reconceptualization" or, in Geertz's terms, "refiguration."

I want to contrast Geertz's example with a claim for conceptual change I consider unfounded. Critics have recently developed a body of criticism that has been named the New Historicism. The eminent critic Stephen Greenblatt, who is the chief figure in this group, has asked for a *poetics of culture*. Greenblatt is against an essentialistic literary history and any self-regarding closed system. His history mixes literary with nonliterary discourses because these properly represent the mixed nature of human discourse. Greenblatt rejects the view that history is a unified narrative because our lives indicate its disjointedness and its occasional randomness. Thus an adherence to coherence falsifies the world we know. And these views are borrowed from anthropologists like Clifford Geertz and Victor Turner. Greenblatt writes that he has attempted to practice "a more cultural or anthropological criticism."[3] What he borrowed is the conviction that men are born "unfinished animals," that the facts of life are less artless than they look, that "particular cultures and the observers of these cultures are inevitably drawn to a metaphoric grasp of reality, that anthropological interpretation must address itself less to the mechanics of customs and institutions than to the interpretive constructions the members of a society apply to their experiences" (4).

It is these very practices that Geertz declares he has taken from the humanities: the need for anthropologists to consider behavior in terms of metaphor (Ricoeur); to consider the interpreter as involved in constructing the interpretation (Fish); to see the act of reading as offering a finishing or completion of the text by the reader (Iser). I say that Greenblatt offers no new concept of knowledge because he borrows from anthropology what the anthropologists have borrowed from literary study. But perhaps these remarks are unfair to him, since all he claims to do is to practice a *more* cultural or anthropological criticism than his predecessors.

But if Greenblatt is merely extending a received concept, we must note that Geertz's borrowing from the humanities means that he is extending the conceptual change established in literary study and history to social science. We thus have evidence of the extension of a conceptual change to still another discipline, a confirmation of its power, however much its specific examples may differ from those in literary study. For differ they do, since Geertz's notion of blurred genres is based on an outmoded notion of the purity of genres. Mixtures have been characteristic of genres, and Renaissance critics sought to defend both generic purity and generic mixture. But Geertz is surely right about the significance of particular mixtures as an indicator of change.

When he describes James Watson's *The Double Helix* as an example of "methodological polemics got up as personal memoirs," he does not pursue the relation of a scientific history to autobiography. But the book offers a resistance to and a personal attack upon the fictions of scientific method and on the idealized model of scientific teamwork. By joining a personal memoir to the history of the search for the genetic chain—joining, therefore, an autobiographical to a so-called scientific genre—is deliberately to use one discourse to undermine another. This genre of scientific history parodies the professional procedure of omitting the actual behavior of men and women in the scientific community. In this respect the mixed genre offered Geertz an opportunity to provide still another characteristic signal of change, namely parody. For parody undermines earlier textual practices and in doing so implies a return to personal honesty. Indeed parody in *Pale Fire*, to which Geertz referred, marks a rejection of New Critical and scholarly apparatus while exhibiting what a multidimensional text is.

We can see that these combinatory genres that are hinted at here by Geertz or by MacIntyre represent a concept in search of an adequate explanatory model. If we pursue the intrusion of the autobiographical element in the conceptual model of a feminist who is also a literary theorist, we can, I believe, begin to see some possible new directions in discourse. I refer to Annette Kolodny's essay "Dancing through the Minefield: Some Observations on the Theory, Practice, and Politics of a Feminist Literary Criticism."[4] The author autobiographically describes her indoctrination by male scholars. This move supports her theoretical argument for an adequate feminist criticism. And her mixed discourse demonstrates the partiality of so-called impartial objective criticism. Its combinatory procedure removes from theory the authority it possesses for readers and surrounds it with political implications that render it subservient. Overtly the essay welcomes a pluralist view of theory, but actually it presents a theory that ignores or conceals the personal element.

I have been describing some of the shifts that have taken place in writings governed by the assumption of contemporary conceptual change. I want now to inquire into how changes in language itself take place. Critics often refer to the training of Derrida, to the Husserl-Heideggerian tradition out of which he came. But I do not find in that history an explanation of his metaphoric choice and his concept of decentering. It should come as no surprise that many of the major figures who urge the need for a conceptual change in texts are Europeans. Derrida is an Algerian Jew, a member of a former French colony, a marginalized figure from a colonized country. It seems to me no historical accident that Derrida's geographical image of boundary crossing should assert the democratization of what previously in criticism was considered dependent and subordinate. The arguments for decentering texts and for attending to the repressive aspects of language in texts seem, at least potentially, to stem from a colonial environment. And I believe the argument for the indeterminacy of the text rests on rejection of the localization and stabilization of place, a rejection of any one place as the origin and center of one's commitment. That critics like Hillis Miller who have not undergone this experience share Derrida's views in no way denies the validity of this hypothesis; it merely indicates that some other historical contexts were at work in his case.

I speak with considerable reservation in aligning theoretical concepts with personal experience. But such speculation is not foreign to Derrida's own way of thinking and it would help explain why the notion of release in play and signification is important in his reconceptualization of philosophy. It may be said that at times Roland Barthes argued for decentering, multiple discourses, the play of signifiers, without possessing Derrida's personal experience. But Barthes was neither systematic nor burdened by marginality.

The appeal to personal experience in providing an explanation of the devices of conceptual change is far trickier in the work of Paul de Man, a Belgian who came to our country after the Second World War. The characteristic of autobiographical exposure that is an element of the assumed conceptual change that I have been tracking is called into question by the changes de Man underwent: from a New Critical advocate to a deconstructionist. One notes the certainty with which he located the key to poems as a New Critic and then the certainty with which he argued for the loss of such keys as a result of the self-contradictoriness of language. And now we are informed of a prior change. For there has been uncovered a large body of his writing at age twenty-two that is said to be anti-Semitic (writings I must say that have not as yet been published). It is thus possible to recognize among scholars who support the principle of conceptual change a disagreement about "exposure," for what is exposed may turn out to be concealment, the assertion of a concept that represses as much as it expresses. It may indeed be that for de Man self-contradiction was not a skeptical view of authority, as it is for Derrida, but a justification for holding any kind of opinion, since all texts were equally unreliable.

In this respect it is pertinent to note how the conceptual change from a pragmatic to a historical conception led to concealment. In arguing for the recovery of a historical context, eighteenth-century critics introduced the principle of "authenticity." An adequate historical interpretation required complete trust in the time identification of a past text, for otherwise works would be mistakenly identified and mislead the critic to impose wrong historical contexts. It was for this reason that the Ossianic poems became a threat to historical accuracy. For these poems were not the work of Ossian but of James Macpherson, who created a world of the past that might be taken as genuine. Thus the so-called documentary evidence can be compared to the mistaken conception of blurred genres. Geertz and Macpherson were both wrong about their evidence but right about the possibilities their writings offered. Genre could indeed be the example of a concept of writing and thinking. The Ossianic poems did indeed demonstrate that a historical consciousness involved the imaginative creation of history.

The most obvious but often least reliable basis for conceptual change is the direct argument against a present model. One example is the argument by Edward Said, who as spokesman for the Palestinians developed a literary theory based on the awareness of the power wielded by states over the production of texts and the way these and their readers are controlled by authority: "The realities of power and authority—as well as the resistances offered by men, women, and social movements to institutions, authorities, and orthodoxies—are the realities that make texts possible, that deliver them to their readers, that solicit the attention of critics. I propose that these realities are what should be taken account of by criticism and the critical consciousness."[5] For Said, culture is national culture and seeks to make citizens in love with and willing to support the values of those who rule the state. But there arise difficulties in such a culture when some of its members resist the love of place or the readiness to support its values. At this time pressures develop "to produce new and different ways of conceiving human relationships" (17). These lead to new relationships, new systems that form a kind of "compensatory order ... whether it is a part, an institution, a culture, a set of beliefs, or even a world-vision" (19). Such new groups convert the earlier forms of authority *into what appear as* "transpersonal forms," and "can easily become a system of thought no less orthodox and dominant than culture itself" (20). Criticism, therefore, "is always situated; it is skeptical, secular, reflectively open to its own failings" (26). But it is predominantly oppositional, suspicious of totalizing concepts, discontented with reified objects, impatient with guilds, special interests, imperialized fiefdoms, and orthodox habits of mind.

Said's theory of power presents us with some of the most perplexing problems in rejecting one critical theory and replacing it with another. The critic is not to replace a theory but to resist and expose all theories that impose authority upon texts. But Said believes that a critic can be oppositional without being partisan. It is a utopian view because the opposite of "political" is to be situated but committed only to opposition. What is missing in Said's statement is what Benjamin recognizes: that "there is no document of civilization which is not at the same time a document of barbarism."[6] What Said does not see and what has, indeed, confounded his and other studies of conceptual change is that texts are not single documents but palimpsests, documents of multiple discourses and of multiple time frames. To proceed with this hypothesis requires a theory of genre that makes no effort to essentialize texts. But it does imply some similarities with genre members of the recent past and shares with them one or more constituents. Such a theory is implicit in the references to combinations and to traditions or continuities, and this theory I shall mention below. For genre members do have some continuity.

If we argue that *theory* has replaced interpretation, then we are misled. Neither "theory" nor "interpretation" are texts: as genres they are interpretive or theoretical essays and as an essay genre they make it possible for critics to discuss what has changed and what has remained the same. For Said, the "critical consciousness is directly reflected not only in the subjects of these essays but in the essay form itself" (26). And he explains that "the essay—a comparatively short, investigative, radically skeptical form—is the principal way in which to write criticism" (26). But such a definition shows no interest in the way critical essays are written or have been written. If it "situates" Said, it does so by making his essay linear, successive, short like other academic essays, and distinctive—if distinctive by its subject matter. One need only compare his definition to that of Roland Barthes, who remarks that the essay uniquely offers the possibility of a "plural" text made up of multiple networks that "interact, without any one of them being able to surpass the rest; . . . it has no beginning; it is reversible; we gain access to it by several entrances, none of which can be authoritatively declared to be the main one."[7] Said's radically skeptical form must presuppose a dominant skeptical discourse that replaces, or is replaced by, Barthes's view of the genre.

Early in this paper I stated that I wished to study what conceptual change involves. I explained this change using definitions from different disciplines. From these I offered the hypothesis that such change referred to the way we organize our knowledge or think about the way we think. I then claimed that such change always implied relations among disciplines, not reference to one. But within any one discipline clues of such change were to be found in the altered usage of words, in the extensions of vocabulary, in the borrowed imagery to describe values previously expressed in a different language, in changes within generic mixtures, in parodies of genres that are being displaced, or in the creation of new genres. Any study of conceptual change entails recognition that earlier genres and discourses do not completely disappear.

My second task involved giving reasons for introducing claims of a change. These reasons I found to be least reliable when overtly directed at the reader. They were more reliable when one could provide the grounds for the changes of metaphors, the presentation of new genre combinations that served as ostensive definitions, the specific examination of cases that took account of the continuities and discontinuities. For example, is the change from modernism to postmodernism merely a variation of the first or a replacement of it? Defenders of modernism point to literary continuities, to elements or features of the works of Pound and Eliot. Defenders of postmodernism point to the changes in painting and architecture as well as in fiction. The simple truth is that the evidence is still insufficient to make a judgment.

But in turning to the procedures to convince readers, it is necessary to call upon theoretical expositions that can help us answer this question. The first is a generic theory which implies that all texts are members of more than one genre. This theory also provides a relation among contemporary genres as well as a temporal sequence to which one can refer. Moreover, genres can be defined by constituents that can connect and disconnect. Genre theory is only now coming to be seen as possessing an ideal possibility for recording historical change. Even in Hans Robert Jauss's aesthetics of reception, a work that tended to ignore conceptual change because of its concern with continuing horizon change, Jauss found it necessary to write an essay on the special nature of medieval genres.

I thus conclude my study of conceptual change by referring to this centennial occasion. This symposium is a genre in which mixed discourses offer presentations of contemporary humanistic knowledge. I thank you for permitting me to be a member of this genre.

NOTES

1. Clifford Geertz, "Blurred Genres: The Refiguration of Social Thought," in *Local Knowledge: Further Essays in Interpretive Anthropology* (New York: Basic Books, 1983), 20; hereafter cited in text.

2. John Drakakis, ed., *Alternative Shakespeares* (New York: Routledge, 1985), 25; "unbridled subjectivity" comes from Perry Anderson, *In the Tracks of Historical Materialism* (London: Verso, 1983), 54.

3. Stephen J. Greenblatt, *Renaissance Self-Fashioning: From More to Shakespeare* (Chicago: Univ. of Chicago Press, 1980), 4; hereafter cited in text.

4. Annette Kolodny, "Dancing through the Minefield: Some Observations on the Theory, Practice, and Politics of a Feminist Literary Criticism," *Feminist Studies* 6, no. 1 (1980): 1-25.

5. Edward Said, "Introduction: Secular Criticism," in *The World, the Text, and the Critic* (Cambridge, MA: Harvard Univ. Press, 1983), 5; hereafter cited in text.

6. Walter Benjamin, "Theses on the Philosophy of History," in *Illuminations: Essays and Reflections,* ed. Hannah Arendt (New York: Harcourt, Brace & World, 1968).

7. Roland Barthes, *S/Z: An Essay,* trans. Richard Howard (New York: Hill and Wang, 1974), 5.

Interpreting Interpretations

In *Poetry and Repression* Harold Bloom remarks that every strong poem, at least since Petrarch, has known implicitly what Nietzsche has taught us explicitly: that there is only interpretation, and that every interpretation answers an earlier interpretation, and then must yield to a later one. But this statement is undercut by another made at the outset:

> Strong poets present themselves as looking for truth *in the world,* searching in reality and in tradition, but such a stance, as Nietzsche said, remains under the mastery of desire, of instinctual drives. So, in effect, the strong poet wants pleasure and not truth; he wants what Nietzsche named as "the belief in truth and the pleasurable effects of the belief." No strong poet can admit that Nietzsche was accurate in this insight, and no critic need fear that any strong poet will accept and so be hurt by demystification.[1]

This desire for pleasure based on the belief in a strong poet's truth of what he has written points to the moral basis of interpretation. Each strong poet and critic is driven by the truth of his belief but his belief in truth is the belief in his own truth. If, indeed, there is only interpretation, belief surely governs it. Where does this truth come from? For Bloom it comes from the sources of his religion. For other critics, from other sources. But what does he mean by a "poem"? Are "poems" epics or lyrics, satires or parodies? Are they critical theories or histories? The two quoted statements indicate the interpretive strategies of our time. One strategy argues that all texts are interpretive and the other argues that the world is a text. These propositions convert all explanations into interpretations and thus provide a totalizing hypothesis about language and interpretation. Every text is interpretive and interpretable, but not necessarily coherent.

Bloom is concerned with the diverse strategies of interpretation—what

---

This essay is published for the first time. It was delivered June 1988 to a conference on interpretation at the Hebrew University, Jerusalem.

he calls revisionary ratios—and the differences in interpretation which result from particular rhetorical strategies. For him, every text is an interpretation of some other text. Bloom is not interested in discussing what can be called "weak" texts. These are excluded because their interpretations do not involve what strong texts do: "A poetic 'text,'" he writes, "is a psychic battlefield upon which authentic forces struggle for the only victory worth winning, the divinating triumph over oblivion" (2). A strong poem is for him a kind of usurpation, it displaces another poem from the canon. Poetic strength "involves a self-representation that is reached only through trespass, through crossing a daemonic threshold" (7).

In this context, interpretation is a deliberate misprision, that is, a deliberate resistance to and attempt to replace another poem. It is not an attempt to restate, to translate, or to remain open to another poem. Interpretation operates by power, by usurpation, by deliberate selection and repression. The poet, Bloom writes, "strives for a selection, through repression, out of the traces of the language of poetry: that is, he represses some of the traces, and remembers others. This remembering is a misprision, or creative misreading, but no matter how strong a misprision, it cannot achieve an autonomy of meaning, or a meaning *fully* present, that is, free from all literary context" (4).

Bloom's conception of interpretation as distortion or misreading is obvious enough. One need only consider the role of translator or interpreter as translator to realize that translation always involves distortion as one language system is transposed into another. In examples where translation is involved as an agreement written in two languages, it seems possible for agreements to be concluded and signed despite the inevitable distortion. And this is possible because such agreements are conceived as promises or include verification procedures that involve observation and examination.

But translation in literary texts, confined as they are to language, inevitably involves distortion or misreading. Not that there is a proper reading; for Bloom, "misreading" is used to characterize the phenomenon of language as polysemic and, therefore, always possessed of possibilities that are in excess of any selection. What a strong poet or critic does is create a new moment in the history of poetry and criticism, and such moments are recognized and grasped by normal or average or weak readers and writers who merely replicate in lesser ways the major texts.

Bloom is not interested in weak or uncombative poets or critics; and he is not interested in them because their misprisions do not present themselves as looking for "truth in the world." In giving an example of the "High Romantic

British and American poets," he names Blake, Wordsworth, Shelley, Keats, Tennyson, Browning, Yeats, Emerson, Whitman, and Stevens. I am not interested in quarreling with Bloom about "strong" poets and critics—though the names of Coleridge and Byron are puzzlingly omitted from the list. Rather, I wish to pursue the premise of language as "interpretation." I have given the example of translation in which distortion is inevitable because we have two different language systems in operation. But the use of one's own language system is equally untrustworthy; that is, any use of language is composed of prior uses. The mark of a strong poet is deliberately to alter such uses and thus to mark them by his desire for power or pleasure. Such desires are of the greatest value for readers and writers because they open for them possibilities that have been repressed.

Strong poetry and criticisms, therefore, are generated for Bloom by the poet's or critic's belief in the truth of his insight. And it is this notion of belief that triggers interpretation. Belief is an intuition, a sense that underlies self-representation. What this belief is, is a resistance to an earlier presentation of language and what it means. And this belief has its source in a primal sense of oedipal conflict.

If we return to the initial assumption that all language is interpretation, then we can see that it necessarily follows that "interpretation" is a term that includes numerous diverse and even contradictory procedures. This is obvious in the disagreement between Paul de Man and Meyer Abrams on the nature of language and its interpretation. Abrams argues that language is a human construct and that human beings can use it well or ill, but the determination of proper or improper use is not problematic. De Man, on the other hand, argues that although human beings do have intentional meaning-functions, there is no a priori certainty that the mode of meaning, "the way in which I mean, is intentional in any way."[2] Abrams suggests that he and de Man offer two different perspectives on language and interpretation. But it seems very difficult to conceive of such disagreements as "perspectives," since one directly contradicts the other. If language is a human construct, it is to be understood by human use; but if it is a human construct that operates in opposition to whatever use is made of it—this poses an irreconcilable contradiction.

This disagreement is irreconcilable because Abrams believes language use demonstrates its understandability, and when this alters, it is possible to chart the alterations. But de Man's position is that whether people use language well or ill is irrelevant, since the deconstruction of language reveals its inner contradiction, a belief which makes de Man's own explanation equally inadequate—and he grants this. It is necessary for de Man to deny the appeal to use, since any use falls into the category of self-contradiction. And Abrams's exposition with his optimistic view of language control and alteration rests on empirical evidence that, in view of the normal difficulty of human communication, makes such evidence less than persuasive. It is often argued that people normally understand one another, but this seems to be the case only if they have prior agreement about the processes of language understanding. Otherwise agreements turn out to be apparent rather than actual.

When such dilemmas arise, it seems proper to refer to what Bloom and de Man and Alasdair MacIntyre offer as a necessary practice: the need to expose as clearly as possible the position one espouses. But in doing so, can such interpretations do anything more than add further mystifications? What is the relation of the reader to the text in these interpretive disagreements? Any interpretation is a selection from a text, and any presentation of this selection is, when read, subject to another selection. In Paul de Man's word—using translation as interpretation—a similar dilemma is offered: The text about translation is itself a translation, and "the untranslatability which it mentions about itself inhabits its own texture and will inhabit anybody who in his turn will try to translate it, as I am now trying, and failing, to do. The text is untranslatable: it was untranslatable for the translators who tried to do it, it is untranslatable for the commentators who talk about it, it is an example of what it states, it is a *mise en abyme* in the technical sense, a story within the story of what is its own statement" (86).

I want now to examine the validity of those comments on interpretation by providing a test case which includes *mise en abyme*, and thus seems especially suited to these arguments. Of course, my test case is, in de Man's terms, another example of a failing interpretation, but perhaps something more is at issue. At any rate we need not foreclose the possibility that language as interpretation may prove an inadequate hypothesis.

The example I wish to study is the play within a play in *Hamlet*, the presentation of *The Murder of Gonzago.* You will recall that the ghost of Hamlet's father appears and tells Hamlet of his vile murder by his brother Claudius. The story is a Cain and Abel allegory in which one brother murders the other in order to seize his inheritance; Claudius through murder, seizes his brother's throne, wealth, and wife. But Claudius is not identified as a murderer, although Hamlet considers his uncle and mother guilty of incest. The interpretive option that this implies is taken for granted by Hamlet. The ghost, however, presents Hamlet with an interpretive problem: to discover, in the behavior of the king, the confirmation of his guilt.

Although Hamlet takes the ghost to be an honest spirit, he decides to put on an "antic disposition" in order to ascertain the truth of the spiritual message. It is during these scenes that Rosencrantz informs Hamlet that the city players are on tour and that they are headed for the castle. It is this accidental event that sparks the idea of a manipulated stage production.

This accident, then, provides the occasion for the generation of a text that provides an interpretation which can confirm Claudius's guilt. And this confirmation will be based on Claudius's response to the play. Hamlet asks Horatio to observe carefully the response of Claudius to a scene imitating the circumstances of the murder of his father:

> There is a play tonight before the King.
> One scene of it comes near the circumstance
> Which I have told thee of my father's death.
> I prithee, when thou seest that act afoot,
> Even with the very comment of thy soul
> Observe my uncle. If his occulted guilt
> Do not itself unkennel in one speech,
> It is a damned ghost that we have seen,
> And my imaginations are as foul
> As Vulcan's stithy. Give him heedful note;
> For I mine eyes will rivet to his face;
> And, after, we will both our judgements join
> To censure of his seeming. (3.2.75-87)

Now we have here the interpretive issue of the reader's response, not a generalization about the responses of the audience, but that of a specific member of the audience. Why does Hamlet trust to what today we would consider an uncertain response to interpretation? The answer is that Hamlet's assumption of a particular reaction rests on the conventional claim that guilty observers react in self-accusing ways to scenes that replicate their crimes. Hamlet's expectation about such responses is that they lead, in his prepared addition to the text, to self-accusation or confession. The grounds of these expectations are hypotheses that Hamlet treats as absolute. There are for him only two possible responses. Either Claudius will interpret the play as a mirror image of his actions and thus confirm his guilt or he will interpret the ghost's comments as the discourse of some fictive character.

> I have heard
> That guilty creatures sitting at a play
> Have by the very cunning of the scene
> Been struck so to the soul that presently
> They have proclaimed their malefactions;
> For murder, though it have no tongue, will speak
> With most miraculous organ. I'll have these players
> Play something like the murder of my father
> Before mine uncle. I'll observe his looks,
> I'll tent him to the quick. If he but blench,
> I know my course. The spirit that I have seen
> May be the devil, and the devil hath power
> T' assume a pleasing shape; yea, and perhaps
> Out of my weakness and my melancholy,
> As he is very potent with such spirits,
> Abuses me to damn me. I'll have grounds
> More relative than this. The play's the thing
> Wherein I'll catch the conscience of the King. (2.2.584-601)

Hamlet believes in the convention of criminal response and thus in Claudius's response as indication of guilt or innocence. Interpretation here is marked by closure, and the king's response reinforces the convention. But the play is preceded by a dumb show in which the action of the play is mimed. This mime, however, does not elicit any response from the king and Ophelia asks Hamlet, "What means this, my lord?" So, too, it is only to the verbal performance that the king reacts. When the player king's nephew pours poison in the king's ear Hamlet explains: "He poisons him i' th' garden for his estate. His name's Gonzago. The story is extant, and writ in choice Italian. You shall see anon how the murderer gets the love of Gonzago's wife" (3.2.255-58).

It is at this point that the king rises and cries, "Give me some light. Away!" The unfinishing of the play, the cry for light to hide the dark revelation indicates that Claudius's confirming response does not require a viewing of the whole play. Interpretation operates as mirror reflection when a particular scene replicates the crime. But the original event must have been done without words, since the king was murdered in his sleep; thus the dumb show was a more accurate replication of the original event than the verbal exhortation of Lucianus, the murderer, to the poisonous mixture: "Thy natural magic and dire property / On wholesome life usurp immediately" (3.2.252-53).

The language of usurpation is addressed to the drug, just as Hamlet's remarks to Claudius are about the forthcoming events in the play—how the murderer gets the love of Gonzago's wife. The king's response is to the words that promise an action analogous to his own deed. This act of interpretation that confirms belief does not do as much for Gertrude or Ophelia, Polonius, or Rosencrantz and Guildenstern. The king is not the sole audience of the play, and his interpretation in no way leads the others to interpret the play as an allegory of his behavior. Hamlet's and Horatio's interpretation of this behavior is at odds with that of the others. What prevents them from sharing Hamlet's interpretation? On the surface it appears a matter of sharing information. Hamlet is prohibited from sharing his information, but if he did, would other observers see in Claudius's interpretation of the play a demonstration of his guilt? Would they, not being relations and not hearing the ghost, belong to Hamlet's interpretive community? There is, of course, no answer to this question, but it does raise the problem of the kind of knowledge necessary to interpret responses to a tragedy.

The narrow example of criminal knowledge of Claudius leaves no room—so far as Hamlet is concerned—to have Claudius stonewall his response to the play or indicate his boredom with it or interpret it as an unlikely situation not worth pursuing. Interpretation here is historically and conventionally fixed. Questions of closure or openness seem inappropriate in Hamlet's use of interpretation. But in interpreting the play as a whole, the notion of openness of interpretation seems obvious. If we assume that interpretation is selective, then we can suggest that one meaning might be the unresolvable situation of Hamlet: his private obligation to revenge his father is countered by his public obligation as prince not to commit crimes for personal ends.

My purpose in drawing attention to the two very different meanings of "interpretation" is to point to interpretation as a *process* which functions in diverse ways within a single text. It reveals multiple meanings in the same way that "wit" reveals multiple meanings in Pope's *Essay on Criticism*. Not only is interpretation multivalent, but it is so because it rests on beliefs that differ. The model of the play within a play very carefully limits the range of interpretation, but the interpretation of the play as a whole can locate *The Murder of Gonzago* as an example of antithetical structure. For the interpretation of further events are not controlled by narrowly defined conventions. In fact, these events acknowledge the contingency of human experience.

Now my statements about the inset play and about the play as a whole place me within the realm of interpreters and my version is thus another interpretation, supporting the claim that interpretations are based on, complement, or resist, or ramify, or refine other interpretations. In claiming that belief is a *structuring principle* in interpretations, and thus demonstrating the hermeneutic circle, I in no way undermine the argument of texts as interpretation. In identifying interpretation as a term that implies a diversity of meanings and functions even within the same text, I merely correct the assumption that strong poets seek to overthrow the poems of earlier poets by indicating the contrary practices of interpretation within a single text of a strong poet. And I mean to resist the assumption that interpretation is necessarily self-contradictory by illustrating that contradictions need not lead to aporia.

In order to do this, I wish to pursue the consequence of interpretation in *The Murder of Gonzago*. What effect does the confirmation of an interpretive hypothesis have? Once Claudius is revealed as a murderer or once the play of *Hamlet* is persuasively argued as an inescapable conflict between private obligation and public responsibility, what follows? Hamlet proceeds without caution or convention in the thoughtless killing of Polonius. The behavior that guides the inset play is in marked contrast to the unplanned actions that follow it. In this example, the powers by which interpretation is controlled do not provide, as a consequence, an understanding of future behavior. The purpose of interpretation in this example seems locked within itself. When Paul de Man argues that interpretation permits us to understand how language is used, he refers to only one function of interpretation, and he sees interpretation as responsive to the nature of language. But insofar as there are several interpretations within a single text, the responder must analyze not only the nature of language but also the nature of the interconnection of discourses.

His view of interpretation, however, alienates language from the social, religious, and political context out of which it grows. I have indicated that the reliance on belief in interpreting the text, indeed in accepting a text to interpret, is fundamental to interpretation.

Questioner: I am not persuaded by your example. What do you take Hamlet's "belief" to be?

Answer: Hamlet's belief is that a particular convention exists about the behavior of a criminal in watching a play that replicates his crime. He believes certain responses—blanching, rising, or speaking—will confirm that Claudius is a murderer. He holds these truths to be self-evident so that if Claudius behaves otherwise he will assume him innocent and the ghost to be a devil "in a pleasing shape."

Questioner: If what you say is true, then Claudius should have reacted to the dumb show, but he did not. Doesn't this mean that Claudius may have killed the king some other way? After all, it is the player king's nephew not his brother who is the poisoner in the play.

Answer: You are, of course, right about the dumb show, and I believe, too, that we do not know which passage Hamlet added. But this much seems implied: when Hamlet tells the king that the poisoning occurs in the garden in order to seize his uncle's estate and that the poisoner gets the love of Gonzago's wife, the king suddenly reacts. I assume that the nephew (Hamlet) telling his uncle (Claudius) of what is happening and what will happen triggers the response.

Questioner: These assumptions seem to me not very strong confirmation of Hamlet's plan. And they do not explain the relation of the dumb show to the reaction.

Answer: The relation of the dumb show to the speaking play is puzzling and I don't wish to minimize the puzzle. But the dumb show stops with the poisoning and thus is not a necessary narrative of the king's behavior, since the occurrence is not in the garden and the marriage with the widow is not shown. Hamlet's goading of his uncle, however, sets off Claudius's reaction. Is it not reasonable to assume that the words make the difference? Is it not the sudden realization that his nephew might know of his deed that causes Claudius to react? Doesn't the play make a point about "words, words, words"?

Questioner: How do you know that Claudius has interpreted the play in this manner?

Answer: Well, Hamlet states that he will observe Claudius's looks and that nonverbal signs will indicate their interpretation of it. Remember that Hamlet says:

> I have heard
> That guilty creatures sitting at a play
> Have by the very cunning of the scene
> Been struck so to the soul that presently
> They have proclaimed their malefactions;
> For murder, though it have no tongue, will speak
> With most miraculous organ.

I take this last clause—"For murder, though it have no tongue, will speak / With most miraculous organ"—to mean that the murderer will react in such a way as to indicate his guilt—and that his guilt can be read by those who suspect him and that, further, "presently / They have proclaimed their malefactions." And, indeed, in the prayer scene, Claudius is discovered by us (the audience watching the play *Hamlet*) proclaiming his malefactions. Thus we know that Hamlet's assumptions that the king is guilty are correct, even though Hamlet may or may not have him confess his guilt (depending on the performance). After all, the purpose of this example is to demonstrate Hamlet's sorrow and determined interpretation of a response to the play in contrast to the quite other responses of the audience on stage.

Questioner: Well, I know you wish to show that two kinds of interpretation are active in *Hamlet*. I just wonder if this is the best example you could have chosen.

Answer: I take the play within a play to be a model example of at least two different kinds of interpretation within the same work because I believe that all inset narratives—for example, in the novels of Fielding or Sterne or later novelists—offer interpretations that differ from those pertinent to the main narrative.

Questioner: Shall we get on with your argument?
Answer: You shall probably be even more perturbed by the next example.
Questioner: Try me.

I wish in this section to illustrate a series of interpretive strategies that satirize the practices of interpretation while relating them to belief systems. My own strategy here may prove disturbing because I select for discussion the narrative of the three brothers in Swift's *A Tale of a Tub*. Swift used this narrative to satirize practices of theologians of his own time who used various interpretive strategies to alter and distort what Swift believed were the stable and reliable texts of primitive Christianity. For him, such procedures were examples of the madness of clerics who were analogous to the mad hack writers of his own time. That these mad theologians held their wrong views with total belief indicated for Swift the madness of their interpretive procedures. I use this example to suggest some of the practices of modern critics and to raise the question whether madness lies in these interpretive strategies or in the assumption of a so-called stable and legal text.

I am not proposing to interpret *A Tale of a Tub*. What I am proposing is to select a section of it pertinent to the strategies of interpretation and to analyze these in relation to the notion of a stable text. I wish, however, not to support

Swift's view of a stable text but to illustrate how interpretation must undermine it. Whether that puts me with the fashionable madmen of our time, you the reader will have to interpret.

Swift's narrative deals with three sons born triplets. Their mother is absent from the narrative (is she excluded from irony or from our serious consideration?) and their father lies on his deathbed. He hands the young orphans his will with these words:

> Sons, because I have purchased no estate, nor was born to any, I have long considered of some good legacies to bequeath you; and at last, with much care as well as expence, have provided each of you (here they are) a new coat. Now, you are to understand, that these coats have two virtues contained in them: one is, that with good wearing, they will last you fresh and sound as long as you live: the other is, that they will grow in the same proportion with your bodies, lengthening and widening of themselves, so as to be always fit. Here, let me see them on you before I die. So, very well; pray children, wear them clean, and brush them often. You will find in my will (here it is) full instructions in every particular concerning the wearing and management of your coats; wherein you must be very exact, to avoid the penalties I have appointed for every transgression or neglect, upon which your future fortunes will entirely depend. I have also commanded in my will, that you should live together in one house like brethren and friends, for then you will be sure to thrive, and not otherwise.[3]

The narrative begins with a privileged document that provides no interpretive problems because the sons accept the document and its provisions. But when the sons grow up, they are rejected by society because of the suits they wear. The story is a satire as well as a religious allegory. I overlook the religious allegory in order to stress interpretive issues. The sons find themselves confronted by a system of belief in which the worshippers assume that the "universe is a large suit of clothes." In this universe, "those beings which the world calls improperly suits of clothes, are in reality the most refined species of animals, or to proceed higher, that they are rational creatures, or men" (283). The narrator informs the reader that in providing this context, he provides a ground for understanding the behavior of the brothers.

The brothers now find themselves "strangely at a loss." They have a will which stipulates that no changes are to be made in their unadorned suits, but they find themselves in a society governed by a philosophy of clothes that posits the need for adornment of different kinds at different times. Choosing to live within society rather than as outsiders governed by a paternal philosophy of clothing, the sons seek to mediate between the two philosophies, between will and desire. They seek to adorn the clothes, but to do so in accordance with their father's will.

The sons wish to adorn their suits with shoulder-knots, but the will does not sanction such adornment: "Obedience was absolutely necessary, and yet shoulder-knots appeared extremely requisite" (285). The interpretive procedure, therefore, was to adjust the boundaries of the will. The first procedure was to argue that sanction would follow if each of the syllables of "shoulder" and "knots" could be found in the will. When this search proves unavailing, the book-learned brother proposes an interpretation based on the letters. This proves more satisfactory, for letters for "s, h, o, u, l, d, e, r" and "-n, o, t, s" appear, but no letter "k." The brother then argues that "k" is an illegitimate letter and that the proper spelling should have been "cnots." Thus shoulder-knots are then attached to the suits in accordance with paternal law.

Now the procedure of interpretation arises from a conflict of obligations. On the one hand the father's will must be obeyed; on the other the brothers subscribe to the current philosophy in order to participate in the social life of society. Interpretation thus becomes a process by which conformity to change is located within the text of the inherited will but the term "will" is defined as a compilation of letters. The readers' response to the will, their "completion" of it, is located in finding individual letters. The reasons for redefining the will are located in the desire of the sons to participate in the changing world of their time. For the will was drawn by a father who had no estate and was born to none. And the ladies the sons wish to address are in the refined part of court and town. The interpretive strategy is to make social elevation possible, without disobeying the father's authority. The procedure is to argue that language is a combination of letters (based on an alphabet) and that combinations of letters when completed provide the proper solution to the interpretive crossword puzzle.

The nature of this strategy is to adhere to the will, but to redefine of what the language of the "will" consists. The consequence of this interpretative strategy is not only to undo the text composed of sentences and propositions, but to make interpretation of the will conform to the shared desires of the sons. Thus when the court fashion changes to include fifty yards of gold lace on the suit, the interpretive situation has once again to change to accommodate what the will obviously did not include.

The strategy here is to treat the text in terms of exclusion. Since the will included no mention of gold lace, the exclusion is affirmed. Thus the concept of exclusion can be demystified by considering the oral contexts of the maker.

> "For, brothers, if you remember, we heard a fellow say when we were boys, that he heard my father's man say, that he heard my father say, that he would advise his sons to get gold lace on their coats, as soon as ever they could procure money to buy it." "By G—, that is very true," cries the other; "I remember it perfectly well," said the third. And so without more ado they got the largest gold lace in the parish, and walked about as fine as lords (286-87).

The principle of oral evidence or hearsay as the basis for completing gaps or demystifying exclusions involved substituting one's desire as the exclusions. In this procedure, the will is seen to have an unmentioned subtext and this subtext is then provided. It is not surprising that the subtext coincides with the aims of the interpreter.

Three other interpretive strategies are introduced to meet the fashionable needs of the times. The first adds a codicil to the will which, the learned brother declares, "is indeed a part of the will, and what it contains hath equal authority with the rest" (287). The codicil, it turns out, is intertextually related to the language of contemporary philosophy of fashion. The codicil tenet is especially important because it is written by a member of the lower classes—"a dog-keeper of my grandfather's"—and talks "a great deal (as good luck would have it)" (287) about the very fashion that the brothers wish to adopt. The interpretive procedure is to indicate that the term "will" requires a codicil for completion, and what the codicil must do is legitimate a flame-colored satin lining for the suit. The codicil is then added on the principle of family resemblance, the father's will providing for suits that change with the times and the dog-keeper's document addressing clothing change in the future. There is no question, it seems, about forgery or authenticity, since the process of interpretation is to adhere to the stable text but accommodate it to changing conditions.

The next interpretive problem is the result of economic changes. The corporation of fringe makers introduce, through the hired services of an actor, the use of silver fringes. The play takes, and silver fringes become the fashion. But in this case the will specifically forbids the wearing of silver fringes: *"I charge and command my said three sons to wear no sort of silver fringe upon or about their said coats."* The learned brother, however, is not daunted, and proceeds to discover that, philosophically, the word "fringe" was used by a certain author to signify "broom-stick." But although another brother indicates that "silver broom-stick" seems unreasonable in the context of the will, he is told that "silver" is used in a mythological and allegorical sense. The wearing of a silver broom-stick on one's coat was indeed a mystery, and that it in no way prohibited the actual silver fringe. The silver fringe of the will signified a religious mystery that was not to be interpreted in the language of reason.

The resort to language change in interpreting the will and to the argument that it is composed of mixed discourse in which a word or phrase can be taken as allegorical and others as natural language thus formed the basis for justification. But it was apparent that the processes of interpretation had called into question the stability and authority of the will. Interpretation is, of course, a procedure of selection and the nature of selection involves a philosophy of clothes different from that specified in the will. The authority of the will is not disputed, but in order to live within the society the sons wish, it becomes necessary to give dominance to their interpretation rather than their father's. Only through interpretation can their religious and paternal authority be made to support conformity to the changing forces in society. Interpretation, therefore, began in the family with the elementary process of the signifier in the will referring to a signified meaning. But accommodating interpretation involves unhinging the signifiers and the signified in order to make the will conform to the desires of the brothers. If we think of them as the readers or interpreters of the will, it is obvious that a change takes place in their reading once they have grown into mature men. The belief in their father's way of life inscribed in the will and in his deathbed address comes in conflict with the new philosophy of clothes and the groups that profit from the new philosophy, including the refined women in country and city who live by it.

As mature men, the brothers seek the company of refined women to elevate their own status by satisfying their sexual desires by making themselves a part of the new society of clothes. The notion of belief that I have been urging is thus clarified by Swift when he illustrates how the conflict of adherence to the will is confronted by accommodation to society. Belief is a way of thinking, living, and thus expressing the values one accepts. Interpretation becomes central when it becomes necessary to adhere verbally to a text that enunciates a set of values that do not support the new values one has selected. Swift ironically describes the strategies by which what he takes to be stable texts become destabilized in order to make them justify beliefs that contradict the "norm" of interpretation.

The readers of the text are also responders to the text and they for some time represent a unified family. And what unifies them are the strategies that interpret the will so that it becomes a justification for the beliefs that contradict those formerly accepted as represented in the will. The process of interpretation, that is the rewriting of the will and the explanations of it, replaces the notions of the priority of the will for interpretation. The will itself was written to resist relativity or the instability of the inheritance, since the suits change with time and are thus self-correcting and self-adjusting. What the sons wish, however, are quite different changes and adjustments resulting from changes in society. Interpretation, therefore, uses the text not as a self-referential and developing doctrine, but as a source which can be used to undermine itself, since the purpose is to legitimate beliefs different from those assumed to be inherent in it. Thus interpretation as a new text, by its selectivity and by revising the very notion of "will," undermines the notion of a stable interpretation, of a philosophy that authorizes belief as an inherent aspect of a text, and substitutes for it a text that is discontinuous, unstable, composed of multiple and contradictory words and discourses. And this interpretation as explanation, as a text itself, becomes a procedure for confirming the beliefs the brothers now hold.

There is no need here to relate this process to Swift's view of madness nor to point out that this interpretive process leads to placing the will in a strongbox and to referring to it as authority. The process of reinterpretation comes to provide authority to the interpreters. Interpreters come to possess the authority previously identified with that of the father. It is the sons who become the authority for what the will contains, their comments now having the weight of authority. "'Tis true, indeed, the fashion prescribed somewhat more than were directly named in the will; however, that they, as heirsgeneral of their father, had power to make and add certain clauses for public emolument, though not deducible, *totidem verbis,* from the letter of the will, or else *multa absurda sequerentur.* This was understood for canonical. . . ." (289).

The sons become the basis for establishing canon law with regard to the will and thus their interpretations replace the authority of the will. The narrator goes on to tell of the breakup of the brothers and in time some effort is made to restore the suits to their original state, but this cannot be done. I can only point out that the cyclical theme develops from a change in the economic and social status of two of the brothers and that the breakup of the family results in a reconsideration of belief.

Questioner: You were right to say that I would be perturbed. For someone concerned with genre, you surely pay little attention to it in your analysis.

Answer: If you mean that I have not interpreted the anatomy—the genre to which *A Tale of a Tub* belongs, for it is also a satire and an allegory—you are right. But I said that I had no intention of interpreting this work. What I have done is to replicate an anatomy in my own essay with its questions from Bloom, de Man, and Abrams. Shakespeare, Swift (and others still to come) combine these with fictive dialogue, serious explication, and satiric analyses of interpretation. I have no wish to provide a text with single discourses or with the assumption that it can be a member of one and only one genre. In fact, my Swift example illustrates the procedure by which interpretation inevitably contributes to the undermining of a text.

Question: But aren't you disregarding the historical context of *A Tale of a Tub?* Don't you ignore its otherness?

Answer: This is a good point. Although I wish to relate some of the interpretive strategies and problems to contemporary practices, I should also draw attention to the otherness of these procedures. The primary otherness of Swift's text is its concept of accommodation. The brothers for a time are an interpretive community that wishes to adhere to the will. All the interpretive strategies are aimed to accommodate the wishes of the father and the sons' obligation not to disobey. This notion of accommodation to a will—God's will—is held by Pope and others even though they hold it in somewhat different ways. When one turns to contemporary critics like Bloom and de Man, we see that their view of interpretation is to disaccommodate contemporary institutionalized texts and values. Their views are that interpretation should deliberately resist other texts, especially those that seek accommodation to institutional values. The brothers seek to accommodate, to adhere, to the will and to society. For Edward Said, in our time, the very function of interpretive criticism is to be "oppositional."

Questioner: But what about Abrams? Doesn't he believe in accommodating interpretation to inherited humanistic values?

Answer: Yes he does. And this makes clear that interpretation is carried on by critics with opposing beliefs in our time no less than in Swift's.

Questioner: But how are you going to deal with opposing beliefs honestly held? And before you answer this, tell me how you discover the "beliefs" that interpreters hold?

Answer: To discover such beliefs one must ask questions about the choices and selectivity (or exclusions and inclusions) of critical commentary. Why does a critic choose to interpret a particular work? In what sense is the disclosure important for others? What is at stake for him in writing an anatomy or an accommodating essay? One seeks answers because these relate writing to the thinking, feeling, and expressing of one's values, to what can easily become a mere exercise without commitment. I don't think it is a simple matter to locate beliefs, especially since I believe that particular works express contrary or complementary beliefs. And surely one would wish to handle with considerable skepticism the overt statements writers make. Nevertheless, one must undertake the inquiry.

Questioner: Well, this is not a very complete answer about how one discovers "beliefs." Can you tell us anything further?

Answer: Well, the pleasure seems to have gone out of this exchange. Let me be the questioner and put your question more specifically. How does one discover the beliefs of an unknown ballad writer? I think we try to derive them from the text, but I admit that this is not very satisfactory. Ignorance sometimes can't be helped.

Questioner: But what purpose is served by beliefs if I argue, as Paul de Man did, that language operates contradictorily without any interpreter?

Answer: How can one tell that it acts in this way without interpreting it; and if there is an interpreter making such claims, why does he wish to make them in this way—repeatedly?

Questioner: Do I understand you correctly when you say that interpretation undermines the stability of a text and for that reason every text is unstable because it is itself an interpretation subject to interpretation?

Answer: You do.

When later in the century Hume came to discuss the role of a standard of judgment, the role of interpretation as authoritative became the basis for a standard. Swift had satirized what might be called the varied perspectives on the text, and he implied that insofar as interpretation was governed by beliefs antithetical to those that resulted from the original text, there was no likelihood of an equilibrium or mediation that was useful. The procedure by which one interpretation cannibalized the prior text left no possibility for balance of perspectives.

The problem that confronted Hume was the same that resulted in Swift's satire, but Hume refuses to concede that the sons' interpretations are to be accepted as reliable interpretations. He grants that there is a species of philosophy that "represents the impossibility of ever attaining any standard of taste" because "the difference, it is said, is very wide between judgment and sentiment. All sentiment is right; because sentiment has a reference to nothing beyond itself, and is always real, wherever a man is conscious of it. But all determinations of the understanding are not right; because they have a reference to something beyond themselves, to wit, real matter of fact; and are not always conformable to that standard."[4] A thousand different sentiments may be excited by the same objects and all would be right. Beauty is no quality in things themselves; it exists merely in the mind that contemplates them.

There is, however, another species of philosophy or common sense which opposes or at least modifies and restrains this view:

> Whoever would assert an equality of genius and elegance between Ogilby and Milton, or Bunyan and Addison, would be thought to defend no less an extravagance, than if he had maintained a mole-hill to be as high as Teneriffe, or a pond as extensive as the ocean. Though there may be found persons, who give the preference to the former authors; no one pays attention to such a taste; and we pronounce, without scruple, the sentiment of these pretended critics to be absurd and ridiculous. The principle of the natural equality of tastes is then totally forgot, and while we admit it on some occasions, where the objects seem near an equality, it appears an extravagant paradox, or rather a palpable absurdity, where objects so disproportioned are compared together. (7)

This passage has come to be known as one of Hume's howlers, for who today would want to defend Addison over Bunyan. Hume then goes on to develop a theory of literary interpretation based on the characteristic practices of critics. He proceeds to define uniformity by always introducing limiting cases. Hume's list of limiting cases is so large that Hume himself recognizes his utopian vision in agreeing on the model responders.

> Thus, though the principles of taste be universal, and nearly, if not entirely, the same in all men; yet few are qualified to give judgment on any work of art, or establish their own sentiment as the standard of beauty. The organs of internal sensation are seldom so perfect as to allow the general principles their full play, and produce a feeling correspondent to those principles. They either labor under some defect, or are vitiated by some disorder; and by that means excite a sentiment, which may be pronounced erroneous. When the critic has no delicacy, he judges without any distinction, and is only affected by the grosser and more palpable qualities of the object: the finer touches pass unnoticed and disregarded. Where he is not aided by practice, his verdict is attended with confusion and hesitation. Where no comparison has been employed, the most frivolous beauties, such as rather merit the name of defects, are the object of his admiration. Where he lies under the

influence of prejudice, all his natural sentiments are perverted. Where good sense is wanting, he is not qualified to discern the beauties of design and reasoning, which are the highest and most excellent. Under some or other of these imperfections, the generality of men labor; and hence a true judge in the finer arts is observed, even during the most polished ages, to be so rare a character: strong sense, united to delicate sentiment, improved by practice, perfected by comparison, and cleared of all prejudice, can alone entitle critics to this valuable character; and the joint verdict of such, wherever they are to be found, is the true standard of taste and beauty. (17)

Hume believes, however, that men of delicate taste, the model interpreters, "are easily to be distinguished in society." In time, prejudices of a society are overcome and great writers receive their due. But even here Hume has to enter disclaimers, for there are two ineradicable sources of variation in human beings—different humors of particular men and the particular manners and opinions of their age and country. These situations create variations in taste but these variations or preferences are unavoidable "and can never reasonably be the object of dispute, because there is no standard by which they can be decided" (20).

Hume realizes that interpretations of past texts must make allowance for changes in manners, customs, and speculative principles. To do otherwise would be to analyze past texts by the prevailing fashions. But there is a major reservation that Hume identifies and that in Gadamer's terms could be called a "good" prejudice. It is a moral prejudice that makes the model critics rest their case on a belief in the rightness of eighteenth-century moral views—as though there were agreement upon what these were.

> But where the ideas of morality and decency alter from one age to another, and where vicious manners are described, without being marked with the proper characters of blame and disapprobation, this must be allowed to disfigure the poem, and to be a real deformity. I cannot, nor is it proper I should, enter into such sentiments; and however I may excuse the poet, on account of the manners of his age, I can never relish the composition. The want of humanity and of decency, so conspicuous in the characters drawn by several of the ancient poets, even sometimes by Homer and the Greek tragedians, diminishes considerably the merit of their noble performances, and gives modern authors an advantage over them. We are not interested in the fortunes and sentiments of such rough heroes; we are displeased to find the limits of vice and virtue so much confounded; and whatever indulgence

we may give to the writer on account of his prejudices, we cannot prevail on ourselves to enter into his sentiments, or bear an affection to characters which we plainly discover to be blameable. (21-22)

It is not surprising, therefore, to find that the essay concludes with a final limiting case: religious principles that rise up to superstition and intrude themselves into every sentiment create ridiculous hopes. "It must for ever be ridiculous in Petrarch to compare his mistress, Laura, to Jesus Christ" (24).

What Hume undertook to do was to stabilize the interpretive transaction. He assumed that the "principles of taste," that is, the capacity of men to agree on a standard, was potentially available to all mankind. But this unfortunately required perfect organs of internal sensation, and these are hardly found to be without defect. Readers acquire understanding of texts through practice, and this phenomenon is reasonable unless the practice is, to begin with, marred by prejudice. So, too, comparison with other works of the same kind aid, in interpretation, to discriminate the various beauties. But here, too, discrimination, when under the influence of prejudice, goes awry.

One of the most interesting aspects of Hume's essay on interpretive standards is his account of the interpreter's response to the alterity of a text. The reader must make allowance for changes in manners, customs, speculative opinions. The critic can relish, can take pleasure in responding to such differences. And the absurdities of the "pagan system of theology must be overlooked by every critic, who would pretend to form a just notion of ancient poetry" (23).

Ideas of morality and decency that differ from our own sentiments of humanity and decency, even though accountable as resulting from the manners of the age, should not be accepted. As critics and readers, "we cannot prevail on ourselves to enter into [such] sentiments, or bear an affection to characters which we plainly discover to be blameable" (22). Hume points out how the critic takes pleasure in the prior text, but the limits of pleasure result from the critic's moral beliefs.

Hume wants the reader to respond to the text so that it can be presented with all its virtues and vices, for this will make accurate judgments possible. But his limiting cases reveal the idealized version of the reader's transaction. If we then ask for the model of contemporary interpretation, we find that claims for openness, for exposure, always lead to selections that inevitably conceal aspects of the interpreted text and one's approach to it.

Hume begins the professionalization of interpretation, even though for him the aim is judgment rather than mere interpretation. He concentrates on the interpreter as responder, not on the prior text as response; he seeks to keep interpretation as close to practice as possible, but he sees both the text and the interpreter as responsive to the morals and manners of their time. In order to avoid relativism, he makes morality and decency of his own time into absolutes; past works that offer contrasting behavior cannot and should not be countenanced because these would undermine contemporary behavior. All immoral actions and behavior in prior texts must be considered serious faults.

Hume is not interested in the relation of this moral attitude to philosophical, social, or economic views. The function of interpretation is to set up a hierarchy of texts—a canon of the best. But the distortion involved in the most comprehensive selection becomes apparent in Hume's disregard of those who place Bunyan above Addison or who find in the Koran a text no more bloody than the Bible. Hume's interpretive procedures make conformity to present moral attitudes a virtue. In this respect moral conformity to present values leaves no place for texts considered immoral, superstitious, or fanatic.

The stability of the text was the ideal that Swift and Hume proposed although Swift was allegorically referring to religious and Hume to literary texts. Both granted that the human interpreters were flawed, but that, despite flaws, reasonable agreement could potentially be achieved. There was no disagreement that beliefs controlled interpretation; they assumed that the distortions beliefs introduced had to be weighted against those aspects of a text that could be supported by readers or responders with other beliefs.

These problems are inherent in interpretation, in the production of one text that revises, explains, rewrites, intersects with another. What matters are the strategies that interpreters introduce to deal with the limitations of interpretation.

What is the relation between the development of beliefs and the interpretation of texts? It is obvious that if we put the question in these terms, beliefs or traditions or interpretations seem ideas existing outside texts and that interpretations are inside them. Such a hypothesis is based on a misunderstanding. Beliefs, traditions, interpretations are writings, but the term "writing" blankets the kinds that writing includes. So, too, I have argued that interpretation is not one procedure but many. If, therefore, we refer to beliefs, we mean attitudes that are expressed in poems, in philosophical texts, in political treatises, in historical theories, etc.

Each text is composed of numerous components; we can call these discourses or elements such as intertextual statements, quotations, rhetorical features; it is thus easy to note that a text is a combinatory phenomenon. In this respect interpretation is a procedure by which texts are composed, but the different kinds or genres identify interpretation as allegory, as satire, as invocation, metaphor or other trope, as evidence or exclusion.

Tradition thus is a component of a text that is repeated or an entire text that is taken as privileged; in the first case the component is always interpreted as dominant and in the second case the text is interpreted as privileged by relation to other texts. The development of a tradition must be related to other texts that argue for it as inspired or possessing special powers. The undoing of a tradition is established by altering the status of components in a text or denying the special properties attributed to it.

Where I refer to beliefs, I refer to the acceptance by a person or a community of attitudes and behavior that they value. This may be due to the authority the statements or attitudes possess or the love one feels for the maker of the statements or some religious or legal sanction which is taken for granted. Reshiftings of belief occur in Swift's *Tale,* when the brothers modify the authority of the original belief document. This results from interpretations that revise the meanings of the text, that undermine its authority by additions, that invoke another authority because it more adequately serves their self-interest.

When contemporary interpretations of literary texts resist the authority given to interpretation as analysis of nonreferential, autonomous texts, they do so because they find this procedure clearly exclusive. They do not deny the usefulness of analysis, but black critics and feminist critics point to slave narratives, journals, freedom songs, and confessional documents that are clearly referential. They resist this view of interpretation because it is directed at middle-class Americans who do not even notice the exclusionary procedure.

In attempting to remedy this social and literary exclusion, an exclusion that is identified with the humanist values of Western industrialized countries, critics have offered a number of alternatives based on the beliefs they hold. These cannot and do not prevent exclusion (or selectivity), but they offer valuable interjections of components of the text. There are Marxist critics who connect text production with economic production; psychoanalytic critics of various persuasions who interpret texts on the basis of some primal scene; there are phenomenological critics, structural critics, minority and feminist critics, New Historical critics, and various combinations of these.

The obvious conclusion that has been drawn from this assemblage of interpretations is that we need to accept pluralism, the phenomenon that interpretations stem from different belief systems. But this conclusion disregards the fact that no provision is made for calling different systems into question. I have indicated above that a theory of the text as combinatorial or componential might prove useful in dealing with belief systems and diverse kinds of interpretation. Suggestions for such an approach are to be found in the work of Bakhtin, Yuri Lotman, and Jacques Derrida.

I began this essay with the discussion of the interpretive approaches by Harold Bloom and Paul de Man. I did so in order to examine important strategies that address problems of interpretation: the assumption that all writing is interpretation and that exposure of one's assumptions about interpretation is necessary to limit the damage resulting from exclusion and mystification.

Both these assumptions seem to me useful, but they seem to me also incapable of indicating the kinds of interpretation that are practiced, and the interrelation of the different components within each interpretation. It is useful and honest to be explicit about the exclusion of weak poets and to interpret poems as engaged in combat with predecessor poems, but to do so is to disregard other relations not involved in a military trope. As for Paul de Man's assumption of the irreconcilable conflict between grammar and rhetoric, about the always destabilized text, this assumes that generic wholes exert no control over the grammar and rhetoric. And I take this to be a mistake in such traditional forms as tragedy or the sonnet.

What conclusions are to be drawn from my discussion of interpretation? The first is that certain accepted assumptions about interpretation—such as that of a stable text or the predictable effect of interpretation—are not refuted, but abandoned as a result of new texts. The second is that certain kinds of interpretation such as judgments or description or narration become dominant or subordinate at different historical moments. Another is that all texts should be treated with suspicion especially those which claim self-consciously to expose their aims. This applies as well to interpretations based on gender, place, or religious affiliations. All texts are founded on or committed to beliefs; when several interpret one and the same situation, they sometimes prove irreconcilable. It is, I suggest, unduly optimistic to urge openness, when openness is resisted. But texts, especially poetic texts, possess features such as rhythm and music that are accessible by sign systems other than verbal. Such components may make alterations possible even though the words prevent reconciliation. It is necessary to emphasize, in a conference on interpretation, that some interpretive components can become more prominent than others. Setting a canon, urging a standard, locating scenes of class struggle can be more powerful at certain times than the rewriting of another text. It may very well be that the effect of holding a conference such as ours may prove more important than any paper provided for it.

NOTES

1. Harold Bloom, *Poetry and Repression: Revisionism from Blake to Stevens* (New Haven, CT: Yale Univ. Press, 1976), 2; hereafter cited in text.

2. Paul de Man, *The Resistance to Theory* (Minneapolis: Univ. of Minnesota Press, 1986), 87; hereafter cited in text.

3. Jonathan Swift, *A Tale of a Tub,* Section II, in *Gulliver's Travels and Other Writings,* ed. Louis A. Landa (Boston: Houghton Mifflin, 1960), 280–81; hereafter cited in text.

4. David Hume, "Of the Standard of Taste," in *Of the Standard of Taste and Other Essays,* ed. John W. Lenz (Indianapolis, IN: Bobbs-Merrill, 1965), 6; hereafter cited in text.

Renewing the Eighteenth Century

The past decade has seen the publication of *The New Eighteenth Century* (1987), "A New History of the Enlightenment?" (1992), and a considerable number of reinterpretations of the century. Writing the interpretation of an earlier historical time, contemporary critics and theorists correctly insist that they see the past through the eyes of the present. But what in our divided and fragmented world governs our visions or perceptions of the past? We insist on the need for self-reflection, on the analysis of our principles, but these are inevitably governed and constricted by the perceptions we have received and constructed.

It is, therefore, understandable that John Bender, for example, should include in his theory of the new Enlightenment an autobiographical statement about his training by the "New Critics": "Having been trained myself in graduate school during the 1960s on a combination—uneasy to be sure but then customary in American English departments—of historical philology and formalist poetics (chiefly those of the New Criticism), I have personally undergone the change of referential framework I am describing."[1]

What he is describing is his shift from the framework of the New Criticism to that of the New Historicism. What remains unsaid are the reasons for the change, why he came to believe in "the dissolution of boundaries between venerated aesthetic objects like novels or paintings and tracts, pamphlets or legislation; the reading of institutions as 'texts'; the treatment of subjectivity as a socially constructed—and therefore historically changing—phenomenon rather than as a permanent feature of human nature; and, perhaps above all, the view that manifestly fictional texts like plays and novels are culturally constitutive—not mere reflections of a 'reality' that exists prior to and outside them" (64-65).

Who can fail to be impressed by the range and thoughtful description of

---

This paper is published here for the first time. It was delivered April 22, 1993, to the American Society for Eighteenth-Century Studies at Brown University.

the new framework? And yet the very notion of a framework, of a controlling system that has historically changed, would seem to demand, above all, a study of how frameworks change. The change that is being described is that of a single theorist, albeit a highly sensitive one. Nevertheless, as many theorists have remarked, no single framework permits us to understand the variety of differences and distinctions particular New Critics or New Historicists reveal.

It is important to realize that critical positions are shaped by particular aspects of culture—not only by political, social, religious, sexual relations, but by responses to, engagements with, and differences from one's contemporaries or critical predecessors. The substitution of one "framework" for another parallels Thomas Kuhn's view of the replacement of one paradigm by another. But even Kuhn acknowledges that the new paradigm includes discourses, images, and terms from that which has been replaced. Can we have a new history of the Enlightenment without dragging some of the baggage of the old history along with us? And how can there be only one Enlightenment if theorists proceed from different premises? If we have enlightenments, against what or from what were writers to be enlightened? How much writing continues to be unenlightened?

One problem is that a framework like New Historicism or cultural materialism is composed of texts and that each New Historical contribution also constitutes a framework. If we make a framework out of frameworks that are often in opposition to one another, we reduce the usefulness as well as the accuracy of our criticism. For example, Nancy Armstrong and Laura Brown are both valuable cultural critics of the eighteenth-century novel, but Laura Brown declares, "despite a superficial resemblance of orientation, Nancy Armstrong's claims for women's access to domestic power are actually incompatible with the argument advanced here, as is her grounding notion of the essential role of discursive forms, and particularly the novel, in the production of major bourgeois social structures."[2]

We cannot do without generalizations, but we might want to consider how to limit the intellectual damage of misinformation we create. Generalizations about cultural implications, Freudian implications, feminist and cultural implications, need to be derived from texts so that readers can at least be aware of what is being included or excluded. This means, as in the quotation I just read, that our distinctions require close comparison with the texts of those with whom we differ. There are other methodological discriminations we need to make, but my point here is that if we pay no attention to the particular generic text to which we are referring, we risk assuming that a statement in a specific *Spectator* can be generalized into the writings and thinking of a whole century. If distinctions govern present critical choices, need we not ask what distinctions governed those of the eighteenth-century writers? Otherwise, how can we deal with eighteenth-century texts without making them appear as inadequate contemporary writing? Hans Robert Jauss suggests that we seek to fuse horizons based on the model of past texts entering into present ones while retaining their alterity. Or we can select an eighteenth-century theme like that of taste or beauty or sublimity and compare our discourses of it with those of the eighteenth century, or we can insist on a particular cultural composition. But such procedures lack the social construction of texts that reveal them as discourse mixtures that are tentative and combinatory.

Elaine Showalter has written that gynocriticism has generated "important books on what is called 'gender and genre': the significance of gender in shaping generic conventions in forms ranging from the hymn to the Bildungsroman."[3] Her statement implies that genre is a procedure for grouping individual texts because they share discourse conventions of a new kind. Forget genre as library classifications or rule-generated texts. Think rather of genre as an interpretive tool for texts that have varied discourses. It is neither a paradox nor—if I may say so—a theoretical problem when one eighteenth-century reader treats *Gulliver's Travels* as a travel book and another as a fictional narrative. But both designations are pointless unless it is apparent why one wishes to make these separations rather than inclusions. And the why leads us to genres as social constructions. And those of us who believe in social construction of texts are not helped by claims that such constructions must be only political deliberations.

I want to suggest that if we seek to see eighteenth-century British literature anew, we need to recognize that generic conventions undergo changes in a hundred or more years and that the most expeditious procedure for creating cultural change is a new kind of genre criticism, because it primarily provides demonstration and explanation of social construction. The most obvious example is the work done on the novel by critics like Ronald Paulson, John Richetti, Lennard Davis, Michael McKeon, Paul Hunter, Nancy Armstrong, and others who have questioned, examined, supplemented, resisted, or ignored Ian Watt's study. What is most pertinent to the argument I am making about the present study of past texts are the practices of these critics. They have demonstrated that the novel was constructed from prior genres such as news reports, conduct books, sermons, ballads, letters, tracts, and other nonfictional texts. No matter how different particular novels—or what we now call novels—are from each other, novels are constructed by combining texts or discourses of texts that previously were separate. This combination narrativizes texts that had, with the exceptions of the sermon or letter, no scholarly or social status. They addressed literate audiences that included readers as diverse as the discourses themselves. Yet it was an audience that was divided in its moral responses to *Pamela* and to *Tristram Shandy,* one that seemed to have divided interpretations of the as yet unsettled conventions. But it does seem reasonable to assume that the social constructions of particular novels from Defoe to Austen undergo shifts and changes in the discourses that they combine.

If we ask what cultural questions about the text as a genre might stem from this type of cultural criticism, I might begin by asking what new genres other than the novel are developed in eighteenth-century British literature. The periodical paper, the magazine, the encyclopedia, the historical dictionary, the Gothic novel, and domestic tragedy. No doubt you can mention others. The point I wish to make is that these forms are not only combinatory, they are genres that provide bodies of knowledge.

If you wonder what I take culture to mean with such neutral statements as "bodies of knowledge," I should share with you the direction this paper is taking. I began with a statement about the new eighteenth-century studies and gave an example of the turn of frameworks from New Criticism to cultural criticism. I then raised questions about the adequacy of the conception of framework, arguing that what seemed to be lacking was the explanation of how a cultural change occurs. I supplemented this with a demonstration that cultural critics did disagree about the operation of culture and that cultural criticism required greater sophistication than appeared in the examples of some of its practitioners. In place of some of the present practices, a redeployment and redefinition of genre criticism began by suggesting that the example of novel criticism indicated support of the view of genre as a practice of social construction. And I followed this with a series of new eighteenth-century genres that could be the basis for study similar to that of the novel. And it was at this point of genre as a combinatory, not a rule-governed, practice that I have now arrived.

This is the place to draw attention to a different combinatory text of philosophy to provide a rationale for the genres I have been naming, a philosophical discourse that would explain the grounds of combinatory procedures. The original source was association of ideas in Locke's *Essay,* but a later justification was found in 1748 in David Hume's *An Inquiry Concerning Human Understanding* under the section called "connexion" and later (in 1750) association of ideas. Hume listed three principles of association—resemblance, contiguity in time or place, and cause and effect.

But the most extensive analysis of associations of ideas was developed in David Hartley's *Observations on Man*. This constitutes one of the major texts for explaining the relation between the body and the mind in the writings of the second half of the century. Hartley writes:

> My chief design in the following chapter is briefly to explain, establish, and apply the doctrines of *vibration* and *association*. The first of these doctrines is taken from the hints concerning the performance of sensation and motion which *Sir Isaac Newton* has given at the end of his *Principia*, and in the *Questions* annexed to his *Optics;* the last, from what Mr. *Locke*, and other ingenious persons since his time, have delivered concerning the influence of *association* over our opinions and affections, and its use in explaining those things in an accurate and precise way, which are commonly referred to the power of habit and custom, in a general and indeterminate one.
>
> The doctrine of *vibrations* may appear at first sight to have no connexion with that of *association;* however, if these doctrines be found in fact to contain the laws of the bodily and mental powers respectively, they must be related to each other, since the body and mind are. One may expect, that *vibrations* should infer *association* as their effect, and *association* point to *vibrations* as its cause. I will endeavour, in the present chapter, to trace out this mutual relation.[4]

Hartley's work became important to writers in the late eighteenth century—to Priestley, Alison, Whiter, and to Dugald Stewart, who extended association of ideas to any two ideas. When we come to identify the ideas of the eighteenth century by the writers of the century we ought to find association among them. I think it appropriate to consider what views a New Historical critic indicates that he is rejecting. I take John Bender's expression of these views because his statements have had considerable support. Bender's view of Enlightenment studies, if I do not do him an injustice, is an attack upon the views of earlier critics of the Enlightenment. There are, he writes, "four assumptions characteristic of the Enlightenment framework within which criticism has proceeded." These are the "invention of the aesthetic as an autonomous discursive realm," "authorship," a "faith in transparency, neutrality, and disinterestedness as ideals of critical discourse," and "gendered sexuality" (70-74). And Bender stresses the important contributions of feminist critics in critiquing eighteenth-century gender construction as it works in literature.

But whoever the modern critics of British literature are to whom Bender refers, neither Shaftesbury nor Hutcheson nor Hume argues for the aesthetic as an autonomous discursive realm. Indeed, Hume points out in "Of the Standard of Taste" that "where vicious manners are described, without being marked with the proper characters of blame and disapprobation, this must be allowed to disfigure the poem, and to be a real deformity. I cannot, nor is it proper I should, enter into such sentiments; and however I may excuse the poet, on account of the manners of his age, I can never relish the composition."[5] The custom of an aesthetic realm could not, for Hume, be without a moral component governed by his view of ideal Christian morality.

The realm of authorship—for example Johnson's letter to Chesterfield or the legal documents urging copyright—can be seen as a rejection of patronage and an important claim to one's text as property. Authorship is a revolutionary step in asserting the right to the work one does. It is a corollary to the assertion of the rights of women in the household work they do. It is part of the project of the invention of the individual that remains one of the incompleted projects of the Enlightenment. The genres in which these discourses appear constitute clues to the social construction of an argument.

This is self-evident, for example, in the dialogue *The Progress of Romance* by Clara Reeve, which begins as a battle between the sexes over the role of romance. In this battle Hortensius is opposed by his two friends Sophronia and Euphrasia. And although the women persuade Hortensius, the dialogue is framed as a narrative about a duel. And although the patriarchal language is ironic—"What Madame, do you think you can give a challenge and go off with impunity? I am come hither to demand an explanation of your behaviour last Thursday evening at Sophronia's house . . ."—Euphrasia takes up the challenge and defeats the male. The dialogue becomes a gendered lesson rather than an inquiry among companions.

Together with and against Bender's view on gendered sexuality, I want to place Dianne Dugaw's argument that the woman warrior in eighteenth-century literature, "long a popular subject in lower-class ballads, moves to a middle-class format and finds a larger and more sophisticated audience in the eighteenth century."[6]

I want to use this reference to the rise of ballads as an entry into the major section of my paper: a study of how ballads can be interpreted as social constructions. But before doing this I want to make a slight regression. Although the woman warrior of the ballads is elevated to a more sophisticated audience in *The Rape of the Lock,* that process of elevation is matched by a process of declination. Pope marks the epic genre by applying it to a private situation and satirizing the very changes it introduces—a gentle woman who becomes a woman warrior. The changes that the poem describes apply not merely to Belinda, but to the objects on her dressing table and to the "deadly Bodkin." For this bodkin was originally three eminent seal rings that through transformation became no more than an adornment for Belinda's mother's hair and now a weapon.

> Now meet thy Fate, incens'd *Belinda* cry'd,
> And drew a deadly *Bodkin* from her Side.
> (The same, his ancient Personage to deck,
> Her great great Grandsire wore about his Neck
> In three *Seal-Rings;* which after, melted down,
> Form'd a vast *Buckle* for his Widow's Gown:
> Her infant Grandame's *Whistle* next it grew,
> The *Bells* she gingled, and the *Whistle* blew;
> Then in a *Bodkin* grac'd her Mother's Hairs,
> Which long she wore, and now *Belinda* wears.) (5.87-96)

The bodkin's various meltdowns trace the shift from rings of status to the weapon she uses to avenge her loss of status. The transformation tells of a symbol of male authority that becomes a female plaything and finally a female weapon to attack male rape. This mock epic raises one genre while reducing another. Culturally what is taking place is the movement of a ballad character into a higher social role, while the social behavior of Belinda loses its luxurious lethargy. If one thinks of Dryden's view of satire that can become a heroic poem, then Pope's transformation of play with the epic alters social implications, for it indicates that the noble diction and the noble warrior have been replaced by the language of social and sexual behavior.

A deliberate construction of social values can be seen in Addison's effort to make the ballad of "Chevy Chase" a respectable work of art. Ballads were used to paper the walls of coffeehouses or to do service in baking dishes. They were the songs of common people. Addison argued that "Chevy Chase" conformed to the rules of a heroic poem as laid down by the "Greatest modern critics," that the poem about the battle between Scottish and English forces constituted a major work, and that the poem's sentiments and heroic action conformed to the procedures of the epic: "I shall ... shew that the

Sentiments in that Ballad are extremely natural and poetical, and full of the majestic Simplicity which we admire in the greatest of the ancient Poets."[7]

This was a bold move—elevating a common song loved by the "rabble" to one of the highest of literary genres. And it was supported, according to Addison, by the universal approval of the multitude, "Tho they are only the Rabble of a Nation" (*Spectator* 70). Generic elevation was to be achieved without having a learned audience to support the elevation, although he pointed out that Sir Philip Sidney and Ben Jonson both praised the poem. It was not unlike the gesture of the bishop of London who, in 1702, ordered "Chevy Chase" to be translated into Latin so that the work would be treated with proper respect by the learned.

Addison's efforts of generic elevation were part of a larger generic and social transformation. In elevating the ballads, Addison devalued some other kinds. He affirmed the significance of the ballad by contrasting the genuine responses of the rabble with the falsely sophisticated taste of the metaphysical poets and their supporters. In fact, Addison chose Abraham Cowley as the vicious model: "Had this old song been filled with Epigrammatical Turns and Points of Wit, it might perhaps have pleased the wrong Taste of some Readers; but it would never have become the Delight of the Common People nor have warmed the Heart of Sir Philip Sidney" (*Spectator* 74).

His elevation of a low genre makes clear the importance of hierarchical generic distinctions for Addison's argument. The received classifications of poetry, he argued—lyric, ode, epic, tragedy, satire, etc.—had omitted ballads that belonged with the highest genres; and such argument permitted him to imply—whether he intended to or not—that current theory did not need to be revised; it had merely to include what it had overlooked. Addison was not seeking to revolutionize poetic theory, but rather to make it accommodate his nationalistic aims and his support of a rising mercantile economy.

Actually Addison was involved in a contradiction he did not recognize. Historically he wished to make the accepted poetic theory include what it was constructed to exclude. By extending the definition of "Chevy Chase" so that it could be considered an epic, a heroic poem, he was devaluing the genre of heroic poetry. The examples now included within epic rendered it ineffective to make the social and literary distinctions to which it originally applied.

Every text distends and even distances the genre to which it belongs. Every text in some way extends, by its contribution, the genre of an ode, elegy, etc., of which it is a part. There is a point, however, at which a classification ceases to be useful because it can no longer be limited to the discriminations for which it was formulated; at such a time it has to be reconceptualized, merged with other genres or abandoned. Unless specific examples of a genre are seen historically as extending or narrowing or undermining their own genre, we can only describe changes as limited to discourses or ideologies rather than to the combinations of which these are only parts. When ballads were elevated to epics, when satires could, in Dryden's terms, become heroic poems or epics, when novels were amusingly confused by Fielding as comic epics, then the epic itself had begun to be devalued. And its devaluation was replaced by genres addressed to literate people. It was replaced also by a justification of trade with colonies. In the essay preceding his discussion of "Chevy Chase," Addison praised the merchant class for its extension of Britain's economic power and for the harmony of private and public interest between his country and those less advanced. Merchants bring into their own country what is wanting and carry out whatever is superfluous. "Nature," he wrote, "seems to have taken a particular care to disseminate her blessings among the different regions of the world, with an eye to this mutual intercourse and traffick among mankind, that the natives of the several parts of the globe might have a kind of dependence upon one another, and be united together by their common interest" (*Spectator* 69).

Addison described commercial behavior in the imagery of moral and political benevolence; he used the language of commercial reciprocity to invoke a harmony between distant wealthy nations, between Britons and "Mohametans." He touted the merchant as one of the most useful members "in a Commonwealth," although previously merchants had occupied no position of importance in English society.

Just as he praised the elevation of the merchant because of the private and public harmony he created between England and other countries, so, too, he pointed to the elevation of the ballad because it, too, functioned to establish a harmony between the sentiment and taste of the rabble with that of the best critics. The universality of the ballad was based on that aspect of human nature which revealed an "essential and inherent Perfection of Simplicity of Thought."

But assumptions about simplicity of thought were not shared by many of Addison's fellow critics. Neither was the elevation of the ballad despite the obvious nationalistic and mercantilistic functions. The rhetoric that considered ballads unskilled effusions was not readily overturned or made obsolete by Addison's commentary. On the contrary, Addison's arguments for equality with epic were substantively defeated. John Dennis objected to Addison's claim for universality of judgment between uneducated and educated human beings, and he argued further that one ought not to separate simplicity of thought from simplicity of expression, since it was art that joined them. Addison's readiness to justify the thought of a ballad in spite of "a despicable Simplicity in the Verse" confirmed the validity of Dennis's attack. In fact, Addison's essays on the ballads were ridiculed by contemporaries in numerous parodies. These critics were unimpressed by an argument that sought to apply the criteria of epic to ballads that dealt with a local battle or a betrayal of family obligation.

One of his contemporaries declared ironically that "if we were to apply our selves, instead of [to] the Classicks, to the Study of Ballads and other ingenious Composures of that Nature, in such Periods of our Lives, when we are arriv'd to a Maturity of Judgment, it is impossible to say what Improvement might be made to Wit in general, and the Art of Poetry in particular," and he proceeded to analyze "The History of Tom Thumb" mimicking Addison's comparison.[8] Addison's arguments existed insofar as they were entertained as a possibility that needed refutation. Addison's eminence as a critic merited replies; it did not account for the triumph of ballads as an elevated literary genre. What did account for it?

No single genre—like a ballad or a tragedy—can be understood as changing by itself. It changes by establishing new combinatory discourses, and these develop changes in the meanings of the terms that are combined. Thomas Kuhn argues that changes in a paradigm involve changes in the definitions of terms previously used and incorporated into the new paradigm. Genres are indeed governed by developed discourses that become conventionalized. And as I have urged, generic terms like the epic undergo change as their construction is used to develop or articulate different modes of feeling.

Addison's attempt to elevate the ballad was but part of the introduction of new genres in the early eighteenth century. The periodical essay which offered the ballad redefinition was itself an innovative form related to the development of the newspaper.

In the years following Addison's essays ballads were introduced into the writing of recognized and established genres. Nicholas Rowe converted the ballad of Jane Shore into *The Tragedy of Jane Shore* in 1714; a collection of ballads was published in 1723; *The Beggar's Opera* introduced ballads into a new comic form in 1728. George Lillo wrote a ballad opera in 1730, and there were numerous ballad operas performed between 1728 and 1760.

Much has been written about the political implications of *The Beggar's*

Opera and the parody of Italian opera. What can generic criticism contribute to the social construction of this new genre "ballad opera"? First the inclusion of ballad songs in comedy addresses the issue of appropriation. Just as the novel began as a composite of low forms so ballad opera included ballad songs while altering the words. Appropriation was thus an elevation of a street form to that of a public performance. Appropriation moved the status of ballads from the street and home to the public stage. In doing so, the play was analogous to the combinatory procedures involved in the invention of the novel. Issues of boundary crossing, mixing music and satire, inverting the narrative of the origin of the Trojan Wars (by having two women rage singing war over a man), all these transformations enacted the life of rogues and prostitutes as the parodic imitation of pastoral love and marriage, of theft, betrayal, and justice.

The Beggar's Opera was indeed a "Newgate Pastoral." The joyful songs provided the basis for remembering other words and references now unsung. The social construction was self-reflexive, since the opera is a play within a play. The appeal to the audience within the play to determine justice for Macheath, alludes to the myth of people having the authority of judgment. What *The Beggar's Opera* illustrates is the relation between families and gangs—that the appropriation of property like the artistic appropriation of ballads involves exploitation and reward. The play may be an attack on Walpole but it is also an attack upon those that made him possible and those who live off those that made him possible.

What happens when one genre—a confessional ballad—is reworked into a tragedy? I can begin the approach to this question by indicating what happens when Jonathan Miller produces a version of *The Beggar's Opera* in which he has Macheath killed, not freed. It represents Miller's attempt to read the play in terms of the arbitrariness of power. This construction of authority, by insisting on its finality, conflicts with the generic basis of the play as an epithalamion. It is, moreover, obvious that renewing the eighteenth century by changing its texts is more an act of bibliographic vandalism than criticism.

The strategy of generic transformation—of one genre transformed (not transposed) into another—takes place when the ballad of George Barnwel is transformed into *The London Merchant,* a poem into a tragedy. The tragedy begins as a historical drama of the Elizabethan age in which the merchant Thorogood explains the importance of his role in defending the country by preventing Spain from making a loan from the Bank of Genoa. Not only is there no such character in the ballad, but the historical reference is an effort to create for the eighteenth-century merchant a historical role in affairs of state, and thus give traditional status to a character who, in 1731, was not considered a man of quality.

The ballad is a confessional narrative told by a young merchant's apprentice who is seduced by a whore, embezzles his master's money, kills his uncle to support his mistress, but is thrown out of her house when the money is spent. The whore accuses him of murder to the authorities, he escapes and accuses her. She is apprehended and hanged; he gets to Poland and is hanged for a crime he did not commit.

The ballad is a crude work, an act of composition by more than one author, since it entails the narration of the death of the apprentice. The social construction of the play involves more than the praise and glorification of the merchant; it transforms a fringe character and an innocent boy into the protagonists of tragedy. In justification of this innovation George Lillo, the author, offers the following explanation:

> If Tragick Poetry be, as Mr. *Dryden* has some where said, the most excellent and most useful Kind of Writing, the more extensively useful the Moral of any Tragedy is, the most excellent that Piece must be of its Kind.
>
> I hope I shall not be thought to insinuate that this . . . is such; that depends on its Fitness to answer the end of Tragedy, the exciting of the Passions, in order to the correcting such of them as are criminal, either in their Nature, or through their Excess. Whether the following Scenes do this in any tolerable Degree, is, with the Deference, that becomes one who wou'd not be thought vain, submitted to your candid and impartial Judgment.
>
> What I wou'd infer is this, I think, evident Truth; that Tragedy is so far from losing its Dignity, by being accommodated to the Circumstances of the Generality of Mankind, that it is more truly august in Proportion to the Extent of its Influence, and the Numbers that are properly affected by it. As it is more truly great to be the Instrument of Good to many, who stand in need of our Assistance, than to a very small Part of that Number.[9]

The point of shifting tragedy to ordinary life was not only an act of generic elevation, but of class elevation. Ordinary life was as important as the lives of the nobility. But equally important was the reshifting of the aims of tragedy—not catharsis through pity and terror, but the "exciting of the Passions, in order to the correcting such of them as are criminal." The use of law implicit in criminality and explicit in the play becomes necessary for the proper management of a merchant's affairs. The law becomes a measure for containing and controlling the corrupting and dangerous behavior of the aristocracy. And this explains the dominant role of the prostitute Millwood. For she was seduced and practiced on the innocent youth what she was taught by men.

> *Mill.* Men of all Degrees and all Professions I have known, yet found no Difference, but in their several Capacities; all were alike wicked to the utmost of their Power. In Pride, Contention, Avarice, Cruelty, and Revenge, the Reverend Priesthood were my unerring Guides. [4.xviii]

The merchant with his new wealth is made aware of the abuses and misuse of power by old wealth. It is the abused and vengeful Millwood who indicts the patriarchal structure of society, including the priesthood. The merchant acknowledges the truth of her claim, but the tragedy suggests that one's personal life and the law may help control some abuses, but as merchant one supports the government and one seeks to become himself a man of quality.

Lillo's shift in the concept of tragedy to permit presentation of protagonists of private life was based on the assumption that tragedy served to prevent vice. It was a liberation concept that intended to free people from vicious actions. And since the greatest need for such liberation involved the common people, tragedy ought to deal with their situations. This utilitarian function of tragedy connected it with mercantile and monetary concerns, with subjects such as seduction, gambling, and prostitution as well as theft and murder. Lillo's theory moved in two directions—one involved the creation of virtuous models and the other the avoidance of display of the very vices that were to be eradicated. It thus rested on an unreal virtue and on unstated vices. For the tragedy is also about the initiation into sex and the uncontrollable passion it can excite, overpowering money, duty, morality.

But this view lived side by side with the traditional argument for noble tragedy. In the notes that have been published of Adam Smith's lectures on rhetoric and belles lettres delivered at the University of Glasgow in 1762-63 there occur the following statements:

> Kings and Nobles are what make the best characters in a Tragedy. (The misfortunes of the great as the[y] happen less frequently affect us more. There is in humane Nature a Servility which inclines us to adore our Superiors and an inhumanity which disposes us to contempt and trample under foot our inferiors.) We are too much accustomed to the misfortunes of people below or equal with ourselves to be greatly affected by them. But the misfortunes of the great both as they seem connected with the wellfare of a multitude

and as [they seem] we are apt to pay great respect and attention to our superiors however unworthy are what chiefly affect us. Nay such is the temper of men, that we are rather disposed to laugh at the misfortunes of our inferiors than take part in them.[10]

I quote this passage by Adam Smith because it seems a direct response to Lillo's argument for a tragedy of private lives. Even if it is not Smith's comprehensive view of tragedy, it describes and defends a servile behavior to superiors—to kings and nobles however unworthy they may be. This reaffirms the argument I made earlier that no necessary connections exist toward literature between the views of two supporters of a philosophic or cultural position—in this case the support of an expanding mercantile society.

I have been using ballads as a prime example of the generic shifts that were taking place in the early eighteenth century. These shifts provided texts that moved audiences to accept low and popular art. This art introduced changes in the conventional literary hierarchies by repositioning the roles of women, of ordinary characters, and ordinary language. It offered new genres and even reordered older ones; it aided readers and viewers in accepting altered social behavior by offering knowledge on which such behavior could be based. This repositioning supported the acceptance of new economic and social groups and attitudes and at the same time treated exploitation of colonial societies as beneficial for exploiters and exploited. In the general transformation of ballads that I have been tracing, the undoing of one type of subordination created others. No ideological or moral position was free from the retention of some of the discourses of the text that was transformed.

Not to recognize the significance of the multiple aspects of texts is to create an eighteenth century blind to the complicated and often contradictory ideologies inherent in their combinations. Many scholars are today engaged in treating detective stories, westerns, private journals, romances, letters as serious cultural statements. But if we are to treat them as cultural constructions, we have to understand that cultural construction involves study of the transformations that the combinatory discourses have undergone.

The incorporation of ballads into other genres, or the use of ballads as the subject matter for other genres, is a significant aspect of literary history. It was beginning to be practiced by eighteenth-century poets in the early part of the century and when Bishop Percy published the *Reliques of Ancient English Poetry* in 1765 he included the ballad of "Chevy Chase" and the ballad of George Barnwel as well as ballads by William Shenstone and David Mallet. What is of interest for this paper is the anthology as a genre in which the ballads I have discussed find a place.

Percy was aware of this genre and referred to the Elizabethan garland of verses, but he came into possession of a manuscript of ballads and the "manuscript was shown to several learned and ingenious friends, who thought the contexts too curious to be consigned to oblivion, and importuned the possessor to select some of them, and give them to the press."[11] The friends were Samuel Johnson and William Shenstone.

The aims of the collection, according to Percy, were to show "the gradation of our language, exhibit the progress of popular opinions, display the peculiar manners and customs of former ages, or throw light on our earlier classical poets." For Percy the collection exhibited a progress from early poetry to "the present state of improved literature," showing the gradual improvements of the English language and poetry from the earliest ages down to the present. And he hoped in his historical presentation to please both the judicious antiquary and the reader of taste. And included in the collection were four essays: "An Essay on the Ancient Minstrels in England," "An Essay on the Origin of the English Stage," "An Essay on the Metre of Pierce Plowman's Visions," and "An Essay on the Ancient Metrical Romances."

I go into this detail because we have here the first anthology which seeks to establish an authentic British poetic tradition. When Percy referred to the "judicious antiquary" he was making an argument for the authenticity of the selections in his collection.

The concern for authenticity represented a desire to preserve the artifacts of the past. Commerce, which had previously been considered the valuable interchange for use between countries in which manufactured goods were exchanged for raw materials, had become, in addition, a type of exploitation in which items were beginning to be valued not for use but for their scarcity. A few eccentric collectors of ballads were found in the seventeenth century, but the value of authenticity was now formalized in the collections of antiquarians. Old ballads were especially valuable if they were the trusted expressions of an earlier British society. As originators of a British literary tradition, ballads no longer needed the *Aeneid* to illustrate their literary value. Rather, their value lay in the thoughts and sentiments of a primitive time that despite their simplicity revealed some of the virtues still possessed by the moderns. The very first poem in the first volume was "The Ancient Ballad of Chevy-Chase," and although Percy praised Addison's essay, he pointed out that Addison's version was probably written after the praise of Sir Philip Sidney, and he offered a much earlier version. But he also published a more modern version of the ballad for purposes of comparison. Percy wished to please not merely the antiquarians but "readers of taste." For him, one value of the ballads as a literary genre was to demonstrate an evolutionary tradition in English poetry. He thus included a number of contemporary poems in his collection of old ballads in order to illustrate that poetry had now attained its "highest beauties." For him, the model was the modern.

Percy was attacked because his notion of "authenticity" did not prevent him from rewriting or editing the ballads to conform to the beautiful taste of the modern reader. His notion of authenticity had to be reconciled, he thought, with the sophisticated needs of men of taste, and his revisions were intended as necessary mediations. But this behavior introduced historical questions and problems that were primarily historical. How could authenticity be made palatable to an audience that despised the diction of authentic ballads? What kind of value did authentic artifacts possess?

The combinatory character of the collection was now turned to a historical enterprise that, like the Greek and Roman societies of the past, had a poetic tradition. The movement of overseas trade was applied to exploring the British poetic past. Percy was uneasy about saving ballads that had been treated by his countrymen as waste.

But looking at the genres that I have been discussing and the transformations in which they have been involved, it does seem that we have been dealing with collections within the novel, within the periodical essays, within the mock-epic, within magazines, journals, dictionaries, and with regard to ballads, with collections within collections.

In the texts I have been describing we can identify the concern for and about a transformation of values. If we seek a new eighteenth century or a new Enlightenment we might look at what is taking place not only with the novel but with every genre during the years of the century. To know what interpretations we want is not enough. We need to ask not only why the eighteenth-century texts reveal what they do, but why they do not do otherwise. After all, Gulliver never once reaches the destination for which he sets out, but he always can come home again—until coming home is finally the destination he doesn't want to reach.

NOTES

1. John Bender, "A New History of the Enlightenment?" *Eighteenth-Century Life* 16, no. 1 (1992): 1-20, and in *The Profession of Eighteenth-Century Literature: Reflections on an Institution*, ed. Leo Damrosch (Madison: Univ. of Wisconsin Press, 1992), 62-83, on 64; hereafter cited in text.

2. Laura Brown, *Ends of Empire: Women and Ideology in Early Eighteenth-Century English Literature* (Ithaca, NY: Cornell Univ. Press, 1993), 9n7.

3. Elaine Showalter, "A Criticism of Our Own" (1989), in *Feminisms: An Anthology of Literary Theory and Criticism*, ed. Robyn R. Warhol and Diane Price Herndl (1991; New Brunswick, NJ: Rutgers Univ. Press, 1997), 226.

4. David Hartley, *Observations on Man: His Frame, His Duty and His Expectations*, 6th ed. (London, 1834), 1:4.

5. David Hume, "Of the Standard of Taste," in *Of the Standard of Taste and Other Essays*, ed. John W. Lenz (Indianapolis, IN: Bobbs-Merrill, 1965), 21-22.

6. Dianne Dugaw, *Warrior Women and Popular Balladry, 1650-1850* (Cambridge: Cambridge Univ. Press, 1989). This quotation, a reliable summary of Dugaw's argument (as it appears in *Warrior Women* and elsewhere), is by Laura Brown, *Ends of Empire*, 142.

7. Joseph Addison, *Spectator* 74; hereafter cited in text.

8. William Wagstaffe, "A Comment upon the History of Tom Thumb" (1711), in *Joseph Addison and Richard Steele: The Critical Heritage*, ed. Edward A. Bloom and Lillian D. Bloom (London: Routledge, 2013), 233.

9. George Lillo, "Dedication," *The London Merchant: or, The History of George Barnwell* (London, 1731), iii-iv.

10. Adam Smith, "Lecture XXI, Jan. 14, 1763," in *Lectures on Rhetoric and Belles Lettres*, ed. J. C. Bryce, *The Glasgow Edition of the Works and Correspondence of Adam Smith*, vol. 4 (Oxford: Oxford Univ. Press, 1983), 2.90.

11. Thomas Percy, *Reliques of Ancient English Poetry* (1765; London: J. M. Dent & Sons, 1906); this and the following quotation are from the preface.

Generating Literary Histories

My aim here is to inquire why and how some recent literary histories have come to be written or rewritten. I consider this inquiry important because it challenges us to understand our own desire for historicity, our sense of our own mortality; not only because we are conscious of a nuclear possibility, but because in this century we have become conscious of the readiness of human beings to end the lives of others. We live with the consciousness of what has been repressed, and despite our desire to expose the repressed, there always remains a remnant that eludes us. This compels us to recognize that our version of history, while it inevitably exposes that which has been repressed, nevertheless leaves us with incomplete knowledge of history and ourselves as historians.

I can but illustrate this point by offering you a biographical—not autobiographical—sketch of an author who, in our time, has developed a revised conception of literary history, a philosopher who has urged a new history based upon the concept of decentering linear texts, of arguing that textual boundaries must be made unbounded, that texts which have repressed social, political, and philosophical views should be deconstructed to reveal the repressions.

Jacques Derrida, whose views I am describing, is an Algerian Jew, born in a former French colony, a marginalized figure from a marginalized country. It seems to me no historical accident that his geographical image of boundary crossing should assert the democratization of what in previous criticism was considered bounded and fixed. His arguments for decentering texts and for attending to their repressive aspects of language seem, at least in part, to stem from a colonial environment. And I believe his argument for the indeterminacy of the text rests on rejection of the localization and stabilization of place, a rejection of any one place as the origin or center of commitment.

This essay was originally published in *New Historical Literary Study: Essays on Reproducing Texts, Representing History*, ed. Jeffrey N. Cox and Larry J. Reynolds (Princeton, NJ: Princeton Univ. Press, 1993), 39–53, and is reprinted with permission of the publisher.

I speak with considerable reservation in analogizing personal experience to theoretical arguments. But such speculation is not foreign to Derrida's own way of thinking, and it can help to explain why the notion of the play of signifiers becomes important in reconceptualizing philosophy. He is, after all, an outsider encountering or discounting or reconstruing the assumed fixed play of the insiders.

Whatever phenomenological assumptions may govern his theory of writing, I want to suggest that we cannot ignore the sense of alienation, perhaps even of personal oppression, that has bred resentment from actual situations and social practices. For state practices of colonization or deprivation of the rights of minorities or the denial of economic and social equality to women are not forms of imaginary subordination.

Social movements which arise to resist these injustices have, in our time, fostered resistance to received histories, including literary history. They have resulted in histories and theories marked by opposition to exclusion and marginalization. The most obvious of such histories are those of the feminists and the black critics. They are generating histories out of an economic, legal, social, and educational awareness of injustice and deprivation. The problem facing the writers of the new histories is that generation implies that prior generations have established the language and genre of history writing. It is thus impossible to generate a new history without being contaminated by the language and genre of the old.

The complicity of writing a history even in opposition to that which has been received becomes apparent in Henry Louis Gates's effort to generate a black literary theory that will empower a black literary history. The problem is to create a distinctive theory to serve the needs of a black audience.

> We must redefine "theory" itself from within our own black cultures, refusing to grant the racist premise that theory is something that white people do, so that we are doomed to imitate our white colleagues, like reverse black minstrel critics done up in white face. We are all heirs to critical theory, but we black critics are heir to the black vernacular critical tradition as well. Our task now is to invent and employ our own critical theory, to assume our own propositions, and to stand within the academy as politically responsible and responsive parts of a social and cultural African-American whole.[1]

Gates seeks to create a distinctive black literary history, but to do this he must establish a body of black writing about which a history can be written.

In order for this to happen, he must turn to bibliographical research and urge others to do so in order to provide necessary texts. We can thus note that the writing of a black literary history involves the following assumptions: the repressing, ignoring, disregarding a realm of texts by white historians. The history to be written will involve an exposure of texts that have been unknown or excluded from study and thus have not created a black literary consciousness. Such texts have to be uncovered, and black historians have to locate the texts for which a history can be written. Black historians are therefore involved in bibliographical studies pertinent to history no less than they are in expanding the notion of "text" to include oral as well as written expressions. And a black literary history must distinguish itself from a white history, despite the fact that they become entangled.

This distinction results in special problems for black theorists in proposing literary histories. They need to distinguish their history from that written for and by historians of the white majority. Yet such historians are often supporters and sometimes even leaders in opposing prejudice and oppression. Black critics who wish to establish a history of their own literature—with or without support from white critics—do so either by establishing a tradition within slavery or beyond national boundaries to a majority culture in Africa. This tradition can then be used to provide a continuity within the actual national history that is constructed.

Black historians and critics have to place this tradition within a history; they have to historicize tradition in contrast to T. S. Eliot and his followers who separate tradition from history. T. S. Eliot in "Tradition and the Individual Talent" defines tradition as a continuity that is changed by each great work—whatever such a work might be. History in no way impinges upon tradition, for the tradition transcends history. And the development of national historical conditions which alter the nature of writing does not result in altering judgments of literary value. But this separation of tradition from history and making the individual writer the continuator of the tradition no longer describes the condition governing either traditions or history.

For traditions do not exist in some transcendental realm but in genres which explain, as Eliot's essay does, what a specific tradition is. And as a kind of writing it inevitably carries ideological implications. For Eliot, it is tradition that involves the "historical sense."

> It involves, in the first place, the historical sense, which we may call nearly indispensable to any one who would continue to be a poet beyond his

twenty-fifth year; and the historical sense involves a perception, not only of the pastness of the past, but of its presence; the historical sense compels a man to write not merely with his own generation in his bones, but with a feeling that the whole of the literature of Europe from Homer and within it the whole of the literature of his own country has a simultaneous existence and composes a simultaneous order. This historical sense, which is a sense of the timeless as well as of the temporal and of the timeless and of the temporal together, is what makes a writer traditional. And it is at the same time what makes a writer most acutely conscious of his place in time, of his own contemporaneity.[2]

Eliot's description of tradition begins by insisting on a historical sense that a writer must possess, a feeling that the "whole of the literature of Europe from Homer and within it the whole of the literature of his own country has a simultaneous existence and composes a simultaneous order." The historical sense is both timeless and temporal, and it is a sense of the "whole" of literature whether of Europe or one's own country. It is not necessary to point to this Eurocentric view of tradition, nor is it necessary to indicate that new works are seen as conforming—though individually—to a tradition. What is important to note is that, for Eliot, a literary historical sense is never oppositional, nor does he see an opposition between alterity and contemporaneity or tradition and history. Tradition is the archetypal linear development.

Eliot's essay is not, however, without its oppositional function. But what he wishes to attack is not an exclusion but a mistake, one about the personality of the poet. For "the poet has, not a 'personality' to express, but a particular medium, which is only a medium and not a personality."[3] How this medium is generated has to do with a psychological theory, not the historical nature of discourses in society. Eliot's argument is far removed from a society divided by different discourses—political, social, philosophical—and by texts that resist the view of a single tradition. Far removed from Gates's need to find an appropriate language to develop a literary history that can empower it. Ideologically, Eliot's tradition transcends history. Eliot's severing of the "medium" from "personality" shrewdly separates the language of a text from the writer, but it continues to conceive of this medium as a single, unified entity.

I should point out that Eliot conceives of "generation" as the entire body of individuals born and living at about the same time. The historical sense functions as a coherent responsiveness, and we know that, in our country for example, this coherence no longer applies to the writings of males and females nor to the writings of minority authors.

I have been discussing the problems that black theorists and historians have had in generating distinctive literary histories. I have noted their search for a tradition that would serve as a basis for differentiation while making it possible for them to link a national literary history to African traditions. And it is this linkage that created the problem of the language of literary history, one that would distinguish it from a white history. But this posed a dilemma for literary theorists and historians: For whom was this history to be written and what language or languages would be appropriate for it? The histories that are being generated bear the marks of divided authority with regard to the language, audience, and ideological procedures that define "oppositional" literary history.

"Oppositional" literary history is not one phenomenon. One need only consider the writing of the New Historicists and the feminists. It is not even unified within each of these groups. For the New Historicists "oppositional" means not only an attack on a history that has suppressed texts or writers, but also an attack on an ideology that views history as a unity, as a harmony. The generation of new historicisms stems from opposition to received views of the relation of literary texts to society, especially the works of Shakespeare and other Renaissance writers. The so-called New Historicists deny the validity of formalist or New Critical analyses of Renaissance works and condemn the approaches that posit a unified Elizabethan world picture that explains literature as a direct reflection of a stable society.

The New Historicists are themselves responding to a historical moment of dissention, disaffection, deconstruction in our society and in our discipline. This disaffection has led them to emphasize subversions in literary texts and to see such texts as unstable arenas of power conflicts. This is not, it should be noted, the attitude of black critics to black writing. Renaissance studies have become the chief areas of New Historicists' inquiries because our greatest writer—Shakespeare—has been our authorized canonical author; and if his texts can be shown to represent ideological, that is, political power, conflicts, a case can be made for reconceiving the entire English canon. Thus these critics pose a challenge to all other scholars to reconsider their historical concepts and practices.

I do not believe that the "generation" of New Historicists can be identified with any one practice, but it is possible to identify the naming of this group. In 1982 Stephen Greenblatt introduced a selection of essays by stating that "many of the present essays *give voice,* I think, to what one may call the New Historicism, set apart from both the dominant historical scholarship of the past (in Renaissance Studies) and the formalist criticism that partially displaced this scholarship after World War II."[4] The *voices,* as Louis Montrose has pointed out, are less a choral movement than a symphonic orchestration, less a movement than an orientation. Those who are called or who call themselves "New Historicists" often operate with diverse, sometimes even contradictory, hypotheses.

But all New Historicists are intent on abandoning the historical procedures in Renaissance studies developed by Eustace Tillyard, by Douglas Bush, by Helen Gardner, by Lily Bess Campbell and to substitute historical procedures that characterize society as unstable and disunified by power struggle. As Montrose has pointed out: "In Renaissance literary studies, 'history' has traditionally meant the literary and intellectual histories that, in combination with the techniques of close reading . . . misrecognize[s] the dominant ideology of the Tudor-Stuart society [defining it] . . . as a stable, coherent, and collective Elizabethan world picture, a picture lucidly produced in the canonical literary works of the age."[5]

Montrose and Greenblatt find that Renaissance literature indicates an unstable society, revealing explicit or implicit strategies of subversion, conflicts, struggles for power. For them literary texts are not mere reflections of historical facts but highly complex social products related to other forms of social production. Literary texts have aesthetic possibilities but these are linked to the "complex network of institutions, practices, beliefs that constitute the culture as a whole." Above all, New Historicists seek to erode the assumed stable ground of literary works by treating them as places of dissention and shifting interests, occasions for the jostling of orthodox and subversive impulses.

Renaissance writers and critics make no special distinction between a literary and a nonliterary language. Thus, history or philosophy, religious sermons or tracts, poems and plays can be referred to in similar terms. As is sometimes noted, the word "literary" came into use late in the eighteenth century as referring to writings distinguished by their form. But even as late as the 1785 edition of Johnson's *Dictionary,* "literary" is defined with reference to learning: "Respecting letters; regarding learning. *Literary History* is an account of the state of learning and of the lives of learned men. *Literary* conversation is talk about the questions of learning."[6] And "literature" is defined as "learning; skill in letters." It thus seems reasonable to assume that "literature" through the eighteenth century retained its meaning as a part of culture and included what we now identify as nonliterary works.

The New Historicists are prepared to grant that for different centuries we need different "histories"; they are even prepared to argue that there is no one history for Renaissance studies but many histories. But what precisely do they take "history" to be? Although there is no one view of "history" that all New Historicists espouse, most agree that texts are produced at a particular time by particular authors using genres that are socially and culturally conditioned. With regard to social conditioning, disagreement occurs even among New Historicists, because the views that they espouse are drawn from diverse sources. Some New Historicists see texts as emphasizing "the possibilities of subversion of the dominant ideology";[7] others emphasize the hegemonic capacity of the dominant ideology to contain and control subversive moves.

This notion of different histories for different times is not an issue for black historians, since their desire is to create a history in which traditions can have some continuity. The question whether a different kind of history is necessary for slave narratives or the Harlem Renaissance seems an irrelevant question, since no critic would deny that this period created writings that differ from earlier kinds. But such differences do not erase the dominance of similarities.

New Historicists draw upon the ideological studies of members of the Marxist revisionist Frankfurt school, draw upon the works of established Marxists and anthropologists. Stephen Greenblatt, in his seminal historical study—*Renaissance Self-Fashioning* (1980)—entitles one of his chapters "The Work of God in the Age of Mechanical Reproduction" after Walter Benjamin's essay "The Work of Art in the Age of Mechanical Reproduction." The influential study *Dialectic of Enlightenment,* by Adorno and Horkheimer, indicts the ideological premises of the Enlightenment for subverting the practices of reason that it sought to defend.

Some New Historicists derive their views of history from Foucault's studies of power. Others derive their views of contradictions within a text from Derrida. But it is the Marxist works of Raymond Williams—especially *Marxism and Literature* and *The Country and the City*—and those of Fredric Jameson that have proved especially valuable in shaping the historical views of the New Historicists. Still, it is only appropriate to note that while Greenblatt and Montrose are not dependent upon a theory of class struggle, the Marxists are. Not only does Jameson insist on his slogan "Only historicize!" but in his essay on *Paradise Lost* he urges that "we must learn to read theological discourse and discursive production related to it, such as Milton's Christian epic, in terms of class struggle."[8] These views seem more appropriate to the writings of Jonathan Dollimore and Alan Sinfield—British Marxist scholars often called New Historicists (they prefer the name "cultural materialists")—than to the writings of the Americans.

It is simple enough to suggest that the British historicists write in opposition to a government policy that has seriously damaged the prospects of humanities education in universities. The turn to Marxist hypotheses can deliberately challenge the stability of such a society by suggesting that no society is stable, not even that of Shakespeare. But American New Historicists have quite other sources for the generation of their histories. They write in opposition to the modernist separation of literary language from ordinary language. Their argument is that so-called literary texts are expressed in language that characterizes the language of politics and the state. They resist modernist aesthetic criteria and find in religious and political texts aesthetic functions previously disregarded. They are against views of textual holism and in this respect align themselves with Foucault and Derrida. But they are not ready to become complete relativists, since they would then have to assume that their own discourses are as unstable as those of Renaissance writers.

Montrose offers as a New Historical chiastic slogan "the historicity of texts and the textuality of history." For him this formulation emphasizes the "dynamic, unstable, and reciprocal relationship between the discursive and the material domains."[9] What this means for the study of Renaissance texts is that the critic draws attention to the reciprocal and unbalanced relations within a text and relates them in sophisticated ways to imbalances, oppressions, and division within the social order. However, both Greenblatt and Montrose eschew imposing generalizations about class struggle, preferring to argue that subversive moments are often coopted into the dominant ideology. In this respect Montrose shrewdly notes the possibility that the New Historicism may itself be coopted into the dominant academic ideology, and that academic discussions will domesticate New Historicism either by demonstrating that we already have it or that it can readily be appropriated merely as another point of view. He writes that "predictably, English (British) 'cultural materialism' . . . remains a marginal academic discourse, whereas American 'New Historicism' is on its way to becoming the newest academic orthodoxy—not so much a critique as a subject of academic appropriation."[10]

No one in our time can neglect the irony of Montrose's remark that the academy can readily coopt any oppositional theory or history into the dominant academic ideology. Gates has made his own view clear in this regard, although it remains a paradox. And most feminist critics and historians are themselves institutionally based and this delimits both their vocabulary and their contribution to the larger nonacademic audiences they wish to change. This paradox is nowhere more obvious than in the university classroom where students are confronted by different literary perspectives and vocabularies. In such an environment, oppositional critics often find themselves welcomed into mainstream departments and find that some of their oppositional vocabulary is appropriated by theorists and historical critics who do not see themselves as oppositional.

I have been describing the generation of some contemporary literary histories and I have been trying to indicate the reasons for the generation of the New Historicists. But it is necessary to raise questions about the relation of theory to literary history, especially since the New Historicists have, as yet, no full-fledged theory of history. What function does theory serve in the generation of literary history? I have given an example of theory generating black history and the generation of literary history from political dissent by the New Historicists, and I shall be talking about the generation of literary history by feminist historians. However, the audiences for these histories are in the academy, and this is the arena at present for a debate between those who believe that literary history inevitably involves theory and those who deny that literary theory is of significance in the writing of literary history. Gerald Graff argues for theory as follows: "Whatever a teacher says about a literary work, or leaves unsaid, presupposes a theory—of what literature is or can be, of which literary works are worth teaching and why, of how these works should be read and which of their aspects are most worth being noticed and pointed out."[11] And this *resistance* to theory, to altering received formulations or practices, is also found among art historians. Rosalind Krauss notes this resistance: "Art historians are shy of theory, rarely enunciating the ones they must undoubtedly have in order to be able to work at all. Theories of historical change. Theories of continuity. Theories of representation. Theories of the role of form. Theories of referentiality. Theories of function. And most important, theories of verification. For art history is proud of its roots in the German soil of *Wissenschaft,* even before that of *Geschichte.*"[12]

What is meant by the statement that "whatever a teacher says about a literary work, or leaves unsaid, presupposes a theory"? Does theory need to be an overt constituent of history writing or is it that the making of statements about literature presupposes some theory about such statement making? Is the *consciousness* of theoretical statements necessary for the writing of literary history? The very fact that some literary and art historians do not include theorizing in their essays, as these quotations make clear, does not invalidate the statements they make. The selection of texts to discuss in class may be the result of an established curriculum that may or may not have had conscious theorizing behind it.

When Rosalind Krauss remarks that art historians rarely enunciate the theories they "must undoubtedly have in order to be able to work at all," she is implying that their theories ought to be enunciated. But such demands of historians raise questions about the nature of history writing. Must a *necessary* component of history writing be a consciousness of the grounds of history writing? Not if we realize that we are dealing with a generic problem. History is a kind of writing and so, too, is theory. There is no reason why theory should not be a component of history or history of theory, since all genres are combinational. What we wish to know is whether histories *must* include theoretical discourses. After all, history was combined with romance in the seventeenth century and with biography in the eighteenth—as witness *The History of Tom Jones.*

Literary histories are altered by the introduction of different discourses within them. Feminist discussions of literary history can include autobiographical statements, assumptions about race, gender, and class, about ideology and value. History writing has not only come to include ideological components, but personal statements as well. Since the generation of current histories is my subject, I want to suggest that genre and gender have generated conceptions of history that are ideologically connected with political and sexual theories. For example, Jane Tompkins's version of this history is polemical rather than self-assured, assertive about the need to resurrect feminine texts excluded from American literature. She writes in opposition not only to patriarchal history but to received views of literary value as well. In "*Uncle Tom's Cabin* and the Politics of Literary History," she declares:

> Expressive of and responsible for the values of its time, it also belongs to a genre, the sentimental novel, whose chief characteristic is that it is written by, for, and about women. In this respect, *Uncle Tom's Cabin* is not exceptional but representative. It is the *summa theologica* of nineteenth-century America's religion of domesticity, a brilliant redaction of the culture's favorite story about itself—the story of salvation through motherly love. Out of the ideological materials at their disposal, the sentimental novelists elaborated a myth that gave women the central position of power and authority in the culture; and of these efforts *Uncle Tom's Cabin* is the most dazzling exemplar.[13]

In reading *Uncle Tom's Cabin* "as a political enterprise, halfway between sermon and social theory, that both codifies and attempts to mold the values of its time," she introduces a combinatory regeneration of the novel form that makes it a model for the kind of history she is writing. She writes with fervor, and anger, and she has generated other feminist histories. If history writing is a genre, then it is obvious that members of this genre will add or omit components from preceding histories. What identifies it as history is that it tells a story of actual events in a structure that resembles prior versions of such storytelling. Thus, when Tompkins seeks to displace the literary history of F. O. Matthiessen, her history is more like his than it is like *Uncle Tom's Cabin* about which she writes. She introduces into her discussion elements from sermons and household texts—not discussed by Matthiessen—to demonstrate that Little Eva's death, for example, "enacts the drama of which all the major episodes of the novel are transformations, the idea, central to Christian soteriology, that the highest human calling is to give one's life for another."[14] Her history is generated not merely by her sense of the deprivation resulting from the exclusion of feminist writing from the canon, but from her disagreement with some of the assumptions of the received historical genre in which she continues to write.

The resistance to the received view of a genre, I want to argue, generates alterations within it. It is not merely personal resentment or social and economic or literary exclusion or the class opposition, but the omission or addition of components that lead to alterations of writing. This conflict within a genre, this expansion of literary history to include sermons and popular literature, also establishes new relations among the genres. Clifford Geertz notes that histories have begun to include equations and tables and law court testimonies and are thus ceasing to be straightforward narratives. Reflecting on the generic changes in anthropological treatises in which theoretical arguments by Lévi-Strauss are set out as travelogues (*Tristes Tropiques*), Geertz believes that a refiguration of knowledge is taking place, a change in what it is we want to know. But genre has never been the fixed form Geertz and others have taken it to be. The extension of literary history by conflicts within the genre and with other genres for primacy has begun to diminish the significance of theory even for those who include it; and theory itself as a genre has come in the work of Richard Rorty to be narrativized as fiction. What these regenerated genres do is to make us question the generic combinations we have come to accept, and our consciousness of history as a given. In fact, one of the most prominent examples of regeneration in history writing is

Hayden White's. For him history becomes a form of literary history. His argument is as follows: "It is because historical discourse utilizes structures of meaning-production found in their purest forms in literary fictions that modern literary theory, and especially those versions of it oriented towards tropological conceptions of language, discourse, and textuality, is immediately relevant to contemporary theory of historical writing."[15] White points out that theorists of historical discourse cannot ignore literary theorists' new conception of language, speech, and textuality because these have "reproblematized an area of inquiry which, in historical theory at least, had for too long been treated as having nothing problematical about it." The new views of language in literary theory are far from definitive, involving disagreements about the indeterminacy of language, the nature of its acculturation, the interaction between grammar and rhetoric, the distinction between literary and nonliterary language.

But insofar as literary theory is a discourse about discourses, it inevitably analyzes the discourses of history and is, therefore, for White a theory of history as well as of literature. In White's terms, "modern literary theory must of necessity be a theory of history, historical consciousness, historical discourse, and historical writing." The different components of literary theory extend like a web through White's version of history, which obviously is at the opposite pole from those historians who resist theory in history writing.

White conceives of history as narrative and takes for granted that no unmediated — objective — history exists. As a narrative it involves a plot and falls into one of the four types of plots that White envisions. White interprets history writing as a literary structure, since the narrative is composed of facts. Insofar as these are imaginatively plotted, they deny both the objectivity of history and its arbitrariness. It is apparent, however, that White's narratives are coherent rather than examples of aporias. But there is no reason to assume that history as literary history need be one single discourse. It can be structured with intersections from psychoanalytic or Marxist narratives.

What does this story of generic generation have to say about the role of literary history in our understanding of past texts? It compels us to see literary history as a series of transformations derived from generic intersections, conflicts, and oppositions. It provides an awareness of literary history as necessarily involving ideological conflicts, since genres as they change nevertheless have some continuous elements. These are ideologically discontinuous with the additions that literary history includes. One might say that the different discourses in literary history are often at odds with each other. But more problematic is White's claim that history is a fictional genre. A history of the French revolution is indeed like a history of the novel. But both histories are more like other histories than like poems, plays, or acts of violence. Literary history, therefore, can contain selections from the interpretations of fictive genres but these are subservient to the ends of history.

The generations of literary history that I have been describing, the shifting conceptions of genre, compel us to ask as Geertz does what such formulations imply. Literary history as genre is obviously connected with social change, as in the effort to provide blacks with pride in their tradition, women with a new view of the importance of feminine bonding, minority readers with a consciousness of their exploitation, majorities with a sense of shame and guilt for their exploitation of others. The social aims are linked to identifying new relations among texts, including texts that have never been considered worthy of study. Oral texts are part of literary history including the lyrics of ballads and of contemporary songs by various rock groups. Literary history includes the study of publishing practices, editors' revisions of manuscripts, the selection of books to print for profit, the incorporation of publishing into conglomerates that produce books, oil, and cereals. The commodification of books in our time has led critics to recognize ideology where previously was found individual creativity. The varieties of literary history, whether by contending black critics or feminist critics or Marxist critics or psychoanalytic critics, reveal how exclusive has been the literary history we have been teaching, for the audiences for literary history are primarily to be found in the institutions of learning where new histories and old histories still exist door by door.

It is sad to read that our most eminent historian of literary criticism, René Wellek, surveying his own work and the current scene, sees "the fall of literary history."

> The new literary history promises only a return to the old one: the history of tradition, genres, reputations, etc., less atomistically conceived as in older times, with greater awareness of the difficulties of such concepts as influence and periods but still the old one.
>
> Possibly, this is a good and right thing. The attempts at an evolutionary history have failed. I myself have failed in *The History of Modern Criticism* to construe a convincing scheme of development. I discovered, by experience, that there is no evolution in the history of critical argument, that the history of criticism is rather a series of debates on recurrent concepts, on

"essentially contested concepts," on permanent problems in the sense that they are with us even today. Possibly, a similar conclusion is required for the history of poetry itself. "Art," said Schopenhauer, "has always reached its goal." Croce and Ker are right. There is no progress, no development, no history of art except a history of writers and institutions or techniques. This is, at least for me, the end of an illusion, the fall of literary history.[16]

But the assumption that literary history was teleological in an evolutionary sense was a mistake to begin with. The discourses of literary history as a genre should compel us to extend our understanding of what is at stake in the shifting components of a genre. We realize now how inadequate a conception of literature is that takes no account of paintings that include writing or illustrate writing, that disregards the music in sung prayers and oratorios, that sees no relation between Descartes's *Meditations* and the meditative poem or Shaftesbury's and Mandeville's dialogues and the development of the novel, between the narratives of criminals and the parodies of affairs of state.

When we consider the mixed media of fiction and television that no longer privilege words but connect them with images of the body and of the environment and with music, we realize how exclusive our histories of literature have been in ignoring the body in writing. No user of word processors can ignore the physiological role one feels in writing or in the order that appears on the screen shielding the disorder of one's thoughts. The generation of new literary histories opens for us the multiform nature of generation: a literary history possesses vestiges of past histories in a contemporary narrative, a narrative that is knowledgeable about past histories; knowledgeable about such generic practices as the ingestion of other genres for ideological purposes, their borrowings or claims to be what they are not to make the unacceptable respectable, the undermining of social practices by romance strategies. Interrelations revealed by past work result in literary genres shaping the consciousness of readers by avoiding or ignoring authors' autobiographical statements about their aims or ideological strategies such as inset stories or sermons or sermonic procedures. Generating such literary histories makes us conscious that while much of history is unrecoverable, much remains to be discovered. But this discovery may need to be done, if it is to reach beyond the classroom, to a history that includes sounds and sights.

I conclude by returning to the generation of this essay, to the theories of the Algerian Jew that I related to place, exclusion, and colonization. No single statement about ideology or theory or tradition can adequately account for a literary history linked with genres that complicate social aims with autobiographical memories and generic competitions. I ask you to listen to the voice of another Algerian Jew, Hélène Cixous, describing a history of her writing. I do this to illustrate that her history is not one of alienation or resentment, but of love of words, place, and gender. Her writing became intertwined with herself and the Other; it became part of her body, her family, her culture, her ethnic identity, her gender, her sense of alienation, and her awareness of mysteries beyond language. Hers is an autobiographical literary history that reveals to us the possibilities we have missed and the opportunities we have before us.

> My writing was born in Algeria out of a lost country of the dead father and the foreign mother. Each of these traits which may seem to be chance or mischance became the causes and opportunities of my writings.
>
> I have had the luck to have foreignness, exile, war, the phantom memory of peace, mourning and pain as the place and time of my birth. At the age of three I knew, among the flowers and their scents, that one could kill for a name, for a difference. And I knew that uprooting existed. But also good uprooting. I should give you a date as well, 1940 for instance. I saw that human roots know no borders and that under the earth, at the very bottom of the ladder of the world, the heart was beating.
>
> My first others were the Arabs, the scarabaei, the French, the Germans. My first familiars were the hens, the rabbits, the Arabs, the Germans, etc.
>
> And the tongue that was singing in my ears? It was languages: Spanish, Arabic, German, French. Everything on this earth comes from far off, even what is very near. I listened to all the languages. I sang in German. I also cackled with the hens. I lost myself often within the city of my birth. I was a veiled woman: it was a signifier. It was ORAN. I had everything:
>
> OR-AN — HORS EN — ORAN-JE
> (Golden-year) (Outside-in) (Oran-I: Orange)
>
> The first of my treasures was the name of my native city which was Oran. It was my first lesson. I heard the name Oran and through Oran I entered the secret of language. My "sortie" occurred through entrance. I discovered that my city meant *fruit* through the simple addition of me. *Oran-je—Orange*. I discovered that the word held all the mystery of fruit. I will let you unravel to infinity the composition, decomposition of this name. Then I lost Oran. Then I recovered it, white, gold, and dust for eternity in my memory and I never went back. In order to keep it. It became my writing. Like my father. It became a magic door opening onto the other world.[17]

NOTES

1. Henry Louis Gates Jr., "Authority, (White) Power, and the (Black) Critic; or, It's All Greek to Me," in *The Future of Literary Theory*, ed. Ralph Cohen (New York: Routledge, 1989), 344.

2. T. S. Eliot, "Tradition and the Individual Talent," in *Selected Essays of T. S. Eliot* (New York: Harcourt, Brace, and World, 1964), 4.

3. Eliot, "Tradition," 9.

4. Stephen J. Greenblatt, Introduction to "The Forms of Power and the Power of Forms in the Renaissance," special issue, *Genre* 15 (1982): 1-2.

5. Louis Montrose, "Renaissance Literary Studies and the Subject of History," *English Literary Renaissance* 16 (1986): 6.

6. Samuel Johnson, *A Dictionary of the English Language* (London, 1755).

7. Montrose, "Renaissance Literary Studies," 10. Montrose is discussing the work of Jonathan Dollimore and Alan Sinfield.

8. Fredric Jameson, *The Political Unconscious* (Ithaca, NY: Cornell Univ. Press, 1981), 9; and Jameson, "Religion and Ideology: A Political Reading of *Paradise Lost*," in *Literature, Politics and Theory: Papers from the Essex Conference 1976-1984*, ed. Frances Barker, Peter Hulme, Margaret Iversen, and Diana Loxley (London: Methuen, 1986), 39.

9. Montrose, "Renaissance Literary Studies," 8. Montrose has expanded his discussion in "Professing the Renaissance: The Poetics and Politics of Culture," in *The New Historicism*, ed. H. Aram Veeser (New York: Methuen, 1989), 15-36.

10. Montrose, "Renaissance Literary Studies," 7n4. Montrose is contrasting the work of American New Historicists such as himself and Greenblatt with the work of British cultural materialists such as Dollimore and Sinfield who owe a major debt to Raymond Williams.

11. Gerald Graff, "The Future of Theory in the Teaching of Literature," in Cohen, *The Future of Literary Theory*, 250.

12. Rosalind Krauss, "The Future of an Illusion," in Cohen, *The Future of Literary Theory*, 281.

13. Jane Tompkins, *Sensational Designs: The Cultural Work of American Fiction 1790-1860* (New York: Oxford Univ. Press, 1985), 124-25.

14. Tompkins, *Sensational Designs*, 128.

15. Hayden White, "'Figuring the Nature of the Times Deceased': Literary Theory and History Writing," in Cohen, *The Future of Literary Theory*, 36.

16. René Wellek, "The Fall of Literary History," in *The Attack on Literature and Other Essays* (Chapel Hill: Univ. of North Carolina Press, 1982), 77.

17. Hélène Cixous, "From the Scene of the Unconscious to the Scene of History," in Cohen, *The Future of Literary Theory*, 2.

Bibliography of Ralph Cohen's Essays

1951

"Introduction." *Essays on Taste,* by John Gilbert Cooper (1757) and John Armstrong (1770), ed. Ralph Cohen, Augustan Reprint Society, publication no. 30. Los Angeles: William Andrews Clark Memorial Library. i-v.

1954

Review of *The Mirror and the Lamp: Romantic Theory and the Critical Tradition,* by M. H. Abrams. *Philological Quarterly* 33, no. 3: 241-43.

Review of *Theories of Pastoral Poetry in England,* by J. E. Congleton. *Journal of Aesthetics and Art Criticism* 12, no. 3: 400-401.

Reviews of *David Hume on Criticism,* by Teddy Brunius; and *Hume's Intentions,* by J. A. Passmore. *Review of English Studies* 5, no. 18: 197-200.

1957

"S. T. Coleridge and William Sotheby's Orestes." *Modern Language Review* 52, no. 1: 19-27.

"Private Eyes and Public Critics." *Partisan Review* 24, no. 2: 235-43.

Review of *The Diction of Poetry from Spenser to Bridges,* by Bernard Groom. *Philological Quarterly* 36, no. 3: 323-24.

"Association of Ideas and Poetic Unity." *Philological Quarterly* 36, no. 4: 465-74.

1958

Review of *The Beautiful, the Sublime, and the Picturesque in Eighteenth-Century Aesthetic Theory,* by Walter J. Hipple Jr. *Philological Quarterly* 37, no. 3: 291-94.

"The Treachery of Sincerity." Reviews of *Religion and the Rebel,* by Colin Wilson; and *Emergence from Chaos,* by Stuart Holroyd. *Kenyon Review* 20, no. 3: 488-93.

"David Hume's Experimental Method and the Theory of Taste." *English Literary History* 25, no. 4: 270-89.

BIBLIOGRAPHY

1960

"Cannibalization of Art." Review of *On Art and Artists,* by Aldous Huxley. *New Leader* 43, no. 48: 17-18.

1961

"Philosophy and Criticism: The Challenge of Discipline." Advancement of Learning Lecture Series, Univ. of Utah, March 10.
Review of *The Varied God: A Critical Study of Thomson's "The Seasons,"* by P. M. Spacks. *Modern Language Notes* 76, no. 8: 875-79.

1962

"Literary Criticism and Artistic Interpretation: Eighteenth-Century English Illustrations of *The Seasons.*" *Reason and the Imagination: Studies in the History of Ideas, 1600-1800,* ed. J. A. Mazzeo. New York: Columbia Univ. Press; London: Routledge. 279-306.
"The Transformation of Passion: A Study of Hume's Theories of Tragedy." *Philological Quarterly* 41, no. 2: 450-64.

1965

Introduction to *Essential Works of David Hume,* ed. Ralph Cohen. New York: Bantam Books. 1-30. Edition includes prefaces to various of Hume's works.
"Games and Growing Up: A Key to Understanding *Huckleberry Finn.*" Introduction to *The Adventures of Huckleberry Finn,* ed. Ralph Cohen. New York: Bantam Books. 282-91.

1967

"The Augustan Mode in English Poetry." *Eighteenth-Century Studies* 1, no. 1: 3-32.
"Thomson's Poetry of Space and Time." *Studies in Criticism and Aesthetics, 1660-1800, Essays in Honor of Samuel Holt Monk,* ed. Howard Anderson and John S. Shea. Minneapolis: Univ. of Minnesota Press. 176-92.

1968

"An Introduction to *The Seasons.*" *Southern Review* 3, no. 1: 56-66.
Reviews of *Language of Fiction: Essays in Criticism and Verbal Analysis of the English Novel,* by David Lodge; and *The Sense of an Ending: Studies in the Theory of Fiction,* by Frank Kermode. *Nineteenth-Century Fiction* 23, no. 1: 104-9.

Introduction to "Literary and Artistic Change in the Eighteenth Century," special issue, ed. Ralph Cohen. *Eighteenth-Century Studies* 2, no. 1: 1-6.

1969

"A Guide through the Sensory Mazes." Review of *Through the Vanishing Point: Space in Poetry and Painting*, by Marshall McLuhan and Harley Parker. *Virginia Quarterly Review* 45, no. 1: 162-67.
"'Spring': The Love Song of James Thomson." *Texas Studies in Literature and Language* 11, no. 3: 1107-82.
"Transformation in *The Rape of the Lock*." *Eighteenth-Century Studies* 2, no. 3: 205-24.
"A Note on *New Literary History*." *New Literary History* 1, no. 1: 3-6.

1972

"The Reversal of Gender in *The Rape of the Lock*." *South Atlantic Bulletin* 37, no. 4: 54-60.
Introduction to "Symposium: Irrationalism in the Eighteenth Century." *Irrationalism in the Eighteenth Century*, ed. Harold E. Pagliaro. Studies in Eighteenth-Century Culture, vol. 2. Papers presented at the second annual meeting of the American Society for Eighteenth-Century Studies. Cleveland, OH: Case Western Reserve Univ. Press. 223-24.

1973

"The Aesthetic Aspects of Literary History." *Neohelicon* 1, nos. 1-2: 44-51.
"Not So Very New." Review of *Toward a New Historicism*, by Wesley Morris. *Virginia Quarterly Review* 49, no. 1: 157-60.

1974

"Innovation and Variation: Literary Change and Georgic Poetry." *Literature and History: Papers Read at a Clark Library Seminar, March 3, 1973*, by Ralph Cohen and Murray Krieger. Los Angeles: William Andrews Clark Memorial Library, Univ. of California. 1-42.
"On the Interrelations of Eighteenth-Century Literary Forms." *New Approaches to Eighteenth-Century Literature; Selected Papers from the English Institute*, ed. Phillip Harth. New York: Columbia Univ. Press. 33-78.
Introduction to *New Directions in Literary History*, ed. Ralph Cohen. Baltimore: Johns Hopkins Univ. Press. 1-10.

1975

"Literary Theory as a Genre." *Centrum: Working Papers of the Minnesota Center for Advanced Studies in Language, Style, and Literary Theory* 3, no. 1: 45-64.

"Innovation and Variation: A Problem in Literary History." *Studies in Eighteenth-Century Culture*, vol. 4, ed. Harold E. Pagliaro. Papers presented at the fourth annual meeting of the Society for Eighteenth-Century Studies, McMaster University, Hamilton, Ontario, May 7-9, 1973. Madison: Univ. of Wisconsin Press. 297-315.

1976

"On a Shift in the Concept of Interpretation." *The New Criticism and After, John Crowe Ransom Memorial Lectures 1975, Delivered at Kenyon College on April 3-5*, ed. Thomas Daniel Young. Charlottesville: Univ. Press of Virginia. 61-79.

"The Rationale of Hume's Literary Inquiries." *Southwestern Journal of Philosophy* 7, no. 2 (1976): 97-115. Also published in *David Hume: Many-Sided Genius*, ed. Kenneth R. Merrill and Robert W. Shahan. Norman: Univ. of Oklahoma Press. 97-115.

1977

"George Sherburn: Continuity and Definition." *Scriblerian* 9, no. 2: 83-85.

"Pope's Meanings and the Strategies of Interrelation." *English Literature in the Age of Disguise*, ed. Maximillian Novak. Berkeley: Univ. of California Press. 101-30.

1978

"Introduction: Remarks on Formalist and Hermeneutic Features of the Conference Papers." *Interpretation of Narrative*, ed. Mario J. Valdés and Owen J. Miller. Papers read at the International Colloquium on Interpretation of Narrative held at the University of Toronto, March 24-27, 1976. Toronto: Univ. of Toronto Press. 3-7.

"Historical Knowledge and Literary Understanding." *Papers on Language and Literature* 14:227-48.

1979

"On a Decade of *New Literary History*." "Journals about Journals," ed. Paul Hernadi, special issue, *Bulletin of the Midwest Modern Language Association* 12, no. 1: 3-10.

"The Function of Literary Study for the Humanities." *Images and Innovations: Update '70's*, ed. Malinda R. Maxfield. Papers of the 1979 Southern Humanities Conference, Center for the Humanities. Spartanburg, SC: Converse College. 140-57.

"Some Thoughts on the Problems of Literary Change 1750-1800." *Dispositio* (ESSAYS) 4, nos. 11-12: 145-62.

1981

"Secondary Characters and the Structure of *Joseph Andrews*." Paper presented at the annual meeting of the Modern Language Association to the panel "The Implications of the Arrangement and Distribution of Secondary Characters in *Don Quixote* for the Structure of the Novel," December 28, 1979. Published in a festschrift for Vida E. Markovic, ed. Sonja Janoski, University of Nis, Serbia.

1982

Review of *The Creative Imagination: Enlightenment to Romanticism*, by James Engell. *Criticism* 24, no. 2: 174-80.
"Abraham Rothberg's Moral Vision." Review of *The Four Corners of the House*, by Abraham Rothberg. *Virginia Quarterly Review* 58, no. 3: 548-55.
"The Statements Literary Texts Do Not Make." *New Literary History* 13, no. 3: 379-91.

1983

"John Dryden's Literary Criticism." *New Homage to John Dryden: Papers Read at a Clark Library Conference, February 13-14, 1981*, by Phillip Harth, Alan Fisher, and Ralph Cohen. Los Angeles: William Andrews Clark Memorial Library. 59-86.
"A Propaedeutic for Literary Change." *Society for Critical Exchange Reports* 13:1-23. Reprinted, with guest editor's preface and seven commentaries, *Critical Exchange* 13 (Spring): 1-17.
"The Joys and Sorrows of Literary Theory." *Innovation/Renovation: New Perspectives on the Humanities,* ed. Ihab Hassan and Sally Hassan. Madison: Univ. of Wisconsin Press. 111-30.

1984

"The Impact of Changes in Scholarship in the Humanities upon Research Libraries." *Advances in Library Administration and Organization* 3:271-76.
"Blake Nevius: An Appreciation." Special issue dedicated to Blake Nevius, *Nineteenth-Century Fiction* 38, no. 4: 377-83.

1985

"Afterword: The Problems of Generic Transformation." *Romance: Generic Transformation from Chrétien de Troyes to Cervantes,* ed. Kevin Brownlee and Marina Scordilis Brownlee. Hanover, NH: Univ. Press of New England. 265-80.
Introduction to *Studies in Eighteenth-Century British Art and Aesthetics,* ed. Ralph Cohen. Berkeley and Los Angeles: Univ. of California Press. 1-15.

BIBLIOGRAPHY

"Literary History and the Ballad of George Barnwel." *Augustan Studies: Essays in Honor of Irvin Ehrenpreis,* ed. Douglas Lane Patey and Timothy Keegan. Newark, NJ: Univ. of Delaware Press. 13-31.

1986

"Commentary." *Society for Critical Exchange Reports,* "Institutional Issues in the Humanities," 19:56-62. Part of a three-day conference, "The Ends of the Humanities: Redefinitions," held at the Univ. of Miami, October 1984. "Roundtable on Institutional Issues in the Humanities" was held October 21.

"History and Genre." *Neohelicon* 13, no. 2: 87-105; *New Literary History* 17, no. 2: 203-18.

"The Aims and Roles of *New Literary History.*" *The Yearbook of English Studies: Literary Periodicals,* ed. C. J. Rawson. Literary Periodicals Special Number 16. 177-87.

1987

"The Fictions of Rhetoric." *The History and Philosophy of Rhetoric and Political Discourse,* ed. Kenneth W. Thompson. Miller Center for Public Affairs, Univ. of Virginia, November 12, 1985. Lanham, MD: Univ. Press of America. 1:83-101.

"Reviewing Criticism: Literary Theory." *Literary Reviewing,* ed. James O. Hoge. Charlottesville: Univ. Press of Virginia. 1-18.

"Do Postmodern Genres Exist?" *Genre* 20, nos. 3-4: 241-57. Reprinted in *Postmodern Genres,* ed. Marjorie Perloff. Norman: Univ. of Oklahoma Press, 1989. 85-113.

1988

"Generic Sites and Literary Criticism." *Hebrew University Studies in Literature and the Arts* 16:215-40.

1989

Introduction to *The Future of Literary Theory,* ed. Ralph Cohen. New York: Routledge. vii-xx. Reprinted 2017 in the series Routledge Library Editions: Literary Theory, with prefatory note by John L. Rowlett.

1990

"Notes on the Teaching of Eighteenth-Century Poetry of Natural Description." *Teaching Eighteenth-Century Poetry,* ed. Christopher Fox. New York: AMS Press. 75-102.

1991

"Genre Theory, Literary History, and Historical Change." *Theoretical Issues in Literary History,* ed. David Perkins. Harvard English Studies 16. Cambridge, MA: Harvard Univ. Press. 85-113. Translation by Jesús Lázaro Garía in *Teorías de la historia literaria,* ed. Luis Beltrán Almería and José Antonio Escrig. Madrid: ARCO/LIBROS, 2005. 221-52.

1992

"Introduction: On Studies of Historical Continuity and Change." *Studies in Historical Change,* ed. Ralph Cohen. Charlottesville: Univ. Press of Virginia. 1-17.

1993

"Generating Literary Histories." *New Historical Literary Study: Essays on Reproducing Texts, Representing History,* ed. Jeffrey N. Cox and Larry J. Reynolds. Princeton, NJ: Princeton Univ. Press. 39-53. Originally delivered at a conference held by the Interdisciplinary Group for Historical Literary Study, Texas A&M University, fall 1989.

1995

"Afterthoughts: Historical Intervention and the Writing of History." *History and . . . : Histories within the Human Sciences.* Charlottesville: Univ. Press of Virginia. 396-409.

2001

"The Return to the Ode." *The Cambridge Companion to Eighteenth-Century Poetry,* ed. John Sitter. Cambridge: Cambridge Univ. Press. 203-24.

2003

Introduction to "Theorizing Genres I." Special issue, *New Literary History* 34, no. 2: v-xv.

"Introduction: Notes toward a Generic Reconstitution of Literary Study." "Theorizing Genres II." Special issue, *New Literary History* 34, no. 3: v-xvi.

2008

Introduction to "Remembering Richard Rorty." *New Literary History* 39, no. 1: vii-xx.

Introduction to "Literary History in the Global Age." *New Literary History* 39, no. 3: vii-xx.

2009

"History and Change: An Interview with Ralph Cohen." By Jeffrey L. Williams. *New Literary History* 40, no. 4: 919-43.

"Notes for a History of *New Literary History*." *New Literary History* 40, no. 4: A1-A28.

Index

Abrams, Meyer H., 52-53, 58, 115, 129, 131, 245-46, 258, 281, 319-20, 332
Addison, Joseph, 7, 10, 24, 27-28, 31, 208, 213, 294-306, 334, 337, 343; on "Chevy Chase" ballad, 98, 101, 294-300, 301, 305, 347-49; *Spectator* 10, 9, 27; *Spectator* 69, 298, 349; *Spectator* 70, 297, 348; *Spectator* 74, 295, 296, 299, 348; *Spectator* 125, 28
Adorno, Theodor W., 364
Aeschylus, 177
age of sensibility, 248
Akenside, Mark, *The Pleasures of the Imagination*, 22, 28
Alison, Archibald, 345
allegory, 11, 25, 132, 164, 207, 320, 327, 332
Alpers, Paul, 196
Althusser, Louis, 145
Altieri, Charles, 79
Altman, Rick, 146-47, 167 n. 2
ambience of *concordia discors*, 197
Analytical Review, 129
Anderson, Perry, 315 n. 2
annihilation of history, 178
anthologies, 111, 117, 355
anthropology, 310, 364
anti-Semitism, 312
Apuleius, 277
Aristotle: aesthetic view of literature and, 248; as critical theorist, 53; on drama as apogee of literary forms, 40; on evolution of genres, 101; on *Iliad* and *Odyssey*, 222; literary theory and, 51, 52, 58-59, 63; on pleasure in imitation, 53-54; *Poetics*, 53-54, 58; on poetry vs. history, 263, 264; on tragedy and epics, 6, 89, 106, 108, 138, 154, 177, 292-93, 304
Armstrong, Nancy, 342, 343
Arnold, Matthew, 81
art history, 257, 366
association of ideas, 345
audience considerations. *See* readers
"Augustan Mode in English Poetry, The" (1967), xxv n. 16
Augustan writers, xxii, 8, 20, 22, 24-25, 28, 29, 210, 215, 249
Augustine, St., 197
Austen, Jane: *Emma*, 96; *Pride and Prejudice*, 155
authenticity, 305, 312-13, 355
authoritarianism, 175
authorship, 25, 27, 28, 346
autobiography: female/feminist, 149, 156, 158, 162-63, 168 n. 11; historical change and, 133; joining scientific genre to, 109, 310-11; literary history and, 358-59, 371-72; testimonies genre, 179-80

Babbitt, Irving, 108
Baker, Houston, 145
Bakhtin, Mikhail, xviii, 105, 108, 110, 139, 155-56, 273, 278, 339; *The Dialogic Imagination*, 145; *Speech Genres and Other Late Essays*, 145
ballad opera, as new genre, 301-2, 350-51
ballads, 96-98, 294; Addison writing first critique of, 294-300, 301, 305, 347-49, 356; authenticity of, 305; "The Ballad of George Barnwel," 96-99, 300, 302,

INDEX

ballads (*continued*)
304, 351, 355; "The Ballad of Jane Shore," 283, 300, 350; ballad parodies, 282; "Chevy Chase," 98, 101, 294-300, 301, 305, 347-49, 354, 355-56; Dennis's disagreement with Addison on, 299, 349-50; generic elevation of, 98, 294, 297, 301, 347-51; as genre of its own, 300; importation into other texts/genres, 96, 109, 160, 300, 303, 350-51, 354-55; literary history's inclusion of, 370; medieval ballads, 215, 294, 305; parodies of Addison's views on, 299-300, 350-51; Percy's publication of, 305, 354-56; as social constructions, 346-52; translation of, 300-301, 348; "Two Children in the Wood," 294
Barthes, Roland, 68, 118, 265, 312, 314
Bate, W. J., 129
Bazerman, Charles, 176, 184
behavior principles, 53, 225-26, 310
Bender, John, 341, 345-46
Benjamin, Walter, 274, 314, 364
Bensmaïa, Réda, 118
Bernal, J. D., 81
black literary theory and history, 165-66, 359-60, 364, 365; censorship of *Huckleberry Finn*, 175; exclusion from the canon, 370; generic analyses, 145, 148. *See also* slave narratives
Blair, Hugh, 10, 14, 24
Blake, William, 81, 249, 268, 319; "London," 243, 259-60
Blanchot, Maurice, 36-37, 113, 239
Bloom, Harold, xiii, 123, 127, 268, 301, 339; *Poetry and Repression*, 317-19, 332
Bloomsbury group, 265
Borges, Jorge Luis, 112
boundary crossing, 156-57, 289, 311
Bowen, C., 263
broadsides, 96-97
Brooks, Cleanth, 294
Brower, Reuben, 71-72, 79
Brown, Laura, 341, 342, 357 n. 6
Brown, Richard Harvey, 85, 100, 102
Brown, Robert, 80

Browning, Robert, 319
Brunetière, Ferdinand, 108
Bruss, Elizabeth, 93
Bunyan, John, 57, 132, 334, 337; Hume on, 334, 337
Burke, Kenneth, 70, 132
Bush, Douglas, 363
Butrym, Alexander J., 145
Byron, Lord (George Gordon), 134, 319

Cairns, Francis, 42, 222
Calinescu, Matei, 117
Calvino, Italo, 105, 155-56
Campbell, Lily Bess, 363
Caramello, Charles, 119 n. 7, 120 n. 15
Caribbean countries, 166
Carlyle, Thomas, 268
Cartland, Barbara, 162
censorship, 175, 225, 265, 288
Cervantes, Miguel de, *Don Quixote*, 278
Chalker, John, 208-9, 220 n. 23
Chandler, Raymond, 183
Chatterton, Thomas, 215
Chaucer, Geoffrey, 215
Chicago Critics, 127-28
children's stories, 294
Cicero, 55, 197
Civil War (English), 8, 192, 209, 223
Cixous, Hélène, xx, 168 n. 9, 372; "From the Scene of the Unconscious to the Scene of History," 156-59
Clarendon, Lord (Edward Ward), *The History of the Grand Rebellion*, 55
Clarey, Jo Ellyn, 145
Clark, John, 26
classics. *See* Augustan writers; Greek genres; Latin originals and translations; *specific Greek and Roman authors*
classifications: genres vs., 170; for great libraries, 177; purpose of using, 293. *See also* genres
Clive, John, 129
Cohen, Ralph: bibliography of essays by, ix, 375-82; characteristics of essays by, xxi; Cixous on editorship

384

of, xx; complicated nature of work of, xviii; as editor-teacher, xvii-xix, xxiii; as essayist-theorist, xvii-xviii; evolution of essays by, xxii; failure to collect essays into volumes, xi-xii, xvii, xxii; innovative conceptual features of, xiv-xv; pre-postmodern influences on, xiv; public delivery of papers or lectures by, xx; reasons for (re)publishing essays of, xi-xii, xxii-xxiii; self-effacement of, xviii, xxiii; as speaker and commentator, xvii; technological humanism of, xxiv; unpublished lectures of, ix, xi, xxii. See also *New Literary History*

Coleridge, Samuel Taylor, 58, 246, 250, 319

Colie, Rosalie, 5, 12, 106, 145, 147

collectivism, 74-75

Collins, William, 248

colloquium as example of history of a genre, 140-42

combination and intermixing of genres, xii-xiii; ballads mixed with other genres, 109, 160, 300, 302; blurring of genres, 108-9, 309-10, 313; combinatory genre theory, 111-12, 222, 292, 304; Derrida questioning, 100-101; in eighteenth century, 11, 14, 27-28, 31, 87, 344; Greenblatt on literary history's need to be open to, 310; in Homer, 106, 114; impossibility of studying genre without recognizing, 278, 295; lyric mixed with other genres, 10-11, 39, 96, 109; part-whole relationship and, 149-50; in Renaissance, 5, 6, 14, 24, 106, 139; Rorty on, 152; scientific genre joined to autobiography, 310-11

commentary, debate over status as genre, 174

communication, 137-44; colloquium as example of history of a genre, 140-42; meanings and mismeanings of, 138; nonverbal elements of, 138; television, generic approach to, 142-44

conceptual changes, 307-16; authenticity and, 312-13; borrowing from humanities and other disciplines, 310-11, 314; continuing and enduring traditions confirming partiality, 308-9; criticism as oppositional and suspicious of totalizing concepts, 313; Derrida and, 311-12; generic blurring and, 309-10, 313; human relationships, new and different ways of conceiving of, 313; multiple discourses and, 308-9, 312; new and borrowed vocabulary incorporated in, 309; New Historicism and, 309-10; *New Literary History*'s role in, 307-8; reconceptualization or refiguration, 91, 309, 312; resistance to, 308

Conrad, Joseph, 91-92, 166

contemporary critical theory, 139

continuity and discontinuity: in descriptive poetry, 37, 41, 49; in genres, 181, 279, 280, 314, 369; in genre theory, 138, 161, 293; history as continuity, 209; in literary change from 1750-1800, 243-45, 247-48, 250-51, 260; in literary study, 277; narrative as element of continuity among different genres in generic alteration, 99; social change and, 214-15

contractual relation of author to reader, 107, 160, 162

conventions: importance of genre conventions, 94; poetic, 197; theory of, 65-66, 218; transgressions of, 184

Cooper, James Fenimore, 181

Coopers Hill (Denham), 8, 191-206, 212-13, 219 n. 5, 233-34; allusion to Waller's "Upon His Majesty's repairing of Pauls," 195-96; altering poetic techniques characteristic of a form, 200-201; anxiety and sense of crisis in, 212; compared to "To Penshurst," 191, 193-94, 197-98; Denham's revisions to, 198-99, 203; as descriptive poem, 44-49; Henry VIII's tyrannical behavior illustrated by ruins in, 198, 202; hope for peace and contentment

Coopers Hill (continued)
  in, 201-2; influence of, 213; injunction for king and subjects to show restraint in, 203; Johnson, Pope, and Dennis declaring as new species of composition, 192-93; as local poetry, 219 n. 6, 246; Milton's *Masque* compared to, 206; nature's role in, 197-98, 202, 211, 213; perceptual survey as journey in, 202-3, 206; as a Renaissance pastoral, 196-97; river image in, 45-46, 203-4; Swift on, 199; Thames couplets of, 45, 199, 233; Virgilian technique adapted in, 194, 204-5
copyright, introduction of, 346
Corti, Maria, 106, 108, 149, 278, 279
country-house poems, 194-95, 219 n. 6
couplets, 191. *See also* Thames couplets
Cowley, Abraham, 11, 297, 348
Cowper, William, *The Task*, 21
Crane, R. S., 60, 128, 132, 145, 205-6, 239, 251-52, 273-74
Critical Inquiry, 307-8
Critical Review, 128, 129
critical theory as part of university curriculum, 308
criticism: cultural criticism, 342, 344; genre of, 240, 295; as integral to literary theory, 123; Romantic critics, 249, 250; transaction between literary work and the critic, 37, 293; unreliable language of, 288; vocabulary of, 241. *See also* reviewers/reviewing
Criticism without Boundaries (Buttigieg, ed.), 111
Culler, Jonathan: *Structuralist Poetics*, 63, 64-65; "Towards a Theory of Non-Genre Literature," 106-7
cultural materialists. *See* New Historicism

Darwinian biology and evangelical religion, dialogue between, 174-75
Davenant, William, 197
Davis, Lennard, 343
Day, William Patrick, 179

De Bruyn, Frans, 182
deconstructionists, 71-73, 130, 238-39, 268, 269, 312
decorum. *See* propriety and decorum
Defoe, Daniel, 222, 231
Deleuze, Gilles, xxi
de Man, Paul, 71-73, 82, 122, 123, 127, 288, 301, 312, 319-20, 324, 332, 333, 339; *Blindness and Insight*, 72, 269; "Symbolic Landscape in Wordsworth and Yeats," 133
Denham, John, 11, 191-92, 193; imitating Virgil, 194, 195, 204-5, 209; *The Progress of Learning*, 202, 203. *See also Coopers Hill* (Denham)
Dennis, John, 191, 192, 299, 349-50
Derrida, Jacques, 76, 86-88, 94, 108, 113-14, 129, 132, 293, 311-12, 339, 358, 364, 365; *Of Grammatology*, 132; "The Law of Genre," 10, 139
Descartes, René, *Meditations*, 151, 371
descriptive poetry, 36-49, 195; combinational features and genre change, 41-43; continuity and discontinuity of forms in, 37, 41, 49; defined, 44; genre hypothesis and, 37-41; historical retrospection and, 44-45, 48; origins of, 43-49; problem of diachronic or synchronic relationships, 36-38; referential quality of, 46
detective novels, 183
diachronic vs. synchronic relationships, 36-38, 40, 42, 245, 254, 288
Dickens, Charles, 28, 256, 260
didactic poetry: ambiguous interrelation of "didascalick" and "heroic," 33 n. 23; change to lyric form, 252; genre of, 4; mixed with lyrics, 10-11; purity and impurity of form, 21; religious and political factionalism and, 28; in seventeenth century, 7-8, 190. *See also* epigrams
Dilthey, Wilhelm, 150
discontinuity. *See* continuity and discontinuity
Dollimore, Jonathan, 365

Donne, John, 233
Donoghue, Denis, 27
"Do Postmodern Genres Exist?" (1987), 105-21
Dos Passos, John, 110
doxography, 150-51, 160
Drakakis, John, 308
drama: eighteenth-century genre, 4, 5, 14, 21; Greek drama, 95; as highest literary form, 40; narration combining, 39
Dryden, John, 5, 25, 108, 199, 233, 281, 297, 347; "Alexander's Feast," 10; *Second Miscellany* (1702) containing "The Ancient and Most Famous Ballad of Chevy Chase," 300
dualism, 246, 248, 274, 314
Dubos, Jean-Baptiste (l'Abbé Dubos), 55
Dubrow, Heather, 174, 176
Dugaw, Dianne, 346
Dyer, John, 15, 16

Eagleton, Terry, 122, 127, 128; *Literary Theory*, 123
eclogues. *See* pastorals; Virgil
Edinburgh Review, 129
eighteenth-century genres, xvi, xvii, xxi, xxii, 3-35, 341-57; allusion, 14, 19-20, 31; ballads as social constructions, 346-52; changes to generic conventions leading to new kind of genre criticism, 343; conclusion as assertive element, 21-22; diction, 14-18; eighteenth-century critics on, 4-5, 10, 14, 30; female roles, 113, 346; form vs. mode, 12-13; georgic poetry in, 205; Gothic novel and, 179; hierarchy of, 3-12, 14, 21, 140; historical development from homogeneity to heterogeneity, 24; individuality of forms, 12-23; interrelationship of forms, 5-6, 14, 18; "kind" as defined by effect upon the reader, 23-24; Latin originals and translations in relation to, 12-13, 20, 31, 196, 214, 220 n. 23; literary change and, 218-19 n. 1; lyric, ascendancy of, 21; model applied, 23-32; most popular of, 231; newness and mixing of forms, 5-6, 11, 14, 18, 250, 344, 354; periodical essays linked to postmodern critical and theoretical essays, 112-13; postmodernist genres sharing features with, xxii, 106, 112-13; principles of unity, 20, 23, 31; purpose of literature, 9, 31; reviewing journals, 128-29; rhetoric, 14, 18-19; rules governing interrelations, 30-31; sonnet, disappearance and reappearance of, 96, 175; *Spectator*'s thinking used to characterize an entire century, 343; style, 14, 18-19; theory of harmony, 14, 28. *See also* literary change from 1750-1800
elegies: diction and, 14-15; in eighteenth century, 4, 5, 6, 10, 11, 12, 21, 24, 29, 30, 222; genre theory of, 145; as subgenre of lyric, 229. *See also* Gray, Thomas
Eliot, George, 256
Eliot, T. S., 132, 270, 315; "Tradition and the Individual Talent," 360-61
Elizabethan age, 303, 305, 351
Ellis, John, 51, 52
e-mail, 179
Emerson, Ralph Waldo, 127, 319
emotions, 55-57, 68
encomia, 229
English Augustanism, 249
Enlightenment, 345-46, 364
epics: Addison's attempt to classify "Chevy Chase" ballad as, 295-99, 301, 347-49; Greeks consider highest genre, 40; literary change and, 24; lower forms incorporated in, 4-5, 6, 14; mock epic, 232; *nostos* (classical motif of homecoming) in, 174; *Paradise Lost* as last successful English epic, 207; Pope's satire of, 347. *See also* Aristotle
epigrams in eighteenth century, 4, 6, 7, 9-10, 12, 24
epistles and letters, 7, 14, 19, 20, 30, 222, 231

INDEX

Erikson, Erik, 287
essays: Barthes on, 118; critical essay, defined, 314; Derrida on genre of, 139; genre theory of, 145; periodical essays, xviii, 14; postmodern critical and theoretical essays, 112-13, 117-18; unreadability of postmodern essays, 119 n. 7
Euripides, 177
exclusion, 148, 162, 256, 338-39, 360, 367-68, 370-71
expectations: contractual relation of author to reader and, 107, 160, 162; Culler on, 107; for interpretations, 64-65, 93; of readers, 93, 106, 237; set of, 106
explanations: of change, 285-89; implicit explanatory mechanisms, xiv; literary history providing, 267, 272; reason-giving and historical explanation, 208-14

fables, 175
Farquhar, George, 9
Faulkner, William, 96, 110
Federman, Raymond, 119 n. 7
Felski, Rita, 163
feminism: boundary crossing and, 156-57; detective novels and, 183-84; eighteenth-century novels and, 342, 346; exclusion of feminist writing from the canon, 368, 370; feminist autobiographies, 162-64; feminist criticism, 109, 128, 132, 168 n. 9, 311, 339, 345-46, 365-66; gender and genre, 343; genre criticism and, 145, 148; Gothic novels and, 178-79, 182-83; multiple discourses in, 308
fiction: Culler's theory of fictional forms, 64; diction in, 17-18; division into more genres, 158-59; in eighteenth-century genres, 14; genre theory on, 105; historical writing as form of, 370; mixing truth and fiction, 28-29; theoretical writing as form of, 301. *See also* novels

Fielding, Henry, 29, 225, 297, 326; *Joseph Andrews*, 11, 17-18, 105, 112, 155, 233, 278; *Tom Jones*, 18, 87, 233, 367
film, generic approach to, 146-47, 173, 264, 283
Fish, Stanley, 78, 94, 129, 310
Fitzgerald, F. Scott, 180
flower imagery, 15-16
Fokkema, Douwe, 113
folktales, 41-42
Fontenelle, Bernard Le Bovier de, 55, 207, 208
formalist theories, 68, 73, 116, 166, 341, 362-63. *See also* Russian formalists
form vs. code, 40, 42
Foucault, Michel, 76, 86, 261, 307, 364, 365; "The Discourse on Language," 139; *The Order of Things*, 273, 285-86
Fowler, Alastair, 108, 147; *Kinds of Literature*, 145
Fowles, John, 264
Frankfurt School, 92
Freadman, Anne, 172-74, 176
free text, 147
Freud, Sigmund, 81, 127, 239
Freudians, 68, 73-74, 240
Frow, John, 145
Frye, Northrop, 39, 61, 62, 74, 89-90, 94, 107, 132, 145, 147, 252, 293; *Anatomy of Criticism*, 106, 132; "Towards Defining an Age of Sensibility," 247-48

Gardner, Helen, 363
Garrick, David, 256
Garth, Samuel, 192
Gates, Henry Louis, Jr., 145, 165-66, 359-60, 361, 365
Gay, John, 216, 301; *The Beggar's Opera*, 11, 233, 301-3, 350-51
Geertz, Clifford, 70, 79, 307, 309-11, 313, 368, 370; "Blurred Genres," 108-9
Geistesgeschichte, 150-52
gender and genre, 343. *See also* feminism
generalizations, dangers of, 342
"Generating Literary Histories" (1993), xxii, 358-73

388

"Generation of Conceptual Changes in Literary Study, The," 307-16
generic change and transformations, xiii, 92, 96, 140, 149, 180-81, 279, 350, 368-69. *See also* combination and intermixing of genres; generic hierarchy
generic hierarchy: accommodation within, 301; of eighteenth-century genres, 3-12, 14, 21, 140; general application of, 140, 279; Miller's recognition of, 171; movement within, 40, 140, 215, 231, 279, 289, 294, 300, 303, 347-49, 368; of poetry, 5-7, 21, 24; rates of change, effect on, 286; synchronic hierarchy, xv, 36-38, 40, 43
generic history, xviii, xxi, 112, 145-69, 291-306; Addison's critique of ballads and, 294-96; Altman on, 146-47, 167 n. 2; of ballads, 294-305; combination of genres and, 292, 295, 302; combinatory consciousness in intellectual history, 155-59; cultural change in oppositional genres and, 147, 160-66; discipline-controlled vs. nation-controlled, 148; generic elevation to be considered "literary," 294, 297, 301, 347-51; importance of, 148-49, 293; methods employed in, 166; of period or movement, 164-65, 182; of philosophy and intellectual history, 145, 150-55; recent recognition of historical process, 147; view of future history of a genre, 163. *See also* literary history
"Generic History as New Literary History," 291-306
generic turn/return, xvi
Genesis, 229
Genette, Gérard, 265-67, 271
genres, xii-xiii, 85-104, 170-86; abandoned when no longer functioning, 152, 175, 279; Bakhtin's broad view of language applied to, 172; belonging without belonging and, 87; blurring of, 108-9, 309-10; ceremonial vs. commentary, 174; characterized by form and substance, 171; choice of, as social act, 283, 306; classification of, 146, 148-49, 293, 297; constructs based on, 306; cultural change in oppositional genres, 147, 160-66; cultural formation of, 148, 223; defined, xiii, xiv-xv, 39, 78, 85-87, 146, 153, 167 n. 2, 171-73, 177-78, 184, 221, 278; Derrida on, 86-88; differences within a genre, 175-76; distinctiveness among, 154, 172, 174; erosion of boundaries between, 289; expectations for interpretations created by, 64-65, 93; gender and, 343; genre markers, 88-89, 175; groups or families of genres, xiv, 40, 102, 146; history of, xv, 88-92, 177, 222; human personality as metaphor for, 176; ideology and, 101, 118, 368-69; importance of genre conventions, 86, 94, 139, 151-52; as interpretative guide, 93-96, 343; intra-active within genre and interactive with other genres, 154; "kind" as term preceding use of "genre," 177; location or setting as determinant of type of, 173-74; Miller's dislike for terminology of, 170-71; new genres, admission of, 4, 114-15; nonverbal procedures included in, 172-73, 304; norm within a genre, 193; as open systems, xix, 92, 137; opposition within, 368-69; oral traditions and, 222; origin of term and etymology of, 176-77, 279; perfection of, 101; purity of, 107; purpose of criticism by, 90; "radical of presentation," 89; reconceptualization of, 91, 368; relationship of individual text to its genre, 77, 93-94, 96-100, 114, 182, 278; rule-governed nature of, 171-72, 176; semantic vs. syntactic approach to, 146, 155; television as, 142-44; text belonging to multiple genres, 96, 278, 292; theorizing as a genre, 38, 186 n. 17; transgeneric description of style analysis, 283-84; variety of, 86. *See also* combination

INDEX

genres (*continued*)
and intermixing of genres; continuity and discontinuity; eighteenth-century genres; newness; postmodern genres; seventeenth-century genres; *specific types*

genre study: countering argument to abandon, 92; diachronic system and, 42; as method to discuss change in literature, 96, 282; postmodern genre evaluated through, 118; scope of, xviii-xix

genre theory, xxi, 145-69; advantages of using, xxiv n. 9, 108, 118-19; application of, xvi, 147-49, 297, 315; Cohen's articles on, xviii; Colie on usefulness of, 119 n. 3; combinatory genre theory, 111-12, 222, 292, 304; compared to literary theory, xix; as critical force, xxiv n. 9; defined, xiii; discipline-controlled vs. nation-controlled, 148; formulations for change in, 149; Glissant on accommodating newly independent countries, 166; historical nature of, xiv, 293, 315; mixed forms or shared generic features, 106; of the novel, 105; overlooked texts of the past and, 148, 369, 370; part-whole relationship enabled by, 149-50; reemergence of, xxiv n. 9, 148-49; rhetorical vs. literary, xxiv n. 9; specifications of genre hypothesis, 37-41, 138-39; temporary stability of, 154-55, 293; theory of change and, xx, 140; units of discourse and, 40

"Genre Theory, Literary History, and Historical Change" (1991), xvi, xxiv n. 9, 145-69

georgic poems, 6-7, 14, 21; Denham as model for innovation in, 191-206; development of English version relating to pre-Augustan Rome, 208-9, 220 n. 23; in eighteenth century, 231; movement in generic hierarchy, 40, 140, 231; new subjects and new perceptual techniques introduced into, 190-91,
194, 216; rejection of, 246; relationship to pastoral, 190, 193, 205, 206-8

Gerhart, Mary, 174-75
Gibbon, Edward, *The History of the Decline and Fall of the Roman Empire*, 69, 294
Gilbert, Sandra M., 108, 178
Giovannini, G., 263
Glissant, Edouard, 166
Golden Age, 10, 206-8, 210, 228
Goldsmith, Oliver, 234
Gothic, the, 178-79, 182-83, 256, 258, 297, 299
Graff, Gerald, 75-76, 78, 366
Grafton, Sue, 182-83
Gray, Thomas, 15, 16, 215, 232-33, 248
Gray, Zane, 180
Greek genres, 40, 42, 85-86, 95
Greenblatt, Stephen, 309-10, 362, 363, 364
Gross, John, 128
group awareness, 269
Guattari, Félix, xxi
Gubar, Susan, 108, 178
Guillén, Claudio, 254-55

Haldane, J. B. S., 81
Hammett, Dashiel, 183
Hardy, Thomas, 239
Harlem Renaissance, 364
Hartley, David, 345
Hartman, Geoffrey H., 17, 36-37, 82
Hassan, Ihab, 80-82, 105-6, 116-17, 119 n. 7
Havelock, Eric, 95
Hebrew poetry, 18
Heidegger, Martin, 75, 239, 311
Heisenberg, Werner, 81
Heraclitus, 243
hermeneutical theories, 68, 75, 78, 240
Hernadi, Paul, 146
heteroglossia, 139
hierarchy. *See* generic hierarchy
high literature, 92, 95, 98, 182
historical change, xiii, xvi, xxi, 145-69, 180. *See also* generic change and trans-

formations; generic history; literary change; literary history
historical in nature, xiv, 133-35, 293
historical knowledge, xv, 221-42; adaptations and innovations, 233; Crane on narrative history of forms, 239-40; cultural influence of temporal sequence, 238-39; definition of historical knowledge, 223-24; historical existence of a literary work, xv, 223; historical hypothesis and, 238, 240; knowledge acquisition related to genres, xix; literary understanding and, 226, 228, 229, 236-42; norm model for variation, 233-34; perpetual reexpression of a theme by different authors, 238-39; rejection-affirmation pattern, 230, 236; social behavior and, 225-26; subgenres of lyric and, 228-29; synchronous placement of a literary work with other literary works, 222; temporally defined systems of a literary work, 222-23; writer's basis on historical precedents, 221; writer's oeuvre as temporally defined system, 221-22
"Historical Knowledge and Literary Understanding" (1978), xvi, 221-42
historical reconstruction, 150-52, 270-72
historical retrospection, 11, 44-45, 48
historiography, 152, 178, 263
history: antiquarian, 267-68; critical, 268, 269; cultural history in relation to literary history, 265; as a discipline, 263; historical writing as form of fiction, 370; history writing as genre, 368-69; of ideas, 153; identification with narrative, 264; as integral to literary theory, xxi, 123; of modern period, 77; monumental, 267, 268; Nietzsche on, 267-69; truth-value of, 264. *See also* generic history; literary history; philosophy and intellectual history
"History and Genre" (1986), xvi, 85-104

Hobbes, Thomas, 5-6
Hogarth Press, 265
Holton, Gerald, 80
Homer, 40, 106, 114, 253, 273, 297; *Iliad*, 222; *Odyssey*, 44, 222
Horace, 209, 215, 233, 273; *Ars poetica*, 183; *Epistle to the Pisos*, 20; *Sermones*, 25
Horkheimer, Max, 364
host and parasite, 73, 82, 239
Howard, June, 181-82
Howell, James, 182
Hoy, David, 75
humanist tradition, 249
Hume, David, 51, 52, 54-57, 63, 333-37, 345, 346
Hunter, J. Paul, 9, 343
Hurd, Richard, 20
Husserl, Edmund, 153, 311
Hutcheon, Linda, 114, 116, 117
Hutcheson, Francis, 346
Hymes, Dell, 80
hymns, 11, 24, 29, 229, 260, 261, 343
hypertext, 179

imitation, 53-54. *See also* georgic poems; pastorals
immanence, 75
individualism, 74, 270, 291
innovation and variation, 189-220; altered hierarchy of forms, 214-15; author's revisions or drafts offering interpretative insights, 198; change not always signaling, 280; Crane considering innovations as more consequential than variations, 206; Denham as model for innovation in georgic poetry, 191, 192-206, 213; difference between extensions of a form and transformations of a form, 197; distinguishing between, 190, 192, 198, 206; evolutionary change or discontinuity as catalyst for innovation, 214-15; function and convention in relation to, 192-99; interaction of convention or allusion with other works, 198; interpretation of individual works

innovation and variation (*continued*) and, 217-18; mid-seventeenth century innovation of georgics, 209-10; new relations of poetic features to poetic ends, 190-91; norm model for, 233-34; order in variations that occur between innovations, 216; reason-giving and historical explanation, 208-14; resolution of anxiety as theme, 212; scientific-religious controversies and, 211-12; strategies that vary norms vs. strategies that overturn them, 304; uniqueness vs., 217; value of a poem and, 218; variety of poems within a period made understandable, 217; Wilkins's *A Discourse concerning the Beauty of Providence*, 210-11. See also *Coopers Hill* (Denham)

"Innovation and Variation: Literary Change and Georgic Poetry" (1974), xvi, 189-220

intellectual history. *See* philosophy and intellectual history

intermixing of genres. *See* combination and intermixing of genres

interpretation, xxiv n. 10, 317-40; accommodation and, 332; belief's role in, 317, 319, 323, 324, 331, 332-33, 336-38; conclusions about, 339-40; contemporary interpretations of literary texts, 338; distortion and misreading in, 318-19, 337, 339; expectations for, 64-65, 93; *Hamlet*'s play within a play (*The Murder of Gonzago*), 320-26; Hume on, 333-37; pluralism and, 339; as procedure of selection, 330; professionalization of, 336-37; revisionary ratios of, 318; stability of text undermined by, 333; strategies to deal with limitations of, 337-40; strong poetry and, 317-19; *A Tale of a Tub*, 326-33; teaching the student a method as purpose of, 71-72; theory vs., 314

"Interpreting Interpretations," 317-40
intertextuality, 120 n. 15, 151, 265, 266, 292

Inter-University Centre, Dubrovnik (IUC), 140
irony, 11, 20, 164
Isaiah, 18
Iser, Wolfgang, xxiii, 73, 78, 94, 291, 310

Jabès, Edmond, 119 n. 7
Jackson, Wallace, 249
Jakobson, Roman, 119 n. 9, 282
James, Henry, 182, 270
Jameson, Fredric, 74, 85, 90-91, 93, 108, 110, 115-16, 127, 140, 145, 146, 269-70, 287, 364
Jauss, Hans Robert, 63, 78, 93-94, 265, 291, 292, 315, 343; "Literary History as a Challenge to Literary Theory," 63-65
Johnson, Samuel: on Denham's *Coopers Hill*, 191-92; on descriptive poetry, 44; *Dictionary*, 21, 363; letter to Chesterfield, 346; "Life of Denham," 11-12, 191-92, 230; on literary history, 178; on mingled drama, 10; Percy and, 355; "Preface to Shakespeare, 1765," 60; *Rambler* 23, 9; on Thames couplets, 199; theory of literature and criticism of, 60-61
Jonson, Ben, 204, 209, 348; *Georgics*, 193; "To Penshurst," 191, 193-94, 197-98
journals, 111, 225-26, 294
Joyce, James, 107, 147, 160
"Joys and Sorrows of Literary Theory, The" (1983), 68-84
Jungian theories, 68
Juvenal, 20

Kant, Immanuel, 75
Keast, W. R., 60
Keats, John, 235-36, 282, 319
Kelley, Donald R., 153-54, 160, 162
King, Edward, drowning of, 206, 212. *See also* Milton, John: *Lycidas*
knowledge. *See* historical knowledge
Knox, Vicesimus, 24-25
Kolodny, Annette, 109
Krantz, Judith, 78

INDEX

Krauss, Rosalind, 115, 366-67
Krieger, Murray, 123, 124
Kristeva, Julia, 120 n. 15
Krupat, Arnold, 145
Kuhn, Thomas, 70, 79, 124, 212, 214, 257, 262 n. 15, 284, 342, 350; *The Structure of Scientific Revolutions,* 102

LaCapra, Dominick, 85, 100-102, 301
La Mettrie, Julien Offray de, 137
language: of change, xiv, 282-83; diction in eighteenth century, 14-18; as heteroglot, 273; new and borrowed vocabulary incorporated in conceptual changes, 309; vocabulary choice in eighteenth century, 258; vocabulary of criticism, 241
Latin originals and translations, 12-13, 20, 31, 101, 191, 196, 214, 220 n. 23. *See also* Augustan writers
Leavis, F. R., 124, 269, 294
legality and tragedy, 304, 352
letters. *See* epistles and letters
Lévi-Strauss, Claude, 368
Lewalski, Barbara, 147, 229
Lillo, George, 350, 352-54; *Arden of Faversham,* 303; *The Country Burial,* 303; *Fatal Curiosity,* 303; *The London Merchant,* 97-99, 300, 302-4, 351
literary change, 189-220, 276-90; change, defined, 276; changelessness, defined, 276; in eighteenth century, 218-19 n. 1; evolution and, 287; explanations of change, 285-89; within a genre and between genres, 279; innovation, function, and convention, 192-99; kinds of change, 281-85; linguistic code, changes in, 282; literary norms and, 284, 305; meaning of "periods," 280; from Milton to Keats, 221; nature of change, 276-81; pastoral and georgic role changes, 206-8; period change and, 284-85, 289; problem presented by, 189-92; randomness and, 287; reason-giving and historical explanation, 208-14; relationship of technique to concepts, 200-206; revisions by authors as, 281; revolution and, 287; scientific change, applicability to, 215-16; semantic change and, 276-77; social change in relation to, 287. *See also* conceptual changes; generic change and transformations; generic hierarchy; innovation and variation; literary change from 1750-1800
literary change from 1750-1800, 243-62; anticipations of new period, 246-47; contemporary explanations of, 245-50; continuity and discontinuity in, 243-45, 247-48, 250-51, 260; Crane on, 251-52; English Augustanism and, 249; evolutionary explanations of, 245-47; Frye on how to view periods, 247-48; humanist tradition, 249; as independent period (disjunctive approach), 247-48; Jackson on, 248-49; meaning of "periods" for, 253-57; product vs. process poetry, 248, 258; rejection of prior poetic procedures, psychological hypotheses, and thematic conceptions, 255-61, 280; reversing functions served by prior structure, 261; revolutionary explanations of, 247-50; Rothstein on fiction writing patterns in, 256-57; simultaneity, 252-53; social origin of genres and, 256; vocabulary choice and, 258
literary hierarchy. *See* generic hierarchy
literary history, xvii-xviii, 31, 160, 263-75, 358-73; applicability of, 264-65; autobiography and, 358-59, 371-72; black literary history, 165-66, 359-60; as collective name for series of genres, 178; Crane's view of, 273-74; definition of "literary," 363; Derrida and decentering texts, 311-12, 358-59; discontinuous view of, 247-48; disintegration and fragmentation, 270; Eliot's description of historical sense of tradition, 360-61; failure to evolve, noted by Wellek, 370-71; as genre, 265-66, 271, 292, 370-71; genre system

393

literary history (*continued*)
attached to chronological time of, 43; genre theory important to explain, 140; Gothic history as, 178-79; historical writing as form of, 368-69; history as a discipline, 263; imitation and, 53-54; intellectual and cultural history related to, 265; introduction of different discourses, effect of, 367; multimedia dimensions and, 371; of narrative, 264; objections to this conventional way of conceiving, 272; oppositional, 362-63; ordering and explaining of texts by, 267, 272; Percy's ballad demonstrating evolution of low to high genre, 355-56; personal experience used in construing, 311-12, 358-59; procedures of, 271-75; relationship to literary theory, 268-71, 292, 366; Renaissance studies and, 362-63; social movements related to resistance and, 359, 370; varieties of, 370. *See also* generic history; historical knowledge

"Literary History and Literary Theory," 263-75

literary norms as descriptive system, 237-38, 284, 305

literary theory, xx, 50-67, 68-84, 122-36; assumption that every text has a subtext, 73; assumption that every text involves a reader who constructs it, 73, 75; behavior principles linked to, 53, 310; as Cohen's topic in 1950s, xxii; compared to genre theory, xix, xx; Culler on readers' expectations and, 64-65; defined, xx, 122-25; Eagleton considering as illusion, 122-23; emotions and, 55-57, 68; general humanistic inquiry encompassing, 70; generic continuity of, 50, 54; as genre, 50, 63, 265-66, 271, 304; history's relationship to diverse kinds of writing, 264; ideology and, 123, 368-69; incorporating criticism and history, 123, 369; interaction between theory and practice, 124; logical procedures and, 51; as model for other disciplines, 80; nature of literary meaning and theorizing, 59, 66; needed for systemization of knowledge, 61-62, 66, 127-28; purpose of, 50; rational inquiry applied to, 80-81; readers and reviewers of, 125-26; referring to writing generally, 123; rejecting autonomous view of literature, 70; relationship to literary history, 268-71, 292, 366; relativism and, 75; scientific discourse's relationship with, 80; selectivity and, 75-76; suitable for all possible writing, 62; theory of conventions and, 65-66; types of theoretical reviews, 127-29. *See also* reviewers; theory

"Literary Theory as a Genre" (1975), xvi, 50-67

Locke, John, 246, 258, 344
Lodge, David, 76-77
logic, uses of, 50-51
Lohafer, Susa, 145
Longinus, 19, 51, 52, 248
Lotman, Yuri M., 40, 41, 43, 127, 149, 239, 339
Lovejoy, A. O., 150, 153-54
Lowth, Bishop, 11, 18, 29
Lucretius, 183, 191
Luhmann, Niklas, 137
lyric: ascendancy of, 21; ballads combined with, 96; changes in image making in, 244-45; drama combined with, 39; genre theory of, 145, 222; as hymns, 29; as part of other texts/genres, 10-11, 39, 96, 109; Romantic lyric, 115, 193, 245-46, 281; types of poetry under genre of, 222. *See also* ballad; hymns; odes; pastorals; poetry

MacIntyre, Alasdair, 308, 320
Maclean, Norman, 5
Macpherson, James, 215, 313
Mallet, David, 355
Mandeville, Bernard, 371
Marcuse, Herbert, 274

marginality, 311-12, 358, 360. *See also* exclusion
Martial, 297
Marvell, Andrew, 191, 206; *Upon Appleton House,* 8
Marxists: as alternatives to exclusionary humanist views, 338; on classes and groups through history, 269; differences among, 127; literary history and, 63, 96, 140, 166; literary theory and, 68, 90-91, 291; multiple discourses among, 308; New Historicists drawing on, 364-65; postmodernism and, 111, 116, 117; reading as historical dialectic for, 74; relativism and, 75; on social contract between author and reader, 162; social formations related to literature by, 145
masculinity and Westerns genre, 181
mass culture genres, 110
"Materialities of Communication: Genre/Media," 137-44
Matthiessen, F. O., 368
McDowell, Deborah, 145
McGann, Jerome, 133, 134
McHale, Brian, 116, 307
McKeon, Michael, 145, 343
McPherson, James, 233
meditative poems, 36, 151, 229, 246, 258, 371
melancholy, 235-36
Meletinsky, E. M., 41-42
merchant's role in society, 298-99, 303, 349
metaphor: generative metaphor, xiv; human personality as metaphor for genre, 176
Miles, Josephine, 258
Miller, Carolyn R., 170-74, 176, 178
Miller, J. Hillis, 73, 238, 312
Milton, John, 96, 165, 175, 192, 206, 213, 215, 234-35, 272; Addison on, 297; *Areopagitica,* 230; *Il Penseroso,* 19, 226-30, 236, 253; *L'Allegro,* 253; *Lycidas,* 206, 212, 223, 245; *A Masque presented in Ludlow Castle,* 206, 212; *Paradise Lost,* 19, 28, 90, 110, 207, 229, 364; *Samson Agonistes,* 229
Minturno, Antonio Sebastiano, 5, 6
Mitchell, Lee Clark, 180-81
modernism's relationship to postmodernism. *See* postmodern genres
Monthly Review, 128, 129
Montrose, Louis, 363, 365
Moretti, Franco, 140, 145
Morson, Gary Saul, 86, 94
muckraking, 182
Mukarovsky, Jan, 254, 284
Musil, Robert, 156
Musser, Joseph F., 102
myths and mythology, 41-42, 203, 277; Gothic novels treated as, 178-79; *Il Penseroso*'s mythological references, 228-29

Nagel, Ernest, 52
narrative, 21, 25, 28, 99, 264. *See also* novels
narrative history, 239, 252
nationalism, 45, 295, 299, 313, 348, 349, 360
naturalism's evolution from realism, 181-82
nature imagery, 15-17, 45, 48, 244. *See also* pastorals
neo-Aristotelians, 58, 127-28
neoclassical criticism, 3-4, 8, 10, 32 n. 4, 115, 246-47
New Criticism, 71, 133, 172, 311, 312, 341, 342, 344, 362
new Enlightenment, 342, 345, 356
New Historicism, 309-10, 339, 341, 342, 345, 362-66
New Literary History, xi, xvi, xviii, 291, 307-8; introduction to journals of, ix, xxiii; "Theorizing Genres" issues (Cohen and White, ed.), xviii-xix, xxii
newness: in eighteenth-century genres, 11, 14, 250, 344, 354; georgics, new subjects and new perceptual techniques introduced into, 190-91, 194, 216; interpreting through oldness,

newness (*continued*)
  293; reasons to add new genre, 4, 114-15, 301; in synchronic genre system, 38, 43; of testimonies genre, 180
Newton, Isaac: *Optics*, 345; *Principia*, 345
Nietzsche, Friedrich, 239, 267-69, 271, 272, 317; *The Birth of Tragedy*, 81
nineteenth-century lyric genre, 21
Nisbet, Robert A., 212, 214, 276
nostos (classical motif of homecoming), 174
novels: detective novels, 183; genre theory of, 105, 145, 222, 292, 343-44; Gothic, 178, 256, 258; literary change from 1750-1800 and, 256; literary history of, 264; movement in generic hierarchy, 140; multiple discourses in, 105, 156, 368; postmodern genre incorporating elements of eighteenth-century genre, 112; satire and, 257. *See also* fiction
Nussbaum, Felicity, 341

objectivity, 78
odes, 5, 21; Blair on, 10, 24; as type of lyrics, 36, 115
"On a Shift in the Concept of Interpretation" (1975), xxiv n. 10
"On the Interrelations of Eighteenth-Century Literary Forms" (1974), xxi, xxv n. 16, 3-35
oral texts and oralism, 88-89, 222, 289, 370
originality, 37, 127, 191. *See also* innovation and variation
"Origins of a Genre, The: Descriptive Poetry," 36-49
Ossian's poems, 233, 312-13
Ovid, 19

panegyrics, 6, 8, 11, 12, 21, 29
paradigms, 262 n. 15
Parmenides, 243
parody: of Addison's views on ballads, 299-300, 350-51; ballad parodies, 282; in comic epic of *Joseph Andrews*, 17-18; as its own genre, 114; Jameson on, 116; Keats's *Ode on Melancholy*, 235; relationship to original works, 31, 114; scientific genre and, 311; *A Tale of a Tub* as parody of Dryden, 25
pastorals: diction and, 14-17; form vs. mode, 12; Pope on, 7, 12, 208; role changes of pastoral and georgic, 206-8; setting or place as determinant of genre of, 174; in seventeenth century, 6-7; as subgenre of lyric, xv, 222, 228-29; variations in, 216; Virgilian eclogues as model, 10-11, 196, 205, 207, 209, 216. *See also* georgic poems
Patrizzi, Francesco, 5
Paulson, Ronald, 24, 343
perception, 44-45, 201, 206
Percy, Bishop, *Reliques of Ancient English Poetry*, 98, 233, 300, 305, 354-55
Percy, Thomas, 305
periods. *See* time
Perloff, Marjorie, 112
Peterson, Gilles, 113
Petrarch, 106, 317, 336
phenomenological theories, 68, 73, 74, 166, 240, 339
phenomenon of change, xiv, 149
Philips, Ambrose, 12, 15
Phillips, Edward, 4-5, 12
philosophy and intellectual history: combinatory consciousness in intellectual history, 155-59; genre history of, 145, 150-55
Plato, *Symposium*, 81
Platonists, 58
pluralism, 117, 128, 311, 339
poetry: change in way of writing, 243-44; combinatory nature of, 222, 234; defined, 237, 263; emotions and, 55-57; epistemological concepts governing, 252; genre of, 139, 245; hierarchy of, 5-7, 21, 24; historical knowledge and, 237; historiography and, 263; innovative shifts in, 216; metaphysical poetry, 297; monumental history and, 268; postmodern poetics, 112; product

vs. process poetry, 248; shared structure with rest of literature, 69; strong poets, 317-19; vocabulary of, 258; Wordsworth's theory of origin of, 56-58. *See also* descriptive poetry; specific types

Poirier, Richard, 71

Pope, Alexander: on Denham as innovator, 191-92; on diction, 14; *Discourse on Pastoral,* 208; Donne's satires reworked by, 233; *The Dunciad,* 21-22, 25, 31; eclogues of, 11, 42; *Eloisa to Abelard,* 19; *An Essay on Criticism,* 20, 22, 139, 277, 278, 296, 323; *An Essay on Man,* 29; imitating Virgil, 205, 209, 216; irony of, 20; lyric dealing with solitude, 245; matching genre to audience, 8; "Ode for Music on St. Cecilia's Day," 10; on pastoral poetry, 7, 12, 208, 216; *The Rape of the Lock,* 15, 22, 232, 244, 258, 347; on unity of parts, 23; *Windsor Forest,* 191, 208

popular culture, 92

postmodern genres, xix, 105-21; anatomization of thought and, 109; attempts to avoid generic classification, 107-8, 110, 113, 118-19, 178-79; combinatory genre theory of, 111-12; critical and theoretical essays, frequency of, 117-18; cultural dominants and, 116, 120 n. 25; eighteenth-century genres sharing features with, xxii, 106, 112-13; electronic world's effect on, 111; explanation of, 113-14; falsehood of genre without boundaries, 111; generic continuity and, 111; Hassan on, 105, 116-17; humanistic aims of, 117; Jameson's new systematic cultural norm of, 115-16; multiple discourses and discontinuous structures in, 105; oral delivery and written text in same compilation, 111; poetics, 112; postmodern critics' role, 106-7; relationship to modernism, 117, 118, 307, 315; social and political attitudes in, 109-10; *Tristram Shandy* employing features of, 105-6; trivial vs. canonized genres, 108, 119 n. 9; as unreadable, 107, 119 n. 7

Post-Restoration tragedy, 215

Pound, Ezra, 110, 293, 315

power and authority, 313

Prague structuralism, 291

praise poems, 222, 228-29

Priestley, Joseph, 345

principles of taste, 57, 71, 336

principles of unity, 20, 23, 31, 122

"Propaedeutic for Literary Change, A" (1983), xvi, 276-90

Propp, Vladimir, 37

propriety and decorum: aesthetic custom in eighteenth century, 346; in ballads, 99; breaches of, 76; as comparative guides, 13; interrelations of forms and, 6, 20, 23, 28, 30; in neoclassical criticism, 3-4; social action and, 8, 288

Proust, Marcel, 265, 267

proverbs, 109

Psalms, 11, 29

pseudoscience, 81

psychoanalytic theories, 132, 166, 338, 370

Puttenham, George, 6, 207, 229

Pynchon, Thomas, 78

Rabinowitz, Peter J., 182-84

race. *See* black literary theory and history

Rader, Ralph W., 62

Radford, Jean, 160-62

"radical of presentation," 89

Rapin, René, 207, 208

Ray, John, 211

readers: aim of genre to target certain type of public, 16; assumption that every text involves a reader who constructs it, 73; changes of taste and values, 57, 71; concept of reading as a historical dialectic, 74; contractual relation of author to, 107, 160, 162; cooperation in construction

readers (*continued*)
of theoretical ideas, 82; eighteenth-century readers, 8-9, 23, 113, 226, 256, 344; expectations of, 64-65, 95, 106; interrelationship of forms mirroring interrelationship of readers' interests, 28; Iser's phenomenological explanation of the reader-text transaction, 73; Jauss on reader as active agent, 63-65, 78; knowledge of poetic conventions, 65; literary history's need to look beyond contemporary readers of a work, 273; literary response created by education and exposure, 79; of literary theory, 125-26; relationship with reviewers, 130; seeking self-awareness and assurance of progress in history, 150-51; sensibility of readers, 57; teaching the student a method as purpose of interpretation, 71-72; transaction between literary work and the reader, xv, 69, 223, 292, 293

realism's shift to naturalism, 181-82
reconceptualization or refiguration, xviii, 91, 309, 312
Reeve, Clara, 346
referential truth, 13, 46
Reinitz, Richard, 264
rejection-affirmation pattern, 230, 236
relativism, 75, 83
religion: religious nature of poetic expression, 268-69; Swift's satire in *A Tale of a Tub*, 326, 337
Renaissance and Renaissance studies, 362-63; English, 139; genre system in, 40, 108, 147; Italian, 139; mixing of genres in, 5, 6, 14, 24, 106, 139; oppositional literary history and, 362; pastoral compared to Virgilian pastoral, 197; poetry, 12
"Renewing the Eighteenth Century" (1993), xxii, 341-57
Restoration comedy, 9
reviewers/reviewing, 122-36; historical inquiry by, 133-35; impact on academic and economic advancement of the author, 129-32; of literary theory, 125-26; reconceiving process of, 135; types of theoretical reviews, 127-29
"Reviewing Criticism: Literary Theory" (1987), xx, 122-36
rhetoric, xxiv n. 9; description as feature of, 44; in earliest genres, 42; in eighteenth-century genres, 14, 18-19; genres of, 171; as method for analyzing texts, 103
Richardson, Samuel, *Pamela*, 222, 225-26, 230, 240, 273, 344
Richetti, John, 343
Richter, David, 178-79, 181
Ricoeur, Paul, 132, 310
Riffaterre, Michael, 46, 238, 283
romance genre, 148, 160-61, 174, 346
Romantic ideology, 134, 239
Romanticism, xvii, 247-50; High Romantic British and American poets, 318-19. *See also* literary change from 1750-1800
Romantic lyric, 115, 193, 245-46, 281
Rorty, Richard, 368; "The Historiography of Philosophy: Four Genres," 145, 150-54, 160
Rosmarin, Adena, 145
Røstvig, Maren-Sofie, 209-10
Rothstein, Eric, 256-57
Rowe, Nicholas, 300, 350
Russell, Alvin Melvin, 174-75
Russian formalists, 39, 82, 108, 140, 172, 176
Russian literature, 265

Sacks, Sheldon, 308
Said, Edward, 313-14, 332
satire: as diachronic genre, 42; in eighteenth-century genres, 5, 7, 8-9, 13, 21, 31, 347; Gay adapting pastoral to, 216; genre theory of, 145, 183; movement in generic hierarchy, 40, 140, 231; Pope's satire of epic genre, 347; Swift in *A Tale of a Tub*, 326, 332, 333
Scaliger, Julius Caesar, 6
Schaeffer, Jean-Marie, 139

INDEX

Schapiro, Meyer, 257
Schmidt, Siegfried J., 80-81
scholarly reviews. *See* reviewers/reviewing
Scholes, Robert, 125
Schopenhauer, Arthur, 371
scientific change, applicability to literary change, 215-16, 310-11
scientific genre, melded with autobiography, 109, 310-11
scientific literary theory, 80
scientific-religious controversies, 211-12
scientific theory, 52, 124
Scott, John, 14, 44
sculpture, expanding genre of, 115
Sedgwick, Eve Kosofsky, 178
Seneca, *Epistles*, 25
seventeenth-century genres: ballads, 97; *beatus ille* tradition, 209-10; didactic mixtures, need for, 7-8; digressions, 26-27; georgics in, 6-7, 209-10; hierarchy of genres in, 40; historical consciousness in, 8; interrelationship of forms, 5-6, 24; Latin originals and translations in relation to, 191, 196, 214
Shaftesbury, Lord (Anthony Ashley Cooper), 9, 346, 371
Shaitanov, Igor, 172, 176
Shakespeare, William: adaptations in later periods, 165, 233; classification of tragedy by, 89; eighteenth-century influence of, 215, 272; Frye on, 61; *Hamlet*, 61, 160, 320-26; idolatry of plays of, 256; Johnson on, 60; *The Merchant of Venice*, 303; oppositional literary history and, 362; period study of genres and, 110; sonnets and, 175; *As You Like It*, 12
Sheffield, John (Duke of Buckingham), 5, 9
Shelley, Percy Bysshe, 239, 245, 319; "Adonais," 245; *A Defence of Poetry*, 81; "Mont Blanc," 124; *Prometheus Unbound*, 39; *The Triumph of Life*, 239
Shenstone, William, 355
Sheridan, Richard, 234

Shklovsky, Viktor, 293
short stories, 109, 145
Showalter, Elaine, 133, 343
Sidney, Philip, 6-7, 190, 207, 300, 305, 348; *Apology*, 5, 32 n. 12
signifier and signified, distinction between, 73
Sigworth, Oliver F., 3
similitude in dissimilitude, 58
Simon, Irène, 4
Sinfield, Alan, 365
slave narratives, 148, 294, 364
Smith, Adam, 353-54
Smith, Barbara Herrnstein, 21, 123, 237
Smith, Sidonie, 162-63, 168 n. 11
Smith, William, 19
social realism, 286
society reflected in genre, xiii, xviii; ballad opera reflecting social history, 301, 303; bourgeois individualism, 270; Brown's cultural analysis of continuities in science and literature and the arts, 102; cultural formation of genre, 148; descriptive poetry and, 44-45; dissension of society and New Historicist views, 363; in eighteenth century, 27-28, 113, 226, 256, 298-99, 344, 354; generic alteration and, 99, 181-82; human decency and norms, 233; merchant's role, 298-99, 303, 349; postmodern genres, 109-10; reviewer's consideration of, 132, 292; social change, types of, 287; social movements related to resistance to literary history, 359, 370; testimonies genre and, 179-80. *See also* Marxists
"Some Thoughts on the Problems of Literary Change 1750-1800" (1979), 243-62
sonnets, 96, 175, 207, 222
Sophocles: *Oedipus Rex*, 95, 138; tragedy, 95, 177
speech act theory, 168 n. 2
Spenser, Edmund, 196, 215; *Faerie Queene*, 253
Sprat, Thomas, 11

Stallman, Robert, 111
Steele, Richard, 27
Sterne, Laurence, 326; *Tristram Shandy*, xxii, 105-6, 112, 281, 344
Stevens, Wallace, 239, 319
Stewart, Dugald, 21, 345
Stone, P. W. K., 249-50
Stowe, Harriet Beecher, 367-68
sublime style, 18-19
Sukenick, Ronald, 114
Sutherland, James, 3, 15
Swift, Jonathan, 199; "Apology" to *A Tale of a Tub*, 11, 25, 29; *Gulliver's Travels*, 26-27, 87, 101, 343, 356; *A Tale of a Tub*, 21, 24-27, 31, 112, 258, 326-33, 337-38
synchronic hierarchy of genres and member texts, xv, 36-38, 40, 43. *See also* diachronic vs. synchronic relationships

Tatham, Campbell, 119 n. 7
television, effect of, 142-44, 173, 371
Tennyson, Alfred, 319
testimonies/*testimonio* genre, 179-80
texts: analogy to body as an entity, 114; assumption that every text involves a reader who constructs it, 73, 75; belonging to multiple genres, 278, 292; choice of genre for, 292-93; dissecting concept of, 82; as historical phenomenon, 272; history vs., 77; relationship of individual text to its genre, 77, 93-94, 96-100, 114, 182, 278; rhetoric as method for analyzing, 103; subtexts, 73, 301-2; text-code relationship, 39. *See also* intertextuality
Thackeray, William Makepeace, 256
Thames couplets, 45, 199, 233
Theocritus, 207; *Idylls*, 10
theory: abundance of theories in disciplines becoming the norm, xvii; argument against contemporary theory, 78-79; in the arts, 52-53; critical works of, 240; desire to theorize, 70; as form of discourse, 50; formulations of, 68; as genre, 296; good critical theory, 58; Graff on objective truths and, 76; institutional theory, seduction of, 79; interpretation vs., 314; logic and, 51-52; scientific theory's components, 52; systematic nature of, 64, 69; theoretical writing as form of fiction, 301. *See also* literary theory
Thomson, James, 15-16, 206, 209, 216, 245; *The Seasons*, 22
Tickell, Thomas, 7
Tillotson, Geoffrey, 14
Tillyard, Eustace, 363
time: in *Coopers Hill* (Denham), 201; literary history's need to span different time periods, 272-73; meaning of "periods," 253-57, 280; newscasts vs. newspapers and, 143; perception and, 201; period change linked to literary change, 284-85, 289
Todorov, Tzvetan, xviii, 43, 59, 61, 62, 107, 120 n. 25, 139, 146, 278
Tompkins, Jane, 367
Tom Thumb, 25, 31
Toulmin, Stephen, 262 n. 15
tradition: *beatus ille* tradition, 209-10; continuing and enduring traditions confirming partiality, 308-9; Eliot's description of historical sense of, 360-61; humanist tradition, 249; interpretation's use of tradition as textual component, 338. *See also* conventions
tragedy: ballad incorporated into, 300, 303, 351-53; comedy mixed with, 10; in generic hierarchy, 300, 303; genre theory of, 145; Hume on, 54-55, 57; legality and, 304, 352; Lillo and tragedy in ordinary life, 98, 351-54; materialities of genre of, 140; nobles as best tragic figures, 353-54; pleasure in imitation and, 54; post-Restoration, 215. *See also* Aristotle
translation: of ballads, 300-301, 348; as distortion, 318
Trapp, Joseph, 6, 7, 10, 14
trust, xvii, 79, 130, 234, 312

truth and truth statements, 13, 28, 75, 213, 269, 317
Turner, Victor, 80, 310
Twain, Mark, *Huckleberry Finn*, 175
Tynyanov, Yury, 39, 119 n. 9
typefaces and typographical techniques, 172-73

uniqueness, 37, 46, 163, 217
units of discourse, 40
unity. *See* principles of unity
University of Virginia, vii, 308
utopianism, 334

values and attitudes, effect of, 57, 71, 75-76, 79
variation. *See* innovation and variation
Varronian satire, 8
Virgil: Addison on, 208, 297; *Aeneid*, 101, 295, 296; allusion in works of, 20; *Eclogues*, 10, 42, 196, 205, 207, 229; in eighteenth century, 215, 220 n. 23; *Georgics*, 7, 193, 195, 204, 208, 209, 220 n. 23; influence of, 194, 195, 204-5, 209, 216, 273; pastoral poetry and, 7, 14, 197; Pope on, 296; Rapin denying Pollio a true pastoral, 207; in seventeenth century, 191
vocabulary. *See* language

Waldrop, Rosmarie, 119 n. 7
Waller, Edmund, 191-92, 195, 204; "Go, lovely Rose," 15; "Upon His Majesty's repairing of Pauls," 195
Walpole, Horace, 258
Walpole, Robert, 351
Warhol, Robyn R., 182-83
Warren, Austin, 3, 107; *Theory of Literature* (with Wellek), 123, 132
Warton, Joseph, 10, 19, 20, 249
Warton, Thomas, 249; *The Pleasures of Melancholy*, 234-35, 257-58
Wasserman, Earl, 197
Watson, James, 109, 309, 310
Watt, Ian, 343

Weinberg, Bernard, 8, 13
Weinbrot, Howard D., 220 n. 23
Wellek, René, 59, 61, 246-47, 254, 292, 370-71; *A History of Modern Criticism*, 4; "Literary Theory, Criticism, and History," 123; *Theory of Literature* (with Warren), 123, 132
Westerns genre, 180-81
"What Are Genres?," xxii, xxiv n. 9, 170-86
White, Hayden, 263, 272, 282, 283, 301, 369; "Theorizing Genres" (with Cohen), xviii
Whitehead, A. N., 81
Whitman, Walt, 319
Wiles, Roy M., 27, 33 n. 28
Wilkins, John, 210-11
Williams, Raymond, 143, 160-61, 243; analysis of Blake's "London," 259-60; *The Country and the City*, 364; *Marxism and Literature*, 364
Wimsatt, William, 244, 252
Wollaston, William, 201
Wordsworth, William: adaptations and innovations of, 233, 280; "Composed by the Side of Grasmere Lake," 71-72; on contract between author and reader, 162; on emotions expressed through poetry, 56-57; as High Romantic poet, 319; literary theory and, 51, 52, 54, 63; "Lucy Gray," 17; on lyric, 96, 245; *Lyrical Ballads*, 248; poetic revolution of, 249, 250; on poetic theory, 250, 280; "Preface" (1800), 56-58; pre-Romantic period in anticipation of, 246; on readers' sensibility, 57; Romanticism and, 246; six genres recognized by, 21, 96; sonnets and, 175; "Yew-Trees," 36, 46-49
World War II, 180

Yeats, W. B., 239, 319
Young, Edward, 15, 21

Zola, Émile, 182